The Sound of Cinema

The Sound of Cinema

Hollywood Film Music from the Silents to the Present

SEAN WILSON

Foreword by Amon Warmann

McFarland & Company, Inc., Publishers
Jefferson, North Carolina

Library of Congress Cataloguing-in-Publication Data

Names: Wilson, Sean, 1987- , author.
Title: The sound of cinema : Hollywood film music from the silents to the present / Sean Wilson.
Description: Jefferson, North Carolina : McFarland & Company, 2022. | Includes bibliographical references and index.
Identifiers: LCCN 2022014667 | ISBN 9781476687575 (paperback : acid free paper) ∞
ISBN 9781476646480 (ebook)
Subjects: LCSH: Motion picture music—United States—History and criticism. | BISAC: PERFORMING ARTS / Film / History & Criticism | MUSIC / History & Criticism
Classification: LCC ML2075 .W55 2022 | DDC 781.5/420973—dc23/eng/20220401
LC record available at https://lccn.loc.gov/2022014667

British Library cataloguing data are available
ISBN (print) 978-1-4766-8757-5
ISBN (ebook) 978-1-4766-4648-0

© 2022 Sean Wilson. All rights reserved

No part of this book may be reproduced or transmitted in any form or by any means, electronic or mechanical, including photocopying or recording, or by any information storage and retrieval system, without permission in writing from the publisher.

Front cover images © 2022 Shutterstock

Printed in the United States of America

*McFarland & Company, Inc., Publishers
Box 611, Jefferson, North Carolina 28640
www.mcfarlandpub.com*

Contents

Acknowledgments	vi
Foreword: What Constitutes a Great Film Score? by Amon Warmann	1
Preface	3
ONE. Tremolo: The Onset of Film Music	5
TWO. Forte: The Romantic Era Takes Shape	28
THREE. Glissando: Jazz, Rock and Roll and the Slide Towards Experimentalism	69
FOUR. Allegro: *Star Wars* and the Resurgence of the Symphonic Score	109
FIVE. Atonal: The Role of Film Music in the Era of Franchising	156
SIX. Dissonance: Gender Disparity, Temp Scores and Rejected Scores	200
Coda: The Future of Hollywood Film Scoring	223
Chapter Notes	235
Bibliography	251
Index	259

Acknowledgments

I owe a considerable debt of gratitude to those editors and journalists who have informed my knowledge of film music, but most notably to those who have given me the opportunity to articulate my own thoughts on the subject. This book would not exist without the influence, either direct or indirect, of Jon Broxton, Christian Clemmensen, James Southall, Jim Paterson, Kristen Romanelli, Amon Warmann, Tim Burden, Loren Sunderland and A.J. Black, all experts in their respective fields.

Above all this book is dedicated to my family, specifically my mother, father and sister, upon whose support I can always rely.

Foreword

What Constitutes a Great Film Score?

BY AMON WARMANN

Think of your favorite film scenes. Now try imagining them without music.

Kind of hard, isn't it?

That's because music in film is the bridge between the mind and the heart. A selection of notes played by a collection of instruments that somehow speaks to what's unfolding on screen. At its best, it feels like real time alchemy. A magic trick that not only enhances emotions but unlocks unforeseen ones.

So what must all great film scores do?

For one thing, a great film score is its own form of storytelling. In the same way that characters in a movie are introduced and drift in and out of a story, so too should the score reflect that musically by establishing themes and then evolving them. Sometimes, that means a change in tempo. Other times, it means using a different instrument. But when it's done well, a simple musical cue is all that's needed to signal to audiences which character has arrived on the scene.

An effective score also articulates mood. That speaks to the second thing all great movie scores should possess: an understanding of what each given scene requires. What emotion is the sequence trying to convey? Whose perspective are we following? Only once the right answers to these questions have been found can the composer work towards accentuating what's transpiring on screen. And even then, sometimes there are moments that demand music that works against the dialogue, communicating a story that goes beyond words and images with the ultimate universal language.

It's much easier to achieve these goals when the director and composer are on the same page. Some of the greatest music to ever be composed has been the result of a pitch-perfect tandem, from Sergio Leone and Ennio Morricone to Steven Spielberg and John Williams to Barry Jenkins and Nicholas Britell. It's little wonder that these artists often choose to work with each other repeatedly; finding someone who is on the same wavelength is hard, so when that creative synergy is discovered, they do everything they can to hang onto it.

Taken altogether, these elements help distinguish the functional scores from the memorable, instantly hummable ones. That's when you get Hans Zimmer's "Barbarian Horde" in *Gladiator* (2000), Howard Shore's "The Bridge of Khazad Dum" in *The Lord of the Rings: The Fellowship of the Ring* (2001) and Alan Silvestri's "Portals" in *Avengers: Endgame* (2019). These are tracks that are intrinsic to the scenes they elevate, so much so that listening to the music on its own immediately reconnects you with the emotions you felt when you watched the movie for the first time. Even without the visuals and the dialogue, they still retain their potency.

That's the power of a great film score. There's nothing quite like it.

Amon Warmann has been a film and TV critic in the UK for the past decade. He is a contributing editor and monthly columnist at Empire *magazine and Talk Sport Radio's weekly film reviewer. He has written for* Variety, Yahoo! Movies, *the* Daily Mirror *and* Heat *magazine and he regularly conducts interviews for* Composer Magazine.

Preface

First and foremost, this book is a passionate salute to a majestic medium: film scoring. It's hard for me to recall when my enthusiasm for film music first took hold. As a child of the late 1980s, I was fortunate to ride the extraordinary creative swell of artists such as John Williams, Jerry Goldsmith, James Horner, Alan Silvestri and others, all symphonic traditionalists and masterful practitioners of melodies that sink, surreptitiously, into the subconscious.

My first exposure to these artists would have come during the 1990s, as I watched the films that they scored on both TV and VHS. That said, I would have been far too young to recognize their status as professional composers, nor would I have been old enough to articulate the spellbinding impact of film music. But it would be hard to deny that my first viewing of, say, *Raiders of the Lost Ark* (1981) on British television wasn't made all the more extraordinary by the multifaceted impact of John Williams' music, variously triumphant, romantic and terrifying by turns.

It should be stressed that although I write from a relatively informed editorial position about film music, I'm not a musician. Barring a stretch playing the violin in my school orchestra during adolescence, I have never played an instrument, nor am I able to sight-read. For that reason, this book is not written with an eye towards music theory (barring some choice phrases and terms and other, more involved sections that arose entirely out of careful research).

More significantly, I intended to write this book to address what I perceive as a somewhat startling gap in the academic market. Music has been bound up with the visual image since the onset of cinema, yet relatively few books have traced the aesthetic development of film scoring from the 19th century through to the present day. I emphasize the words "relatively few"—there are a handful of writers who have attempted such a feat with clarity, wit and insight, and to those people I owe a not inconsiderable debt. But more often than not, academic literature on film music (which isn't especially extensive in the first place) tends to focus on very specific periods. Silent cinema music and scores from the so-called "Golden Era" of film music (broadly speaking, the 1930s to the 1950s) are fairly well-traversed, editorially speaking, but I wanted to address the overall evolution of the medium: where it started, where it's been and where it's going in the future. In turn, this allows me to put a fair amount of emphasis on contemporary franchise scoring, which by and large is not well anthologized in academic circles (largely because we're living through that phase at the moment and the need for retrospective appraisal hasn't yet reached a critical mass).

Additionally, in the process of writing this book I desired to put the thoughts and ideologies of leading film composers front and center. I've had the pleasure of interviewing several of Hollywood's finest musical artists over the years, and this book presents pertinent highlights of my conversations with Howard Shore, Alexandre Desplat, Terence Blanchard, Michael Giacchino, John Powell, Laura Karpman and David Arnold. Said content begins with the epigraphs at the start of each chapter and is interpolated in the body copy thereafter. It's all well and good to invoke the legacy and technique of specific composers on an anecdotal basis; by allowing these prodigiously talented individuals to speak for themselves, I aim to fashion a greater sense of emotional directness and credibility with the reader.

The art of film music is now more than 100 years old and yet, when I discuss film scoring with people, it still seems like something of an elusive, alchemical dark art. This book is written specifically for those individuals who are curious and want to know more. The turbulent story of the development of film music acts as a mirror on the social, historical and political movements that have occurred over the last century. Film music encapsulates all that is inspiring and troublesome about the human condition, a sweeping odyssey worthy of the grandest David Lean epic.

ONE

Tremolo

The Onset of Film Music

"Film music is very much about point of view.... You're approaching it on the basis of human interaction."—HOWARD SHORE[1]

The Early Relationship Between Music and Picture

At the beautifully atmospheric Curzon Cinema in Clevedon, southwest England, audiences can take a step into the past. This is down to the presence of the Christie pipe organ, dating from the 1930s, which contains 723 pipes, three keyboards each with 61 notes, and the facility to mimic various percussion instruments including drums and the tambourine.[2]

But this is no mere art deco gimmick. The Christie was installed to mimic the technique of silent cinema music accompaniment. In the early 20th century, the pipe organ was a key factor in picture houses around the world, emboldening and enlivening the on-screen action with its richly profound notes. In short, it gave voice to the voiceless.

Moving picture entertainment in the 1890s was traditionally located in the context of fairground attractions, travelling shows and vaudeville entertainment. Vaudeville was defined as an upmarket variety show (smoking and drinking were both banned) consisting of 8 to 12 acts at a length of 10 to 20 minutes.[3] The format was commonplace across the United States at the end of the 19th century: in 1896 it had around 200 locations, which had doubled just 10 years later.[4]

Such formats would traditionally have been accompanied by music, sound effects and narration. Music was often played live at the entrance to the shows or recorded on a barker's phonograph ("barker" being an archaic word for a carnival promoter) and projected into the street in a bid to lure in audiences (a publicity approach known as "ballyhoo").[5]

Another popular staple of the late 1890s was the magic-lantern show. The intricate narrative sequencing of these shows was further bolstered by the careful application of narration and music. So-called "illustrated songs" took place whereby popular tunes accompanied the magic-lantern projection as the audience sang along.[6] Already, spectators were getting a distinct taste of the power that could be conjured from the marriage between sight and sound.

In Paris in the 1890s, a series of cinematic presentations fused visuals and music to dazzling effect. Émile Reynaud's animated films *Pantomimes lumineuses* made their debut in 1892 at the city's Musée Grévin, set to a composed piano score by Gaston Paulin.[7]

The Lumière brothers later presented a series of short films in 1895, accompanied by pianist Emile Maraval. (A later showing in London made use of the harmonium.)[8] Later in 1895, the Lumière brothers were to become infamous for their short reel *The Arrival of a Train at La Ciotat*, projected in a Parisian café. The film's startlingly immersive qualities (for the time) allegedly caused the café patrons to flee the building, an early sign of an audience's visceral reaction to the moving image.

Similar landmarks followed from the likes of Georges Méliès, a silent cinema pioneer who was championed in Martin Scorsese's fantasy-drama *Hugo* (2011). Méliès' *A Trip to the Moon*, released in 1902, is a triumph of imaginative form, with the shot of the capsule landing in the "eye" of the moon one of the most enduring images in motion picture history. In fact, during the Paris premiere of *A Trip to the Moon*, Méliès played the piano accompaniment himself.[9]

Many would contest that the progenitor to any kind of film score came courtesy of Thomas Edison. The scientist was a key figure in the early days of moving pictures, and in 1889 he began work on the Kinetograph (camera), which would provide supplementary visuals to the music already being deployed by his phonograph.[10] Edison then attempted full synchronization of image and music with the combination of the Kinetograph and the Kinetoscope (projector), but the limitations of the technology meant it wasn't possible.[11]

Edison's *The Dickson Experimental Sound Film* (1895) contained a sampling of string music, played by director William Dickson during the film itself, along with its two minutes of recorded sound. This could arguably be seen as the moment where film music took its first steps, crude as they were. The piece in question was Robert Planquette's 1877 composition "The Chimes of Normandy," and if it's not the first full-length film score, it's almost certainly the first example of tracked-in, pre-existing classical music in cinema history.[12]

Edison's example was soon followed by the likes of German inventor Oskar Messter, a pioneer of early silent cinema. By 1896, Messter's films were a popular fixture on the program at Berlin's Apollo Theater, and this necessitated a stream of topical, interesting material. To that end, Messter developed his own camera and projection mechanism and took to the streets. In the manner of his contemporaries, the Lumière brothers, Messter observed the rhythms of everyday life, including commuting workers and parading soldiers.[13]

At the start of the 20th century, Messter developed his Kosmograph disc system (1903), which purported to synchronize gramophone music with the moving image. Nevertheless, the crudeness of the technology, the poor levels of sync and the absence of a standardized system, doomed the initiative's commercial opportunities.[14] It would, in fact, be another two decades before visuals and accompanying music enjoyed full synchronicity.

At the start of the 20th century, the supremacy of vaudeville was challenged by the emergence of so-called "nickelodeon" cinemas. In the early days, these were storefront theaters with a basic set-up: folding chairs, a sheet for a screen and $75 for the projector.[15] Each theater featured a repetitious program of 15- to 20-minute films, and the brevity of the presentation, not to mention the sheer variety on offer, saw the average nickelodeon explode in popularity. Despite the aesthetic differences, there were shared elements between nickelodeon presentation and vaudeville; the use of a barker's phonograph, for instance, to draw in customers at the entrance, or play throughout the auditorium.[16]

At the same time, organic instrumentation was also found in the most commonplace nickelodeon, foreshadowing the developments to come as silent cinema became more sophisticated. Live pianists were mainstays from the outset, and they were often supplemented by mechanical devices such as player pianos.[17] Thereafter, as theaters expanded, audiences grew and the demand for music became more urgent, the concept of the live film score performed to picture swiftly became a standardized approach.

The organic versus mechanical principles of early silent cinema are deeply embedded in the aforementioned *Hugo*. Scorsese's wondrous adventure, set in Paris in 1931, tells of young orphan Hugo (Asa Butterfield). Living in a Parisian train station, he is left a mysterious, non-functioning automaton by his late father (Jude Law). Hugo's destiny brings him into contact with the embittered filmmaker Georges Méliès (Ben Kingsley) who is seeking his own measure of redemption. We are then taken into the past to witness Méliès at his creative peak in 1902, as he constructs his seminal *A Voyage to the Moon*, whose production is joyously recreated by Scorsese.

Fittingly enough, for a filmmaker so steeped in the tactility and practicality of cinema, Scorsese champions a complex host of sound elements from the hissing of the steam engines to the clanking of the station clock behind which Hugo lives. This extends to Howard Shore's Oscar-nominated, lyrical score, which integrates seamlessly with the bustling sound of mechanization that earmarked the early days of filmmaking. Shore explains: "When I was writing the score ... the sound designers were matching the whistle of the trains to the key of the score. I like those collaborative relationships. If I can work with the other filmmakers and create something interesting, then I'm all for that."[18]

Around 1904, contemporaneous with the events depicted in *Hugo*, an increased emphasis on narrative-driven cinema, propelled by continuity editing, necessitated the use of music that was expressive, as well as illustrative. In other words: music seeking to capture mood, as opposed to simply reflecting movement and incident. A soundtrack accompaniment had the capacity to act as a commentary on an audience's feelings, further investing them in the narrative themes.[19]

It was at this point that film music started to embrace its destiny as a manipulative, non-objective form, one capable of amplifying a sense of heightened fantasy. The increasingly luxurious nature of movie theaters, which were undergoing a boom in construction, offered the space required for musical accompaniment. The orchestra pit of the Regent Theater in New York, opened in 1913, was reserved not just for a musical ensemble but also live performance and opera. Popular orchestras and conductors were imported specially for the occasion, forging greater links between the thrill of projected visuals and a sense of musical prestige.[20]

Film music can be split into two camps: diegetic and non-diegetic. The former is broadly defined as music whose source is visible within the scene. The latter refers to music outside the world of the film that is seemingly streamed in from nowhere. It's been suggested that the increasingly popular "fantasy" of non-diegetic music in the early 20th century owed itself to the wide-ranging influence of opera, ballet and melodrama, where music and imagery coalesced to form a seamless whole.[21] Many silent film directors had been schooled in the melodramatic arts, including the use of organs and incidental orchestral pieces to help guide an audience's emotions, and subsequently transferred these principles over to cinema and cinema music.[22]

Industry practices that we now take for granted also took hold around this time. As early as 1909, Thomas Edison (in his Edison Kinetogram bulletin) started to make "musical suggestions" for his own films, which later led to the development of the cue sheet.[23] Today, as they did then, these unassuming bits of paper act as a catalogue for all aspects of music used during a film or TV production.

Rumor has it Edison advocated this practice to curate a sense of appropriate musical numbers for in-theater pianists, whose abilities tended to vary wildly.[24] It also signaled the level of interest from production companies who were clearly starting to recognize the power of film music in exhibiting and selling their product. One can see that, as early as the first decade of the 20th century, commercial practices were beginning to intrude on the art form of the film score.

As the power of narrative-driven cinema started to take off, picture houses began to install their own pneumatic and mechanical instruments, including pipe organs and keyboard photoplayers, to steer around the limitations of human players. The pipe organ's ability to capture the heart of a particular movie went far beyond its initial brief; such instruments (later commercialized by companies including Wurlitzer) could also replicate sound effects including birds, whistles, aeroplanes and more, adding greater veracity and atmosphere, and further enveloping audiences in the drama. These would often be engineered to rise above the auditorium floor for added dramatic effect. Several distinguished musicians were apprenticed in the art of cinematic organ and piano playing, including Dimitri Shostakovich and Dimitri Tiomkin in the Soviet Union, and jazz artist Fats Waller in the United States.

Many films can claim to have incorporated the first film score. However, *The Assassination of the Duke of Guise* (1908) is widely credited as the inception point of the contemporary movie soundtrack.[25] Directed by Charles le Bargy and André Calmettes, the film depicts the real-life events of 1588 when King Henry III summoned his powerful rival, Duke Henri de Guise, to his chambers at the Château de Blois and had him murdered. Renowned classical composer Camille Saint-Saëns, much loved for such pieces as "Carnival of the Animals" (showcased in Terrence Malick's 1978 film *Days of Heaven*) penned the music for this pioneering 15-minute short.[26]

Technically speaking, the veteran Frenchman was pipped to the post by a few months. Earlier in 1908, *The Fairylogue and Radio-Plays*, a two-hour production (now lost) of L. Frank Baum's *The Wizard of Oz* stories that combined magic lantern, live performance and film, showcased a 27-cue score from Nathaniel D. Mann.[27]

Nevertheless, purists would argue that the contemporary film score was conceived with Saint-Saëns' landmark work. Noted film music critic Craig Lysy writes for website MovieMusicUK: "The composer worked out the music scene-by-scene while watching the film, reworking extracts from his unpublished symphony *Urbs Roma*, and developing small-scale drama within a larger form."[28]

This was revolutionary for the time, and an especially impressive achievement given Saint-Saëns was then aged 73. Music with its own residual sense of character and narrative structure could now be applied to moving pictures, enhancing a film's implicit meanings and emotional undercurrents. The notion of a scene-by-scene soundtrack is something we now take for granted, but it all began with Saint-Saëns' extraordinary work.

Although he couldn't have known it at the time, Saint-Saëns had anticipated (if not exactly invented) that pivotal aspect of film scoring known as "spotting." Standard procedure dictates that a composer and a director will sit down and identify the natural musical breakpoints in the proposed score, proceeding on a sequential basis throughout the movie. This process is now par for the course in Hollywood music production, but it owes itself to technical trailblazers like Saint-Saëns. Howard Shore is among those to have benefited from Saint-Saëns' pioneering abilities, saying: "Spotting is always really important to me. How music is used in the film, why it's there, and the point of view."[29]

The Assassination of the Duke of Guise exerted a considerable influence on the technical development of the film score. "Just as the score adheres harmonically to the measure of Saint-Saëns' mastery, so too does the music enjoy enormous freedom in its classical nature," Lysy elaborates. "The range of dynamic and articulate expression by comparison to film music as we know it today is unmistakable. No discretion is required to accommodate dialogue or sound effects. Instead we can recognize this music as an aspect of the composer's oeuvre, akin with his earlier tone poems; heavy-handed in its presentation but manifestly clear in how it interacts with the screen."[30]

Saint-Saëns may have been a pioneer, but L. Frank Baum was also a progressive figure in the history of film music. Not just a celebrated children's author, Baum also carved out a reputation as a filmmaker in his own right. He's noted for his collaborations with American composer-conductor Louis Ferdinand Gottschalk, which first came about with 1913 *The Tik-Tok Man of Oz*.[31]

Later on, Baum became affiliated with the production company The Oz Film Manufacturing Company, and appointed Gottschalk as its vice president. Gottschalk's ensuing film scores further helped develop the medium of the feature-length film score. In 1914, he composed several film scores, all based around Baum's wonderful world of Oz, for films including *The Magic Cloak of Oz* and *His Majesty, the Scarecrow of Oz*.[32]

Had Gottschalk anticipated the eventual trend of franchise film scoring? Although the various movies weren't strictly connected, they were bound together thematically by Baum's dazzling Oz mythology. Gottschalk's ability to associate himself with a particular genre of storytelling may have portended later composers like John Williams, who found himself largely defined by his work on the *Star Wars* franchise.

Another significant step forward came in 1915 with the soundtrack for D.W. Griffith's hugely controversial *The Birth of a Nation*. Widely credited as the first long-form narrative drama, this contentious epic of racial segregation appallingly favors the Ku Klux Klan as white saviors. (It was originally titled *The Clansman* after Thomas Dixon, Jr.'s, play, which served as the film's inspiration.) Nevertheless it's a technical milestone in cinema history, with overlapping narrative strands stitched together via the newfound liberty of "montage." This was later explored to even more dynamic effect by Russian director Sergei Eisenstein in his film *Battleship Potemkin* (1926), particularly in the intercutting of the famous "Odessa Steps" sequence. (Edmund Meisel's original score has subsequently been covered by an eclectic range of artists from Pet Shop Boys frontman Neil Tennant to Michael Nyman.)

The score for *The Birth of a Nation* was no less radical. Composer and tenor musician Joseph Carl Breil, who co-composed the music with Griffith, threaded his original material around existing works to craft a dynamic tapestry of conflicting emotion, and it's often credited as the first-ever film score for a feature-length narrative drama.[33] *The Birth of a Nation* is, therefore, an important bridging moment between the reliance on existing classical standards, and the eventual autonomy of the designated film composer.

In fact, there were two scores composed for the film. Breil and Griffith's work accompanied the East Coast roadshow presentation of the film while the West coast presentation (including the Los Angeles premiere) was composed by Carli Elinor. At the time, as part of an extensive publicity drive it was common practice for movies to open in a limited number of theaters in selected American cities. Breil made liberal use of the organ and the orchestra during these roadshows, but it was noted that when the movie went on wide release, the score as performed in picture houses was replaced by ad-hoc instrumentals. This is possibly because the logistics and complexity of the score were too much for the in-house musicians to master.[34]

The nature of this score throws up an important question: does a film composer actually possess any autonomy? Their key brief is to fulfill the vision of the director, subsuming their ego, or at the very least tempering it, so that the music augments and enhances the vision that the filmmaker has in their head. Breil was compelled to use existing classical works, not to mention many familiar folk tunes from America's Deep South, in his score, suggesting that the film score medium was, at this point, yet to attain full independence.[35]

Nevertheless, the notion of a musical tapestry composed of different themes and emotions was hugely influential. Breil's work on this film was actually preceded by an earlier effort named *The Love of Queen Elizabeth* (1912), so he was clearly well-positioned in terms of writing music that would serve the images.

In *The Birth of a Nation*, not only did Breil track in music from German composer Richard Wagner, but he also deployed the Wagnerian "leitmotif," an operatic device whereby certain musical themes, motifs and impressions are used to depict individual characters, locations and situations. This was first developed by Wagner in his four-opera masterpiece *Der Ring des Nibelungen*, composed between the years of 1848 and 1874. A case in point is Breil's swooning love theme: designed to off-set the offensive "menace" of the film's black characters, it's a clear precursor to later romantic epics from the likes of Max Steiner and Erich Wolfgang Korngold. In fact, it was later published with lyrics as "The Perfect Song," to great success.[36]

In total, Breil's work comprised over 200 individual music cues including the aforementioned love theme, waltz-like dance idioms and a central piece titled "The Bringing of the African to America."[37] Misguided and revolting though the film's politics are, the scale and intricacy of the music was unprecedented for the time, and one must also credit the exacting Griffith for his oversight in these matters.

Revered French pianist Erik Satie ("Gymnopedie No. 1") expanded the parameters of the medium in 1924, as the silent period was drawing to a close. His score for director René Clair's 20-minute silent movie *Entr'acte* diverged from the so-called "illustrative," surface-based approach of film scoring, common to the era. Satie's use of momentum, tone, melody and rhythm didn't comment directly on the action but instead occupied a more subservient role, using its inherent qualities to suggest hidden meanings beneath the fabric of the visuals. In his own way, Satie had intellectualized the concept of film scoring, although such stylistics were described by the composer, seemingly derisively, as "furniture music."[38]

Should an audience be able to perceive film music in the first place? Or should it work surreptitiously on the emotions? Satie was among the very first film composers to highlight the critical juncture between the obtrusive and the unobtrusive. Many, if not all, film composers prior to Satie aligned their music explicitly with the rhythm and content of the visual imagery. Satie, on the other hand, took a more insidious tactic and elucidated those themes that could not be seen, but felt on an instinctive level.

Film lecturer and festival director Laraine Porter notes that the majority of silent cinema scores performed a strictly utilitarian purpose, which had the effect of diminishing a composer's profile. She observes: "Music needed to harmonize with the mood, genre, story, characters and narrative trajectory, and to help audiences relate to the film."[39] Few composers of the era, with the possible exception of Erik Satie, were able to imprint a sense of their own singular personality onto the medium because they weren't hired "to provide a counterpoint or contradict the film."[40]

Whether a composer's role in a film is overt or covert, whether they're scoring a silent movie or a sound picture, they are compelled to serve the narrative to the best of their ability. Howard Shore says that coherency of presentation is key to the success of a completed film score. He says he wants audiences "to be swept into the world of the film. I like to feel that it's seamless between all aspects of music in the film. I like to be involved in all the music. To know what it is and be able to write around it. It's fun to work with directors when you have this musical cornerstone or bedrock."[41]

Outside of Hollywood and France, advances were also being made in Germany. In 1927, towards the end of the silent cinema era, director Fritz Lang helmed the influential *Metropolis*. This science-fiction story of a futuristic dystopia is a key text in the German Expressionist film movement and had a huge impact on later seminal works such as Ridley Scott's *Blade Runner* (1982).

The score for *Metropolis* was originally composed by Gottfried Huppertz, although various artists have provided their own scores for *Metropolis* in the decades since. These have ranged from electronic pioneer Giorgio Moroder to Abel Korzeniowski, composer of *A Single Man* (2009), and it demonstrates that *Metropolis*, both as a film and as a soundtrack, has had a lasting, fascinating impact.

Like the earlier *The Birth of a Nation*, the *Metropolis* score deploys a Wagnerian leitmotif structure, incorporating original themes for various characters. It also makes use of established classical tracks such as "Dies Irae" (later adapted by Wendy Carlos in Stanley Kubrick's *The Shining*, 1980) and French revolutionary anthem "The Marseillaise" (dramatically distorted during a key moment of worker rebellion).

The score's rich canvas is noted for its ability to stitch together a sense of mechanization, Viennese waltzes for scenes of altogether more human flirtation, dark subterranean textures, bustling movement as the Tower of Babel is constructed and impressionistic effects for the construction of the robot, Maschinenmensch.[42] Together, Huppertz and Lang demonstrated that science-fiction, in particular, is a magnificent canvas to show off bold musical brushstrokes, with the later likes of Jerry Goldsmith (*Planet of the Apes*, 1968; *Star Trek: The Motion Picture* and *Alien*, both 1979) picking up the baton.

We conclude this section by once again invoking Erik Satie and Camille Saint-Saëns, whose move from live classical performance into the more programmatic realm of film music anticipated the journey of many other distinguished artists. One such musician was Soviet master Sergei Dmitri Shostakovich who, in 1929, just as the silent era was concluding, composed an orchestral score for *The New Babylon*, directed by Grigori Kozintsev and Leonid Trauberg.

Shostakovich is said to have deployed a sense of sardonic irony in the music, including grandiose waltzes to reflect a sense of bourgeois decadence.[43] In that sense, his music maybe owes a debt or two to Satie, emboldening illusory themes and not just supporting the outward imagery. Several songs from the French Revolution, including the "Marseillaise" (already used in *Metropolis*) were used also to underpin the film's reactionary Soviet politics.[44] Shostakovich would enjoy great success in the sound era with *The Gadfly* (1955), as his contemporary Sergei Prokofiev had with the earlier *Alexander Nevsky* (1938).

Composers such as Shostakovich bridged the all-important divide between the silent and sound eras, helping to advance the language of film music. However, one must also credit the lasting influence of a certain Charlie Chaplin and his endearing creation, The Tramp.

Charlie Chaplin: The Composer Behind the Comedian

Which genre poses the greatest challenge for composers of film music? Many would contend that only a composer of real skill could compose lavish Wagnerian bombast for epic dramas or rousing themes for Westerns. However, it's relatively easy to play on an audience's emotions as far as action, romance or horror are concerned. Each of those genres strikes a primal note of raw emotion or adrenaline, and very often a composer can be unashamed in reflecting the impulses of the audience.

Comedy, however, is a different story. Accentuating humor through music walks the finest of lines between annoyance and wit. After all, if one is faced with a priceless bit of physical comedy, what possible good can come out of, say, honking tubas or prancing woodwind arrangements? Surely, it's redundant and distracting when the physicality of the performer is the greatest effect of all, and the thing that's designed to hold our attention? All too often, comedy scores can be all about the surface, whereas dramatic scores have, perhaps, the easier job in stimulating the emotions that toss and turn beneath the skin.

Right from the earliest years of silent cinema, careful orchestration and harmonics were matched with visible human movement to evocative effect. A few repetitious, dainty keys on a piano could match the airy grace of a ballerina; or, perhaps, some phrasing from a bassoon, with its low pitch, could give a sense of sneaky, skulking mischief. The tone and pitch of certain instrumentation has the ability to bypass the intellect, all the while connecting to our own visceral sense of humanity.

These techniques were put to memorable use by the esteemed Charlie Chaplin, one of the early 20th-century's most recognizable movie stars, a mercurial, maverick talent who not only directed and starred in his own films, but regularly composed music for them as well. The notion of Chaplin as a composer has perhaps been overlooked amidst the sheer breadth of his extraordinary achievements; nevertheless, he was an auteur who highly valued the power of film music, and he helped pave the way for non-diegetic comedy scores. Born in Walworth, London on April 16, 1889, Chaplin suffered an impoverished childhood. This included his mother, a former vaudeville star, being incarcerated in a psychiatric institute when he was just 14.

A keen amateur performer and musician from a young age, Chaplin got his first taste of the limelight when theater impresario Fred Karno enlisted him to star in burlesque sketch "The Football Match" at London's Coliseum, starring opposite popular comedian Harry Weldon.[45] Interestingly, in his autobiography, Chaplin specifically remembers the clarion call of the music as he first walked out on stage, an implicit acknowledgment of its visceral impact on both audience and performer.[46]

Chaplin proved a roaring success with the crowds, eventually signing a year-long contract with Karno as "The Football Match" went on a UK tour.[47] This did, however, come at Weldon's expense who was said to be seething with jealousy at the young upstart's sudden burst of popularity.[48]

Despite his success with the Karno Company, Chaplin eventually desired pastures new. He looked towards America, that land of boundless possibility where he could throw off the shackles of stuffy British music hall revue. His dream came true when Karno selected him to play the lead in the American tour of "The Wow-wows."[49] Nevertheless, he would leave the company for good in November 1913.

A tectonic shift in Chaplin's life came when he was drafted into Keystone Studios, to replace outgoing star Ford Sterling.[50] The company's owner, Mack Sennett, claimed he had spotted Chaplin while playing "A Night in an English Music Hall" at New York's American Theater. Sennett was allegedly convinced of Chaplin's humorous and distinctive qualities by his girlfriend, Mabel Normand.[51]

During his time at Keystone, Chaplin was having to grapple with the demands of appearing in front of the camera for the first time, and he became fascinated with the processes of filmmaking. His soon-to-be-iconic character The Tramp (also known as The Little Tramp) made his screen debut in *Kid Auto Races at Venice* (1914), although Chaplin claimed to have first donned the costume in *Mabel's Strange Predicament*, filmed earlier but released two days later.[52] Under the auspices of Sennett, a revered slapstick comic in his own right, Chaplin gave birth to one of cinema's most enduring individuals.

Chaplin would say of The Tramp's creation: "I wanted everything to be a contradiction: the pants baggy, the coat tight, the hat small and the shoes large.... I added a small moustache, which, I reasoned, would add age without hiding my expression. I had no idea of the character. But the moment I was dressed, the clothes and the makeup made me feel the person he was. I began to know him, and by the time I walked on stage he was fully born."[53]

Interestingly, it appears that The Tramp went through a character evolution of his own. The movie *The Tramp* (1915) marked a turning point of sorts in which the figure transitioned from a relatively unsophisticated individual into more of a romantic archetype. This may have resulted from Chaplin's affection for co-star Edna Purviance, who went on to appear in over 30 of his films.[54] This gentle and melancholic sense of whimsy would soon extend to The Tramp's accompanying film soundtracks. Although outlandish in appearance and clumsy in his body language, The Tramp spoke a universal truth through his physicality, and Chaplin's music would give him an inner soul.

Not just a major movie star and emblem of the silent era, Chaplin also transformed into one of the most powerful film moguls of his day. In January 1919, along with D.W. Griffith, Mary Pickford and Douglas Fairbanks, Chaplin became a partner in the newly formed studio United Artists. The company was formed in order to benefit actors and filmmakers, particularly in the face of other studios which were increasingly asserting creative control over budgets, salaries and creative decisions.

For Chaplin, the freedom offered by United Artists was vital as he sought to wield his influence behind the camera, as well as in front of it. This was a revolutionary step for all involved, allowing each of the quartet to become their own producers, financiers and distributors, and scooping up the profits that would otherwise have gone to their employers.[55]

Ultimately, Chaplin's desire for creative control would extend to the realms of writing, directing and film scoring. Chaplin achieved trailblazing successes with the likes of *The Kid* (1921), *The Gold Rush* (1925), *City Lights* (1931) and *Modern Times* (made in 1936, after the silent era, but centering on a silent lead character). However, the sheer comic force of his physical personality, tiny moustache, wonky cane, baggy clothes and all, has perhaps overshadowed Chaplin's notable work as a film composer in his own right.

What really surprises about Chaplin's scores, when listening to them again in retrospect, is how accomplished and literate they are. No mere exercise in "mickey-mousing" (the term used, sometimes in a derisory manner, for illustrative music that over-emphasizes visual humor or action), Chaplin's music is symphonically attractive, detailed and complex.

Of course, one could focus on any number of silent comedy scores that went hand in hand with their respective star's personalities. The extraordinary sequence in Buster Keaton's *The General* (1926) when he dislodges a railway sleeper in front of a moving train before it ultimately crashes is boosted immeasurably by its music. It builds up a head of brassy suspense, paradoxically building a sense of tension and awe even as our outraged laughter escalates in pitch. Various artists have interpreted the music for the film including William P. Perry, Studio Ghibli veteran Joe Hisaishi and British composer Carl Davis.

When it came to the 1989 re-scoring of the 1923 Harold Lloyd classic *Safety Last*, Davis' talents were once again sought. The British composer, famous for Thames Television's *The World at War* theme and many other noted works, augments Lloyd hanging from the clock face with airy piano and bubbling orchestrations. The score is humorous yet bristling with an underlying tension. What better way to accompany one of the most famous images in motion picture history?

Chaplin, however, is a special case study. He fully immersed himself in the film scores for his own movies, working carefully, even fanatically, with composers to establish a singular sense of character, note by note. He recognized that silent film scores, particularly in the realm of comedy, could do more than merely replicate the act of physical movement. Such scores could get to the heart of narrative themes, becoming both expressive and illustrative at the same time, to echo the earlier philosophy regarding Erik Satie.

Chaplin's love of film music stemmed from his childhood years. He was a self-taught musician, having learned to play the piano, violin and viola at a young age, although he never learned to read music. Chaplin reminisced that he carried his violin and cello within him during an early Karno vaudeville tour in America. Elaborating, he said: "Since the age of 16, I had practised from four to six hours a day in my bedroom.... I had great ambitions to be a concert artist or, failing that, to use it in a vaudeville act, but as time went on I realized that I could never achieve excellence, so I gave it up."[56]

In 1921, Chaplin returned to England. He visited Kennington Cross in the London borough of Lambeth, where he had spent his childhood, and it reminded him of where he had first fallen in love with classical music. He claimed it was here that music "first entered my soul" after hearing, when he was a boy, a clarinetist play the music hall tune "The Honeysuckle and the Bee."[57] Although Chaplin downplayed his own musical abilities, as a filmmaker he would prove to be an exacting and demanding presence on the recording stage, with a keen ear for melody. Rather than simply hand notes over to musical arrangers, he took an active interest in the form and was determined to sculpt his own scores.

Chaplin historian Theodore Huff highlights *City Lights* (1931) as an example. Huff writes: "Arthur Johnston and Alfred Newman arranged and orchestrated the music for *City Lights*, Chaplin's outstanding score. But the melodies, with the exceptions noted above, used for the associations they would evoke, were composed by Chaplin."[58]

Huff notes: "As was customary in the scoring for silent pictures, the Wagnerian leitmotif system was followed—a distinctive musical theme associated with which character and idea. The musical cues in *City Lights* come to some 95, not accounting the passages where the music follows or mimics the action in what is generally known as 'mickey-mousing' from its use in the scoring of animated cartoons."[59]

"Although he relied upon associates to arrange varied and complex instrumentation," writes film historian Jeffrey Vance, "the musical imperative is his, and not a note in a Chaplin musical score was placed there without his consent."[60] This was another side of Chaplin, the creative auteur and multi-tasker: actor, writer, director, producer, studio founder and composer. Chaplin's exacting control of his film scores was another sign of how he carefully calibrated his screen personality, both on camera and off.

"I tried to compose elegant and romantic music to frame my comedies in contrast to the Tramp character," Chaplin explained, "for elegant music gave my comedies an emotional dimension. Musical arrangers rarely understood this. They wanted the music to be funny."[61]

Warming to his theme, Chaplin elaborated: "Nothing is more adventurous and exciting than to hear the tunes one has composed and played for the first time by a 50-piece orchestra."[62]

Composer David Raksin is famous for his haunting theme to 1944 noir *Laura*, directed by Otto Preminger and starring Gene Tierney; the theme was later covered by artists such as Frank Sinatra and Nat King Cole. But before becoming a celebrated composer in his own right, Raksin started out as Chaplin's musical assistant on *Modern Times*. In 1979 Raksin co-authored an article with Charles M. Berg titled "Music by Charlie Chaplin: Auteur or Collaborauteur?," which examined Raksin's involvement in the picture. The piece delves into Chaplin's creative process, while also raising the notion of authorship in film music. It's a subject that would become increasingly controversial as the years went on, particularly in the modern era of shared credit on massive franchise blockbusters.

Raksin stresses that Chaplin was actively involved in the composition process, to the extent that the development of a score could take months. Even if he wasn't directly reading the music, Chaplin was imprinting his personality onto it. He would sing or dance the tune that he wanted, often stemming from pieces that he'd improvised at the piano, and it was the responsibility of the composer or composers to orchestrate the themes and make them practical for usage in the movie.[63]

Nevertheless, for all Chaplin's enthusiasm and the skill of the symphonic musicians, the technology of the era was often lacking. It was noted that the nuances of the *City Lights* recording failed to resonate owing to poor microphone quality. Later, in 1989, the aforementioned Carl Davis re-recorded the score to mark the centenary of Chaplin's birth, for the first time exposing the score's charm and warmth.[64]

Chaplin's exacting demands for his film scores could occasionally pose problems. For David Raksin, it became personal when he was initially fired from *Modern Times*. Raksin recalled: "In the area of music, the influence of the English music hall was very strong, and since I felt that nothing but the best would do for this remarkable film, when I thought his approach was a bit vulgar, I would say, 'I think we can do better than that.' To Charlie, this was insubordination, pure and simple—and the culprit had to go."[65]

However, Raksin was later re-appointed to the project after reinforcing to Chaplin that he would not merely act as a musical secretary, one who simply transcribed Chaplin's ideas. Impressed by Raksin's tenacity, Chaplin brought him back on board, resulting in what the composer described as "four and a half months of work, and some of the happiest days of my life."[66]

Raksin later spoke of his collaboration with great affection, and reinforced Chaplin's seriousness of intent with regard to the music. "Charlie and I worked hand in hand," Raksin recalled. "We spent hours, days, months in that projection room running scenes and bits of action over and over, and we had a marvellous time shaping the music until it was exactly the way we wanted it. By the time we were through with a sequence, we had run it so often that we were certain the music was in perfect sync. Very few composers work this way ... the usual procedure is to work from timing sheets, with a stop clock, to coordinate image and music."[67]

Like D.W. Griffith, Chaplin was a director who tended to treat music with the same gravity as the picture itself. Chaplin's scores would yield timeless gems such as "Smile," first composed for *Modern Times* and later covered by Nat King Cole. (In the 1992 biopic *Chaplin*, starring Robert

Downey Jr., composer John Barry adapted the theme for director Richard Attenborough, putting his own uniquely poignant spin on the material.) The 1973 re-issue of *Limelight*, meanwhile, waltzed away with the Oscar for Best Original Score, beating two scores from John Williams in the process (*Images* and *The Poseidon Adventure*).

One might wonder how a movie that was originally released in 1952 could claim an Oscar nearly two decades later. Intriguingly, it's because *Limelight* was shown in Los Angeles for the very first time in 1972, which put it in contention for the Academy Awards the following year. Remarkably, it was Chaplin's only competitive Oscar win—how fascinating that, amidst such a glittering career, it was the realm of film scoring that clinched him the prize. (He won an honorary award that same year and had landed another honorary Oscar in 1929 for *The Circus*.)

It's a stirring reminder of the power of film music. The passage of time clearly hadn't dimmed the vibrancy of the *Limelight* score (composed by Chaplin and arranged by Raymond Rasch). In fact, it says a lot about the relative timelessness of an orchestral ensemble that Oscar voters were able to overlook a 19-year gap in film history and still recognize the potency of the music as a narrative and emotional device. One could say the same thing about all the classic film scores whose reputations have increased over the years. There's an ageless quality to the orchestral ensemble that is only enhanced when it's placed in conjunction with the moving image.

The film scores of Charlie Chaplin and his contemporaries were an important bridge between the earliest days of film music, and the eventual onset of talking pictures, or "talkies."

The Transition to "Talkies" and Sound Cinema

There's a marvelous moment in the classic musical *Singin' in the Rain* (1954) that encapsulates an epochal (and tricky) shift in Hollywood history. During the sequence, movie director Roscoe Dexter (Douglas Fowley) must coach squeaky-voiced diva Lina Lamont (Jean Hagen) through the intricacies of recording live dialogue on a film set. Quite apart from Lina's lack of commanding vocal chops, there's also the logistical challenge of wear to place the microphone on her person, so it can pick up the volume whilst also remaining incognito.

A riotously funny sequence plays out in which the increasingly harassed Roscoe picks up Lina's heartbeat, attempts to hide the mic in a prop bush and inadvertently causes chaos with the placement of the mic cable. The sublime joke is further compounded with a later sequence showing the premiere of Lina's movie, named "The Duelling Cavalier." Not only is the dialogue wildly out of sync, prompting guffaws from the attendant audience, but certain sound effects are exaggerated owing to the mic placement (the rattle of Lina's pearls, for one).

Not just a memorable instance of humor (and *Singin' in the Rain* is hardly lacking in those), this is also an affectionate and honest account of an epochal turning point in Hollywood history. Namely, the transition from silent cinema to pictures with sound, or "talkies" as they were referred to.

As the 1920s advanced, there was a sea-change in attitudes towards motion pictures. Developments in technology meant audiences could now hear their beloved stars, instead of imagining their voices through intertitle sequences. Films could also now convey added layers of meaning through a complex sound design. Music had been compelled to carry the emotional meaning of a movie in the silent era, acting as both the inner monologue and outer commentary on the actions of the characters. With A-listers now empowered to speak with their own voices, surely this would relegate film music to a position of lesser importance?

This is arguably the moment where the illusory and complex nature of film music as we know it today first started to take shape. Around the time of the early sound era, music became just one facet of a layered sound design encompassing dialogue and Foley effects (named for the pioneering sound effects artist Jack Foley), among other things. Whereas a film score would once have taken on this responsibility single-handedly, now a more complex power dynamic was taking shape.

There's no denying that silent pictures were propelled by a suite of orchestral tones, either culled from library tracks or composed specifically for the project (as discussed in the previous section "The Early Relationship Between Music and Picture"). But the steady march towards sound pictures invited the trickier question: what makes a truly great film score? Does it actively make one sit up and take notice, or does it subtly manipulate the emotions from a background position?

The struggles faced by the hapless Lina Lamont reflected the turnaround confronting Hollywood stars and craftsmen. With the stars now speaking, their neuroses, phrasing and timing would be all the more nakedly exposed, as would imperfections in the soundscape. Composers, meanwhile, now had to consider the juxtaposition of their own creations with a myriad of warring elements that brought their own meaning.

In the modern era, a composer must consider tonality, time signatures, textures and orchestration as measured against sound effects and dialogue. The inception point for this delicate balancing act began in the talking pictures period, where a harmonious aural blend would be used to communicate meaning. All of a sudden, a film score could be accused of being too overwrought, or, at the end of the scale, too underplayed, when pitted against the other elements in the sound design.

It's a balance that film composers have long struggled with, and these difficulties likely started with *Don Juan*. This 1926 adventure movie doesn't, in fact, contain synchronized dialogue, but it does showcase a synchronized score (from William Axt) and sound effects. Although the triptych of synced-up dialogue, music and sound wouldn't properly take off until *The Jazz Singer* (1927), the cutting-edge production techniques utilized in *Don Juan* would quietly (or not-so-quietly) revolutionize Hollywood.

Directed by Alan Crosland, *Don Juan* is based on Lord Byron's irresistibly seductive lover of the same name. John Barrymore is the amorous hero, Don Juan de Marana, and Mary Astor and Estelle Taylor play the women who fall under his spell. Yet the real star of the show was a largely unseen figure operating behind the scenes: a man named George Groves, who carved out a place in film history as cinema's first-ever soundtrack mixer.

Nowadays, the concept of a sound mixer is routinely accepted within the construction of a film's aural language. Broadly speaking, a mixer's role is to harmonize the tone and texture of the movie relative to the other competing elements in the soundscape. Or, to put it in the words of Tom Bailey, engineer at London's pre-eminent AIR Studios: "A successful score mix for me is when you get a piece of music on the dub stage where the music stems essentially remain untouched. The composer has achieved their vision and we've successfully navigated all of the obstacles in the dialogue and effects."[68]

Bailey elaborates: "Someone once described dubbing to me as big levers. You're essentially turning three main things up and down, music, dialogue and effects. At any one point it's difficult for them all to be flat-out."[69]

Lancashire-born George Groves was the unassuming figure who paved the way for Bailey and his fellow sound engineers the world over. Initially an employee of New York's Bell Labs (originally known as Western Electric Research Laboratories), Groves brought his musical intuition (he was an accomplished French horn player) to bear on some truly cutting-edge technology.[70]

During his time at Bell Labs, Groves helped develop what is described as "sound on disc technology." In 1922, following early experiments with loudspeakers, condenser microphones and "vacuum tube amplifiers," Groves and his team succeeded in synching picture and sound to an animated movie produced by Bell itself, called *The Audion*. The film explored the making of the aforementioned amplifier, and the team's sound efforts were accurate to within one second.[71]

By 1925, sufficient enhancements and upgrades to the system allowed full synchronization between sound and picture, although it took a while to convince the studios of its efficacy. Out of this came the Vitaphone system, the most successful example of early sound-on-disc synchronization. It was developed by the Western Electric Company and later purchased by Warner Bros. Initially, the studio was queasy about attempting to record and synchronize dialogue; their sales strategy was to play on the limitations of movie houses, selling the technology as a convenient solution to cumbersome live orchestral accompaniment.[72]

The success of *Don Juan* eventually convinced Warner Bros of the efficacy of the format. The Vitaphone technology was sought by the *Don Juan* filmmakers who aimed to fully synchronize a mixture of sound effects and symphony orchestra with the moving image. Groves and the rest of the Vitaphone engineers looked to record the New York Philharmonic (enlisted to perform William Axt's score) in the vast and beautiful Manhattan Opera House.

Groves would later say: "This was the start of big things because now they had decided to score some pictures with a big orchestra and to make Vitaphone short subjects with famous talent." Groves then took the unprecedented step of close-miking individual sections of the wider symphony (strings, brass, woodwind and so on), and later creating a live mix from each of these elements.[73]

Groves had also been asked to mix the sound and music for six Vitaphone short movies, which would play alongside the main feature. The end result caused a sensation, and lines stretched around the block outside the majestic Manhattan Opera House. For the very first time, both atmospheric sound effects and the sweep of the symphonic accompaniment had been captured on disc, playing along with the film itself to widespread acclaim.

Groves and the rest of the Vitaphone team may not have known it at the time, but they had established a watershed moment in Hollywood history. Together, they had created spine-tingling synergy between objective sound and subjective score. No longer was there a need for a live orchestra to play along to the picture in the manner of past silent movies.

A door had been opened into the future of immersive filmmaking. So successful was *Don Juan*'s New York premiere that the Vitaphone show was swiftly exported to the newly opened Grauman's Egyptian Theater in Los Angeles. And yet, studio executives still questioned the need for audible dialogue to sit alongside synchronized sound effects and music.

Towards the end of his career, in 1973, Groves reflected: "One thing that has impressed me during the passing of time is that nobody thought at that time of putting talking sequences in. Everything we did, somebody was singing, either an opera or a vaudeville act of some kind.... Somehow or other it never seemed to dawn on anybody that they should talk in motion pictures."[74]

Enter *The Jazz Singer* (1927), which established itself as Hollywood's first talking picture, or "talkie." This time, the trifecta of talking, music and accompanying sound effects would be perfected, drawing a line in the sand between the silent and sound eras. *The Jazz Singer* was the moment where the talking picture came of age in Hollywood, dazzling audiences with a brave new way of embracing popular cinema.

The Jazz Singer, directed by *Don Juan*'s Alan Crosland, is based on Samson Raphaelson's 1925 play of the same name. It stars Al Jolson, a hugely popular early 20th-century entertainer who's been unfortunately commemorated in hindsight as "the king of blackface." Jolson plays Jakie Rabinowitz, a Jewish man who defies his father's wishes to become a jazz artist. To that end, Jakie blacks up and takes to the stage, adopting the alias "Jack Robin."

Unfortunate racial politics aside, *The Jazz Singer* broke down multiple technological boundaries in Hollywood. The film deployed Vitaphone's "sound on disc technology," used to such successful effect in *Don Juan*, this time integrating Jolson's own voice into the sound design. This would include six songs performed by Jolson himself, including the famous "My Mammy" with lyrics by Samuel M. Lewis and Joe Young. Other performances included the Irving Berlin staple "Blue Skies" and traditional Aramaic declaration "Kol Nidre."

The score for *The Jazz Singer* was composed by Louis Silvers. Interestingly, Silvers had collaborated with Al Jolson for the song "April Showers." The piece made its debut in the 1921 musical production *Bombo*, which opened at the Jolson's 59th Street Theater (later renamed The New Century Theater). Jolson regularly included the song in his repertoire after first recording it with Columbia Records, a move which undoubtedly helped pave the way for Silvers' appointment on *The Jazz Singer*.

Although his name may not resonate as strongly as a John Williams or a Hans Zimmer, Louis Silvers put his cultural imprint on Hollywood, starting with his collaboration with D.W. Griffith. The latter first collaborated with an uncredited Silvers on 1920's *Way Down East*. Such was the success of their collaboration that they worked together again on 1921 drama *Dream Street*.

Largely forgotten today, London-based movie *Dream Street* adapts two short stories by British author Thomas Burke, bringing to life a turbulent love triangle. Despite the presence of noted silent performer Carol

Dempster, the movie is best remembered as providing Silvers' debut film score. The filmmakers also attempted a synchronized song sequence that was swiftly abandoned owing to poor sound reproduction.[75]

In the wake of *Dream Street*, Silvers would cement himself as one of Hollywood's pre-eminent musicians and conductors, eventually rising to become the Head of Music at the Columbia Studios Music Department. That posting would later yield critical and artistic success. In the meantime, his music for *The Jazz Singer* was one of several elements juggled by the Vitaphone engineers.

Groves and his fellow team members were established on Stage Three of the Warner Bros studio backlot to capture the mix for *The Jazz Singer*. For the first time ever, Groves was able to enjoy a glass-partitioned mixing booth, placed adjacent to the set, in which to do his work; such things are now a mainstay of even the most standard recording. Warner Bros, newly emboldened by the process, was itself responsible for the construction of the recording set, and their investment would soon pay off handsomely.

Groves recalled the epochal moment where Jolson's voice was first captured on the recording, the actor ad-libbing his lines. Groves said: "It was all planned that he should sing. In one sequence he came into the set to sit down and play for his mother and, purely ad-lib, he said, 'Mother you ain't heard nothing yet.' When they saw this stuff, [they said] 'My gosh he talked.' It seemed to be a tremendous surprise…. It was done completely ad-lib without rehearsal. Everybody held their breath, then he sang. It took everybody by storm that he just came out with spoken words."[76]

With just a smattering of spoken dialogue, Jolson, in conjunction with Vitaphone's technological marvel, had offered Hollywood stars and craftsmen a glimpse into the future. *The Jazz Singer* was a notable success on its release in October 1927, grossing $2.5 million against its $400,000 budget. Little wonder it was billed on the promotional posters as "Warner's Supreme Triumph." And the approach to the movie's sound design sent ripples all the way through the upper echelons of Hollywood.

At the inaugural Academy Awards, held on May 16, 1929, at the Hollywood Roosevelt Hotel on Hollywood Boulevard, Los Angeles, *The Jazz Singer* caused a sensation. The movie walked away with a special honorary Oscar, awarded to Warner Bros studio head Darryl F. Zanuck "for producing … the pioneer outstanding talking picture, which has revolutionized the industry."[77]

The Jazz Singer was the first movie of its kind, and studios and filmmakers became increasingly emboldened by the opportunities that synchronized dialogue, music and sound effects offered. In 1928, Walt Disney, spurred on by *The Jazz Singer*'s success, utilized synchronized sound and visuals in Mickey Mouse animation *Steamboat Willie* (including a cow's teeth being played like a xylophone) with help from composer Wilfred Jackson.

The latter supplied "bar sheets" in advance to indicate the rough placement of the music while Disney (working off Jackson's metronome markings) produced exposure sheets for the animators, indicating where the frames and music should match up.[78] The music, conducted by Carl Eduoarde in New York, followed the tempo of a bouncing ball to attain full synchronization and synergy with the imagery. *Steamboat Willie* anticipated the full synchronization between music, sound and dialogue in the seminal likes of *Snow White and the Seven Dwarfs* (1937), and all feature-length Disney animations thereafter.

The Jazz Singer also marked the beginning of a beautiful friendship between Al Jolson and George Groves. The latter warmly reminisced: "Jolie, I thought, was a wonderful, wonderful man.... We were very good friends and I had to do all of his shows.... He was a greater entertainer off the stage than on, in my observations.... Any time he was off stage and relating some story or anecdote to a group of people, they would stand around absolutely spell-bound."[79]

In return, Jolson affectionately dubbed the unassuming yet pioneering Groves as "the quiet little Englishman."[80] It was a synergy of creative minds that sent motion pictures careering in a thrilling new direction. Together, the two men would collaborate on the likes of *The Singing Fool* (1927), *Say It with Songs* and *New York Nights* (both 1929), and *Mammy* (1930).

If the story of George Groves proves anything, it's that heroes can come from anywhere. A British-born man, Groves' work at Bell Labs in New York ushered in a brand-new chapter in motion picture history. Groves' inspirational story continued long after *The Jazz Singer* wrapped production, including a stint in World War II, serving, appropriately enough, in the 1st Motion Picture Unit of the American Air Force.

A 1946 report from Hollywood Quarterly Magazine notes how Hollywood craftsmen like Groves were drafted into World War II, sought for the filmmaking skills that would encourage prospective soldiers to enlist. The so-called "Celluloid Commandos" began operation in October 1942 and continued until October 1945. A self-contained film unit, they turned out 288 movies in that period, each running at various lengths, with the combined running time for all emerging at 78 hours and 37 minutes.[81]

Groves further asserted his credentials with Oscar wins for *Yankee Doodle Dandy* (1942), *Sayonara* (1957), starring Marlon Brando, and the Audrey Hepburn musical *My Fair Lady* (1964). The last of these, in particular, demonstrated Groves' remarkable flair for harmonizing and integrating a busy, bustling mixture of dialogue, sound and music, one of many sophisticated accomplishments in a remarkable career. He would forever be immortalized as the first mixer in the history of Hollywood cinema.

As for Louis Silvers, he made his mark several years later. In 1935, as the aforementioned Head of Department for Columbia Music, he won the inaugural Oscar for Best Original Score (then credited as Best Music—Scoring). The Oscar was awarded for *One Night of Love*, a musical drama about an American opera singer (Grace Moore) who, against the wishes of her family, makes the decision to study in Milan.

The effect of Silvers' Oscar win would establish film scoring as a competitive and credible art form amidst awards circles. Although the dramatic underscore itself was credited to Victor Schertzinger (also the film's director) and lyricist Gus Kahn, it was Silvers' intuition and studio clout that created a sea-change in the attitude towards film music.

Also nominated at the Oscars that night: a rising composer named Max Steiner. This talented craftsman had turned heads in Tinseltown just two years earlier, with his score for a movie about a giant gorilla. The film was called *King Kong*, and Steiner's music had portended a richly engrossing new era for Hollywood film scores. The resulting period would be one of sweeping romance, bold themes, adventurous tones and an irresistible sense of derring-do.

Two

Forte
The Romantic Era Takes Shape

"There are thousands of sounds that I have in my head that have influenced me, from Nino Rota to Bernard Herrmann to Maurice Jarre to Georges Delerue to Miles Davis. There are many, many voices."—ALEXANDRE DESPLAT[1]

Max Steiner, the Monster Movie and the Romantic Epic

Few movie images are as famous as that of King Kong, the giant ape, standing atop New York's Empire State Building. Before fate intervenes, leading to the classic line "it was beauty that killed the beast," the character of Kong bestrides the silver screen in a mighty display of power. One can only imagine what audiences thought when first seeing the movie in 1933—the technical craft on display was unprecedented by Hollywood standards.

Yet, while Willis O'Brien's tactile creature designs broke new ground, it was the accompanying film score that made audiences feel Kong's bulk. For the first time in Hollywood history, a dramatic symphony was attached to an outlandish and fantastical central character. This was, essentially, the first narrative-driven monster movie/adventure score, and no-one at the time could have foreseen its lasting effects.

The music was written by Max Steiner, at this point 47 years old, and already an established presence in Hollywood. But where did Steiner come from, what were his influences, and how did he come to exert a remarkable, lasting legacy on the medium of the film score?

The composer was born in 1888 in Austria, and the innate, romantic stylistics of Steiner's home country would course through his eventual Hollywood film scores. Steiner came from illustrious and wealthy Jewish stock, and his family had already exerted a considerable influence on the Viennese cultural scene. Steiner's grandfather, Maximilian Raoul, collaborated with Johann Strauss II, bringing Strauss' operetta *Indigo and the Forty Thieves* to a live audience in 1871 to huge success.[2] In 1873, Raoul Steiner purchased the rights to French play *La Réveillon*, later adapted by Strauss into the seminal operatic work *Die Fledermaus*.[3]

Steiner's father, Gabor, was an influential theater impresario who was credited with bringing the tango to Vienna.[4] Although Gabor encouraged his son to become an engineer, the musical instincts of the younger Steiner weren't about to be suppressed. He owed much of his gift to the inspiration of his godfather, the esteemed "The Blue Danube" composer Richard Strauss. It was clear that an appreciation for, and skill with, music flowed within and around the Steiner family. The rich era of romanticism would instill in Steiner a gift for melody, counterpoint and theme, a gift that would immeasurably elevate the film projects to which he became attached.

"The dramatic language Steiner helped create was quickly adapted by others: recurring leitmotifs linked to specific characters, climbing key modulations to intensify emotion, precise orchestral colors to evoke place and psychology," writes Steiner historian Steven C. Smith. "But Steiner's own musical genius was sui generis. No other film composer possessed such a seemingly inexhaustible gift for melody. His choice of musical key signatures carefully considered the pitch of an actor's voice, as well as sound effects (Steiner would compose above or below them)."[5]

Later, whilst enrolled at the illustrious Imperial Academy of Music in Vienna, the adolescent Steiner was tutored in the art of conducting by Gustav Mahler, another 20th-century musical figurehead who would influence the genesis of Steiner's film compositions.[6] Mahler was just one of several revered musical figures who encouraged and furthered Steiner's gift with melody and musical dramatism.

Steiner achieved an extraordinary amount while still in his teens: at the age of 14, his own self-penned operetta, *The Beautiful Greek Girl*, was highly successful, and ran in Vienna's Orpheum Theater for 12 months.[7] The adolescent Steiner would eventually seize the opportunity to conduct all over the world, travelling with his father Gabor as the latter toured the globe with his new theater company.

Steven C. Smith writes: "By his early teens, the boy who once yawned over Bach and Beethoven had fallen madly in love with the classics. 200 years of concert music became his daily study."[8] It helped that Steiner came of age during a dazzling cultural crossroads in Europe, with the likes of Wagner, Debussy and Ravel swirling on the ebbs and flows of the musical scene.

Steiner's young mind became a soup of complex cultural intermingling, mixing ethnic traditions and folk music with his already-established love of operetta and romanticism. Leaving Vienna, he finally alighted in London where he conducted musicals at a number of noted venues, including the Opera House, the Adelphi and the London Pavilion.[9] In 1912, he became infatuated with an old flame with whom he'd reconnected in London: actor Beatrice Tilt, whom he would later marry. It's perhaps not hard to see where the lusty and yearning side of Steiner's musical personality stemmed from, although his later marriage to Tilt would end in divorce.[10]

In 1914, Steiner left England for America, and he eventually landed in New York. It coincided with the outbreak of World War I, the first of two global conflicts that led to a mass exodus of European Jews to America during the 20th century. It's remarkable to note the artistic breakthroughs that came out of this turmoil and strife: destabilized, ostracized composers and craftsmen whose destinies aligned perfectly with the ever-expanding motion picture business.

Nevertheless, accounts of Steiner's arrival in the United States tend to vary. Studio publicity indicated that he was personally invited to America by conductor Florenz Ziegfeld whereas Steiner said that, upon arriving in New York, he offered his services as a conductor and was pointed towards a job working on the railroads.[11]

Either way, Steiner was enlisted by Ziegfeld and began working as a conductor and orchestrator on Broadway musicals. He worked with the cream of the crop, including George Gershwin, composer of "Rhapsody in Blue" that's memorably heard at the start of Woody Allen's *Manhattan* (1979).[12] At the same time, Steiner began to serve as music director for Fox Films in Manhattan, which led to his first film composition project.

A fledgling motion picture studio, Fox was headed by the tenacious ex–Nickelodeon owner William Fox who recognized Steiner's nascent skills.[13] In 1916, Steiner composed a score for a silent movie called *The Bondman*, which arose, in his words, out of a desire to do "something new." He would later describe the project as a "perfectly terrible picture," but it was an early outlier in the realm of fully dramatized film music.[14] That said, full synchronization with additional sound elements didn't come until the late 1920s, as noted in the previous chapter.

Alas, Steiner's technical accomplishments on *The Bondman* came to nought. The film offers dried up, or, rather, were thwarted when he was lured back to Broadway. One knee injury and a mixed run of productions later and it wasn't clear if Steiner had missed the movie boat altogether. He then became involved in the tumultuous production of *Rainbow*, on which he served as musical director. Staged by Oscar Hammerstein II, the show ran for just 29 performances, a black mark on Steiner's illustrious career.[15] However, things were about to change.

In 1929, Steiner was personally selected by the in-house composer at studio RKO (Radio-Keith-Orpheum), Harry Tierney, to act as an orchestrator in Hollywood. Broadly speaking, an orchestrator translates the composer's work for the purposes of the live orchestral ensemble, physically arranging the musicians to facilitate the correct level of nuance in the performance. Very often a composer will undertake this duty his or herself (Howard Shore, cited in Chapter One, is such a person).

Tierney was in the process of bringing his musical production *Rio Rita* to the big screen, and thenceforth Steiner was enmeshed in the Hollywood studio system.[16] On December 10, 1929, Hollywood history was made when Max Steiner officially joined RKO Pictures, a decision that would eventually yield several of the greatest film scores of all time. He would begin by working as an orchestrator for the prolific Roy Webb, later recognized as the Oscar-nominated composer of *Quality Street* (1937).[17]

In another example of strange cultural-political dovetailing, Steiner's entrance into Hollywood coincided with the devastating Wall Street Crash in 1929. It's been suggested that this economic strife is what propelled Steiner from Broadway to RKO, although the scoring industry was itself still struggling with the studio stigma against non-diegetic music accompaniments.[18]

Not long after Steiner's arrival, RKO itself ran into financial difficulties, largely down to the box office failure of the musical *Dixiana* (1930), which Steiner had orchestrated (yielding his first screen credit in the process). Yet despite this turbulent socio-cultural backdrop, a wave of singularly talented individuals was sweeping East to West across America, in anticipation of opportunities within the motion picture industry.

As Steven C. Smith observes: "The westward migration of New Yorkers included not only Steiner, but other future masters of the craft—Alfred Newman, Herbert Stothart and Dimitri Tiomkin among them."[19] And as post-production techniques began to improve, the consensus on non-diegetic scores began to change for the better, facilitating Steiner's rise to the top. The main evolutionary leap came in the form of the click track, which allowed infinitesimal synchronicity between the tempo of the music and the on-screen action.

Composer and score academic Peter Wegele explains that a sound technician fixed "an additional track onto the film that was punched with holes. When playing the film, the hole running through the projector would produce an audible click. The distance between these holes was determined by the tempo desired. For example, if the tempo was 60 beats per minute, the film had a click every 24 frames…. If the composer wanted to hit a cue in the sixth second of the film (the 144th frame of this reel), the cue would be the seventh click."[20]

Steven C. Smith elaborates: "The conductor of a score wore

headphones, through which he heard the clicks while watching the movie projected above the orchestra. The movie had visual 'punches' corresponding to key moments needing synchronization, and 'streamers'—rolling lines—indicating the imminent appearance of a 'punch.'"[21]

As with the Vitaphone sound-on-disc technology, this breakthrough helped establish a more technically sophisticated approach to film scoring. To this day, the click track is used by musicians in all fields, not just film, to attain a perfect level of synchronicity. Many cite the invention of the click track to Steiner himself or, failing that, aforementioned cartoon composer Carl Stalling.

Steiner's earliest use of the process came in 1931 when he scored the RKO picture *Beau Ideal*. Although another unfortunate flop for the studio, the movie would play an important, if unassuming, part in the development of the film score as we now know it.

"Well, I had what I thought was a brilliant idea," Steiner recalled. "I hired 20 men, all of whom played two instruments; the trumpet, flute, trombone, etc. I orchestrated the march for approximately 40 men. Then I made one recording with 20 men—maybe all brass against this tempo track, because they had to be in sync with the men marching. Then I had my men double and I did the same thing over again with all the woodwinds. When I got through with that, I used about six drummers, also the same men. In the dubbing we put the three tracks together according to the click track. When we were finished, it sounded like a 60-piece band."[22]

Whether or not Steiner was the inventor of the click track form, he's widely credited with popularizing it. By the early 1930s, the ability to record and mix multiple layers of the orchestra had lined up with synchronization technology. The end result: film scores attuned perfectly to every nuance of the visible action. Nowadays, we take it for granted when, say, a Marvel Cinematic Universe (MCU) score vigorously skims around an action sequence, hitting all the requisite cue points to further enhance our excitement. But in the early days of Hollywood, this was astonishingly radical.

The stars were therefore aligned perfectly for Steiner's *King Kong* score to induce a sense of awed reverence. By the time Steiner came to scoring it in 1933, he'd achieved critical success with his music for *Cimarron* (1931), a Western starring Richard Dix and Irene Dunne. (Steiner would later experience more success in the Western genre, notably John Ford's *The Searchers* in 1956, starring John Wayne.) When *King Kong* arrived on the big screen, the composer's dramatic intuition meshed with the expansion of, and increased confidence in, the non-diegetic score medium. It was an extraordinary convergence of the artistic and the practical.

It took two directors to bring the oversized simian known as Kong to the big screen. They were Merian C. Cooper and Ernest B. Schoedsack, although it was Cooper who developed the idea and initiated the project. Fascinated by gorillas from a young age, he imagined a movie scenario whereby a whole group of them would battle monstrous Komodo dragons.[23] Eventually, the focus was narrowed to just one gorilla, while also throwing in a female character to encourage a more romantic element.

Cooper pitched the idea to Paramount Studios in the midst of the Great Depression in 1931. Yet there was understandable queasiness about budgets, particularly if far-flung, exotic locations were to be involved. He then brought the project to RKO, where it fell under the auspices of the studio's new vice president: the soon-to-be-infamous David O. Selznick, whose own story would regularly intertwine with that of Max Steiner. Cooper later became Selznick's assistant, and he drew his attention to a mooted RKO project named *Creation*.

Effects artist Willis O'Brien was to use stop-motion creature designs in what was essentially a remake of Arthur Conan Doyle adaptation *The Lost World* (1925), in which humans discover a dinosaur island and bring the creatures back to civilization. Although Cooper wasn't interested in the project per se, O'Brien's concepts arrested his attention. O'Brien's stop-motion skills prevented the need for creature footage to be captured in far-flung locations—instead, it could be achieved in a cost-effective manner on a soundstage. Cooper eventually combined these principles with the DNA of the *Creation* story to give birth to *King Kong*.[24] (The "King" section of the title reportedly came from Selznick.[25])

The final movie, released in the United States on April 7, 1933, was the very first creature-feature epic in cinema history. *King Kong* was a technical spectacle the likes of which the world had never seen. O'Brien's palpably tactile Kong design, while potentially clunky looking now, was the first time that special effects had been put in service of a film's title character. Everything was set up to fail, but Kong was given tangible life by the filmmakers, the first monster to act as the star of his own movie.

One reason why the film continues to endure is the seamless use of forced perspective and clever camera angles. The effects mesh perfectly with a scrupulous array of matte paintings, rear projection, foreground props and miniature sets. Optical and practical came together to fully immerse audiences in a fantastical landscape, an early example of the wonders wrought by painstaking Hollywood craft. And while Kong was given an actual roar by the sound designers, it was Max Steiner who really communicated the awe-inspiring heft and make-believe majesty of this ill-fated great ape.

King Kong would have been catnip for any composer, let alone one of Steiner's abilities. He deployed a sizeable orchestra (financed by Cooper himself out of his own pocket[26]) to articulate and embellish the movie's central themes of exotic bestiality and inescapable romance. In Steiner's own words: "It was the kind of film that allowed you to do anything and everything, from weird chords and dissonances to pretty melodies."[27]

Nowadays, it's very easy to take Steiner's approach in *King Kong* for granted. The memorable main titles introduce the guttural theme for the title character, largely carried on the French horns, trombones and tubas. The notion of low-range brass conveying a bestial roar is par for the course now, but in 1933, audiences had never heard anything like it.

This wasn't a live orchestral accompaniment or an improvised piano melody, but a film composer actively getting beneath the skin of the main character and extracting his personality through music. That we hear Kong's theme long before we first see him is key to the devilishly clever intent: we're already anticipating his animalistic rage and overpowering size in the first few seconds, keeping us gripped as to what will follow.

There are multiple themes threaded throughout the *King Kong* score. Outside of the imposing main theme, there's also a winsome, romantic piece for Fay Wray's imperiled Ann Darrow, the beauty who tames the beast. The wavering strings mesh with the soft-focus close-ups in a manner that recalls the approach of early silent cinema, while also advancing the language of narrative-driven music into a new decade. By aligning specific themes and motifs to certain characters and situations, Steiner honored Wagnerian tradition while also fashioning a musical tapestry that proved singular to the movie.

The malleability of Kong's leitmotif is seen as pivotal to the score's impact. At key moments Steiner reduces it to just three notes, which allows him to sneak into various sequences in a host of guises. This includes at least one diegetic cue and the all-important climax where it meshes with the love theme to heartbreaking and tragic effect.[28] At the same time, it's also noted that the stereotyped musical depiction of Skull Island's natives is unreconstructed by today's standards. That said, it proved hugely influential on practically every Hollywood score that came afterwards, particularly when it came to dealing with "exotic" other cultures such as Native Americans and Romans.[29]

It's the marvelously complex overlap and collision between these ideas that further cements *King Kong* as the first-ever blockbuster Hollywood film score. Yet Steiner is also to be commended for his restraint, particularly in the early stretches of the movie. Following the main title reveal, the composer makes us wait before unveiling his next piece of original score music, an indication that the movie is brilliantly spotted, as well as brilliantly composed.

For British composer Ilan Eshkeri (*Stardust*, 2007; BBC's *A Perfect*

Planet, 2020), this is the crux of Steiner's genius. He explains: "For the first 20 minutes of the movie, there isn't a single note of music. Then, this mist descends and the boat heads into it. They're all lost, but there still isn't any music. As the boat comes out of the mist and they see Skull Island for the first time, it marks the moment where you've left reality and entered fantasy for the first time."[30]

Eshkeri applauds this approach, saying it's the key to managing audience expectations. "At that moment, you get the first bit of film music ever," he explains. "It's a great bit of music, but there's also something incredibly poetic about that music being cued up at that moment. All of the ideas encompassed in that are foundational ideas as to how film music works."[31]

The cue to which Eshkeri refers, titled "A Boat in the Fog," is a sign of how carefully Steiner treated both the incidental music cues and the central themes. Tentative, prickly harp chords swirl as the boat crew gets its first glimpse of Skull Island, creating an eerie, almost spectral, atmosphere while tribal drums (heard diegetically) implicitly suggest the Kong-level savagery that's about to be unleashed. One can clearly hear, in retrospect, the influence on John Williams' later *Jaws* (1975), an Oscar-winning score that uses similarly crystalline harp textures to suggest the terrifying fathoms of the deep.

In fact, it was Steiner who encouraged the level of musical discretion in the film's early stages. He recommended to Cooper that the first 18 minutes of the movie remain unscored, to better reinforce a sense of verisimilitude in the early New York sequences.[32] This would have the effect of heightening the music's impact during the more fantastical sequences.

The power of *King Kong*'s music, in combination with the click track synchronization, creates a marvelous audio-visual hybrid. Just as Steiner's score is led by the film, so does the film itself gain added resonance and meaning from the non-diegetic soundtrack. As a project, *King Kong* solidified the cyclical relationship between sound and vision, making a virtue out of narratively music that seemingly materializes from nowhere. This ought to have been an almighty distraction, and indeed studio heads at the time were still doubtful about the age-old question: "Where's the music coming from?"

That those fears were immediately put to rest is a testament to Steiner's skill. And audiences in 1933 didn't notice the joins; they were instead being swept up by Steiner's brassy outbursts. Crucially, no music is present as Kong swats the biplanes atop the Empire State Building during the finale. It's a testament to the power of careful spotting, and the skill of a composer capable of recognizing sound effects as their own kind of musicality.

For the first time in Hollywood history, music itself became an organic, mutable character, rife with contradictions. At the same time that the film score is subservient to the image, it also emboldens and deepens the picture, transforming Kong from stop-motion puppet into a tragic, oddly relatable figure who meets his doom. Rumor has it that the filmmakers were, from the very start, not convinced of the animated Kong's efficacy and subsequently relied heavily on the score to reinforce a suspension of disbelief.[33] There's no denying that the strategy worked.

Upon its release, *King Kong* was a huge box office success, and one cannot imagine the film having the same impact without its music. After premiering at Grauman's Chinese Theater in Los Angeles, the movie grossed more than $5 million against a total production budget of $672,000. It officially ushered in the era of action-adventure entertainment, with visionary directors and egotistical producers increasingly punch-drunk on the notion of high-concept narratives for a mass audience. *Jaws* would later adopt and adapt the mantle, introducing audiences to the notion of the "summer tentpole blockbuster" spectacular.

Tragically at the time of *King Kong*'s release, the Oscar scoring category hadn't been formed. Regardless, *King Kong*'s legacy is borne out not in arbitrary Oscar wins, but the sheer number of electrifying film scores that have emulated its approach. One need only listen to Akira Ifukube's similarly impressive work for the original *Godzilla* (1954), which uses relentlessly driving strings and a booming brass section to suggest the bulk of the irradiated giant lizard.

At the same time, Ifukube added plenty of avant-garde techniques of his own, including a resin-coated glove that was rubbed up and down the strings to simulate Godzilla's roar. This, in turn, would inspire countless future *Godzilla* scores, including a powerfully exciting iteration from David Arnold for Roland Emmerich's 1998 remake. Then, in 2014, Alexandre Desplat unleashed a darkly turbulent and brilliant score for director Gareth Edwards' big-budget remake. It's heartening to note that, in the genetic code of all these spin-offs and reboots, Steiner's influence is still churning away in there.

Returning to John Williams, his score for Steven Spielberg's *Jurassic Park* (1993) uses guttural French horns and strings for the dreaded velociraptors. The music attains an animalistic, vicious air, channeling the spirit of Max Steiner at the same time as Spielberg mirrors the visual stylistics of *King Kong*'s approach. Williams' use of low-register brass in conjunction with Spielberg's low-angled shots of the T-Rex, for instance, call to mind the spellbinding blend of Merian C. Cooper's direction and Steiner's music in *King Kong*. One can also hear the dissonant, propulsive influence of Stravinsky's ballet *The Rite of Spring* (1913), principles that would later be transferred into the turbulent, terrifying *War of the Worlds* (2005).

In truth, the wide-ranging impact of Steiner's *King Kong* score is too multifaceted to cover in a few sentences. A microcosmic, and perhaps better, example, is emphasizing its legacy through the various *Kong* remake scores that have emerged throughout the decades. In 1976, John Barry tackled the story of Kong in director John Guillermin's movie, playing up the languid romance of Jessica Lange's performance as Dwan (effectively the substitute for the original film's Ann).

Although Barry largely favors his yearning, romantic side (later to flower in the Oscar-winning *Out of Africa*, 1985), he does pay clear homage to Steiner. The opening titles pit seat-shaking trombone blasts against high-register strings in the manner of Barry's classic *James Bond* scores. In deference to the period in which he was recording, Barry also throws in a light synthesized touch (a somewhat unusual approach for him). It's a sign of how the genetic code of the original Steiner score had evolved and mutated over time.

The most acclaimed of the *King Kong* reboot scores came from James Newton Howard. He wrote the music for Peter Jackson's mega-budget 2005 movie, a relentless three-hour epic that unleashed not just Kong, but dinosaur stampedes and giant creepy crawlies. Newton Howard's Golden Globe-nominated score (replacing work from Howard Shore) is pleasingly aware of its origins, an old-fashioned symphonic blast right from the brassy menace of the main titles.

Thunderous musical set-pieces such as "Head Towards the Animals" and "Tooth and Claw" showcase Newton Howard's own style, excitingly bold and dynamic in its execution. Chugging strings and brass approximate not just Kong's size, but the scale of the creatures faced by the film's human characters, including Ann Darrow (Naomi Watts). Yet it's important to remember that the foundations of all contemporary blockbuster action music owe themselves to Steiner, from the clarion call of the brass to the jitteriness of the violins. The latter is an instrument whose register is said to best approximate the tone of the human voice, making it consistently effective in engaging a viewer's attention during an action sequence.

Away from the more bombastic scenes, Howard pays due diligence to the romantic, sensitive side of Steiner's original score. Howard's love theme for Ann and Kong (brilliantly realized by Andy Serkis via motion capture) is a largely piano-led, delicate theme that belies the species differences between the two characters. It's a meeting of minds and souls, not physicalities, and Howard's delightful music reinforces this, playing up the fairy tale aspects of the narrative in a manner that Steiner would no doubt have admired.

Recent Kong reboot *Kong: Skull Island* (2017) brings the classic Max Steiner sound into the era of the digitized blockbuster score. Composed by

Henry Jackman, *Kong: Skull Island* can never escape from the central use of the brass section to convey the iconic monster's overwhelming mass. In this instance, the aggressive brass is taken to the extreme with a Kong who is far bigger than any other we've seen before. Yet the central tenets of Jackman's music date all the way back to that fateful day in 1933 when Steiner essentially gave birth to the first full synchronized action film score.

The next part of Steiner's story threads together his destiny with another character cited earlier in this chapter: producer David O. Selznick. Following his appointment to RKO, Selznick would quickly ascend the ranks to become one of the most tempestuous and incendiary producers in Hollywood history: brash, outspoken and never reticent to indulge in an outlandish vision.

By 1936, Selznick had established himself as an independent producer via Selznick International Pictures. He then purchased the film rights, for $50,000, to Margaret Mitchell's American Civil War–set novel *Gone with the Wind*. One year later, the book itself had sold one million copies, and Hollywood expectations had started to skyrocket. The project would eventually draw together two creative titans of the film world, Selznick and Steiner, the former's incorrigible bluster mirrored in the latter's garrulous, full-blooded approach to life.

In fact, by 1937, composer and producer had already parted ways. The two strong personalities had appeared to cancel each other out, temporarily at least. Newly installed at Warner Bros, Steiner had started to produce scores (for a much-reduced salary) at a startling rate, averaging 12 a year by 1939 (the year of *Gone with the Wind*'s eventual release). His classics in this period are too numerous to mention but encompass the likes of *The Informer* (1935) for director John Ford, which won him his first Oscar, and *The Charge of the Light Brigade* (1936). However, the soon-to-be-composed *Gone with the Wind* would cast a long shadow over most other scores in Steiner's career (with the exception of *King Kong*).

That said, the ever-erratic Selznick would not choose *Gone with the Wind*'s composer until three months into filming. The producer had always championed Steiner for the project, and yet, when the composer discovered the news, it put him in a bind. Now contracted to Warner Bros, Steiner had to write an apologetic letter to studio head Jack L. Warner.[34] His aim: to secure a temporary release to score the MGM/Selznick picture centered on Scarlett O'Hara, a project with which Steiner had been enamored for several years.

Warner approved Steiner's temporary release, but on the condition that Selznick would pay top dollar to once again employ the composer's services.[35] In the meantime, Warner would squeeze Steiner as much as possible prior to starting on *Gone with the Wind*, eventually extracting another four scores in that period from the prolific musician. By June 27, 1939, *Gone with the Wind* finally completed principal photography.

An extensive and elaborate post-production process now stretched out, with Steiner at the center. He would be on call for Selznick between July and December of that year, deploying every skill, nuance and technique he had learned in his 51 years. Officially signed to the project in August 1939, Steiner would become engulfed by the chaotic maelstrom that was *Gone with the Wind*, which had already burned through three directors during the difficult shoot (George Cukor, Victor Fleming and Sam Wood). The demanding Selznick didn't make allies among the cast or crew, pursuing a vision of Hollywood opulence never before seen on the big screen. And Steiner was next in line to grapple with Selznick's exacting, even tyrannical, approach.

That said, the composer already had experience in this area, having clashed with Selznick during his RKO years. The creative conflict between the two men is very likely the first documented spat between a producer and a composer in movie history. As is always the case, two strong-minded individuals set out with the best intentions for the movie but go about it in different ways. The composer is naturally beholden to the whims of the picture, but he or she is not about to take notes from a non-musician while lying down. This problem has only intensified in the decades since *Gone with the Wind*'s release, as producers and franchise owners have asserted more control over the post-production process.

An immediate concern on *Gone with the Wind* was Selznick's insistence that Steiner incorporate existing classical pieces into the score, not to mention pieces that originated from America's Deep South, but this idea was compromised following disagreements with the composer.[36] Aping, rather than directly referencing, existing music staples became the order of the day, but naturally, the real star of the show is a Steiner original. "Tara's Theme," which opens the film and is incorporated throughout. It remains one of the most sumptuously romantic in the history of cinema. If one were to point towards the single cue that embodied Steiner's style, this would be it.

The elegiac sweep of the strings and the nobility of the brass counterpoint complements two critical areas of the narrative. The first is the central character of Scarlett O'Hara, the fiery Southern belle played by Vivien Leigh in a star-making performance. Steiner was said to have been enraptured by Leigh's screen presence, and upon hearing the yearning, sweeping tone of his main theme, it's hard to disagree. The tone of the theme is beautiful yet bold, tender yet defiant, brilliantly summing up the contradictory facets of the character. The narrative accomplishments of Steiner's storytelling would directly influence all the romantic composers in his wake, including the aforementioned John Barry. It's hard to listen to Barry's *Out of Africa* theme without acknowledging the lingering influence of *Gone with the Wind*'s music.

As the title of the theme suggests, the Tara music is indicative of the film's broader narrative sweep. The track is named after Scarlett's beloved plantation, which becomes the eye at the center of the brewing Civil War storm. Both the personal and the political, the intimate and the wide-ranging, are summed up in a single piece of music, arguably marking the moment where the epic Hollywood drama score came of age. Naturally, the romantic nature of the music belies the unsavory stereotyping and undercurrents of *Gone with the Wind*, which have only soured further with the passing of the decades.

However, Steiner has few charges to answer on this front. As a composer, he was tasked with scoring the movie in front of him, not the movie that we, the 21st-century audience, wish it could be. Scale, grandiosity and operatic emotion are largely the order of the day throughout the score, as Scarlett's tempestuous romance with Rhett Butler (Clark Gable) is mirrored in the wider turbulence of the American Deep South.

And yet, even amidst *Gone with the Wind*'s overblown budget and escalating, laborious sense of scale, Steiner seeks to keep the music rooted in something recognizable. This plays into a key philosophy of his: that volume and bombast is no substitute for depth of feeling. Such an approach would be carried into countless other Steiner classics, including *Casablanca* (1942) and *The Big Sleep* (1946), but *Gone with the Wind* is the epitome of this ideal.

Steiner would later say in his film scoring lectures:

> The hardest thing in scoring is to know when to start and when to stop. Music can slow up an action that should not be slowed up and quicken a scene that shouldn't be. Knowing the difference is what makes a film composer.
>
> Some composers get carried away with their own skill—they take a melody and embellish it with harmonies and counterpoints. If you get too decorative, you lose your appeal to the emotions. My theory is that music should be felt rather than heard.[37]

Steiner elaborated: "Many so-called serious composers are still unwilling to give serious attention to film music. They insist on weighing it against the symphonic music of the classicists and find it wanting. In the first place, their intention and function is completely different. Good film music is written for a specific purpose and if the film composer refuses to recognize the dictates of the picture, he may write a great symphony, but it will serve the film badly."[38]

This tussle between the emotional and technical requirements of a film score is writ large in the personality of every film composer. However, it was Steiner who first gave voice to this dichotomy, articulating the battle for supremacy between the gut and the intellect. Many decades later, composer Jerry Goldsmith would tell a group of students that, when faced with a sequence of a rider on a horse racing away from his enemies, one shouldn't score the chase. Instead, one should score the fear of the rider, therefore bringing truthful emotional impetus to the scene.[39] In articulating these thoughts, Goldsmith was echoing Steiner's own philosophy.

Ironically, Steiner very nearly missed out on scoring *Gone with the Wind* altogether. He found himself under immense pressure from Selznick, whose fickle changes of mood mirrored that of Scarlett in the finished movie. The micro-managing producer repeatedly rejected many of Steiner's ideas and also confessed disappointment in the themes for Scarlett and Rhett, although he was delighted with the pieces for Melanie (Olivia de Havilland), the Tara plantation and Mammy, the latter played to Oscar-winning effect by Hattie McDaniel. The themes for Scarlett and Rhett were, in fact, reduced in prominence in the finished film.[40]

In late 1939, close to the movie's December release date, Steiner truly believed he would not be able to finish the project. Despite a troubled relationship with Steiner, Selznick believed the composer performed best when under the thumb. However, this didn't stop him enlisting a back-up composer, Herbert Stothart, to prepare new themes and compositions in the event that Steiner couldn't succeed.[41] Upon hearing the news, an enraged Steiner was motivated towards the bitter end, and finally wrapped up the score, albeit with the help of several orchestrators. (One of these was Hugo Friedhofer, later to become a composer of repute himself.) Was this the devious psychological game planned by Selznick all along?

It's hard to say. Either way, Steiner was guided towards an eventual Oscar nomination at the 12th Academy Awards, although he was denied the prize, pipped to the Best Original Score post, ironically enough, by Herbert Stothart for *The Wizard of Oz*. (There was also a separate Scoring category, which went to John Ford's *Stagecoach* and its musical team of Richard Hageman, Frank Harling, John Leipold and Leo Shuken.)

The Wizard of Oz was a significant hit for studio MGM (Metro-Goldwyn-Mayer); shifting from muted Kansas-sepia to glorious Technicolor for the scenes in Oz, it's widely credited as the first feature-length fantasy musical. It remains celebrated for its yearning Harold Arlen song "Over the Rainbow," performed by Judy Garland, and initially earmarked for deletion by impatient studio executives who deemed it tedious. Garland would enjoy further success with MGM with the musical *Meet Me in St. Louis* (1944), directed by her eventual husband Vincente Minnelli; Garland's single-take performance of the exuberant "Trolley Song" is regarded as a high watermark of the genre.

Returning to Steiner, his nomination was one of 13 bestowed on *Gone with the Wind*. Selznick's relentless pursuit of perfection paid off with 10 wins out of those nominations, including Best Picture, Best Director (awarded to Victor Fleming), Best Actress for Vivien Leigh and Best Supporting Actress for Hattie McDaniel (making her the first person of color to triumph at the ceremony). The movie became the highest-grossing release of all time up to that point, and adjusted for inflation, *Gone with the Wind* still holds that accolade. Going by 2020 ticket prices, the movie's global adjusted lifetime gross is $1.85 billion, above *Star Wars: Episode IV—A New Hope* (1977) with $1.668 billion.[42]

So was this a pyrrhic victory for Steiner? Was that maddening scoring schedule, and the stress of collaborating with Selznick, worth it, given he was denied at the Oscars? In truth, it's all too easy to put faith in facile awards ceremonies. The sumptuous romantic legacy of Steiner's music speaks for itself, and the story of the score's creation, serves as a testament to the creative process. Deadlines, hair-pulling frustration and combative colleagues were mitigated by Steiner's essential flair for the dramatic. Ultimately, his essential love of, and skill with, the medium pulled him through even the most turbulent of times. It is the archetypal account of how a composer writes a large-scale film score, taking the positive and the negative in their stride.

It would be wrong to suggest that Steiner peaked with *Gone with the Wind*, although he was already approaching middle age when he embarked on the project. It says something about Steiner that his creative mojo wasn't sapped by the exhausting process of writing the score. In fact, the masterpieces kept coming for years afterwards, including *The Treasure of the Sierra Madre* (1948), *The Caine Mutiny* (1954) and *A Summer Place* (1959). Throughout the remainder of his career, Steiner demonstrated both boundless enthusiasm and a fierce loyalty to the medium that had put his name on the international map.

Nevertheless, if one is pinpointing the archetypal Steiner sound, it has to be *Gone with the Wind*. It's the ideal case study through which to explore the ongoing evolution of the film score as a concept, while also binding up everything that is fulsome and impressive about the man and his music. Steiner's last film score project was a Walt Disney Studios movie named *Those Calloways* (1965), and he died several years later on December 28, 1971.

As with all film composers, Steiner's creative impulses were subservient to the needs of others, be they directors or producers. Steiner was compelled to inject his own personality into film scores, but only to the extent that it wouldn't swamp the picture. His struggles reinforce the notion that film scoring is a paradoxical medium, one that's never truly autonomous, yet at the same time possessed with remarkable emotional impact.

Steiner's legacy can also be recognized outside of the sphere of Hollywood cinema. In particular, his delicacy and love of melody would be imprinted on European composers such as Ennio Morricone and Georges Delerue. The sweep of the strings in Morricone's scores carries a distinct echo of Steiner's voice, famously in the Oscar-nominated likes of *The Mission* (1986), with its awe-inspiring ascent to heavenly beauty. As for Delerue, he emerged as one of film music's all-time greatest melodists, equally adept at working on films in his native France (his "Theme du Camille" from 1963's *Le Mépris* is justly famous) and America (1985's Oscar-nominated *Agnes of God*). Both composers naturally bear singular melodic voices of their own, but it's hard to deny the origins of that sumptuous romanticism.

Steiner possessed the ability to skip between idioms and genres, all the while staying true to his own maverick voice. This philosophy has been adopted by every successful film composer in his wake, including the aforementioned Alexandre Desplat who says: "I want to write for different types of stories, and this allows me to write for different kinds of orchestras, bands or group of instruments. If you're a concert composer you're in the same position: you can write for a solo piano or a clarinet duet or a string quartet or an opera. There's variety but ultimately the person who writes the string quartet is the same composer. He's just spreading his wings."[43]

Desplat adds: "My voice, I guess, is still my voice but it takes different shapes, different volumes, different dynamics, a different type of orchestration. Yet my obsessions remain the same—that same kind of restrained emotion, my love of woodwinds, especially flutes, and strings. Whether it's for a full orchestra or a jazz chord or a different rhythmic pattern altogether, it's still me."[44]

When any noteworthy film composer passes away, it always leaves a gaping hole and an air of sadness. However, there is always optimism as contemporaries and rising stars take up the baton, both figuratively and literally. Although Steiner's personal chapter had ended by the early 1970s, by virtue of his astonishing legacy, he never truly disappeared from the Hollywood scene. Instead, his sound was adapted, translated and extended throughout the decades—and which composer could ask for a higher honor than that?

Erich Wolfgang Korngold: Pioneer of the Swashbuckling Adventure Score

When we imagine a particular scene from a movie, can we picture the imagery in our mind's eye without thinking of the accompanying film score? This, of course, will vary widely from person to person depending on one's own knowledge. And in certain movies there may be a minimum of original score anyway, so thoughts will naturally gravitate towards the visual language. But what about those irresistible classics where our knowledge of the film is intrinsically bound up with the cut and thrust of the narrative symphony?

Think of an elaborate stunt that's been staged on a grandiose movie set. Hours of preparation and set-ups have, one assumes, established sufficient safety protocols while also providing the framework for something truly spectacular in the completed film. However, it's only when the movie is edited and the score laid down that the concept evolves from the theoretical to the tangible. It's the composer who speaks to the subjective, illusory and intangible emotions underpinning the most fantastical of sequences. In essence, the composer is anticipating what we're going to be feeling long before the audience arrives at the cinema to see the end result.

Erich Wolfgang Korngold was an early master in this area, the high prince of the symphonic ear worm, and a composer who could seemingly conjure stirring, addictive melodies on a dime. His career was contemporaneous with that of Max Steiner, swiftly bringing a lavish and unashamedly bold approach to increasingly ambitious Hollywood action productions. In the process, he was also able to bolster the ego and luster of many of the period's biggest movie stars. Let's take, as an example, Errol Flynn, the quintessential debonair Hollywood hero of the 1930s and 1940s. Utilizing the earlier stunt analogy, as Flynn swings from rope to rope in high-seas epics like *The Sea Hawk* (1940), it's impossible to imagine his derring-do without Korngold's brass-fuelled music.

Korngold was born in 1897 in Brunn, Austria-Hungary (present-day Brno in the Czech Republic), and brought up in Vienna. Like Steiner, Korngold, a Jew, was uniquely positioned to absorb the political turbulence and cultural contradictions of the late 19th and early 20th centuries. A combination of ethnic exile, technological breakthroughs and his own deep-seated symphonic flair would soon propel Korngold to becoming one of Hollywood's greatest musical dramatists.

His father, Julius Leopold Korngold, was a noted music critic and scholar, so one need not look too far as to the source of this inspiration. By the age of five, Korngold was a prodigiously talented pianist, and by the time he turned seven, he was turning his hand to original compositions. Little wonder that the aforementioned Gustav Mahler labeled the boy as "a musical genius," upon hearing his cantata *Gold*, sentiments shared by Richard Strauss. (It's fascinating to note the role both of these men had in the development of two of Hollywood's most accomplished composers.)

There were many parallels between Korngold's youth and Max

Steiner's early life. In fact, Korngold likely surpassed Steiner when, at the age of 11, his two-act ballet *Der Schneemann* (translated as *The Snowman*) played in front of Emperor Franz Josef of Austria. The ballet made its debut in 1910 at the Vienna Court Theater, a truly astounding achievement for one who hadn't even reached adolescence.

The accomplishments kept on coming as Korngold reached his teenage years. He wrote his first orchestral score, the *Schauspiel-Ouvertüre*, at the age of 14, with a sinfonietta arriving the following year. Music clearly wasn't just a passion for the young Korngold, but a calling, one that would eventually beckon him across the ocean to America to compose some of the most memorable film music of all time.

Both Korngold and Steiner would become Tinseltown contemporaries, churning out extraordinary works in parallel with one another. Although Steiner was first out of the traps with *King Kong*, Korngold wasn't far behind in the adventure stakes, eventually snagging the Oscar for 1938's *The Adventures of Robin Hood*.

The two became friends and even shared offices close to one another, although their methods differed. Korngold firmly believed that film music was opera without the singing,[45] and subsequently treated each film script with reverence as if it were an operatic libretto. On that basis, he scanned each script prior to starting work on the music, unlike Steiner, and he also strenuously avoided the use of the click track. Instead, Korngold relied on his own, innate sense of synchronization and tempo.[46]

Korngold's approach would appear to clash with Steiner's maxim, quoted earlier, that less is more in terms of film music. Nevertheless, that mellifluous and unashamedly forthright gift would serve Korngold well in the early years of Hollywood, where subtlety was rarely allowed to get in the well of full-blooded emotion. Prior to his arrival in Hollywood, opera and concert music fuelled Korngold on a hugely successful career through Europe. He composed his first one-act opera, titled *The Ring of Polycrates*, in 1914. It premiered, along with another one-act production, *Violanta*, in 1916 in Munich's Hoftheater. At the age of 19, he was the toast of the continent with many of the period's great artistes, ranging from Mahler to Puccini, lauding his compositional skills. When, during the 1920s, Korngold turned his hand to adapting the operettas of Johan Strauss II, he gained an additional level of critical respect.

Die Tote Stadt (translated as *The Dead City*) was Korngold's first full-length opera, first performed in 1920. A lavish production in three acts, it proved a huge hit and went on tour throughout the continent. Yet it's undeniably true that Korngold's film music went on to overshadow his earliest achievements. For a man who set out as an operatic composer (and who increasingly sought a return to the medium as he got older), it's somewhat ironic that his creative aspirations would swing towards the relatively more commercial medium of cinema.

By the late 1920s, Korngold had established himself as a man with a keen awareness of tradition and an ability to skip between genres, all the while remaining loyal to an intuitive sense of melody. In 1929, Korngold struck up a partnership with the man who would change his life forever: legendary Austrian-born theater impresario and director Max Reinhardt. Initially, they collaborated on opera and operetta, including Strauss' *Die Fledermaus*, another artistic success for the prodigiously talented Korngold.

In the opinion of New Yorker music critic Alex Ross, it's unfortunate why Korngold's operas aren't held to the same impossibly high standards as his contemporaries. Ross writes: "I cannot fathom why [*Die Tote Stadt*] is not as popular as anything by Puccini—its melodic writing is no less indelible, its expressive urgency no less intense."[47]

Ross also hits on a raw nerve. He highlights the snobbery that often ensues when a celebrated classical composer like Korngold is seen, in the eyes of some, to "sell out," taking his or her skills onto the recording stage in Hollywood. Ross says: "Hollywood composers have employed so many different styles that the term 'film music' has little descriptive value. Worst is when the pejorative is used to discount figures who brought distinctive personalities to the scoring business, thereby elevating it. Such was the fate of the composer Erich Wolfgang Korngold."[48]

Whether Korngold's reputation did indeed suffer as a result of his film work is debatable. Nevertheless, the siren call of Hollywood proved hard to resist, even if the draw towards America wasn't exactly of his own volition. By the early 1930s, the lives of both Korngold and Reinhardt would forever be shaped by circumstances beyond their control. Continental Europe was seething with political turmoil and in Germany, Adolf Hitler's Nazi party was on the swift ascent to power. Fearful of the circumstances, Reinhardt fled Vienna for California, via Britain, and established a new life for himself. And then, in 1934, he chose to adapt his own 1927 Broadway staging of William Shakespeare's *A Midsummer Night's Dream* for the big screen.

The movie production attracted a stellar cast of talent led by Jimmy Cagney, Mickey Rooney and Olivia de Havilland. And, naturally, his cohort Korngold was present and correct, re-orchestrating the music of Felix Mendelssohn's 1826 concert performance of *A Midsummer Night's Dream*.[49] Korngold jumped at the chance, keen to exercise his musical muscles in a different medium, while also escaping the volatility of the situation in Europe (although at this stage, it wasn't a permanent escape). This was one of the most significant assignments in the composer's career, setting in motion his own love affair with the synchronized film score while establishing his reputation in Hollywood. It's a reputation that has only grown in stature in the decades since, borne out in the sheer number of composers who've assimilated his style.

For the next four years, Korngold vacillated between California and Vienna, maintaining important cultural links with his home country and family. However in 1938, at the same time that Korngold began work on *The Adventures of Robin Hood*, Adolf Hitler annexed Austria, forcing the composer into permanent exile in California. And yet he never truly abandoned his Viennese roots. Instead, these latent abilities were enhanced and empowered by a still-youthful cinema industry greedily devouring creative talent from all over the world.

Of course, the reason why Korngold's film scores resonate is precisely be*cause* of their intrinsically operatic nature. He was able to thread his cultural background and knowledge through every swoop of the string section, every minute phrase of the brass, every trill of the woodwind. One might accuse his approach as "mickey-mousing" the action, that derogatory phrase directed at film music that over-emphasizes the visual cue points. But given that the movies of the period were designed to be larger-than-life, Korngold's approach adapted perfectly to cinematic conventions.

Between 1934 and 1938, Korngold experienced divided loyalties between Europe and America. It's a brisk period of time in relative terms, but one that encapsulated a wealth of change in terms of the film score. At either end of the scale, this four-year stretch was bookended by two Steiner classics, *King Kong* in 1933, and *Gone with the Wind* in 1939. However, during this time, Korngold also asserted himself and exerted a significant cultural impact.

Korngold's first significant Hollywood film score was 1935's *Captain Blood*, the stirring pirate adventure that made a star out of Errol Flynn. It's fascinating to note how Korngold's movie career ascended at the same time as Flynn's; there was clearly a synergy between the composer's brassy bombast and the actor's cavalier charisma. Nowadays, we're used to film scores routinely bolstering the inherent charisma of a lead performer. But this was arguably the first time that film music had crafted, from scratch, a star persona in the collective mind of the audience.

Captain Blood is directed by Michael Curtiz, who would later strike gold with his collaboration with Max Steiner on *Casablanca*. The film is based on the novel of the same name by Rafael Sabatini, and stars Flynn as the eponymous Peter (later Captain) Blood. An Irish doctor who is arrested for treason and sold into slavery, Blood becomes a buccaneer who sets out to avenge those who wronged him. By today's standards it's an amusingly unreconstructed, but still thrilling, romp that rides high on Flynn's performance. And, coincidentally, the movie co-stars Olivia de Havilland, who had already starred in the Korngold-scored *A Midsummer Night's Dream*.

A critical and commercial hit for Warner Bros, *Captain Blood* clearly owed a lot of its impact to Korngold's accompanying soundtrack. Interestingly, he was initially averse to scoring a pirate picture, stating that he didn't have the right frames of reference. Nevertheless, Korngold eventually accepted the offer and would receive his first Oscar nomination for his efforts. This, despite the fact that time constraints forced him to incorporate sections from composer Franz Liszt (hence why Korngold takes a "music arranged by" credit at the start of the movie).

Wholly original or not, the *Captain Blood* score is still rousingly entertaining, nine decades on. Film music critic Craig Lysy observes the score's complex thematic construction, one brimming with symphonic vigor and warmth. Lysy writes: "For his soundscape, Korngold composed 12 themes. For his two primary themes, 'Peter's Theme' has a classic ABA form, with the A Phrase born by proud horns bravura supporting his heroic actions as a fighter, while the B Phrase is emoted warmly by lyrical strings, which reveal his more intimate and sensitive side. Later in the film a new thematic identity arises for Peter, the 'Pirate Theme,' which is kindred to the A Phrase of 'Peter's Theme' in that it is horn declared, but it has a more martial sensibility to it, and emotes with more aggression."[50]

The notion of splitting the main character's musical identity wasn't completely original around the time of *Captain Blood*'s release. Indeed, one can point towards Max Steiner's earlier work on *King Kong* on that basis, with the mutable fragments of Kong's theme varying in tone relative to their visual context. However, Korngold's technical expertise and melodic exuberance was a real bolt from the blue for 1930s audiences, cementing in their minds the notion of cinema as an inherently escapist medium populated by larger-than-life individuals.

Lysy states: "Worth noting is that this film, in large part because of Korngold's score, launched the swashbuckling genre in Hollywood. This score drove home the point to studio executives how rousing and inspiring orchestral music could enhance and elevate their films. Warner Brothers contracted Korngold immediately after the film and the other studios all created music departments and hired directors to manage them. So, we must conclude that Korngold's effort with *Captain Blood* was a transformative event in the history of film score art, a catalyst, which ushered in for all practical purposes the grand orchestral scores that exemplified the Golden Age."[51]

Film music historian Mervyn Cooke concurs with Lysy's thoughts, stating: "Like Steiner's, Korngold's film music followed what were already becoming well-established conventions: it cultivated a leitmotif-based romanticism ('symphonic' was the term used by Korngold himself to describe it), with fundamental narrative orientation, the music almost always subordinate to the primacy of the visual image and dialogue... [The music] demonstrated a lush self-confidence that was ideally suited to the Flynn swashbucklers, and at the same time achieved the kind of structural sophistication only to be expected of someone from Korngold's background."[52]

In the wake of *Captain Blood*'s success, Warner Bros was so thrilled to have Korngold on its books that the studio acceded to his many demands. He'd signed an exclusive contract with Warner, allowing him to assert his right to score no more than two films a year (a sharp contrast with Max Steiner's situation). Additionally, he was granted more time to work on his scores than his contemporaries, reserved the right to decline projects he disliked, was assured of prominent accreditation and, because he hadn't signed the copyright over to Warner, was allowed to incorporate his film score work into his concert hall arrangements.[53]

It was official: Korngold had arrived in Hollywood. Yet it's remarkable to note that, including *Captain Blood*, Korngold composed just 19 original film scores in his lifetime. (As a point of comparison, Ennio Morricone is alleged to have scored more than 400.) Of those, six were collaborations with Errol Flynn, the two artists clearly feeding off one another to the delight of audiences. Another of Korngold's key collaborators was Olivia de Havilland, and he would score several more pictures with her as the lead.

One of these was the critically praised *Anthony Adverse* (1936), which won Korngold his first Oscar. Korngold established a place in popular history as the third person to win the Academy Award for scoring a feature film (as mentioned, Louis Silvers was the first while Max Steiner was the second). However, given the Academy politics of the time, the trophy was personally handed to the head of Warner Bros' music department, Leo F. Forbstein, a veteran composer, conductor and arranger. Forbstein had been nominated in the same capacity for the *Captain Blood* score, and he would be nominated again for overseeing the Max Steiner scores *The Charge of the Light Brigade* (1936) and *The Life of Emile Zola* (1937).

By today's standards, it no doubt seems like a slap in the face for the actual composer not to be personally recognized for their work, but such was the position of film music at the time. In 1936, the concept of the large-scale symphonic score was still a relatively new one, not to mention that the Oscars had only recently formed the Best Original Score category. The cinematic landscape was increasingly starting to embrace the work of

Korngold and his fellow composers, but at the same time it was still struggling to measure up film music's artistic worth and sense of authorship.

In-keeping with Korngold's other works, *Anthony Adverse* is a score buoyed by a propulsive set of themes and motifs that interlock in dazzling fashion. Directed by Mervyn LeRoy, it tells the story of the titular Anthony, an orphan raised in poverty who learns to embrace life's challenges. The movie is based on Hervey Allen's book of the same name and draws great appeal from the central performances by Fredric March and Olivia de Havilland. Korngold's score, as one would expect, is also a warm presence, pointing towards the burgeoning romance between Anthony (March) and Augusta (De Havilland).

However, despite its Oscar win, *Anthony Adverse* was merely a dry run for Korngold's career-topping achievement with the aforementioned *The Adventures of Robin Hood*. Reuniting with *Captain Blood* director Michael Curtiz, Korngold delivered what is likely the seminal score of his career, and one of the most influential ever composed in the history of the medium. One need only listen to the fulsome opening brass of John Williams' *Star Wars* scores to hear the lingering effect of Korngold's full-blooded work, a soundtrack that places the composer's operatic sensibilities front and center.

As before, the composer was clearly inspired by the presence of dynamic stars Errol Flynn and Olivia de Havilland. The former is unmistakable as the Sherwood Forest outlaw, forever cementing in our minds the image of Robin in pea-green tights and with a feather in his cap. Gallant and brave, Flynn's portrayal of the character defined the era of escapist thrills. Not to be outdone, De Havilland is another strong presence, radiating sincerity and emotional fortitude as Maid Marian.

Initially disinterested in the project, Korngold accepted when Hitler's annexation of Austria threatened the lives of all European Jews, compelling the composer to stay in America.[54] As was the case with Max Steiner and *Gone with the Wind*, Korngold was forced to rely heavily on his orchestrators, including Hugo Friedhofer, to defy the limited turnaround time, but he succeeded in marvelous fashion. Indeed, it's a truism that film composers often deliver their best work when under impossible pressure.

The Adventures of Robin Hood practically invented many of the clichés we've come to take for granted in the contemporary adventure score. The forward-thrusting, barreling brass of Robin's theme, the multitude of oboes and piccolos to represent the homely environment of Sherwood Forest, the wavering strings of Marian's love theme—these are familiar ingredients in today's world, but it was Korngold's emotional foresight that set the ball rolling way back in 1938. As a point of comparison, take Michael

Kamen's score for *Robin Hood: Prince of Thieves* (1991), starring Kevin Costner. That galloping brass theme accompanying the Bayeux Tapestry opening credits sequence is as clear, and as loving, an homage to Korngold as one could hope to find.

In fact, so great were the time constraints on the recording (a familiar bane of any film composer's life), Korngold had to improvise. More specifically, he chose to plunder from his own operatic riches, works that had distinguished him on the European concert stage. His brassy fanfare for 1920's *Sursum Corda* forms the basis of Robin's heroic theme,[55] allegedly a suggestion from his experienced, scholarly father Julius.

Whatever the methodology, the score served to make the movie even more memorable. MovieMusicUK's Craig Lysy describes *Robin Hood* as the prototype Hollywood swashbuckling score: "Korngold music is perfectly attenuated to [Errol Flynn's] heroic persona and expertly captures his irrepressible spirit. From the fanfare of the 'Main Title,' to the lush 'Love Theme' where the Lady Marian succumbs to his charm, to the epic and culminating 'Duel,' this score is a testimony to Korngold's genius, and mastery of his craft. His countless melodies and fan fares are timeless, peerless, and continue to echo through time."[56]

Lysy's thoughts are mirrored in those of film historian Rudy Behlmer. He says that one of the greatest joys of the score comes in identifying the influence of Korngold's musical mentors. Although a narrative symphonic score written specifically for the cinematic medium, *The Adventures of Robin Hood* proudly bears the standard of Korngold's musical upbringing and background.

"Korngold's score was a splendid added dimension," enthuses Behlmer. "His style for the Flynn swashbucklers resembled that of the creators of late 19th century and early 20th century German symphonic tone poems. It incorporated chromatic harmonies, lush instrumental effects, passionate climaxes—all performed in a generally romantic manner. Korngold's original and distinctive style was influenced by the Wagnerian leitmotif, the orchestral virtuosity of Richard Strauss, the delicacy and broad melodic sweep of Puccini, and the long-line development of Gustav Mahler."[57]

As mentioned, the score for *The Adventures of Robin Hood* graced Korngold with an Oscar. (That year the award was split between categories for Original Score and Scoring; the latter went to Alfred Newman for Irving Berlin musical *Alexander's Ragtime Band*.) And yet, despite his artistic success, and the many critically acclaimed success stories to come, Korngold would eventually become restless. If not exactly burned out by the demands of Hollywood (lest we forget, his total tally of film scores was relatively low), he yearned for a return to the European operatic arena.

However much he was able to parlay this spirit into his film music, perhaps it was only a partly satisfactory substitute.

Therein lies one of the great cultural and political tragedies of the era: the separation of cultures throughout the world by the specter of World War II. The conflict eventually resolved itself in 1945, one year before Korngold delivered a soundtrack for another Olivia de Havilland picture, *Devotion*. This was a fictionalized take on the lives of the Brontë sisters, and it allowed Korngold to compose a relatively more intimate, tender work, one that demonstrated another side to his talents.

Korngold's cinematic output eventually started to wane. Instead, he channeled his passions into standalone orchestral works, including *Symphonic Serenade in B-flat major, Op. 39*, composed for a string ensemble between 1947 and 1948. And he never lost that inherent flair for opera, returning to the medium with the acclaimed likes of *Die Stumme Serenade*, worked on and revised between 1946 and 1951.

It's tempting to read between the lines and see this as Korngold pining for the beloved European concert halls of his youth. And yet, poignantly, he was never able to make a permanent return to his home country. Instead, he settled in the United States in 1947, before delivering one final film project in 1955: Richard Wagner biopic *Magic Fire*, for which Korngold personally arranged Wagner's own melodies.

In a way, this brought Korngold full circle back to his Hollywood debut with *A Midsummer Night's Dream*, for which he had arranged the pre-existing work of Felix Mendelssohn. It serves to reinforce not just Korngold's humility, but that of every film composer. They not only have to subsume their ego when it comes to their own ideas, but, when it's dramatically appropriate, foreground and honor the pioneering works of their predecessors and influences.

There's no denying the humanity and compassion that coursed through Korngold's film scores. Without this essential grounding, he would not have been able to score the likes of *Captain Blood* or *The Adventures of Robin Hood* so brilliantly. He clearly felt a deep-seated connection with the characters and their surrounding narratives, and in the process, he communicated this joyousness to the audiences watching in the cinema. The sheer sense of energy and vitality proved a huge influence on his contemporaries and the film composers coming down the pipeline.

Korngold passed away in 1957 at the age of 60. At that time, films and their accompanying scores were radically changing, increasingly embracing the youth movement and casting off the shackles of the old. Yet the works of Korngold would hold nostalgic allure in the coming decades, particularly in the 1970s when the big screen epic once again held sway after several years of experimental, anti-establishment cinema.

This, arguably, was the moment where Korngold finally got his dues. Two decades after his death, his musical imprint was not only revived but championed and extended through increasingly large-scale blockbuster film soundtracks, including John Williams' *Star Wars*. There can surely be no greater measure of an individual composer's impact than that.

Alfred Newman and Bernard Herrmann: Golden Age Godfathers

What is the first piece of soundtrack music you hear when a film begins? It won't necessarily be the opening credits suite, or another piece of introductory scene-setting. Rather, you're very likely to have heard a bold statement of intent during the presentation of the studio logo, more often than not an original creation from a leading film composer.

This is an art form in and of itself, establishing an identity for the studio in question, and getting the audience prepared for the big-screen adventure to follow. Take the Universal Studios fanfare, as an example. Originally composed as a lyrical, freewheeling string elegy by James Horner, it was later given a reworking by Jerry Goldsmith, who fashioned it as a brassy, ballsy, portentous piece. Goldsmith's theme was later re-arranged by Brian Tyler, who added further layers of choral majesty while staying true to the central melody. Another example: the bubbling, balletic xylophone, flute and strings of the attractive StudioCanal theme, composed by Alexandre Desplat.

Logo music is, like so much else in film scoring, very easy to take for granted. Naturally, the approach had to start with someone. That someone is Alfred Newman, one of the godfathers of the so-called "Golden Age" of film music who gave birth to the 20th Century–Fox (now 20th Century Studios) fanfare. This piece of music, although brief, is one of the most famous and easily identifiable in pop culture history, immediately resonating with a feel of pomp and circumstance. In essence, it encapsulates the majesty of cinema.

It's a marvelous achievement, and one that is instilled in audiences young and old whenever the Fox titles appear. Yet it is but one facet of Newman's remarkable contribution to the medium, an illustrious career that encapsulated composing, conducting and arranging. It's already been mentioned, in the previous chapter, how Newman played an early role in conducting Charlie Chaplin's score for *City Lights*. And it says something about Newman's talents that his contribution to Chaplin's movie can get lost amidst the shuffle of his overall career.

As the 1930s and 1940s rolled on, Newman, who was a contemporary of both Max Steiner and Erich Wolfgang Korngold, delivered a near-endless stream of musical masterpieces. In fact, Newman regarded conducting as his true calling, saying: "I studied music composition and counterpoint because I wanted to be a good conductor."[58] The story of how he got to this stage is truly fascinating.

Born in Connecticut in 1900 as one of 10 children, the young Newman, like Steiner and Korngold, demonstrated a prodigious flair for the piano and self-taught composition. Neither of his parents were musicians, but Newman clearly had talent and would develop these skills even further as he advanced into his teens. At the age of 19, he embarked on a career that would establish him as one of New York's most esteemed conductors. He began conducting the musicals of his close friend George Gershwin, among others, on Broadway, a position that Newman held for 10 years. This, combined with his earlier experience touring on the vaudeville circuit with American singer Grace La Rue, instilled in him a level of disciplined, metronomical technique, not to mention a deep-seated love of collaboration.

The conductor is perhaps the unsung hero of any film score. Many times this role is taken by the composers themselves. Few conductors, if any, gain the sufficient level of credit they deserve for wielding the baton and ensuring that every upbeat and downbeat of a live orchestra is synched perfectly to the picture. At the same time, the conductor has to act as a genuine team player, the conduit between the needs of the composer (should they be acting in a separate capacity), the players and the mixers in the recording booth.

This is why Newman was perfectly suited to the needs of film conducting: he savored technique above the spotlight, and his background in live performance earmarked him as a clear communicator. Both of these facets would eventually help him navigate the pressure cooker environment of the Hollywood scoring stage. He was first invited to Los Angeles in 1930 by Irving Berlin, that doyen of timeless show tunes, not to mention enduring film scores including *Top Hat* (1935) and *White Christmas* (1954).

The Irving Berlin movie in question, Douglas Fairbanks musical *Reaching for the Moon*, was looking to enlist Newman's experience as a conductor. However, he instead ended up receiving his first on-screen credit as musical director, forever aligning his destiny with Hollywood. Like Steiner and Korngold before him, Newman's initiation into the world of film music was almost a happy accident, a collision of circumstances that would have significant ramifications for the medium going forward.

Although conducting remained his true love, as a composer Newman racked up an astonishing level of celebrated scores that cemented him as one of the fulcrums of the so-called "Golden Age." This term of affection is regularly used to indicate the sheer breadth of glossy, intelligently handled and star-driven period pictures emerging out of the Hollywood system at the time.

The term "Golden Age" can also be applied to the film music of the period, implying an upsurge in orchestrally sophisticated, thematically driven masterworks that derived rich inspiration from the visual narrative. Some of Newman's most acclaimed scores of this period went hand in hand with emotionally complex dramas, further cementing the bond between the visible and the aural.

Take Newman's score for *The Hunchback of Notre Dame* (1939), for example. This highly praised adaptation of Victor Hugo's novel immortalized Charles Laughton as the disfigured, tormented bell-ringer Quasimodo, and Newman's somber, serious score plugged audiences into its themes of social isolation and betrayal. This psychologically astute approach to film music may have shared the same technical principles as the scores of Steiner and Korngold, but if those efforts primarily went for the gut and the heart, Newman's moody soundscapes aimed, more often than not, for the intellect. A maturation was occurring within the lifespan of the film score, and Newman would be at the vanguard with his litany of applauded works including *Wuthering Heights* (1939), *All About Eve* (1950) and *The Diary of Anne Frank* (1959).

Very often, these movies were driven by their dialogue, which necessitated a fresh approach from Newman. He was compelled to augment not only visually spectacular set-pieces and stunts, but complex verbal tussles penned by some of Hollywood's finest scriptwriters. The film score was increasingly going interior, often suggesting character psychology as well as outward action.

Above all, Newman's sense of prestige, stemming from his experience as a conductor, helped reinforce the sense of the film composer as an auteur. The artistic credentials of musicians imported from Europe, Broadway and elsewhere were finally being recognized as important ammunition in bolstering a particular film's reputation. Newman wasn't just deployed on the films in question; the studios sought his talents to graft a singular musical identity onto their entire operation.

Hence, his recording of the 20th Century Studios fanfare. The company, then called Twentieth Century Pictures, needed a signature theme to impress upon audiences. In 1933, the same year that Max Steiner unleashed his soundtrack for *King Kong*, Newman presented his impactful overture, commissioned by studio executive Darryl F. Zanuck.[59] Later, in 1939, Newman would be appointed as Music Director of the 20th Century–Fox Film Corporation (named after the 1935 merger between Twentieth Century Pictures and Fox Film Corporation). He was later succeeded by his brother, Lionel.

It's hard to assess which of Newman's achievements were the most significant; as the pre-eminent film music director of his age, he was responsible for schooling and nurturing the next generation of great film composers, including the likes of Bernard Herrmann, David Raksin, Dimitri Tiomkin and Elmer Bernstein. As a conductor, he kept his feet planted in the realm of musicals, translating his love of the form into vibrant arrangements for *Tin Pan Alley* (1940) and *The King and I* (1956), both recipients of Academy Awards.

As a composer in his own right, Newman assembled such a line-up of critical successes that he practically became his own brand, a flesh and blood representation of all that film music could attain. During his career Newman attained nine Oscar wins out of a truly remarkable 45 nominations, making him one of the most garlanded individuals in the history of cinema.[60] In terms of film scoring, Newman's success is rivaled only by John Williams who has attained five Oscar wins out of 52 nominations.

The noted Variety music critic Jon Burlingame champions Newman's generosity of spirit, especially in the field of talent-spotting. Burlingame elaborates: "As Fox's music boss, Newman could have assigned all the best films to himself. Instead, more often than not, he gave them to other composers, sometimes jumpstarting careers or just keeping them alive. David Raksin got *Laura*, in the process writing one of film's most memorable themes. Bernard Herrmann wrote his most romantic score for *The Ghost and Mrs. Muir* (1947) and a groundbreaking electronic one for *The Day the Earth Stood Still* (1951) because Newman knew he was right for those pictures."[61]

One of Newman's most gargantuan achievements saw him branch out into the increasingly popular realm of the Biblical epic. *The Robe*, released in 1953, relays the story of the Roman brigade responsible for the crucifixion of Jesus, starring Richard Burton in the role of Marcellus Gallio. Directed by Henry Koster, it unsurprisingly elicits a score of reverential awe from Newman, one that demonstrates his versatility and unparalleled flair for dramatic melody. In turn, he would inspire the later generation of composers to pick up the baton as the 1950s and 1960s progressed, including Elmer Bernstein with *The Ten Commandments* (1956) and Miklós Rózsa with *El Cid* (1961).

Just as impressive as *The Robe* is Newman's sweeping work on *How the West Was Won* (1962). This vast Western is the story of one family's wagon train voyage from East to West, their journey set against the birth of contemporary America. So large in scale was the production, it needed three directors to helm it: Henry Hathaway, John Ford and George Marshall. It was, therefore, a wise move to hire someone of Newman's caliber on the music front, although even he confessed to being overawed by the sheer amount of work necessary.

To that end, Newman enlisted lyricist and arranger Ken Darby to help out. Darby would compose several original folk tunes, to be used in the movie to create an authentic ambience. Newman, meanwhile, dialed up the expansive melodies and themes to complement the film's handsome look, shot in the newly developed Cinerama curved widescreen format.[62] The end result was a soundtrack that fused Newman's long-standing love of song with his now-familiar scoring capabilities, and it yielded an Oscar nomination for both himself and Darby.

Jon Burlingame notes that the majority of Newman's Oscar wins came when he selflessly adapted the music of other people. Yet, at the same time, his original compositions could strike a wide variety of emotional registers.

"His sole Oscar for Original Dramatic Score was for 1943's *The Song of Bernadette*, one of several religious pictures for which Newman (though a non-practicing Jew) had a remarkable affinity," writes Burlingame. "His setting of the 23rd Psalm for *David and Bathsheba*, powerful orchestral-and-choral score for the first Cinemascope picture *The Robe*, the undeniable spiritual quality of his music for *The Diary of Anne Frank* and his moving theme for Jesus in *The Greatest Story Ever Told*, were equally compelling."[63]

One of Newman's greatest and most enduring achievements was establishing a legacy of brilliant film composers through his own family. The Newman dynasty comprises, among others, his sons Thomas and David, and his nephew Randy. As mentioned, Alfred Newman's younger brother Lionel rose to prominence at the same time as his sibling, becoming an in-house fixture at 20th Century–Fox. And yet each of Alfred Newman's successors have carried on his lineage in myriad different ways.

Whereas Thomas Newman is a renowned experimentalist, famous for the use of the detuned marimba and other speciality instruments on the Oscar-nominated *American Beauty* (1999), David Newman has excelled in the realm of comedy. His regular collaborations with Danny DeVito, such as *The War of the Roses* (1989) and *Matilda* (1996), bear this out. And Randy Newman has split his time between bitingly satirical comedy tunes ("Short People") and film scores, including many for animation studio Pixar (the *Toy Story* films included).

Producer Nick Redman, who oversaw the 2012 La-La Land Records re-release of *The Robe*, said that Newman's humanist qualities resonated both on the scoring stage and off. "The legacy of Alfred Newman and his influence on the language of music for the cinema is practically unmatched by anyone in Hollywood history," Redman explained. "As an executive, he was hard but fair. As a mentor to his staff, he was revered. The orchestras under his baton delighted in his abilities as a conductor. The music he himself composed, often under extreme emotional duress, is among the most gorgeous ever written. [...] Not big in physical stature, he was a giant in character, a titan in the world he loved and dominated. He was a true musical force, and one that cannot in any sense be replaced."[64]

In 1954, Newman would embark on a relative rarity in the world of film scoring. He would collaborate with another noted composer, the movie in question being the ancient historical epic *The Egyptian*. His cohort: the aforementioned Bernard Herrmann, another equally tremendous film composer with a penchant for bucking the mainstream, although Herrmann's approach, both in terms of his music and his attitude, was far more forthright and tempestuous.

In fact, the combustible Herrmann likely ignited the notion of the film composer as a "personality," one whose ego and creative choices would frequently challenge the established hierarchy. As film music became increasingly modernistic and experimental, the attitude of the composer in question became more complicated. Or was it the other way around, the inherently iconoclastic nature of the composer informing the music that they were writing? Such questions were directly tied into the deepening battle for supremacy between the moving image and the sonic landscape—which of the two would win out?

More often than not, the former always emerged triumphant. But it remained a bitter pill for expert musicians like Herrmann to swallow, and, as the film score has evolved, it has not become any easier. In the silent era, film composers likely enjoyed the most autonomy they've ever had, largely, if not entirely, reducing the need for creative conflict. In the early days of the "talkies," there was still a semblance of autonomy, inasmuch as the rules of film scoring were still being refined (although, as mentioned earlier, it took several years to convince studio executives of the efficacy of the non-diegetic film score).

However, Herrmann landed at a critical and delicate juncture where dramatically astute sound pictures could potentially be swamped by soupy, overcooked scores. Any film composer, even one as genre-defying and brilliant as Herrmann, is forced to kowtow to the needs of the picture. The question is this: how far can the composer thread the needle? In other words, how many genuinely groundbreaking ideas can one smuggle into a given score without compromising the structural integrity of the director's vision?

Naturally, that depends on the ability of the composer in question, not to mention their communication skills. For all his fiery bluster, Herrmann established strong partnerships with many leading Hollywood directors, none more so than Alfred Hitchcock. Before we explore that cinema-defining collaboration (and its unfortunately abrupt end), let's backtrack and take a closer look at Herrmann himself.

Born in New York in 1911 to a Jewish family of Russian heritage, Herrmann (birth name Max) shared many of the childhood traits of his illustrious scoring predecessors. To wit: an encouraging family (in this case, his father), an early facility with instruments (chiefly the violin) and an education that shaped his musical capabilities. This included attendance at both New York University and The Juilliard School.

In 1934, he was put under contract at the Columbia Broadcasting System (CBS). Composer and orchestrator Johnny Green had become a fixture with his program "Music in the Modern Manner," which alternated challenging classicists such as Arnold Schoenberg with live poetry readings by CBS announcer David Ross.[65] Green recommended that Herrmann conduct the radio adaptation of the play *Mr. Whittington*.[66] It didn't take long for the idiosyncratic Herrmann to make an impression: Green recalled that, within three weeks, "[Herrmann] had the whole building on its ear."[67]

Later on, Herrmann was appointed as musical director of the Columbia Workshop drama series, finding the perfect outlet to unleash his original compositions on an unsuspecting public.[68] At the same time, he was able to stage dramatic arrangements of his most revered influences, including Myaskovsky's *22nd Symphony* and Gian Francesco Malipiero's *3rd Symphony*.

Many of the best film composers find themselves in exactly the right place at the right time. Max Steiner emerged as the talking picture came of age, Korngold, as "talkies" gained in dramatic ballast and entertainment value. Herrmann's ascent coincided with the emergence of then cutting-edge technology. The wireless radio democratized classical music, exposing listeners to a vast range of otherwise obscure artists. This was the perfect medium for Herrmann to both flex his conducting muscles and showcase his own style, which, as demonstrated throughout his later career, plunged film scoring even further into the realms of psychological madness.

As with Steiner, Korngold and Newman, family heritage and ethnic tradition played a strong and fiercely proud role in Herrmann's music. His family had Slavic roots, and, like his predecessors, Herrmann assimilated these influences into his film scores. It's another reminder of the rich Eastern European, Jewish and Russian heritage that coursed through the film music of the early 20th century.

Yet Herrmann's stylistic approach helped move film music away from the predominantly European, romantic sound into something more contemporary, more American, perhaps. His work was contemporaneous with Aaron Copland who, in the course of just eight film scores, established a distinctly Americana sound, incorporating elements of jazz and folksong and moving away from a sense of European operatic romanticism.[69] Copland was one of the first American concert hall composers to legitimize the film score medium; seminal works such as *Appalachian Spring* (1944) spoke of the great outdoors and of wild natural expanse.[70] This proved to be a significant influence on the later likes of Elmer Bernstein's *The Magnificent Seven* (1960).

Andy Hill, former Vice President of Music Production at Walt Disney Pictures, questions whether any film score can be wholly European or wholly American. He argues that individual film scores embody a mixed set of cultural idioms that have been passed down from generation to generation. In essence, he says film music is "a crossbreed, a hybrid, a loveable mutt ... a citizen of no nation."[71] He elaborates: "Whereas once (pre–1940), it might have been asserted that film music owed whatever pedigree it had to Viennese and Italian opera and the late romantic composers, that hereditary thread had already begun to fray when the radio *mélodrames* of the 1930s encouraged such mavericks as Bernard Herrmann to experiment with music that stood apart from the action as opposed to merely miming it."[72] (This refers back to the expressive versus illustrative argument from Chapter One.)

Whatever one's view of alleged cultural "purity" in film music, there's no denying that Herrmann continued to push the medium of scoring into avant-garde areas. At the same time that Herrmann was first making his mark in radio, a certain Orson Welles was also breaking down the boundaries of the medium. In 1938, he delivered a famously evocative CBS reading of H.G. Wells' *The War of the Worlds* (1898), which proved so convincing that many listeners were convinced an alien invasion was upon them, and a full-blown nationwide panic ensued.[73] Although little original music was involved in the actual broadcast, the CBS Orchestra, under Herrmann's baton, simulated radio dance bands and concert hall recitals before and after the eerily convincing "news" interruptions, adding to the air of verisimilitude.[74]

The two men had already worked together on Welles' radio drama series "Mercury Theater on the Air," later to become known as "Campbell Playhouse" after being sponsored by the Campbell Soup Company.[75] From the late 1930s to the early 1940s, there was a true meeting of the maverick minds, the uncompromising Herrmann meshing perfectly, if often explosively, with the increasingly ambitious Welles. And then, the actor and playwright lured the composer to Hollywood to work on his directorial debut, *Citizen Kane*.

Newly appointed at RKO Pictures, Welles set about making one of the boldest and most exciting debut films in movie history. In fact, *Citizen Kane* regularly tops modern-day critical lists of the best movies of all time, and for a long time held the top spot with the BFI (British Film Institute), although it has since ceded its position to Alfred Hitchcock's *Vertigo* (1958), also scored by Herrmann.[76] Forthright in its technique yet elusive and mysterious in its tone, *Citizen Kane* is a film of multifaceted contradictions, and this extends to Herrmann's score.

Welles directs and stars as Charles Foster Kane, the enigmatic media magnate who expires after uttering a final, enigmatic word: "Rosebud." The movie then disrupts the fabric of time as it crisscrosses Kane's richly storied life, from his early childhood to his eventual ascent to power. The movie broke down a multitude of boundaries, from its use of flashbacks to its deep-focus cinematography from Gregg Toland. It's held together by Welles' typically volcanic performance, but beneath Kane's surface bluster there is real pain—and this is where Herrmann steps in.

From the quavering opening notes of the woodwind section to the elliptical string arrangements reflecting Kane's later, more tormented years, Herrmann's music does a fascinating deep dive into one man's psyche. No mere surface score, *Citizen Kane* did more than any soundtrack before it to suggest the emotional depths that cannot be rendered in physical form alone. The make-up of Welles' central portrayal defies expectation at every turn, alternately grandiose, generous, self-absorbed, tragic and ostracized. And Herrmann's music is a masterclass in tonality, often using the orchestra at the lowest end of its range to suggest the dark depths of one individual's heart.

"Herrmann brought a new dramatic language rooted in America to film music," notes Jon Burlingame. "He used much smaller forms than Europeans like Erich Wolfgang Korngold did. He tended to write cells, brief motifs rather than long lines. It took a while for people to catch on. *Citizen Kane* is really a bunch of miniature themes. But they worked dramatically, just as they did in radio."[77]

The composer was given a generous 12-week schedule to write and record the music,[78] unprecedented when so many film scores, particularly contemporary ones, are forced into a mere three- or four-week recording window. It was clearly a sign of how much Welles valued Herrmann's input, and he even edited certain passages of the film around Herrmann's music.

There are many reasons to admire Herrmann's debut film score. One is its sense of economy, clearly honed from Herrmann's days with Welles on CBS. Long passages of the film pass by with no music at all, and when the music does appear ("spotted" by the composer and director), it's subsequently all the more impactful. Another is the sheer amount of variety that's packed within its relatively short running time.

Never one to court convention, Herrmann composed a "Breakfast Waltz" to accompany the marital breakdown montage between Kane and his first wife, Emily Monroe Norton (Ruth Warrick).[79] The usual approach may have favored maudlin sentimentality, but Herrmann keeps things much more playful and unpredictable. He also incorporated a pastiche aria ("Salammbo"), used for the doomed operatic debut of Kane's second wife, Susan Alexander (Dorothy Comingore).[80] These are but two examples of how effectively he dived into the psychology of the central and supporting characters, and it's not hard to see why Hollywood immediately sat up to take notice of Herrmann's capabilities.

Although *Citizen Kane* proved to be a box office flop, for Herrmann, the floodgates opened, and he went on to score a multitude of critical hits. From the atypically tender *The Ghost and Mrs. Muir* (1947), the composer's self-confessed favorite score,[81] to the thunderously aggressive *On Dangerous Ground* (1951), Herrmann was a composer who refused to be pigeonholed.

While Herrmann was a fine practitioner of melody, he was increasingly keen to push the medium of scoring into avant-garde areas. The use of the woozy theremin of *The Day the Earth Stood Still* (1951) is a notable influence on the now-standard extra-terrestrial sound, and an early outlier in the field of the electronic film score. Meanwhile the string-free ensemble of Greek mythological adventure *Jason and the Argonauts* (1963), which instead emphasizes brass, woodwind and percussion, fully conveys the might and gravitas of heroes and monsters from days gone by. Herrmann's ability to push the boundaries was truly remarkable.

However, there was one filmmaker in particular who would define the tone of the score known as "Herrmannesque": Alfred Hitchcock. Born in Leytonstone, London in 1899, Hitchcock would eventually establish himself as one of the most admired, and studied, filmmakers in the history of cinema. His famous (or, rather, infamous) treatment of his blond female characters, his capacity for unnerving voyeurism and his calmly probing camerawork helped take Hollywood filmmaking in directions never before dreamed of.

Having specialized in silent pictures in his native UK, Hitchcock was lured to America to make *Rebecca*, an adaptation of Daphne Du Maurier's novel, by producer David O. Selznick. That movie was scored in lusciously melodramatic fashion by Franz Waxman, one of the leading lights of the "Golden Age" of film music, but he wasn't about to form a lasting partnership with Hitchcock.

For *Spellbound* (1945), starring Ingrid Bergman and Gregory Peck,

Hitchcock deviated to another rising composer of the era: Miklós Rózsa. Before he became pegged as the master of the historical epic soundtrack (*El Cid* et al), Rózsa delivered an Oscar-winning score in the form of *Spellbound*. It was one of the first soundtracks to deploy the unsettling, alien sound of the theremin, which in conjunction with Hitchcock's visual deployment of a Salvador Dali dream sequence, cast a rapturous spell over audiences.

It was becoming clear that Hitchcock encouraged the evocative power of the film score, one that could remain foregrounded and comment on the incidental action while also suggesting the rippling emotional undercurrents beneath the surface. Hitchcock solicited scores not just from Rózsa and Waxman but a host of Hollywood's most acclaimed musicians, including Alfred Newman (1940's *Foreign Correspondent*), Dimitri Tiomkin (1943's *Shadow of a Doubt*, and others) and the aforementioned Hugo Friedhofer (1944's *Lifeboat*).

Interestingly, the Hitchcock/Herrmann partnership wouldn't be established until fairly late in both men's careers. The film in question was *The Trouble with Harry* (1955), a decidedly low-key affair for the director, and one that elicited a superb score from Herrmann. It showcased another side to the composer, a lighthearted and deviously satirical reflection of small-town American life torn asunder by the revelation of a dead body. Bassoons and French horns skip and dart around as if in the manner of the story's busy-body characters, before a heartbreaking oboe line injects an air of melancholy as the consequences sink in.

If there's an air of menace in the music, it's of the decidedly tongue-in-cheek variety, reflecting a somewhat unusual Hitchcock movie that's gained in stature over the years. But *The Trouble with Harry* (1955) is more significant for what it represents: the birth of what is arguably the most famous director/composer partnership in film history. Hitchcock and Herrmann made this union a marketable brand, and audiences and critics eagerly anticipated what the two prodigiously talented individuals would contrive next.

There are countless examples within their oeuvre to demonstrate this, and such musical riches are an important step in the ongoing evolution of the film soundtrack. In *Vertigo*, widely considered as Herrmann's sumptuous masterwork, strings and trombones eddy and spiral to capture the freewheeling madness of James Stewart's haunted private detective Scotty. When tracking seemingly possessed woman Madeleine (Kim Novak) through San Francisco, Scotty falls into a vortex of love and madness, particularly when Madeleine plunges to her death from a bell tower and he later becomes infatuated with her double.

Vertigo is based on the 1954 novel *D'Entre les Morts* by the writing duo of Boileau-Narcejac. The book itself was inspired by the tragic-romantic myth of Tristan and Isolde, which had already inspired Wagner's operatic masterpiece *Tristan und Isolde* (1865). This operatic sensibility directly informs the tone of Herrmann's music, particularly the nature of Wagner's "Liebestod" ("Love Death").[82]

Herrmann's score rises to extraordinary heights during the pivotal "Scene D"Amour' cue in line with Hitchcock's circling camerawork, infusing Wagnerian sweep with his own phrasing, diminished chords and tonalities. This, despite the fact that Herrmann was deeply unhappy with Muir Mathieson's conducting—owing to a musicians' union strike, the score had to be conducted by Mathieson in Vienna, rather than by Herrmann in America.[83]

For comedy-chase caper *North by Northwest* (1959), starring Cary Grant, Herrmann adapted a musical medium that would seem ill-fitting for the narrative, a frenetic fandango. He used this to give a sense of danger closing in on all sides (albeit the tongue-in-cheek kind). In *The Birds* (1963), Herrmann didn't compose a conventional music score but instead sampled layers of what were then sophisticated electronic effects to give an impression of birds squawking and flapping in unison.

Of all the Hitchcock/Herrmann collaborations, the most famous is *Psycho* (1960). It was composed for a string-only ensemble, reportedly necessitated by the film's strikingly low-budget.[84] The film's economy of scale was a deliberate decision by Hitchcock who sought to steer away from the more expansive *North by Northwest*; to that end, he populated the *Psycho* crew with members of his *Alfred Hitchcock Presents* TV show, including cinematographer John L. Russell.

Herrmann's characteristic stabbing strings arrest us right from the very opening credits (designed by Saul Bass), creating a sense of threat without us knowing the context. In doing so, both director and composer brilliantly mislead us, making us think that Janet Leigh's Marion Crane is the psycho of the title, having absconded with her boss's money. The music is very cleverly leading us down a blind alley, culminating in the notorious shower sequence (storyboarded by Bass) in which Crane is murdered, and during which the audience feels appropriately assaulted by Herrmann's blood-curdling music. It makes the audience feel the stabbing even while Hitchcock's editing carefully works around it, yielding, arguably, the most imitated passage of film music of all time. In a magnificent example of expressive scoring, Herrmann's music actually starts stabbing seconds *before* the killer attacks, subtly anticipating Marion's horrendous demise and further adding to the air of discombobulation.

Interestingly, Hitchcock had envisaged the sequence with no music at all, and it was Herrmann who persuaded him to change his mind.[85] The composer recalled playing the shower scene cue against the picture for the first time, to which Hitchcock replied, "Of course, that's the one we'll use."[86] Upon reminding Hitchcock that he had originally envisaged the scene without music, the director said, "Improper suggestion, my boy."[87] Hitchcock would later credit 33 percent of the film's impact to Herrmann's music.[88]

The subtly disturbing synchronicity of Herrmann's score has been observed in sequences other than the genre-defining shower scene. For instance, in the scene where Marion drives to the Bates Motel, the jabbing violins mesh with the slashing of the windscreen wipers to suggest impending violence. In the words of Herrmann himself, without the music, Marion "could have been driving it to the supermarket or to her mother-in-law's."[89] With the music added, the sequence is transformed to an extraordinary degree.

Batman (1989) and *Edward Scissorhands* (1990) composer Danny Elfman is a self-declared fan of Herrmann, and says his legacy extends far and wide. (He also adapted Herrmann's *Psycho* score in stereo for the colorized 1998 remake, directed by Gus Van Sant.) Describing his idol as an "iconoclast," Elfman elaborates: "When I became a composer, it was to strive for his versatility. I consider him the most original composer of the Golden Age, even though he came toward the end. The most iconic scores I can think of are his. The uniqueness of what made cinema great came from artists like him. To not learn from that cuts us off from being great."[90]

Yet, the Hitchcock/Herrmann pairing would meet an ignominious end. Both men united for the 1966 spy thriller *Torn Curtain*, starring Paul Newman and Julie Andrews. But by this stage, Hollywood had undergone some significant ideological shifts, and the working relationship between director and composer would implode as a result. The movie was released just one year before *The Graduate*, a cornerstone in the use of pop music in cinema, particularly Simon and Garfunkel's "The Sound of Silence." Perhaps unsurprisingly, Hitchcock was under considerable pressure to yield to studio demands for a pop-oriented score.[91]

Needless to say, the singular Herrmann didn't take the directive well. Scorning the apparent need for a score that would play to contemporary trends, Herrmann found his toiling, turbulent music removed, and replaced with a somewhat peppier, more buoyant soundtrack from John Addison.[92] The ultimate irony was that *Torn Curtain* largely failed with critics and audiences anyway, making one wonder what would have happened had Herrmann's original work remained. Likely, it would have made an already turgid movie seem all the more portentous and overblown, but it's hard to say.

This would make the end of a beautiful friendship, with both Hitchcock and Herrmann moving onto pastures new. The former would bow out with the blackly comic duo of *Frenzy* (1972), scored by Ron Goodwin, and *Family Plot* (1976), scored by John Williams, before passing away in 1980.

It's a humbling reminder of the egos at stake within the art of film music. Both Hitchcock and Herrmann had emboldened and deepened the art of the film score during their time together, transforming it from a surface pleasure into an insidious, teasing presence that, voyeuristically, took audiences even deeper inside the frame. Herrmann's seriousness of intent, and his refusal to compromise on his own abilities, would throw down a formidable gauntlet to all the film composers in his wake.

All of Herrmann's scores, including his ones for Hitchcock, showcased a maturation of film music as a whole, reinforcing the format's mutability and its capacity to render intangible angst as tangible chords, progressions and rhythms. We may not be able to explain the torment of many of Herrmann's great works, but we certainly feel it and therefore, on a deep-seated level, we understand it. Such is the essence of truly brilliant movie music.

Herrmann's final score was *Taxi Driver* (1976), composed for director Martin Scorsese. In yet another brilliant touch, Herrmann used jazzy, borderline sleazy alto-sax solos to represent the inner inferno of isolated New York cab driver Travis Bickle (Robert De Niro), later praised by Scorsese as "the psychological basis" of the entire film.[93] The music has a melancholic air and yet also carries seedy overtones, the essence of an isolated man moving through a disturbing world that he barely understands, and which he feels he has the power to change. Sadly, Herrmann never got to see the public reaction to his score, as he passed away hours after completing the final scoring session, on Christmas Eve, 1975.

The baton would later be taken up by film composers such as Alex North and Jerry Goldsmith, contemporaries of Herrmann from the 1950s through to his death in the 1970s. North, Goldsmith and many other vaunted composers realized that there was much to be mined from the notion of film music as an interior monologue, building on Herrmann's principles while also taking the medium in exciting new directions.

Jon Burlingame says Herrmann's influence on later generations of composers cannot be overstated. "Danny Elfman's scores for *Beetlejuice* and *Batman* have their roots in Herrmann's colorful and exotic scores for Ray Harryhausen's films from the late 1950s and 1960s," Burlingame explains. "And [*Planet of the Apes* composer] Jerry Goldsmith ... also walked in those footsteps, admiring Herrmann's ability to create an emotional response with the simplest musical means."[94]

Steven Spielberg and John Williams, Robert Zemeckis and Alan Silvestri, Tim Burton and Danny Elfman—these are all strong relationships forged in the fires of the film score. Yet each collaboration owes itself to the mercurial, dynamic partnership between Hitchcock and Herrmann, two men who consistently challenged themselves and each other.

The importance of collaboration is evident in the scores of Alexandre Desplat for director Guillermo del Toro: *The Shape of Water* (2017), which won the Oscar for Best Original Score, *Pinocchio* (2022). As with the films of Hitchcock and Herrmann, Desplat says there must be genuine synergy in terms of visual and musical storytelling.

"In our conversations we talk about cinema, we talk about film music," he explains.

> We go through the great composers we love like Georges Delerue, Maurice Jarre and it helps. It's all a matter of communication with a director, always. But you're building bridges—that's what Maurice Jarre used to say. You have to help the director understand your language and you yourself have to reach the same level of understanding with them.
> The way Guillermo juggles both the real and imaginary worlds is something spectacular because he drags you into the film in just a few seconds. Right from that opening sequence, which is all special effects cinema, you believe in it. And that's the magic of cinema. You sit down, the light comes down and the story is being told to you. That's why cinema has become such a strong medium. It goes right the way back to the ancient stories, from the sagas of the Vikings to the Griot in Africa and Homer with *The Odyssey*. That's why cinema is so strong.[95]

With each passing decade, film music has undergone, and continues to undergo, pulse-quickening and provocative changes in tempo, an evolution of sorts, one that is often necessitated by a wider cultural context, and also the quicksilver moods of the composer in question. The "Golden Age" of Hollywood defined the notion of the film composer as an auteur, a person beholden to the vision of another creative artist, but with the capacity to enhance that vision beyond anything that was expected.

Above all, film music is intrinsically tied to the medium of the moving image, and therein lies the issue. Scoring is not, in and of itself, an autonomous medium, yet in a strange way it can gain autonomy away from the completed picture (especially if the music is excellent and the movie less so). Take Bernard Herrmann, for instance: all of his film scores were willed into existence by virtue of their function in a given movie, and yet many listeners will happily listen to his works, and those of his contemporaries, on a standalone basis.

As movies evolve to reflect a given time period, so too does film music. When it comes to cinema soundtracks, a change in style isn't optional but necessitated, lest the music itself be out of step with the imagery. The movie industry had already gone through numerous watershed moments in the years between the late 19th and early 20th centuries, and more changes were afoot as bold new horizons beckoned.

Three

Glissando

Jazz, Rock and Roll and the Slide Towards Experimentalism

"Jazz themes have led to some of the most iconic film music, and some instruments are steeped in the jazz tradition."—Terence Blanchard[1]

Alex North and the Birth of Jazz in Dramatic Film Scoring

The image of Hollywood icon Marlon Brando, shirt ripped open, shouting an anguished "Stella" in 1951's *A Streetcar Named Desire* defines the word "lusty." Brando's sweaty, rage-fuelled absorption of the newly-in-vogue "method" approach blew apart the parameters of acting. Put simply, here was someone who wasn't merely playing the part of the brutish Stanley Kowalski—he was living it.

Brando had originally played the role on Broadway, embodying the animalistic, broiling undercurrents of Tennessee Williams' controversial 1947 play. However the parameters of the cinema interpretation, directed by Elia Kazan, brought new dimensions to the role, enhancing the sense of claustrophobia and encasing us inside Stanley's sweltering New Orleans apartment. It's there that Stanley clashes with his sister-in-law Blanche DuBois (Vivien Leigh), who represents a tragically fading way of life.

The movie adaptation of *A Streetcar Named Desire* won four Oscars (although not one for Brando), and its upfront, even controversial, approach to sexuality encapsulated the changing attitudes of Hollywood at the time. Steadily, the movie industry was starting to throw off the shackles of the old in order to become more daring. Although the film was forced to edge around Stanley's violent assault on Blanche during the climax, enough was suggested through Kazan's visual languages to leave audiences stunned and deeply uncomfortable. And this was but one scene in the movie that challenged the status quo.

Since the early days of *King Kong*, the European Wagnerian symphony had been entrenched as the main way by which composers could communicate with audiences. However if *King Kong*, and its accompanying score by Max Steiner, marked the zeitgeist of early 1930s Hollywood, by the 1950s things had changed. Spectacle was still very much in demand, but of a different kind.

The A-list movie star was beginning to take hold, and fireworks could just as easily be rendered through body language and dialogue as through showy set-piece stunts. Marlon Brando was at the forefront, but even actors of his caliber found themselves boosted by film music capable of acting as an inner monologue. As Bernard Herrmann's score for *Citizen Kane* (1941) had demonstrated, increasingly challenging and angular scores could connect viewers to the darker side of human impulse. And the score for *A Streetcar Named Desire* would turn out to be the most significant in a generation.

Centrally, *A Streetcar Named Desire* is a story about the fight for America's soul, with Stanley the representative of the immigrant Polish generation, and Blanche the symbol of genteel plantation wealth. As per Tennessee Williams' original play, this was not a narrative that owed itself to grandiose Euro-centric traditions, and therefore a score drawing on the conventions of, say, Erich Wolfgang Korngold, would have been wildly inappropriate. Not to mention the story was set in the heart of New Orleans, that oft-romanticized birthplace of jazz, the quintessential American music idiom.

All of these factors would be critical in underpinning the eventual score from composer Alex North. Remarkably it was his debut film score, and single-handedly marked a stylistic turning point within cinema music, from lush romanticism to jazz. It's surprising to note that no dramatic film scores prior to *Streetcar* had embraced a modernistic jazz approach, but then there had been relatively few films like *Streetcar* in the run-up to the 1950s. The stylistics of North's film score were necessitated by the context in which he was operating—even so, North possessed an astonishing ability to both operate within his brief and establish a new kind of cinematic sound.

In the modern day, it's very easy to take jazz-influenced scores for granted. But North is the person who invented these clichés, beginning with the strident, bluesy nature of the trumpets and saxophones during *Streetcar*'s opening title sequence. It's a relatively brief passage of music but one that resounds with a sense of blusterous, sultry power.

Immediately, North taps into the sort of American cultural idioms that had been established by the likes of Louis Armstrong and other pioneering jazz greats. The tonality and instrumentation are a subconscious siren call, alerting prospective viewers that this is not a soundtrack, or, indeed, a movie, that owes itself to sweeping romanticism in the manner of a Korngold or a Newman. Within the first minute, audiences were aware that they had crossed a cultural boundary in terms of how they engaged with cinema, both visually and aurally.

"[A Streetcar Named Desire] is about male eroticism," observes jazz critic Selwyn Harris, "pointing the gaze of the viewer towards the figure of Brando, something unprecedented in Hollywood at the time. Alex North's score reflects this too as in when Stanley meets Blanche for the first time and a note-bending, bluesy saxophone seems much more in tune with Stanley's sexuality than Blanche's. North does something unusual at the time by bringing out different aspects of the various character's moods and behavior instead of the normal convention of giving each character a specific theme or motif."[2]

Certainly there's a compelling contradiction at the heart of the *Streetcar* score, one that pits the steamy jazz rhythms for Stanley against a heartbreakingly frail string theme for Blanche. The latter eventually builds into a haunting echo of the "Varsouviana" polka, the fateful music forever connecting Blanche with memories of "the boy," her deceased husband Allen Grey who, prior to his death, was revealed to be homosexual. North's approach signals how he brilliantly gets beneath the skin of the movie: his music makes audible the clash between different ideologies, making us feel the intense psychological battle between the two central characters.

Born in Pennsylvania in 1910 to Russian Jewish parents, North (born Isadore Soifer) showed an early talent for piano performance, developed through practice with his brother. At the age of 12, he developed these skills further by enrolling at the Settlement Music School and later, as a teenager, at Philadelphia's Curtis Institute. At this time, he found himself drawn to the jazz and swing artists who performed in Atlantic City—already, one can sense the genesis of the classical/jazz dichotomy inherent in the *Streetcar* score.[3]

North's mentor, accomplished Australian pianist George Frederick Boyle, encouraged him to enroll at the prestigious The Juilliard School in New York. North balanced his emergent compositional skills with a job as a telegraphist, designed to keep the money rolling in. He would later meet dance choreographer Anna Sokolow, his eventual partner and musical collaborator. In 1934, she and North would be invited to the Soviet Union, an invitation resulting from her socially conscious musical work *Homage to Lenin*. Although they later separated, it was a pivotal moment in North's life, as he would compose music for her productions and, in the process, make many valuable contacts in the theater and movie business.[4]

In fact, North's infatuation with Russia extended beyond his relationship with Sokolow. Between 1933 and 1935, he was accepted on a scholarship at the Moscow Conservatory, the first American to receive such an honor. He then served as music director of the Latvian State Theater, but despite being in the land of Prokofiev, his great idol, North found himself pining for the jazz rhythms of his home country.[5]

After serving in World War II, North returned to New York where he established himself first and foremost as a noted composer of ballet. His spell in Moscow had instilled a love of dance—in fact, as a young man he had once entertained the thought of a career as a performer, but dismissed it due to ill-health.[6] Nevertheless, North made a significant impact with critically acclaimed scores for stage productions. The most significant of these was 1947's *Death of a Salesman*—North's soundtrack for the Arthur Miller classic brought him into contact with director Elia Kazan, and the director would later invite him to Hollywood. The project: *A Streetcar Named Desire*.

Author Annette Davison identifies two clear facets of North's scoring personality. She points towards his tendency to alternate between "subjective" and "objective" movie projects, both of which afforded him different dramatic opportunities. The former allowed him to empathize with the characters, and he could subsequently pour more of his own personality into the music. The latter approach was, according to North, more concerned with atmosphere and spectacle.[7] And atmospheric though *Streetcar* certainly is, it's not hard to see the movie falling into North's subjective scoring bracket. This is a movie that can be read in a multitude of different ways, and the characters likewise, allowing its composer to mix a multitude of styles and tones.

In stark contrast to the scoring approach of Korngold on *Captain Blood*, the music for *Streetcar* is very much about what we're not seeing. This is a sign of how the evolution of cinema itself was forcing an evolution of the film soundtrack. North's tightly wound *Streetcar* score offers a profound commentary on different ways of life, ethnic backgrounds and emotional turmoil. And, in its own way, the score uses an oppressive jazz set-up to anticipate the fateful endgame long before we get to see it.

The primary register of the *Captain Blood* score is exuberance and high adventure, and Korngold responds magnificently. It's a score that taps into an audience's primordial adrenaline and appetite for escapism. For *Streetcar*, the emotions are somewhat more illusory, challenging and disturbing. Kazan's film, as per the original play, isn't meant for easy consumption, and the music is therefore free to pull in multiple directions. Not that North's approach is necessarily superior to Korngold's—one of the great draws of film music is its malleability, its ability to take us on specific journeys relative to the film in question. But there's no denying that North had established a watershed moment in the wider history of the soundtrack whereby appealing harmonics and melodies could be shelved in favor of something more textural.

Jazz historian David Meeker says there were financial imperatives for studios enlisting a jazz score: "The score [for *A Streetcar Named Desire*] served to color the sound of the film's steamy New Orleans setting. It has become a well-deserved landmark in the history of film music and paved the way for numerous movie jazz scores. Producers, ever on the lookout for new ways of cutting costs, soon tumbled to the sad truth that jazz musicians were relatively cheap to hire and that a small ensemble, an octet, or even a quartet could satisfactorily provide the necessary musical background to a film's action."[8]

Meeker continues:

> Up until that time all the major Hollywood studios had kept their own full-time orchestras; their days were now numbered. The recent demise of the big band era had dumped hundreds of skilled, hard-working jazz instrumentalists in the Los Angeles and New York areas eager for the rewards offered by the film, TV, and recording studios. They could sight read and could play anything put before them. Jazz scores soon proliferated.
>
> Composer Leith Stevens started the ball rolling with his seminal use of source music jazz cues in *The Wild One* (1953) arranged and played by Shorty Rogers and his Giants. Elmer Bernstein used rhythmic elements of jazz in his influential scores for *The Man with the Golden Arm* (1955), again performed by Shorty Rogers, and for *Sweet Smell of Success* (1957) featuring the Chico Hamilton Quintet. Johnny Mandel used the talents of top West Coast musicians for *I Want to Live* (1958). Suddenly jazz scores were hip.[9]

That said, in the early days of the sound era many of the biggest film studios (Warner, Fox, MGM, et al.) had already put out short films showcasing musical entertainers and dancers, helping to establish jazz as a cultural tour-de-force. Frequently cited: Duke Ellington's *Bundle of Blues* (1933), Billie Holiday in *Symphony in Black* (1935) and Louis Prima in *Swing Cat's Jamboree* (1938).[10] All of these artists, and many more besides, had erupted onto the wider cultural scene at the start of the 20th century—the exciting new medium of cinema would further sculpt their identities, particularly given the breakthroughs in sound technology.

Jazz had also been prevalent in the realm of animation since the earliest days of cinema. The frenetic, improvised melodies and countermelodies worked wonders when placed against the visual medium of animated slapstick, capable of enhancing the humor and absurdism. The music of the noted Cab Calloway was put to use in the likes of Betty Boop cartoon *Minnie the Moocher* (1932), and later on, direct caricatures of certain jazz artists were made visible on the big screen. The likes of Louis Armstrong and Fats Waller found themselves represented, to detrimental and stereotypical effect, in the likes of *Clean Pastures* (1937), *Have You Got Any Castles?* (1938) and *Tin Pan Alley Cats* (1943).[11]

Despite the cultural misappropriation, it was clear that Hollywood had long recognized jazz as a dramatic mechanism. These early efforts were an outlier of the cultural changes that would increasingly grip Hollywood through the 1950s. Despite these antecedents, Alex North's score for *A Streetcar Named Desire* was the first narrative-driven jazz film score. It showcased a level of sophistication, cultural awareness and dramatic intuition that arrested audiences by the throat.

And yet, even North's vision had to be compromised. At the end of Tennessee Williams' original play, following Stanley's rape of Blanche and her subsequent breakdown, her sister Stella (played in the film by Kim Hunter) returns to Stanley, representing a damning and daringly forward-thinking look at the toxicity of relationships. However, Elia Kazan was forced to tone down the ending for the movie, suggesting that Stella has indeed rejected Stanley for his monstrous crimes.

It was an approach that didn't sit easily with North, no doubt because his authentic jazz approach had done such a brilliant job throughout the movie of plugging an audience into the characters' carnal desires. The composer later said that the Warner Bros studio executives "insisted I make a big statement for the end … and there's always the question of retribution. Stanley had to be blamed at the end."[12] Hence the reason why Blanche's devastating final line, "I have always depended on the kindness of strangers," is accompanied not with a muted bass clarinet, suggesting mournful introspection, but a grand upsurge in the string section.

In hindsight, one can perhaps view North's swelling finale as an ironic riposte to the horrors that occurred earlier. Nevertheless, this clearly wasn't his original intention, and it's telling that Hollywood was only willing to embrace the suggestive qualities of a jazz film score up to a point. At this stage in the early 1950s, the codes and conventions of the romantic symphony still needed to be deployed to give audiences a clear moral resolution.

A Streetcar Named Desire proved a huge success at the 1952 Oscars ceremony. Marlon Brando was denied Best Actor, but the film walked away with Academy Awards for Best Actress (Vivien Leigh), Best Supporting Actress (Kim Hunter), Best Supporting Actor (Karl Malden) and Best Art Direction (Richard Day and George James Hopkins). In addition, it was nominated for Best Motion Picture, Best Director, Best Screenplay (for Tennessee Williams), Best Cinematography—Black and White, Best Costume Design—Black and White, Best Sound Recording and, finally, Best

Scoring of a Dramatic or Comedy Picture. It was one of two Oscar nominations that greeted North that year, the other being for the 1951 movie adaptation of *Death of a Salesman*, starring Fredric March in the title role of the hapless Willy Loman.

North had clearly exploded onto the Hollywood scene with a bracing and experimental new musical voice. He accumulated a total of 15 Oscar nominations throughout his career but never won, although he received an Honorary Oscar in 1986 "in recognition of his brilliant artistry in the creation of memorable music for a host of distinguished motion pictures."[13] The only other composer to have received such an honor is Ennio Morricone in 2007. (Morricone was given his dues with a long-overdue win for Best Original Score for Quentin Tarantino's *The Hateful Eight*, released in 2015.)

Despite establishing this newly in-vogue trend for cinematic jazz music, Alex North was more than capable of drawing on thunderous symphonic power when he needed to. Take his score for Stanley Kubrick's Roman epic *Spartacus*, released in 1960. Scripted by blacklisted Hollywood screenwriter Dalton Trumbo (who adapts Howard Fast's 1951 novel of the same name), *Spartacus* tells the story of the titular slave revolutionary, played in brawny and muscular fashion by Kirk Douglas. Outside of the stirring central performance, Kubrick's typically intricate direction and the sublime supporting cast (also including Laurence Olivier, Tony Curtis, Jean Simmons, Charles Laughton and Peter Ustinov), the movie is adorned with North's truly spectacular music.

Recognizing the weight and scope of the material, North composed a score worthy of ancient antiquity. In another indication of his typically intellectual approach to film music, North used a multitude of different orchestras, each showcasing a rich range of traditional symphonic and speciality instruments. Aiming to pay homage to one of his great influences, Prokofiev's *Alexander Nevsky* (1938), North incorporated dulcimers, lutes, marimbas and more to add exotic edge to the standard symphonic accompaniment. It was reported that 102 musicians were employed to perform the main and end titles on the movie.[14]

North later said of the score: "It has something to say about the world, which existed then and which still exists. I decided here to conjure up the feelings of pre–Christian Rome, not by resorting to archaisms and clichés, but in terms of my own contemporary, modern style—simply because the theme of Spartacus, the struggle for freedom and human dignity, is every bit as relevant in today's world as it was then. I wanted to interpret the past in terms of the present."[15]

It was clear that, during the 1950s, there was something of a binary split occurring at the center of Hollywood, epic traditions sitting alongside, and increasingly giving way to, arresting new voices. In the former camp, the likes of *The Ten Commandments* (1956), scored by Elmer Bernstein, *Ben-Hur* (1959), scored by Miklós Rózsa, and *Spartacus*. The latter camp was represented by such films as *A Streetcar Named Desire* and arresting youth movement movies, spearheaded by the likes of James Dean in *Rebel Without a Cause* (1955). As movies became somewhat less homogenized, so too the accompanying soundtracks diversified. That North was able to veer between such ideologically different modes of cinema is not just a showcase of his diversity, but a sign of the changing demands on composers within the wider film industry.

For all his versatility, North would best be remembered for his score to *A Streetcar Named Desire*. It kick-started a new sub-genre of film scores, eagerly embraced by a rising young generation of talented musicians. One of the greatest, cited earlier by David Meeker, is Elmer Bernstein's *The Man with the Golden Arm*. Before he became the revered composer of *To Kill a Mockingbird* (1962) and other dramatic gems, Bernstein embraced the jazz principles of Alex North and embellished them with increased levels of swagger.

The movie is directed by Otto Preminger and stars Frank Sinatra as junkie Frankie Machine. The movie's depiction of drug use was eye-opening and controversial for the time, and Bernstein's score plays up the sense of moral ambiguity. Full-throated, roaring trumpets and trombones kick off the opening titles, immediately establishing an air of decadence and modernity, musical conventions aligned to a changing world increasingly populated with jazz clubs and dive bars.

As with Max Steiner and other greats, the greatest sign of a composer's influence is when the baton is picked up by those who follow. Bernstein would follow up with *Sweet Smell of Success* (1957), another jazz gem eagerly drinking in the fumes of swinging New York on the cusp of cultural change. In 1959, jazz artist Duke Ellington brought an added level of authenticity to Otto Preminger's courtroom drama *Anatomy of a Murder*, starring James Stewart. Ellington's role as the soundtrack composer was an early example of Hollywood using an established popular musician on a soundtrack, a trend that would increasingly take hold as the 1960s and 1970s advanced. He was also a lone person of color within film music, and these shocking disparities were only hesitantly arrested within the industry as time went on. Both Bernstein and Ellington's works owe themselves to North's dramatic intuition on *Streetcar*.

One of the most famous jazz themes of all time, "The Pink Panther," came from the pen of composer Henry Mancini. Like North and Bernstein, Mancini came into his own during the relatively more liberated Hollywood era of the 1950s and 1960s, bringing a distinctly light and delightful touch to many popular comedies of the period. The theme was first composed for 1963's *The Pink Panther*—directed by Blake Edwards, it was the first movie to showcase Peter Sellers' incomparably funny French police bungler Inspector Clouseau.

Mancini's sparkling main theme, with its prominent saxophone solo and tapping triangle, showed how jazz conventions could be deployed with a sense of wit and knowing humor. The piece has a devious, sneaking quality to it, almost bottling the essence of a brilliant joke creeping up on you unawares before the punchline hits. The modes and conventions of jazz in film music were already widening just 11 years after North had debuted *A Streetcar Named Desire*. Whereas the *Streetcar* score evoked a sense of overwrought desire, *The Pink Panther*'s music accentuated a sense of farce.

The piece accompanies the famous animated title sequence showcasing cartoon character the Pink Panther. (This was a technique repeated in multiple movies throughout the series.) If generations have come to associate the theme's comic tone with Sellers' unforgettable comic timing, it's almost certainly happened retrospectively. Mancini admitted that he originally wrote the piece to capture David Niven's suave jewel thief Sir Charles Lytton, later bolting it to the opening credits sequence (the irony being that Niven's thunder was ultimately stolen by Sellers in the finished film).[16]

Regardless of its dramatic intentions, the theme is one of the most famous opening title pieces in movie history, and for good reason. Mancini would later say of its creation: "I told [the animators] that I would give them a tempo they could animate to, so that any time there were striking motions, someone getting hit, I could score to it. [The animators] finished the sequence and I looked at it. All the accents in the music were timed to actions on the screen. I had a specific saxophone player in mind—Plas Johnson. I nearly always precast my players and write for them and around them, and Plas had the sound and the style I wanted."[17]

Almost as an aside, a certain John Williams, then credited as Johnny Williams, was starting to break into the scoring industry as a session musician for Mancini. Years before the likes of *Star Wars*, Johnny Williams was a pianist and composer of featherlight jazz comedy scores such as *How to Steal a Million* (1966). It was a relatively unassuming start for an individual who would soon bloom into one of the most celebrated musicians of the 20th century.

As the 1960s progressed, the conventions of jazz became aligned with a sense of chic, swagger and bravado. Argentinian-born Lalo Schifrin was one of the finest practitioners of such scores, continuing the principle of Alex North's music and adding further layers of atmosphere. His score for *Bullitt* (1968) embodies this perfectly. The film stars Steve McQueen as maverick cop Frank Bullitt who, at one point, engages in a car chase around San Francisco in his Ford Mustang, a seat-gripping sequence that set new standards for vehicular realism and mayhem in cinema.

Interestingly, Schifrin leaves the car chase unscored, but his music leads us into it brilliantly. Alto-saxophone and trumpets build a sense of suspense as Bullitt begins his cat and mouse chase with the bad guys, only for the score to cut out as a different kind of music, the throaty roar of the V8 engine, kicks in to carry us through the next 10 minutes. It's a superb example of musical spotting, courtesy of Schifrin and director Peter Yates, and, like Alex North, it plays on an audience's broad awareness of jazz conventions. The history of jazz carries with it an air of rebelliousness and improvisational flair, and when combined with the imagery, this history implicitly emboldens the ice-cool, outsider status of McQueen's central portrayal. These conventions would later be translated into Clint Eastwood's *Dirty Harry* series, beginning with 1971's *Dirty Harry*.

The lingering influence of North, Schifrin and others can be heard in the works of contemporary artists like Terence Blanchard. A regular collaborator with director Spike Lee, Blanchard balances loyalty to his jazz origins with expansive, symphonic idioms, as heard in critically acclaimed scores such as *Malcolm X* (1992), *25th Hour* (2002) and *BlacKkKlansman* (2018). Blanchard is a visiting scholar in the Jazz Composition department at Berklee College of Music and has won plaudits for his moody interpretations of works by other artists. This includes Jerry Goldsmith's seminal, sensual trumpet theme from *Chinatown* (1974).

"Growing up in New Orleans, it was kind of inevitable," Blanchard says of his exposure to jazz. "You'd hear it all over the place. There was a guy named Alvin Alcorn who gave demonstrations in New Orleans of jazz. I was in 4th grade, in elementary school, and I've been hooked ever since."[18]

"With jazz, there was an inspiration to play on a higher level, which was all down to the people I heard performing live," he recalls. "Then, when it came to film music, once I got into it, that world opened up to me. So I did my homework and I listened to it. John Williams, Jerry Goldsmith, Thomas Newman ... Elmer Bernstein was another. It was then a case of how everything evolved from there."[19]

The improvisational nature of jazz and the more programmatic field of non-diegetic film scoring require different disciplines, says Blanchard. "Jazz musicians are accustomed to telling their story musically, because that's what we do," he explains. "But when it comes to writing music for a film, you're trying to enhance someone else's story. So the challenge is, how do I help the director best do that? The next challenge, with film anyway, is having the discipline not to reach the apex in the score before you reach that in the story."[20]

Blanchard's ability to translate these principles into the world of film owes itself, at least in part, to Alex North's pioneering approach. One can also sense North's influence in the jazz scores of Mark Isham, particularly achingly moody gems like *Quiz Show* (1994) and *The Cooler* (2003). It's also present in Angelo Badalamenti's sultry scores for David Lynch, particularly the *Twin Peaks* feature film spin-off *Twin Peaks: Fire Walk with Me* (1992).

And yet, despite his achievements in diversifying the tone of film music, it wasn't always plain sailing for North. In 1968, he was appointed a plum assignment: Stanley Kubrick's trend-setting sci-fi *2001: A Space Odyssey*. Emboldened by the vision of the *Spartacus* director, North embraced the film's oblique and ambiguous tone, one that would favor the silence of outer-space and therefore throw greater emphasis onto its music. Could there be a more grandiose assignment for a film composer?

Unfortunately, the fastidious Kubrick bailed on the idea of an original film score at the very last minute. The problem was, North had already recorded his score and, with the music in the can, assumed that was that. It was only during a later New York screening that North discovered his music had been junked for an ensemble of classical tracks including "Thus Spake Zarathustra" by Richard Strauss, "The Blue Danube" by Johann Strauss II and assorted works by avant-garde classicist György Ligeti.

The tapestry of music ultimately selected by Kubrick added to the film's eerie, portentous power. Sadly, it came at the expense of North's own time and efforts, a story sadly familiar to most, if not all, film composers the world over. North would later express his disappointment: "Well, what can I say? It was a great, frustrating experience, and despite the mixed reaction to the music, I think the Victorian approach with mid–European overtones was just not in keeping with the brilliant concept of Clarke and Kubrick."[21]

Despite that turbulent and upsetting experience, North's enduring legacy was never in doubt. He passed away on September 8, 1991, and forever made his mark as one of the most daring and brilliant film composers of all time. One of North's greatest protégés was a certain Jerry Goldsmith who'd been mentored by North in the earliest stages of his career. In the process of being taught by North, Goldsmith had assimilated his perfectionism and experimental tendencies seemingly via osmosis. These tendencies would erupt in later scores such as *Planet of the Apes* (1968).

Goldsmith had an interesting take on the *2001* situation. "[The score] was only there as a backstop in case the rights couldn't be gotten for the classical music recordings," he surmised. "There was never an issue whether the music was appropriate or inappropriate for the film. It was not an aesthetic decision. It was a business decision, a political decision. That doesn't make it any easier to swallow."[22]

Goldsmith's diplomatic and informed comments came in 1993 as he prepared to re-record the score for *2001: A Space Odyssey* with the National Philharmonic Orchestra. Goldsmith was, by this stage in his career, long-established, not to mention highly experienced in the political rigmarole of film composing, and his measured analysis underlined his experience. The painful truth behind Goldsmith's words exposes a bitter truth at the heart of the film score: the composer is not the one in charge, and this can lead to significant artistic upsets. Very often, the score will have to yield to the notion of a movie as a business venture, and this is the point at which egos will be bruised and weeks, if not months, of careful musical preparation will be thrown out of the window.

A close friend of North's, as well as his student, Goldsmith had an almost reverential outlook on his music. One year after the re-recording of *2001*, Goldsmith would bring crisp clarity and sultry bravado to his new arrangement of North's *A Streetcar Named Desire*. Recorded in 1994 with the Royal Scottish National Orchestra, the album helped reignite interest in one of North's seminal works, some three years after his death. Upon listening to it, one can clearly hear Goldsmith's passion and reverence for his mentor resonating in the pitch and roll of the trumpet section, especially in the lusciously sultry "Stan and Stella" sequence.

The association between the two composers stretched back to the 1960s, and it was North who helped Goldsmith get his big break. North had been invited to write the music for 1965's historical epic *The Agony and the Ecstasy*, a drama focusing on the troubled relationship between artist Michelangelo and Pope Julius II during the painting of the Sistine Chapel ceiling. A lavishly mounted star vehicle for Charlton Heston and Rex Harrison, the movie demanded a film score to match its sumptuous design and weighty subject matter.

North duly responded with an appropriately cavernous and large-scale symphony. However, he didn't compose all of it, instead handing the responsibility for the album's "Prologue" track to the up-and-coming Goldsmith. In fact, the latter's music would accompany the mini documentary titled "The Artist Who Did Not Want to Paint," a companion piece that was directed by Vincenzo Labella. Goldsmith conjures an air of noble dignity and gravitas befitting one of the most iconic artists of all time, a stunningly beautiful piece that got him noticed in Hollywood circles.

In the wake of this celebrated work, Goldsmith would grow into a genre-defying, chameleonic musician of rare brilliance and insight, one who adopted increasingly exotic and experimental tendencies and rewrote the rules of the film soundtrack in the process. He's regarded by many as the finest film composer of all time and is a key influence on the conceptual development of the film score.

Jerry Goldsmith Spearheads an Era of Extraordinary Cultural Change

Multifaceted changes were afoot in Hollywood during the 1940s and 1950s. Audience demographics were becoming more complex, the boundaries of taste were changing, and the sudden eruption of the American "nuclear" family was a threat to cinema supremacy. As time went on, the idealized image of the white picket fence suburban neighborhood began to assert a seductive hold. But it was what was going on inside these homes that gave powerful movie studios pause for thought. Namely, the increasing popularity of television, which democratized mass-market entertainment and piped it directly into people's living rooms. What could possibly be done to tempt movie fans out to their local cinema?

As for film composers, this would be a turbulent time in which they attempted to assert their rights. After the foundation of the Screen Composers' Association in 1945, Hollywood musicians continued to fight for the intellectual rights to their own work. This was traditionally held by the producers (the aforementioned Erich Wolfgang Korngold being a rare exception), and they were loath to hand over copyright authority to the artists themselves.[23] In 1947, the ASCAP (American Society of Composers, Authors and Publishers) attempted to raise license fees for the use of copyrighted music in movies; however, three years later, the outcome of a court case ruled against the organization, subsequently denting the amount of money composers took from royalty payments.[24]

This was also the era of the notorious McCarthy Communist witch hunts, spearheaded by Senator Joseph McCarthy. The so-called "Red Scare" engulfed the Hollywood elite, turning many members of the establishment against one another and often derailing entire careers.[25] One film composer who weathered the storm was Elmer Bernstein; called in front of the House Un-American Activities Committee (HUAC), he was effectively smeared and reduced to scoring throwaway sci-fi B-movies such as *Robot Monster* (1953). Fortunately, his reputation was later restored, allowing him to return to prestige pictures such as *The Ten Commandments*.

In 1948, the U.S. Supreme Court passed its landmark anti-monopoly ruling. It effectively ended the practice of "block booking" whereby studios would sell their products to theaters as an all or nothing package deal; this gave the studios significant control over the exhibition of their films. The termination of this practice pinched profits even more and eventually compelled executives to loan out their musical equipment to TV studios.[26] (Studio orchestras would eventually be abandoned altogether in 1958.[27]) The upsurge in television, plus the damage to studio supremacy, would force many established composers into the field of independent filmmaking as the 1950s and 1960s wore on (Bernard Herrmann and *Psycho*, 1960, being a prime example).

Added to all this was the softening of the previously cast-iron Hollywood Production Code, used to determine moral standards in American moviemaking. It's therefore little wonder that cinema was proving especially fickle and unpredictable. Of course, this is a large part of what made the era so exciting—filmmakers had access to creative opportunities previously denied them, and the boundaries of taste and social convention were continually being pushed. Director Otto Preminger was just such an example—his movie *Anatomy of a Murder*, mentioned earlier, was noteworthy for its use of terminology such as "panties," "rape" and "spermatogenesis," graphic for the time and never before heard in cinema.

At the same time, technological breakthroughs, particularly television, gave fledgling film composers a huge boost. Whereas in the 1930s and 1940s, radio helped the likes of Bernard Herrmann to reach a mass audience, a decade later it was syndicated TV that proved a boon to creatively minded musicians. Composers could now establish their musical personalities in the living rooms of homes across America, day on day, week on week, continually refining their skills in a distinctly low-budget and deadline-driven arena. It was a striking contrast with the early years of the 20th century whereby concert hall composers were directly imported into America from Europe, sought for their Wagnerian operatic bombast.

Jerry Goldsmith was exactly the kind of composer who benefited from the emergence of television. He first gained attention when working on Rod Serling's *The Twilight Zone*, the cult sci-fi/fantasy series which started in 1959 and offered all manner of eccentric possibilities for budding musicians. Via the medium of this show and others, Goldsmith demonstrated his early flair for electronic experimentation and unusual time signatures, skills that would later flower in some truly extraordinary film scores. With *The Twilight Zone*, Goldsmith was able to introduce a mini symphony every week to rapt audiences across the country, exposing them to new modes of musical storytelling. (Goldsmith would later score *Twilight Zone: The Movie* in 1983, an anthology collection of stories that allowed him to hit a diverse series of registers in one film.)

Born in Los Angeles in 1929, Jerry Goldsmith encapsulated the shift from traditional film scoring norms to something more experimental. His music simultaneously had one foot in the past and one firmly rooted in contemporary trends, classically inclined grandeur often sitting alongside modernistic rhythmic techniques and synthetic experimentation. Composer Marco Beltrami (1996's *Scream*) was a student of Goldsmith's and reiterated his importance in the history of the film score: "Without Jerry, film music would probably be in a different place than it is now. I think he, more than any other composer, bridged the gap between the old Hollywood scoring style and the modern film composer."[28]

Goldsmith was a keen pianist from a young age, and he studied under the renowned concert pianist Jakob Gimpel, before later studying theory and composition as a teenager under Italian composer Mario Castelnuovo-Tedesco. The latter was something of a fixture in Hollywood, and would also school the likes of Henry Mancini, André Previn and John Williams.

When asked to cite his inspiration for becoming a film composer, Goldsmith would credit Alfred Hitchcock's 1945 drama *Spellbound*, saying that he was enraptured with star Ingrid Bergman's beauty and the arresting, unusual tones of Miklós Rózsa's Oscar-winning score.[29] It's not hard to see why: even now, Rózsa's piercing, yearning use of the theremin (an exotically unusual instrument for the 1940s) casts a woozy, romantic spell, so one can only imagine what an impressionable teenage Goldsmith thought of it.

Initially enrolled at the University of Southern California, Goldsmith later sought a more practical program at the Los Angeles City College. There, he became assistant choral director and assistant conductor,[30] initiating his steady ascent into the upper echelons of Hollywood film music. However, there was a great deal of practical experience to be gained first, starting in 1950 with his job as a clerk typist in the music department of CBS (coincidentally, where Bernard Herrmann had made his name many years earlier).

The years spent toiling as a typist, and later as a composer and conductor on network television, instilled in Goldsmith a work ethic and professionalism that would prepare him well for the rigors of Hollywood. As for his precise musical voice, it's hard to pin down exactly where it came from. Clearly, his early musical training as a teenager charged him with an understanding of form, theory and composition, which in turn presumably instigated his enthusiasm for complex time signatures that challenged even the best orchestral players.

When quizzed on the subject of his versatility, capable of leaping from genre to genre and idiom to idiom with ease, Goldsmith replied: "It seems like it's me, and that's that!" Elaborating, he added: "Certain composers are doing the same thing over and over again, which I feel is sort of uninteresting. I don't find that you grow very much in that way. I like to keep changing, trying to do new things. Basically, I'm saying the same thing with a little different twist on it. Once you get caught up in the creative process, something inside takes over, and your subconscious just does it for you."[31]

Goldsmith's struggle to articulate his own abilities speaks of the internal contradictions within film music. Individuals working in this field may struggle to pinpoint their mode of voice or creative vision, simply because they are subject to the singular needs of each movie project they work on. In short, it is very often the film itself that determines the composer's voice, a voice that will naturally shift and evolve on an ad hoc basis.

That said, all truly great composers like Goldsmith have inherent mannerisms that mark a score, or series of scores, as their own. By his own admission, Goldsmith disliked the term "film composer," seeing himself first and foremost as a composer who happened to work primarily within the realm of cinema. He always sought to work beyond the frame, his quest to articulate not what an audience was seeing (in other words, simply reflecting the film's visuals), but those intangible emotions encoded in the very celluloid itself.

From his early days on CBS to his breakout TV work on *The Man from U.N.C.L.E.* (1964–1968) and others, Goldsmith always favored a diverse approach in terms of instrumentation, musical meters and harmonics. The immediately recognizable *U.N.C.L.E.* theme, with its bongos, groovy bass flute and resonant double-bass, encompassed an entire era of popcorn spy thrills. It was contemporaneous with John Barry's thrilling, brassy work on the *James Bond* series, starting with Sean Connery movie *From Russia with Love* (1963), and Lalo Schifrin's rip-roaring *Mission: Impossible* theme (1966–1973). It was a bountiful period for experimentation whereby various composers would redefine the musical zeitgeist, while at the same time feeding off the work of their contemporaries to enhance their own approach.

The *James Bond* theme remains one of the most distinctive in the history of motion pictures. The story of how the piece came together, not to mention who authored it, remains contentious. The generally accepted version of the story states that Eon producers Albert R. "Cubby" Broccoli and Harry Saltzman enlisted songwriter Monty Norman, a regular collaborator with Cliff Richard, to write and compose the theme, resonant with its meaty brass chords and twanging electric guitar undercurrent (performed by Vic Flick).[32]

However, John Barry, who went on to write 11 scores in the franchise, alleged that he was asked to adapt and arrange the rough outline of Norman's work, as well as produce the recording. In Barry's eyes, this effectively made him the co-writer of the theme.[33] During a protracted legal battle over ownership of the theme, the British court system ruled in favor of Norman, to Barry's immense chagrin.

Regardless of the outcome, the Bond theme remains a classic creation, a signifier of latent violence and swaggering masculine charisma in line with Ian Fleming's source material. Whether he was responsible for the theme or not, Barry became the signature voice of the series, despite its revolving door of guest composers. His work on the series is marked by its tonal and cultural versatility, adapting to all manner of exotic locations in the underscore (Istanbul in 1963's *From Russia with Love*; Japan for 1967's *You Only Live Twice*) and performing artists during the opening title sequences. From the piercing Shirley Bassey on 1964's *Goldfinger* to the synth pop of a-ha on 1987's *The Living Daylights* (Barry's final Bond score), the reinvention on display is nothing short of fascinating.

It was clear that symphonic tradition hadn't completely fallen by the wayside during the 1950s and 1960s. One need only look at the sterling work of Elmer Bernstein as a reminder of the power of nostalgia in film music. His music for *The Magnificent Seven* (1960), a candidate for the most famous Western theme of all time, evoked the spirit of the quintessential Americana composer, and Bernstein's mentor, Aaron Copland ("He had a tremendous influence on me"[34]), not to mention early Hollywood works from Max Steiner.

Bernstein said of *The Magnificent Seven*: "I think Aaron Copland and I did that score.... I like the film, but if you watch it without the music it is slow, strangely enough. It develops very slowly. I learned my lesson from [Cecil B. de Mille]. I thought, 'I'm going to infuse this film with energy.' And it worked."[35]

Years later, Bernstein was in Barcelona preparing for some concert work when his attention was caught by a mechanical, coin-activated horse. He recalled: "All of a sudden, it starts to play *The Magnificent Seven*! I thought, 'Now I know what my life has been about!'"[36] Bernstein's capacity for memorable melody would again take flight with the unmistakable theme for World War II movie *The Great Escape* (1963), which conjures an air of whimsical defiance.

Circling back to Jerry Goldsmith, he had a truly unique voice whereby he balanced the Steiner/Korngold ancestry with something altogether more aggressive and modernistic. Breakout Hollywood scores such as *The Blue Max* (1966) showcased this approach. This World War I drama focused on Western Front fighter pilot Lieutenant Bruno Stachel, played by George Peppard. Directed by John Guillermin (the man behind the John Barry–scored *King Kong* remake from 1976), the film benefited hugely from a Goldsmith score that took viewers soaring into the skies while also hitting them in the pit of their stomach as to the dangers of contemporary warfare.

Of course, this was made possible by the film itself, one that takes a decidedly non-chivalrous approach—disenchantment and trauma underpin the story, which allows Goldsmith to let rip with animalistic brass arrangements and uncomfortable percussion patterns. His rhythmic and instrumental choices appear to interrogate the nature of valor, stirring our sense of adrenaline while simultaneously deploying abrasive textures that strike a decidedly non-harmonious note. The music is an act of contradiction in and of itself, a microcosm of how certain soundtracks of the period were becoming more complex in line with their movies. The terseness of Goldsmith's music was mirrored in other militaristic scores of the period, including Ron Goodwin's snare-laden, exhilarating work on *Where Eagles Dare* (1968), starring Richard Burton and Clint Eastwood.

Naturally, Goldsmith wasn't the only composer who was setting new trends. One need only point towards Ennio Morricone who completely reinvented the sound of the Western with his scores for director Sergio Leone. Like Alex North and John Barry, Morricone was a composer with a background in jazz, and he brought this idiosyncratic approach to bear on one of Hollywood's oldest genres. That said, the movies that Morricone scored for Leone were of the Italian "Spaghetti" Western variety, deriving inspiration from the operatic sensibilities of his home country.

This allowed Morricone to let rip with some of the most uniquely thrilling and unusual music ever heard in cinema. His music for Leone's *Dollars* trilogy (1964's *A Fistful of Dollars*, 1965's *For a Few Dollars More* and 1966's *The Good, the Bad and the Ugly*) unleashes a volley of ticking watch chimes, guttural male voices, mariachi trumpets and piccolo flutes. It's a wildly eccentric mix that speaks of Morricone's background in improvisational jazz; that he was able to pull it together with such flair was a sign of his astonishing dramatic abilities. Morricone's music remains consistently grand throughout, applying operatic textures to both the sandswept landscapes and the craggy crevices of Clint Eastwood's face, in the process helping audiences to see, feel and listen to movies in a striking new way.

"In the ocarina/vocal figure in *The Good, the Bad and the Ugly*, we are looking at one of the most primal of aural signifiers," writes music producer Andy Hill. "It is a *call*: a summons, an alert, even a warning. It mimics birdsong in its shape and repetition, just as so many of the most ancient humans did. It is simultaneously (1) a clarion call (i.e., a demand for action); (2) the war cry of an avenging angel.... And (3) a hero's fanfare (in this case, an antihero's, since it wasn't always easy to tell Clint Eastwood from the bad guys."[37]

The later *Once Upon a Time in the West* (1969), again directed by Leone, favors experimentation to an extent, particularly with the harsh electric guitar and harmonica combo for Henry Fonda's ruthless killer Frank. For the most part, though, it carries a much more soulful tone, carried by the piercingly gorgeous soprano vocal of Morricone's regular collaborator Edda Dell'Orso, who represents Claudia Cardinale's settler Jill.

The tone of the score establishes a complex mixture of yearning and mechanized brutality, distilling in musical form the hopes, dreams and despairs of those in the midst of America's Western expansion.

Morricone's music was just one example of how the attitude towards cinema music was undergoing its most radical shift in years. Bernstein's *The Magnificent Seven*, and earlier efforts like Jerome Moross' *The Big Country* (1959), were rooted in the Americana stylistics of Aaron Copland. Now, Morricone and others like him were able to apply a distinctly European sensibility. And plenty of other scores of the era were breaking down technical boundaries. John Barry's work on *The Lion in Winter* (1968), for example, used thunderous Gregorian plainsong to illustrate the war of words between King Henry II of England (Peter O'Toole) and his wife Eleanor of Aquitaine (Katharine Hepburn). The archaic is transmogrified into something relatable and understandable for a contemporary audience, a brilliant approach that duly saw Barry awarded with an Oscar.

That's not to say that pre-existing Hollywood standards weren't finding favor throughout this period of great change. Some of the biggest blockbusters of the 1950s and 1960s were those unashamed big-screen epics that had held sway since the days of *Gone with the Wind*. *The Ten Commandments*, for instance, was brought to audiences in high-resolution VistaVision widescreen, offering an eye-widening feast of Biblical plagues and spectacular sets, held together by Charlton Heston's imperious central performance as Moses.

Elmer Bernstein's gargantuan score moves between incantatory brass and string passages and location-specific speciality instrumentation, evoking the wrath of the almighty and the sin of man in one fell swoop. It's not hard to imagine that Bernstein's score was a critical factor in engaging an audience's attention, helping propel the film to global grosses of $122 million worldwide against a $13 million budget.

Likewise, the musical genre enjoyed some of its biggest success stories during the 1960s. The Julie Andrews–starring *The Sound of Music* (1965), with music from Richard Rodgers and Oscar Hammerstein II, grossed a mammoth $286 million against a relatively slight $8 million budget. Come 1966, it had been cemented as the most financially successful movie of its day, surpassing even *Gone with the Wind* (unadjusted for inflation). Ironically enough, just two years later, the Rex Harrison musical vehicle *Doctor Dolittle* flopped with a mere $9 million against its $17 million budget, a reminder of how notoriously fickle audience tastes are at the best of times.

In the midst of all this cultural and creative turbulence was Goldsmith. And in 1968, he would redefine the parameters of the film score with his work on *Planet of the Apes*. Directed by Franklin J. Schaffner, with whom Goldsmith would enjoy a lasting and fruitful collaboration, the film adapts Pierre Boulle's dystopian sci-fi novel *La Planète des singes*. Charlton Heston plays an astronaut who lands on an unmarked planet to discover, shockingly, that mankind has been knocked down a few places on the evolutionary pecking order. That's because the planet is presided over by intelligent apes, capable of sophisticated communication and dialogue. Meanwhile, the remaining humans are either killed or rounded up for scientific study. Even to this day, it remains a startling vision, even if the rubbery ape make-up (which won an Oscar) doesn't convince as much as it once did.

Regardless, the film's allegorical take on a nightmarish future, not to mention its satirical destabilizing of man's place in the world, still packs a punch. Like all great films, its surface pleasures gain greater resonance through the addition of a truly engrossing score. Goldsmith's arrestingly avant-garde music was unlike anything heard in cinema before, deploying standard symphonic instrumentation in unusual ways, and mixing it with exotic, appropriately alien tonalities. (The influence of Stravinsky's *The Rite of Spring* is evident in the phrasing and eccentric time signatures.) While the film's startling visuals speak for themselves, it's Goldsmith who makes us feel the horror and discombobulation of Heston's character, doing the thing that all great film scores do: translate intangible, complex emotions into something textural and tonal that audiences understand on a base, instinctive level.

Ram's horns, stainless steel mixing bowls (from the composer's own kitchen), woodblocks, Brazilian cuica drums, woodwind instruments blown without reeds—these are just a few of the choices made by Goldsmith to craft a distinctly impressionistic atmosphere. Pizzicato (plucked) strings are filtered through an echoplex (later used by Goldsmith in his score for 1979's *Alien*) to create an unsettling, elongated effect in the soundscape, while the French horn players reverse their instruments and play through the horns instead. Add all this to an onslaught of slide whistles, bells and lots more, and it's no surprise that the score perfectly distilled both animalistic rage and a steadily mounting sense of discombobulation.[38]

It can truly be said that the avant-garde film score came of age with *Planet of the Apes*, not least in the pivotal hunt sequence. It's at this moment that Heston's character, Taylor, discovers exactly what predicament he's landed in on this strange planet, signaled by the astonishing sight of an ape on horseback wielding a gun. The sight is perfectly underscored by the feral blast of the ram's horn on Goldsmith's soundtrack, elucidating the feeling of terror and anxiety.

If the best film music is said to articulate invisible emotions, then there can be few finer examples. The horn is mixed in with a host of woodblocks, low-register piano chords and piercing strings, all of which further compound the shock. One can clearly hear Goldsmith's influence on his aforementioned pupil Marco Beltrami, a composer who emphasizes brass and string instruments at the very end of their tonal ranges in the acclaimed likes of *Scream* and *Snowpiercer* (2013). Like Goldsmith, Beltrami walks that fine line between atonality and recognizably human sounds.

Interestingly, Goldsmith (who, at one point, conducted the orchestra wearing an ape mask) decided not to score the final Statue of Liberty twist (revealing that the planet is, in fact, Earth) with any music. His reason: "Because Charlton Heston was over the top enough."[39] This speaks to the power of spotting in film music, that fine art whereby the director and composer will unite to decide the scene-specific placement of the score. Whereas Goldsmith's music has frightened us all the way through the movie up to this point, in the end it is the absence of music that leaves a lingering chill, reinforcing the sound of the crashing waves and Heston's anguished "Damn you all to hell."

Goldsmith's efforts were recognized with an Oscar nomination, and it cemented his partnership with Schaffner. This collaboration would encompass a host of styles, from fading trumpet triplets in World War II biopic *Patton* (1970) to gorgeously lyrical, accordion-set waltzes in *Papillon* (1973). Later, in 1977, Goldsmith deployed a heart-rendingly intimate ensemble for Ernest Hemingway adaptation *Islands in the Stream*, and in 1978, the composer would deviously fuse Wagnerian and Straussian waltzes to capture latent Nazi evil in *The Boys from Brazil*. Schaffner and Goldsmith made one of the finest director-composer partnerships in the history of the industry.

Planet of the Apes set in motion a series of convention-defying scores from Goldsmith. His career-topping achievement came in 1976 for the horror movie *The Omen*, directed by Richard Donner. Gregory Peck and Lee Remick star in this classic chiller as the unwitting, adoptive parents of the Antichrist, known as Damien, and their dawning realization of this apocalyptic terror is what gives the movie its charge.

Interestingly, Donner envisaged the movie as a psychological horror in which the nature of Damien's evil would be played somewhat ambiguously. Are the main characters mad, or is the boy actually the son of the Devil? Goldsmith's score goes against this brief somewhat, foregrounding the Satanic panic with a litany of spine-tingling Gregorian chants, including the bone-chilling main title theme "Ave Satani" ("Hail Satan"). Yet, perversely, it adds an extra layer of creepy dialogue to sequences otherwise devoid of devilish cliché—a decapitation by a pane of glass is transformed into a shrieking celebration of unholy evil, and, at the other end of the scale, whispering voices reflect the latent menace of the rottweilers deployed as Satan's servants.

The music covers a wide spectrum of orchestral/vocal emotions, charging the movie with an added layer of suspense and metatextual meaning. It's a masterful example of how film music can take an appreciably solid concept and elevate it into something palpably visceral, and it's little surprise that it won Goldsmith an Oscar. (That same year, he beat two scores from his late friend and contemporary Bernard Herrmann: *Taxi Driver* and *Obsession*.)

Remarkably, however, this is the only Oscar Goldsmith would ever win in his career. ("Ave Satani" was, rather amusingly, Oscar-nominated for Best Original Song, a distinct change from the usual wholesome choice.) The score would exert a huge influence on both Goldsmith's own career (the Oscar-nominated use of children's lullaby "Carol Anne's Theme" in 1982's *Poltergeist*) and other composers (Philip Glass' malevolent *Candyman* from 1992).

Goldsmith's love of pushing the envelope was most apparent in his science-fiction, action and horror scores, but he diversified into a wide range of genres. A haunting solo trumpet became the embodiment of Jack Nicholson's jaded melancholy and regret in 1974's *Chinatown* (one must also credit principal musician Uan Rasey for such depth of feeling). Scores such as *Gremlins* (1984) and *Total Recall* (1990) broke new ground with their integration of organic and synthetic elements, a trademark of the composer that had started with his television work in the 1950s, and really flourished from the mid-eighties onwards. He showcased a love of crisscrossing ethnic styles, evident in long-forgotten killer lions movie *The Ghost and the Darkness* (1996).

The score for the latter blends Irish flute melodies with brassy grandeur and a joyous Swahili choir, a distillation of 19th-century colonial expanse and a reflection of Africa's breathtaking Tsavo landscape. Just two years earlier, Henry Mancini, presenting Goldsmith with a lifetime achievement award, said of the composer: "He scares the hell out of us."[40] Certainly, few of Goldsmith's Hollywood contemporaries would have dared tackle such a mundane film as *The Ghost and the Darkness* in such a richly textured manner.

If Goldsmith was synonymous with any franchise, it was *Star Trek*. He scored 1979's *The Motion Picture* for director Robert Wise (with whom Goldsmith had worked on 1966's *The Sand Pebbles*) and in the process conjured an operatic symphony of the unknown. Forced to score an edit that showcased incomplete special effects, the composer let his imagination run wild across a spectrum of orchestral grandeur and experimental, unusual sounds. Goldsmith's score embodied the *Star Trek* philosophy of discovery, wonderment and alienness, from the swirling, Bernard Herrmann-esque strings for the mysterious V'Ger cloud to the piercing drone of the blaster beam. The latter was an instrument designed by Craig Huxley, fusing artillery shell casings with motorized magnets inside a 15-feet-long tube.

Goldsmith was Oscar-nominated for his work, but only after Wise had rejected Goldsmith's original main theme. Somewhat irked, the composer went back and refashioned it into the iconic brassy fanfare we know and love, one of the most famous movie themes of all time. Regarding the musical reveal of the all-important U.S.S. *Enterprise*, film music journalists David Hirsch and Ford A. Thaxton describe it as a "love theme." They elaborate: "As the travel pod moves around to the open front and the shop is revealed in all its glory, Goldsmith pours in the full power of the orchestra."[41]

Goldsmith's work on *The Motion Picture* would kick start a long-running connection with the franchise. Spanning both the original and *Next Generation* eras, he scored 1989's *Star Trek V*, 1996's *First Contact*, 1998's *Insurrection* and 2002's *Nemesis*. In-between, he scored the TV incarnation of *The Next Generation* (1987–1994) and *Voyager* (1995–2001). The franchise offered the perfect canvas on which Goldsmith could paint his signature unusual sounds and heroically thrilling melodies.

When addressing his score for the Pearl Harbor attack epic *Tora! Tora! Tora!* (1970), Goldsmith made an astute observation. He said he only made the decision to add music if "there is a scene so special, where there is something to be said that only music can say. Then the presence of music will bring that extra element you need, and if it's done right, it will elevate the scene."[42] It's a simple statement yet also a deceptively profound one that underlines Goldsmith's philosophy: music in a film can be utterly redundant unless it's correctly tailored to the material, both in terms of spotting and dramatic commentary. (Goldsmith's *Chinatown* score is another fine example of this, consisting of little more than 30 minutes in total.)

In his own way, Goldsmith was honoring the principles laid down by Max Steiner decades earlier, another individual who lamented the over-writing of film scores. There's always an emotional truth at the center of a given narrative, and it's the composer's job to extract it with an appropriate amount of notation. The key difference between the two composers resides not so much in philosophy as in technique. Steiner established most, if not all, of the rules of the symphonic film score. Goldsmith was able to use these as a foundation but came of age as a composer in an era marked with much counter-cultural turbulence and technological expansion. Hence why his music operates via the same parameters as a Steiner score, but tonally sounds very different.

As an artist, Goldsmith was chameleonic, and he eagerly adapted to the changing zeitgeist of a given era. He became the embodiment of a new kind of film composer, one who could adopt new tones and textures relative to the period. In the process, he reshaped the possibilities of film scoring as a dramatic medium. For instance, as Goldsmith went through his heavily electronic stage in the 1980s, he inspired his contemporaries to take up arms and do the same, emboldening the film music community to carve out distinct new textures and sounds. One can clearly hear this in Maurice Jarre's scores of the period—it's perhaps hard to match up the composer of *Lawrence of Arabia* (1962) with the largely synthetic *Gorillas in the Mist* (1988), and one would imagine that Jarre was heavily influenced by Goldsmith's like-minded scores of the period, such as *Gremlins* (1984).

No longer did the battle lines have to be drawn between the "conventional" organic needs of the symphony orchestra and the oblique, unattainable world of electronics. Goldsmith brought these two seemingly different philosophies together, with the recognizably human sound of the string section melding with the abstract nature of, say, a Yamaha synthesizer. The former is often compared to the emotional register of the human voice, whereas an audience can easily divine the absence of that very element, no matter how intangible, in a piece of electronic music. This was a significant step forward in the use of cinematic music as language, capable of more specifically responding to fantastical scenarios, and imagined worlds and characters.

Several of Goldsmith's greatest accomplishments, in fact, came outside the world of film in the form of his concert work. Goldsmith discovered that his intrinsic cinematic style adapted successfully to the parameters of live performance, whether he was composing something original (his critically acclaimed 1999 work *Fireworks: A Celebration of Los Angeles*), showcasing his past movie work or curating a show of pre-existing score pieces from other composers. It's been noted that both Goldsmith and Elmer Bernstein operated effectively within this arena, reinforcing the symphonic power of film music while shining a light on neglected scores.[43] John Williams has also thrived in the live environment, collaborating with the Boston Pops Orchestra on the rousing 1984 "Olympic Fanfare." In 2020, Williams joined forces with the Vienna Philharmonic Orchestra to acclaimed effect, presenting stirring interpretations of some of his most famous works.

Of course, like all the great film composers that had come before him, Goldsmith was being swept along on a current, one not of his own making. Musicians operating on a Hollywood scoring stage are, more often than not, instruments of fate, subject to the extenuating context informing the very film that they're working on. Take *Planet of the Apes*: the film's essential tone distils a turbulent time in Hollywood history when creative voices were diversifying, and conventional feel-good narrative structures could be junked in favor of something much more intellectually probing. Hence why Goldsmith's radical rejection of conventional melody and theme exists in the first place.

One must also point out that the simpatico relationship between composer and technology also predates Goldsmith. In truth, this can be said to go back to the earliest days of Max Steiner and the click track, that fundamental breakthrough that allowed infinitesimal synchronization between music and moving pictures. Goldsmith carried all of this rich heritage in his persona and his music, and yet he initiated a sophisticated upgrade with the surface-level techniques.

Film music is, at its heart, a concept marked by evolutionary upgrades across the decades, in line with the changes continually wrought upon cinema itself. Film scoring possesses the capacity to absorb all manner of dramatic and technical possibilities, but only if a given approach meshes with the whims of the director and producers. And there can be no denying that Goldsmith's tenure as a Hollywood film composer was one of the most significant evolutions in the history of the medium.

His instinctive dramatic capabilities and love of experimentation found its perfect outlet in the changing nuances of the pop culture landscape, but which one fed the other? It's a curious example of the cyclical relationship between film scorer and external context. A musician can only thrive because of the environment or period they're in, and yet in the process they can define that very same era via the power of their own voice. In turn, they are sure to influence and inspire others to do the same. Goldsmith passed away in July 2004, having assuredly elevated film music into a higher state of being, just like Max Steiner, Erich Wolfgang Korngold, Alfred Newman, Bernard Herrmann and other dignitaries before him.

And yet, from the 1950s onwards, a drastically different approach to film soundtracks had started to run in parallel with Goldsmith's breakthroughs. Hollywood no longer needed to simply rely on original music—instead, there was a huge captive audience hanging on the appeal of rock and roll. All of a sudden, film scoring faced another huge challenge to its supremacy, as the tastes of the burgeoning youth market were increasingly courted by major Hollywood studios. The very essence of film music was about to be split down the middle.

Blackboard Jungle Brings Rock and Roll to the Silver Screen

In 1955, a movie about social alienation and inner-city deprivation shook the foundations of Hollywood. The film in question was *Blackboard*

Jungle, directed by Richard Brooks who would go on to achieve critical hits such as Burt Lancaster vehicle *Elmer Gantry* (1960) and Truman Capote adaptation *In Cold Blood* (1967). The former won Lancaster his only Oscar and the latter scored Brooks the Academy Award for Best Adapted Screenplay. However, *Blackboard Jungle* remains, arguably, Brooks' most significant contribution to cinema.

The film (adapted from Evan Hunter's 1954 book *The Blackboard Jungle*) stars Glenn Ford (he of the tough-minded 1953 film noir *The Big Heat*) as a teacher grappling with the most profound kind of juvenile delinquency. His character Richard Dadier has been newly installed at a tough inner-city prep school with a notorious (and, as it turns out, deserved) reputation. In attempting to reach out to his pupils, who have been shaped by poor living conditions and unpleasant upbringings, Dadier finds himself continually knocked back, and is even savagely assaulted at one stage. And yet he remains determined to break through to at least one of his students: the musically gifted yet wayward Gregory Miller (Sidney Poitier, delivering a star-making performance).

The movie was one of several 1950s dramas riding high on a new kind of American phenomenon: the teenager. Disaffected young adults, subject to impressionable new trends in both fashion and music, railing against their place in the world, had started to cause a stir. American teens were well-positioned to enjoy the post–World War II breakdown in norms regarding identity and sexuality, with an emphasis on upward mobility, vehicular ownership and an almost fetishistic attitude towards appearance. Accused of being dissolute and immoral, this generation was instead the harbinger of a bold new era in which the trappings of material wealth could be embraced and critiqued simultaneously.

Behavioral trends were also being put under the limelight like never before. The nature of children emerging from broken homes and violent backgrounds started to hold dramatic currency as far as Hollywood was concerned. Loneliness, melancholy and the nature of the individual versus the wider hegemony all became narratively potent tools.

Films such as *The Wild One* (1953), starring Marlon Brando, centered on the notion of gang culture and mob mentality, exploring the morally corrosive effects such hierarchies have on individuals. In this case, it's Brando's rootless yet essentially principled Johnny Strabler, the leader of a motorbike gang known as the Black Rebels Motorcycle Club. With his detached air of cool, leather jacket and bike, Brando was immediately cemented as a cultural icon.

One cannot discuss this material without a mention of James Dean, the symbol of dispossessed teens the world over, not just in Hollywood. In his tragically short career, Dean carved out vivid portrayals of young men inwardly raging against social convention. His most famous movie, 1955's *Rebel Without a Cause*, targeted that essence of bland, middle-class American suburbia, here exposed as a poor veneer for emotionally stunted lives. His character, Jim Stark, is railing principally because of the disintegrating relationship between his parents, a bold narrative decision for the time, although one we would take for granted in the modern age.

In real life, people of Jim's age found their avatar, their emotional nexus, in the form of this seething, deeply unhappy creation. And yet, the newly formed cultural emphasis on teenagers wasn't solely focused on doom and gloom. As record companies of the 1950s increasingly geared trends towards a youth audience, film studios were quick to pick up on this as a dramatic outlet. In particular, the swing towards the new craze of rock and roll compelled Hollywood studios to reach out to young audiences in exciting new ways, and this in turn changed the essence of the movie soundtrack forever.

Blackboard Jungle was at the vanguard of this movement. The film's opening credit sequence is accompanied by the swinging sounds of "Rock Around the Clock" by Bill Haley & His Comets, a brief interlude but one that would exert a powerful impact on the usage of music in cinema. Although earlier films such as *The Wild One* had subtly integrated jukebox classics into the fabric of certain scenes, this was the first time a pre-existing youth rock staple had been foregrounded at the start of a Hollywood movie.

The song was originally written in 1952 by Max C. Freedman and James E. Myers, and Haley recorded his version with The Comets in 1954 for Decca Records. Interestingly enough, Haley's take wasn't an immediate commercial success, but when later grafted onto *Blackboard Jungle* its profile was boosted significantly. In fact, starting in July 1955 (some four months after the release of the movie), the song spent eight weeks at the top of the Billboard pop charts, a slow burner if ever there was one.[44] It demonstrated how a mass-market medium like cinema could act as a showcase for musical artists and their work. And, in turn, this was a potent strategy for the movie studios in securing the attention of the fickle and unpredictable youth market.

Reports vary as to why the filmmakers settled on "Rock Around the Clock" as the opening number. It's widely accepted that director Richard Brooks was rifling through the record collection of Glenn Ford's son, Peter. From here, Brooks selected several possible candidates and, out of these, "Rock Around the Clock" was the winner.[45] It was perhaps inevitable that a youngster would play a pivotal role in establishing the film's rock and roll credentials—after all, this was the very audience being courted.

On its list of the 15 most influential film soundtracks of all time,

Turner Classic Movies (TCM) defines *Blackboard Jungle* as a watershed moment in pop culture history. It states: "Teens flocked to the film, dancing in theater aisles as the song played over the opening credits. Parents may have been shocked by such uninhibited behavior, but things got worse when screenings also inspired violence and vandalism around the world. Thanks to *Blackboard Jungle*, the song hit number one on the Billboard charts, eventually selling 25 million copies and becoming what Dick Clark called 'The National Anthem of Rock'n' Roll.'"[46]

It's perhaps ironic that the song makes only a few limited appearances in the movie, and yet defines the tone of the narrative absolutely. The nature of music as a cathartic, healing mechanism is a key role within the fabric of the narrative, chiefly in the relationship between Dadier and Miller. There's also a distressing sequence in which one of Dadier's fellow teachers naively brings in his prized record collection to play for his class, only for the students to violently attack him and destroy his beloved music in the process.

In the world of *Blackboard Jungle*, getting those who are emotionally and materially dispossessed to engage in culture and creativity is a hard-fought battle. More often than not, the response is a rage-fuelled and aggressive one, and at the time of the film's release, this was seen as startlingly realistic. The film reflected the thwarted dreams and incandescent anger of overlooked youngsters from all across America, contradictory emotions that were increasingly bound up within the fabric of rock music itself. Many theaters in America's Deep South opted to ban the movie outright, but they were clearly fighting against the tide. Rock and roll was clearly here to stay, and the genre's symbiotic relationship with cinema would only become more and more potent.

In today's world, the notion of a soundtrack album is something we tend to take for granted. A recent successful example is Marvel Studios' *Guardians of the Galaxy* (2014), which does a sublime job off-setting its celestial sci-fi landscapes against recognizably groovy retro music hits. Director James Gunn dusts off an eclectic mix of overlooked gems (Redbone's "Come and Get Your Love," which plays during the opening credits sequence), and established favorites (The Jackson 5's "I Want You Back"). No mere gimmick, the music as heard in the film is key to the character development of Chris Pratt's reluctant hero Peter Quill/Star-Lord, who carries around a series of "Awesome Mixes" on analog cassette tapes as a reminder of his late mother.

Running parallel to the songs in *Guardians of the Galaxy* (and its 2017 sequel) is the score by Tyler Bates. This also carries a somewhat nostalgic tone, favoring major key resolutions in the brass section, plus some gorgeous choral and electronic accents, to emphasize the heroism of the story's unorthodox ensemble. It's an example of how bifurcated modern soundtracks have become: original orchestral music can tease out the subliminal themes of the narrative while, sitting alongside it, crowd-pleasing pop music staples create a euphoric blast of familiarity. The critical aspect is how well these two musical approaches dovetail, and in the case of the *Guardians* films, Gunn pulls it off superbly well.

The use of rock music in *Guardians of the Galaxy* would not have been possible without *Blackboard Jungle*. It changed the game in Hollywood, showing executives that it wasn't always necessary to commission a composer to give a movie its identity. Instead, audiences could be trusted to bring their own pre-existing awareness of rock and pop music to the party, the net result being that when such music is heard in the context of the movie, it fashions greater emotional engagement.

Rock and roll already existed beyond the boundaries of the cinema frame, skyrocketing in popularity in homes, clubs and bars across America—when such music was placed inside the parameters of a given film, it imbued the format with greater socio-cultural relevance. Increasingly, movies could respond to the needs of the zeitgeist, in the process keeping up with changeable audience demands and, hopefully, keeping box office sales healthy.

It didn't take long before many of the era's rising stars embarked on movies geared to their musical personalities. The most famous of these was surely Elvis Presley, the hip-shaking icon of cool from Mississippi who would exert a formidable impact on the evolution of rock music. Born in 1935, Presley honed a singular stage presence that led him to being dubbed "the King of Rock and Roll." Under the constant inspection of his manager, Colonel Tom Parker, Presley eventually diversified into musical dramas that would showcase both his music and his inherent persona.

Several of these films have become deeply intertwined with Presley's mythology. The most famous is surely *Jailhouse Rock*, released in 1957 and directed by Richard Thorpe. Presley portrays Vince Everett, a man sent to prison whose musical abilities are realized by his cellmate. Mentored, trained and later released, Vince looks to embark on a recording career, only to realize that his escalating stardom is having a detrimental effect on his personal life. Although Presley's character is a clear extension of his own personality, his performance is compelling, and the movie has intriguing things to say about the nature of selling one's soul for fame.

Made for the studio MGM, it was Presley's third movie and unleashed the celebrated jailhouse dance sequence, shot in arrestingly lustrous black and white. The scene was choreographed by Presley himself and set to the title track written by Jerry Leiber and Mike Stoller, who had already gifted Presley with hit single "Hound Dog" in 1952. It was reported that Presley was initially unhappy with Alex Romero's original choreography, and he therefore re-staged it himself, in the process cementing one of the most famous musical sequences in film history.[47]

If the narrative is somewhat incidental in *Jailhouse Rock* (although less so than in many other Presley vehicles), then it paved the way for later musical dramas. Namely, those expressly geared around the talents, both physical and vocal, of a specific pop star. In the case of *Jailhouse Rock*, the film is making less of a statement about incarceration than it is about Presley's astonishing ability to captivate an audience. The movie absorbs the electric energy of Presley's life persona and translates it into a widescreen cinematic presentation, existing for a very singular reason: to grab the attention of his existing fans. A gimmick? Perhaps, but it's more of a fascinating touchstone as to how rock and roll was becoming increasingly bound up with cinema.

At the same time, this was creating a headache for composers of original symphonic scores. How could they possibly compete with an onslaught of hits from a bestselling artist? This was new ground for practitioners of film music, requiring even greater spotting not just in terms of their own work, but also when weaving around existing standards. As always, this comes down to clear communication with the director who, if they are good at their job, will quickly identify the most relevant areas for both songs and symphonic score.

Naturally, the presence of songs in a given movie is beyond the composer's remit—their role is to maximize their own skills from the recording stage. If this happens to mesh perfectly with competing music in the soundscape, then all well and good. Even so, from the mid to late 1950s onwards, it appeared to be a case of divided loyalties as to whether an original score or a compilation soundtrack ought to be favored. In keeping with youth trends, the latter option was becoming ever-more popular, particularly as the 1960s beckoned. To refer back to Bernard Herrmann and *Torn Curtain*, composers were increasingly being asked to compromise their work to ensure its relevance to a modern audience.

To play devil's advocate, the 1960s wasn't altogether disinclined towards the orchestral symphony. Far from it—at the start of the decade, Maurice Jarre's score for David Lean's masterpiece *Lawrence of Arabia* (1962) became synonymous with images of shifting, sunbaked sands and Peter O'Toole's piercing blue eyes. Originally, Jarre was one of three composers commissioned to write the score. However, his melodic sense so impressed Lean and producer Sam Spiegel that he was entrusted with sole responsibility for the music. (The latter asked him to do a "Superman job!"[48])

Jarre had a mere six weeks to compose the score for the four-hour movie, and the high-register strings of his famous main theme speak of exploration and colonial expansion. The music is perfectly matched to Lean's all-encompassing visual language, which attains deep focus and solidifies in the hazy, arresting manner of a desert mirage. The score was meant to have been conducted by Sir Adrian Boult, music director of the London Philharmonic Orchestra. However, when he confessed ignorance to conducting music to picture, Jarre took over.[49] Owing to government subsidies, Boult's name remained on the movie although Jarre was credited on the soundtrack album. (Lean said this was the only time where undue credit was given on one of his films.[50]) The sheer scope of Jarre's score saw him awarded with an Oscar, and it was one of several soundtracks capitalizing on the potential of ultra-widescreen exhibition formats.

In a bid to lure audiences away from their television sets and into cinemas, movie executives were forced to think bigger. The cinematic medium had to justify itself, and that meant the scores became increasingly ambitious as well, something of a rebuke to the increasingly pop-oriented landscape. *Spellbound* composer Miklós Rózsa emerged as a master of thematically complex, epic scores, ones that blended singular ethnicities with elements of historical research. His work on 1959's *Ben-Hur* was just such an example, meshed perfectly to the movie's expansive 2.76:1 aspect ratio.

For a film of this size, literally and figuratively, it was necessary for the music to match up, and Rózsa built on his experience with the earlier film *Quo Vadis* (1951). Unusually, he was able to spend a year and a half on *Ben-Hur*, throwing himself into the narrative's onslaught of Christian, Jewish, Macedonian and Roman characters (centrally held together by Charlton Heston's slave Judah Ben-Hur). Stirring tonalities are mixed with uncomfortable dissonance and location-specific instrumentation to add yet more emotional heft.[51]

Clearly, no-one was talking about the symphonic film score dying a death just yet. In movies such as *Lawrence of Arabia* and *Ben-Hur*, the historical emphasis clearly favored original, non-diegetic compositions as opposed to contemporary needle-drops. But as the youth movement increasingly took over from the 1960s onwards, audiences demanded new frames of reference as far as music was concerned. People wanted music that would speak to their experience in terms of the here and now.

Returning to *Jailhouse Rock*, it had clearly started a craze for something thrillingly new, or, at the very least, it escalated that craze to new heights. Specifically, audiences started to enjoy a new kind of movie in which the pop star persona informed the entire narrative. One can see Elvis Presley's lasting influence on 1963's *Summer Holiday*, a movie expressly designed for the talents of Cliff Richard. Like so many of Presley's movies, it's a somewhat threadbare narrative stitched around musical set-pieces, all designed to showcase Richard's collaboration with The Shadows. In total, 16 songs are featured throughout the film, including the title track, and it's little surprise that the accompanying *Summer Holiday* album was a chart-topping hit in the UK.

The notion of the musician as a sellable commodity hit new heights with 1964's *A Hard Day's Night*, centering on British phenomenon The Beatles. Group members Paul McCartney, John Lennon, George Harrison and Ringo Starr were essentially able to harness the hysteria they induced in their fans ("Beatlemania"), turning it into a potent narrative weapon. The movie, directed by Richard Lester, features the Fab Four as themselves, all the while as they prepare for an all-important television performance. Essentially, it's a satirical story of what happens when these musical gods land among us mere mortals, instigating a variety of different reactions in the process.

Genuinely funny, *A Hard Day's Night* also proved astonishingly perceptive in its look at fan worship. More than that, it demonstrated an even greater blurring of the lines between subject and soundtrack—as in *Jailhouse Rock*, they are one and the same thing. In *A Hard Day's Night*, rather than segregating orchestral score and songs into different camps, the film positions The Beatles as both the stars and the musical auteurs of the project.

Further underlining that point, the movie was Oscar nominated for Best Score (Adaptation), the nomination going to the so-called "Fifth Beatle" George Martin, the record producer who was actively involved in the group's development. (He was credited as "music director" in the movie.) It was, perhaps, more proof that the essence of soundtrack authorship was fragmenting as the 1960s progressed, expanding beyond the notion of an in-house studio composer. Cannily, the accompanying soundtrack album, which sold 1.5 million copies, contained songs that didn't feature in the film, a strategy that influenced the Bee Gees' later *Saturday Night Fever* (1977).[52]

Moving ahead even further, one can see the influence of *Jailhouse Rock* on the likes of Prince's *Purple Rain* (1984). The late singer-songwriter essentially fashions a fictional twist on his real-life persona, playing a character named The Kid who is compelled to navigate the pitfalls of fame and its impact on personal relationships. Prince's inherent mystique and cultural appeal defined the tone of the entire narrative, and his presence, plus the accompanying soundtrack album, helped push the movie towards a gross of $72 million worldwide (budget: just $7.2 million). The film's title track won the Oscar for Best Original Song Score, a clear indication of how popular music artists had redefined the landscape of cinematic music in just a few decades.

Bridging the gap between Elvis Presley and Prince are two seminal movies. Both arrived in the late 1960s and redefined what was possible in terms of cinematic pop music. The first of these is 1967's *The Graduate*, the wry and laconic story of youthful dislocation starring Dustin Hoffman and Anne Bancroft. Hoffman portrays aimless young college graduate Benjamin whose affair with older married woman Mrs. Robinson (Bancroft) sets him on the road towards emotional awakening. Directed by Mike Nichols (and adapted from Charles Webb's book), the movie's atmospheric sense of alienation and disenchantment yielded enormous box office success, defining a period of youthful malaise and sociopolitical turbulence. And a significant part of the film's impact was down to its soundtrack.

Nichols tracked in several songs from the hugely popular duo of Paul Simon and Art Garfunkel, which only increased its potency in the eyes of young viewers. The impact of their music is evident right from the opening scene in which Hoffman's disconnected Benjamin drifts along a conveyor belt at an airport as the credits roll. While Benjamin is framed to the right, to his left is an endless strip of wall that speaks of ennui and repetition—and the brilliant camerawork is goosed even further by Simon and Garfunkel's 1964 song "The Sound of Silence." In conjunction with the quietly melancholy visual imagery, the duo's words take on the air of a lament, the sound of a dispossessed 1960s generation crying out for a direction or a purpose (so much so that it's used twice more in the movie).

It was a revolutionary approach for the time, speaking volumes about the nature of Benjamin's character before audiences had even learned his name. In one fell swoop, Nichols had tapped into the power of pop music to convey a sense of cinematic immediacy and deeper meaning. Yet fascinatingly, he had only intended to use the songs as editorial placeholders while the film was being pieced together. Upon viewing the footage, Nichols and his editor Sam O'Steen realized how brilliantly the music worked and decided to keep it in, a somewhat unusual approach for the time, but one that forever changed the course of film music.[53] It also paved the way for a hugely successful soundtrack album, one that reached the top spot on the United States Billboard Top 200 chart. It also went platinum twice over in the United States.

It could be said that this was the point where pop music and the moving image truly synergized for the first time. *The Graduate* was a huge box office success in its day, becoming the highest-grossing movie of 1967 with global takings of $189 million. One must credit the role of the soundtrack in this. Nichols had identified popular artists who spoke to those people who were the same age as the fictional Benjamin. In the process, the movie attained a specificity and texture, embodying a watershed moment in Hollywood history. Not just a smash success with audiences, the movie's artistic credentials were cemented with seven Oscar nominations, one of which was translated into a win (Best Director for Nichols).

Left out of the nominations was original composer Dave Grusin whose compositions were, perhaps unsurprisingly, overshadowed by Simon and Garfunkel's contributions. It was a microcosm of how film composers were becoming displaced within the Hollywood hierarchy. Although Grusin has gone on to enjoy a distinguished scoring career (including an Oscar win for 1988's *The Milagro Beanfield War*), it's hard to deny that viewers continue to associate *The Graduate* with Simon and Garfunkel's back catalogue. *The Graduate* also demonstrated that songs, even those that are several years old, can retrospectively gain additional resonance and currency when framed in a cinematic context. The music fuels the movie and the movie, in turn, exposes yet more people to the music, boosting the artist (or artists) and album sales.

Just as earth-shattering as *The Graduate* was the movie *Easy Rider*, released two years later. Few films are as synonymous with the late-sixties period of Hollywood counterculture, a turbulent and relatively short-lived, yet explosively creative, era that gave voice to the dispossessed like nothing before. Conventional narrative norms and inspirational maudlin story arcs were largely thrown out of the window, as films distilled the anger bubbling up through American society. Disillusion over America's involvement in the Vietnam War and the strides made by the Civil Rights movement informed the deeply political texture of movies from this time.

Such background context influenced cinema on both a visual and musical level. Movies such as Bob Rafelson's *Five Easy Pieces* (1970), starring Jack Nicholson, adopted a greater sense of verisimilitude. Grainy, washed-out and naturalistic cinematography sits alongside realistic ambient sound and, crucially, an absence of an accompanying score, all of which informs the meandering journey of Nicholson's no-hoper character Bobby Dupea. In films such as this, the ordinary becomes the extraordinary, and melodrama becomes redundant. There was a clear desire in this period to ditch idealized Hollywood tropes, in the process engaging rootless young audiences in the here and now.

Hence why a scene like *Five Easy Pieces*' famous toast sequence resonates so much. It's a deeply relatable scenario: Dupea, frustrated and angry at the lack of control over his own destiny, attempts to verbally strong-arm a stubborn waitress into getting the order of toast that she's denying him. The scene proved a microcosmic example of the frustrations underpinning an entire generation, the very banality of the scenario speaking to ordinary American citizens.

Ironically, given that there's no score in the movie, the film uses music as a potent dramatic device. Dupea is a gifted pianist, at one point leaving his car in the middle of a traffic jam and taking over a piano sitting on the back of a truck. This is because he actually hails from a family of upper-class musicians, on whom he has turned his back, and with whom he's forced to painfully reconcile.

As with everything else in the movie, Dupea's creative expression is the equivalent of shouting into the void, his skills ultimately drowned out by the blasts of vehicular exhausts and car horns. *Five Easy Pieces* uses diegetic sound as its own form of musical expression—in the case of this particular sequence, it's the traffic jam that emerges as the dominant melodic force, underlining the film's sense of despair as personal ambitions become tantamount to white noise. Later on, his performance of Chopin's "Prelude in E Minor" audibly resonates with a sense of regret.

Easy Rider, likewise, refrained from utilizing a non-diegetic orchestral score, instead deploying pre-existing rock tunes to bracingly anarchic effect. Directed by Dennis Hopper (who also stars), the film is a discursive and atmospheric reflection of late-sixties hippy culture, focusing on a pair of bikers (Hopper and Peter Fonda, who co-writes) making their way through America's Deep South.

It's a classic embodiment of the maxim "the journey, not the destination," deriving its power not from a conventional narrative but a carefully observed sense of time, place and character. The imagery of Hopper and Fonda (and, later, Jack Nicholson) sitting behind the handlebars of their enormous Harley-Davidson motorbikes is among the most famous in cinema history. And yet, a single song would help catapult the movie into the realm of a cult classic.

The track in question was Steppenwolf's "Born to be Wild," originally released in 1968. Written by Canadian musician Mars Bonfire, it's a raucous statement of intent, describing the euphoric fumes one inhales when hitting the highway and embracing the freedom of the open road. In other words: a song that would eventually be simpatico with the rebellious, feverish atmosphere of *Easy Rider*. As with *The Graduate*, it remains a thrilling example of the synergy that can occur between a pre-existing piece of music, and the eventual cinematic context that houses it. *Easy Rider* gained additional drive from the song's inclusion, and in turn the film boosted Steppenwolf's profile enormously.

Mars Bonfire (aka Dennis Edmonton) recalls: "I was in the Ford Falcon when I first heard 'Born to Be Wild' on the radio. But after it was used in the druggy road movie *Easy Rider*, as the soundtrack to Dennis Hopper and Peter Fonda riding 'chopper' motorcycles, it took on a life of its own. Thanks to its success, I've been able to spend years hiking in the great outdoors and enjoying the freedom I had written the song about. Without it, I'd probably be back in Canada, working at General Motors. It's ironic that a song so associated with motorcycles and rebellion was inspired by a medium-sized family car—although I always drove it with the windows down."[54]

Steppenwolf singer John Kay recalls an amusing meeting with Dennis Hopper as to how the latter secured the songs in the first place. "Years after it was used in *Easy Rider*, I found myself sitting next to Dennis Hopper at an airport and asked how he'd managed to get so many top artists—from Jimi Hendrix to Bob Dylan—to contribute hits to a film soundtrack. He told me they'd just wanted songs to suit the film, adding that another one of our songs, The Pusher, was perfect for the coke-dealer scene. 'We bypassed all the record companies,' he said, 'and just rang all the artists—who then told their labels it was a done deal.'"[55]

With such lighting-in-a-bottle moments as these, was there any longer a need for bespoke orchestral film scores? Audience demographics and appetites had changed, and people wanted cinematic narratives that authentically reflected their personal experiences and tastes. The subjective disconnect of a symphonic soundtrack appeared to no longer fit the bill—it seemed to lack that sense of immediacy that had come to consume movies of the period.

Of course, film scores by established composers still had their place on the cinematic scene. In fact, the 1960s produced some of the most memorable original soundtracks in movie history. These scores flowered alongside the upsurge in rock music to give a bounteous sense of widespread creativity. In the world of the *James Bond* series, John Barry delivered what is arguably his finest score for the franchise: *On Her Majesty's Secret Service*. Written for the 1969 film, which showcased the sole 007 appearance from George Lazenby, Barry's score imported many hip trends from the period to further assert the relevance of the orchestral soundtrack.

Somewhat unusually for a Bond movie, Barry's score doesn't feature a title song performed by a famous artist. This is allegedly because the cumbersome title was impossible to fit into a rhyming structure. No matter, Barry's alternative was a broodingly atmospheric melodic theme for a rousing brass section (typical of the composer), strings and the then-innovative moog synthesizer, which gave everything a distinctly contemporary and psychedelic kick.

Never one to rest on his laurels, Barry also coaxed one final performance out of jazz legend Louis Armstrong. His mellifluous vocals adorn the film's love theme "We Have All the Time in the World," which underscores the burgeoning relationship between Bond and Tracy Draco (Diana Rigg), later married at the end of the film before Tracy is tragically killed. The clear frailty in Armstrong's voice lends the track a palpable texture and poignancy, capping off a landmark career. He died in July 1971, two years after the film's release. It's moving to note how Armstrong's influence helped give rise to Alex North's *A Streetcar Named Desire*, among others, and reached its resolution in the hands of another distinguished film composer, John Barry.

As mentioned already, Ennio Morricone was another innovative composer who refused to be cowed by the spectacle of pop music in movies. His Western scores reached their apotheosis around the time of *The Graduate* and *Easy Rider*, bringing opera into a distinctly cinematic space. His other scores of the period were no less fascinating. In 1966, Morricone delivered a rumbling, terse score for Gillo Pontecorvo's anti-establishment war movie *The Battle of Algiers*, favoring piano chords at the lowest end of their ranges and piercing strings (plus the input of Bach's *St Matthew Passion* from 1727) to capture the horror of conflict.[56] Maudlin patriotism is stripped away from the music in support of something much more troubling.

A few years later, in 1970, Morricone explicitly embraced pop and jazz conventions in his first score for renowned Italian horror maestro Dario Argento. The movie in question was the famous "giallo" horror *The Bird with the Crystal Plumage*, giallo being the Italian word for yellow. This was used to describe the lurid pulp paperback books that inspired Argento's chilling, blood-soaked narratives. This twisted story of a man who's witness to a brutal murder, and the black-gloved killer who begins to stalk him, gains a great deal from Morricone's unusual music. Jazzy snare drums mix with placid yet subtly malicious lullaby vocals, capturing the swinging essence of Italy at the time, plus the teasing revelation of the killer's identity.

The pop and classical worlds crossed over in scores such as these, showing there was no real need for battle lines to be drawn. However, it was imperative that film scores continued to evolve, hastening the need for composers to embrace even more experimental and offbeat techniques. Movies of the period that might have been expected to showcase original film scores increasingly went in different directions, meshing nostalgic, historical contexts with contemporary trends.

A famous example of the latter is 1969's *Butch Cassidy and the Sundance Kid*. Directed by George Roy Hill and written by William Goldman, it's a Western story that gleefully dispenses with the usual genre trappings. As the title characters, Paul Newman and Robert Redford established their peerless on-screen chemistry, portraying two likeable, bank-robbing chancers who find themselves stranded in a changing world. The genre of the Western may be one of the oldest in Hollywood history but as a movie,

Butch Cassidy and the Sundance Kid adopts a distinctly 1960s visual aesthetic (freeze frames, long-lens zooms) that intentionally clashes with one's expectations.

This also extends to the use of music in the film. There's an original score in the movie, composed by Burt Bacharach, but it owes little to the sweeping orchestral style of Max Steiner, Jerome Moross or Elmer Bernstein. Instead, it's in on the joke, deploying a faux pop/jazz sound to further enhance the film's comic atmosphere. The most famous instance of music in *Butch Cassidy and the Sundance Kid* comes with the original song "Raindrops Keep Falling on My Head," a self-consciously anachronistic inclusion that is accepted within the wider fabric of the movie.

Written by Bacharach and Hal David, and performed by B.J. Thomas, the song doesn't sit with the period of time depicted in the movie, but oddly enough, it leaps beyond the frame to suggest the implicit whimsy of Butch and Sundance's friendship. (That said, it actually accompanies a scene of Butch frolicking on a bicycle with Sundance's girlfriend, Etta, played by Katharine Ross.) In that sense, it demonstrated how filmmakers could deploy cognitive dissonance as a dramatic device, making the historical feel contemporary. It also proved that one needn't use a traditional symphonic accompaniment to achieve those results.

It clearly didn't have any kind of negative impact on the finished film. On the contrary, *Butch Cassidy and the Sundance Kid* was one of the biggest box office hits of 1969, grossing $102 million against a $6 million budget and laying the foundations for the buddy movie genre that flowered in the coming decades. "Raindrops Keep Falling on My Head" also won the Oscar for Best Original Song, part of a clutch of Academy Awards that also included Best Original Screenplay, Best Cinematography, Best Sound Mixing and, interestingly enough, Best Original Score.

It was clear that, in the eyes of the Academy, Bacharach's underscore compositions had just as much artistic merit as the song he had composed for the movie. One might imagine that the stark contrast between the film's setting and the stylistics of the music, both song and score, is what set it apart from the competition. Increasingly, it seemed that composers were being rewarded for going off the reservation, so to speak, and for flying in the face of the Hollywood musical conventions that had been in place for decades.

So what did this mean for the typical Hollywood film score? As mentioned already, the medium was in no danger of dying a death and, indeed, just eight years after the release of *Butch Cassidy and the Sundance Kid*, John Williams would unleash a certain cinematic symphony by the name of *Star Wars*. In fact, even before that, Williams delivered some of his most charming and beautiful scores in the midst of the counterculture revolution, including *The Reivers* (1969).

The movie, adapted from William Faulkner's 1962 novel *The Reivers, A Reminiscence*, stars Steve McQueen as a charismatic drifter who embroils a young boy in a series of misadventures. The tone of Williams' unashamedly big-hearted score anticipates many of his later cinematic masterworks, brings out the banjos and fiddles alongside the expected symphonic set-up, throwing listeners into a full-blooded Deep South environment. It demonstrates the composer's brilliance in establishing specificity of location, while the orchestral sections reflect the timeless, enduring themes of adolescence and growing up.

Williams was Oscar nominated for *The Reivers*, so it was clear that the Hollywood establishment hadn't completely given up on the power of nostalgia in film music. Yet many other scores of the time were increasingly deploying a standard orchestra in ways that were rather spartan. The melodic and harmonic principles were in place, but sweeping melodies and clear-cut themes were put aside, replaced by uncomfortable, challenging textures. This had already been demonstrated within the realm of science fiction (*Planet of the Apes*), but the same philosophy was also being applied to that quintessentially American genre, the Western.

Whereas *Butch Cassidy and the Sundance Kid* intentionally melded pop music with cowboy iconography, the likes of *The Wild Bunch* (1969) used the fabric of orchestral music in ways that were strikingly atmospheric. Notions of nostalgia and bravado were increasingly stripped out of Western scores, reflecting the cynical, disillusioned tone of movies that came during the period of Vietnam (and, at the start of the 1970s, Watergate).

One such practitioner was Jerry Fielding, a regular collaborator with *enfant terrible* and hellraiser Sam Peckinpah. The latter was a hard-drinking filmmaker and a famously tough character, and this translated into the movies he made. *The Wild Bunch* is the most famous of Peckinpah's Westerns, breaking down the boundaries of cinematic violence and painting a resolutely nihilistic depiction of the American frontier. This is most clearly evident in the blood squib-laden opening and closing scenes as William Holden's titular band of renegades find themselves, in both instances, in the midst of deadly shootouts with extensive collateral damage.

The artillery-laden finale of the movie shocked audiences with its gory onslaught of chaos, showing how the Western, as a genre, had shed its skin to emerge as something much darker. Fielding's tense music is vitally important in all this. Largely devoid of Elmer Bernstein's enveloping melodies and Ennio Morricone's soaringly operatic grandeur, this is a score that makes the audience feel like they're down in the dirt with Holden and his gang. Tense rhythmic clusters and jangling percussion are designed to create an uncomfortable soundscape, making one feel that possible betrayal lurks around every corner. Fielding would parlay these stylistics into many of his later scores for Peckinpah, including the notorious rape-revenge drama *Straw Dogs* (1971), starring Dustin Hoffman, and *Bring Me the Head of Alfredo Garcia* (1974).

Fielding used symphonic instruments to create this effect of unease, which reinforced how orchestral principles had been turned inside out during this period of immense change. The familiar had become unfamiliar, although, as has been explored, many other scores of the period maintained the heritage of the old-school symphonic set-up. That Fielding was Oscar nominated for both *The Wild Bunch* and *Straw Dogs* demonstrated that Hollywood had finally come to terms with the principles and technique of the dissonant film score.[57]

What it all served to demonstrate was the sheer diversity of approaches from the 1950s through to the end of the 1960s. As a medium, film music was uniquely placed to capitalize on the social upheaval of the time. As movies underwent changes in terms of their narratives, heightening elements of satire, sexuality and violence, scores could embrace dysrhythmic, atonal and unusual approaches, while also absorbing the new-found cultural impetus on jazz and rock and roll.

Far from being outgunned during the period of Steppenwolf and Simon and Garfunkel, film composers instead pushed the boundaries of creativity further than anyone had dared to imagine. Movies showcasing original compositions were able to sit alongside those favoring tracked-in songs, making this an especially rich and lively period for music in cinema. The visual impact of cinema was changing—and there were also multiple ways in which to process the subjective power of music. Film scores had become, for want of a better word, more intellectual, in line with the complexity of the narratives that informed said music.

The early part of the 1970s continued to prove a challenging yet rewarding period for Hollywood's established and rising film composers. Despondency and paranoia reigned, and this informed many scores of the period. At the same time, growing awareness of racial divides would allow a plethora of popular music artists to erupt onto the scene, connecting with audiences of color in ways never before possible.

Yet Hollywood is a fickle place, subject to transience and upheaval. No sooner had the counterculture era taken off than nostalgic norms were swiftly re-established from the mid-1970s onwards. The birth of the contemporary blockbuster would occur with *Jaws* in 1975 and mature with the release of *Star Wars* two years later. In terms of film music, this effectively swung the needle back the other way, inducing a sense of comforting nostalgia and re-connecting audiences with the symphonic heritage of early Hollywood.

FOUR

Allegro

Star Wars *and the Resurgence of the Symphonic Score*

"*Star Wars* ... made me aware of what an orchestra was doing."—MICHAEL GIACCHINO[1]

Electronic Music, Soul and Funk in the Era of Vietnam and Watergate

Before one arrives at the sweeping tone of *Star Wars*, one must address the singular state of film music at the start of the 1970s. At this point the counterculture principles of the 1960s, explored in the previous chapter, still held sway over the film industry. In fact, such trends were about to intensify as America reckoned with itself on a national level.

The effectiveness of tracked-in pop and rock music in cinema had already been established, and there was still a genuine hunger to capture the attention of disaffected youths and post-flower power communities. At the same time, cynicism over America's foreign policy in Vietnam, and a certain Presidential disgrace in the form of the Watergate scandal would shake the country to its core. Liberation and anger went hand in hand, offering rich pickings for filmmakers, and inspiring film composers to take up arms.

Movies of this era weren't afraid of courting controversy, shock and outrage. An especially effective example came not from America but the UK, where director Stanley Kubrick had cultural censors up in arms. His 1971 movie *A Clockwork Orange*, adapted from Anthony Burgess' novel, was perhaps the most savage indictment yet of youth violence and a cruel, unfeeling society. Malcolm McDowell is unforgettable as the feral yet cultured Alex, leader of a gang of "droogs" (thugs) who take delight in rape, robbery and violent assault.

However, when Alex is finally captured by the authorities, he's subjected to a dehumanizing technique, named the "Ludovico," that will ostensibly transform him into a decent member of society. Morality is blurred, and emotions are not so much pricked as assaulted by Kubrick's nightmarish futuristic vision, one that caused such an uproar that he himself withdrew it from circulation. It wasn't until 1999, after Kubrick's death, that *A Clockwork Orange* again became available to the public. Nevertheless, the contradictory and spiky tapestry of the movie inspired a new kind of electronic film score, one that would prove hugely influential.

The score came courtesy of Wendy (born Walter) Carlos, a pioneer in the realm of synthesized music. Throughout the 1960s, organic, symphonic techniques had been used to turn conventional melodies and harmonies inside out. Now, at the start of the 1970s, technological breakthroughs were sophisticated enough to suggest new textures within the realm of electronics. In the case of *A Clockwork Orange*, the philosophy is diabolically effective.

Carlos' pioneering work on the film had been anticipated by her groundbreaking 1968 synth/classical album *Switched-On Bach*. Released during the height of hippy flower power, it had already demonstrated the potential of electronic music, ushering in a new dawn of musical storytelling that would soon leap onto the big screen.

It should be said, however, that Carlos was already building on trends laid down by earlier film and television composers. As always with film music, there's an important sense of heritage coursing through the medium from one decade to the next, as certain stylistic principles are upgraded to embrace increasingly sophisticated techniques. Early harbingers of Carlos' work include Bernard Herrmann's famously eerie, theremin-led theme for *The Day the Earth Stood Still* (1951), representing the alienness of extra-terrestrial Klaatu (Michael Rennie) who has arrived on Earth along with his hulking robot companion Gort.

However, a more exact comparison with Carlos may be the work of British sound engineer Delia Derbyshire. In 1963, while working at the BBC Radiophonic Workshop, Derbyshire arranged a woozy and unusual title theme for a new series named *Doctor Who*, elaborating on the sketches of original composer Ron Grainer. The otherworldly sound created by Derbyshire is among the most immediately recognizable in the history of science-fiction, speaking of exploration, adventure and cosmic menace.

In the days before sophisticated electronics, Derbyshire was entirely reliant on tape recordings. She recorded live sounds like wood blocks and metallic clangs onto the reel, and then undertook the laborious process of cutting each individual note out of said reel. She then formed a new section of tape comprising all the spliced notes, which when played together conveyed Doctor Who's signature aura.² One doesn't have to listen hard to hear the similarities between her work and what Wendy Carlos would be doing just a few years later.

In describing "Switched-On Bach," journalist Jude Rogers explained that the album "made [the moog synthesizer] internationally famous and became the second classical album ever to go platinum in the US. Then came [Wendy Carlos'] extraordinary soundtracks for *A Clockwork Orange*, *The Shining* and *Tron*. She made an ambient album five years before Brian Eno did, and jumped from analogue machines to do leading work in digital synthesis, but worried that her status as one of the first visible transgender artists in the US would overshadow it."³

As a device, synthesized music is shorn of that tonal element found in a symphony orchestra, one that implicitly aligns with the pitch of the human voice. Instead, synths possess a quality that speaks of something inherently robotic and detached, an approximation of humanity but with the intrinsic feel of something far colder. This is brilliantly exploited by Carlos in *A Clockwork Orange* to reflect not just Alex's monstrous side but also the dehumanizing nature of bureaucracy and the invasive air of science that seeks to alter our free will.

Further compounding the irony is the inversion of many celebrated classical pieces. In the film, Alex is a self-professed fan of Ludwig van Beethoven, an indication of how the sophisticated and the animalistic can often sit together inside one deeply disturbed mind. Complicating the situation, when Alex is later exposed to the "Ludovico Technique," he's conditioned to hate all of Beethoven's music, most specifically his *Symphony No. 9* dating from 1824.

To address the complexities of the narrative, Carlos and Kubrick decided to twist pieces like Henry Purcell's "Music for the Funeral March of Queen Mary," first performed at said monarch's funeral in March 1695. However, any sense of historical pedigree and stately prestige is stripped away by the insidious, insinuating synth performance of the piece that accompanies the film's famous opening credits sequence, one that leads into the famous "Kubrick glare" as Alex leers down the lens at the viewer.

Another classical piece that Carlos distorts is Gioachino Rossini's famous "William Tell Overture," here given a warbling, up-tempo synth rendition as it accompanies a frenzied orgy scene. In line with the film's dystopian future environment, what was once pure is sullied and warped out of all proportion, a bold new form of musical dialogue for electric and transgressive cinema.

Carlos' score encompassed a great many things: it had a steely, convention-defying edge that very much sat in line with youth trends, and it also exploited a great many technological opportunities that simply weren't available a decade earlier. It was a score uniquely positioned to raise the curtain on a bold new era of cinematic music. Naturally, one must credit the ever-fastidious Stanley Kubrick as much as anyone—few filmmakers would have thought to apply such an approach to the music, rendering the familiar unfamiliar in a host of unsettling ways. Would that every director showcased such a bold statement of intent, although, sadly, this is not always possible thanks to the pervasive influence of producers and franchise owners.

Carlos' work was, however, just one of several rule-breaking soundtracks to emerge in the first half of the 1970s. In the wake of the Civil Rights Movement, filmmakers of color were finding themselves empowered to fashion narratives about their own experiences, which gave rise to the relatively brief, but much-loved, Blaxploitation period. These films were distinguished by strong black lead characters, men and women, who gleefully blasted away red tape in a funky blur of sex and violence. Amorality was underscored with a sense of cool, as the white cinematic hegemony was, for a short period of time at least, seized upon and torn up.

The presence of Blaxploitation allowed a diversification of musical voices, led in large part by the hugely successful release of 1971's *Shaft*, directed by Gordon Parks and adapted from Ernest Tidyman's novel. Now, funk, soul and jazz musicians of color could take hold of the medium, one that had been traditionally dominated by white composers of European and American origin. In the case of *Shaft*, it was soul master Isaac Hayes who gave a groovy inner voice to the title character: "private dick" John Shaft, played with swaggering charisma by Richard Roundtree.

Narratively speaking, *Shaft* may not be tantamount to much. But it oozes style, and much of that is down to Hayes' indelible contribution, one of the defining Blaxploitation film scores. Hayes was, at one point, considered for the role of Shaft, but although that opportunity escaped him, he still imprinted his personality on the movie. The soundtrack consists of instrumental and vocal performances, the most famous of which is the opening "Theme from Shaft." Lyrically, it carved out a place in pop culture history, asserting a black lead character as a virtuoso, magnetic force of nature.

The soundtrack was produced via Hayes' Stax Records label, on which he served as a musician and producer. He had established himself as a pre-eminent soul and jazz artist throughout the 1960s, often arranging smoothly enticing covers of pop hits from the likes of Burt Bacharach (1963's "Walk on By" being a famous example). In the field of popular music, Hayes was putting his auteurist stamp on established standards, re-authoring them and making them relevant for a new audience. This singular sense of style and authority meant he was well suited to work on *Shaft*.

Initially Hayes wrote just three pieces of music for the film at Parks' request, including the aforementioned title theme. When studio MGM heard these selections, they were so pleased that they requested Hayes compose the entire score.[4] Featuring contributions from Memphis R&B band The Bar-Kays (also affiliated with Stax Records), the *Shaft* soundtrack proved to be an enormous hit, both in context and as a standalone album.

The score topped the American Billboard 200 charts, won a Grammy and made history at the Academy Awards. This occurred when Hayes became the first-ever African American to win an Oscar for a non-acting category—in this case, Best Original Song for the aforementioned "Theme from Shaft." In fact, he was just the third African American person in the history of the cinema to win any kind of Oscar (after Hattie McDaniel for 1939's *Gone with the Wind* and Sidney Poitier for 1963's *Lilies of the Field*). That said, Hayes' Oscar-nominated underscore lost out to Michel Legrand's *Summer of 42*.

Shaft was an example of a film score that transcended the boundaries of the frame, communicating the essential narrative while also serving as an easy-listening experience. Not just a segment of musical storytelling, it communicated a way of life, an attitude that plugged directly into the mood of the period. Film music was no longer being contained—it could embody a counter-cultural attitude, able to seep into people's lives when experienced outside the context of a given movie.

Shaft opened the floodgates and instigated a hunger for Blaxploitation music. A year later in 1972, soul musician Curtis Mayfield delivered a classic of his own with his theme for *Super Fly*. Interestingly, the film was directed by Gordon Parks Jr., son of the aforementioned *Shaft* helmer Gordon Parks—tragically, the younger Parks died in a plane crash at the age of 44. The film traces the exploits of an African American cocaine dealer (played by Ron O'Neal) who's attempting to go straight, and Mayfield's music rides a crest of rebellious cool.

White audiences had already had a taste of what to expect when their favorite musical artists were deployed in cinema. Now it was the time for audiences of color to enjoy their heroes being assimilated into the fabric of the movies. As with Isaac Hayes and *Shaft*, Mayfield's status as a musical icon elevated the status of *Super Fly* from entertaining B-movie into zeitgeist-defining thrill-ride. The film capitalized on Mayfield's extensive experience as one of America's leading soul and blues artists, which had encompassed extensive work with the gospel and soul group The Impressions. Together with Mayfield, they had produced a string of hits including 1964's "Keep on Pushing," a Top 40 smash hit that defined the early years of the Civil Rights movement.

The *Super Fly* score is perhaps best known for its central theme, officially titled "Freddie's Dead" on the *Super Fly* album but subtitled as "Theme from Superfly" on the single release. It cemented many of the Blaxploitation music clichés we've come to take for granted, including a funky bass line, wah-wah guitar refrains and tapping percussion. Scores such as this attempted to get listeners to walk in the shoes of the central character, as they assimilated trace elements of soul, R&B and jazz into one harmonically smooth narrative package. More than just an instrumental piece, the theme from *Super Fly*, just like *Shaft* before it, crystallized a history of popular black music in a mere matter of minutes, shattering white-centric Hollywood norms in the process.

Of course, one must acknowledge the progenitors of the Blaxploitation movement. In 1958, French-language movie *Elevator to the Gallows*, directed by Louis Malle and starring Jeanne Moreau, secured the talents of jazz artist Miles Davis. Unusually, Davis, along with his ensemble, improvised his sultry score directly to the picture, rather than sitting down and spotting each scene with Malle.[5] The rebellious, ice cool codes and conventions of jazz music grafted a distinct atmosphere onto the movie, anticipating the counter-culture rebellion to come in the films and soundtracks of the French New Wave. (This would include the aforementioned Michel Legrand who scored, and appeared in, 1962's *Cleo from 5 to 7*.)

In 1961, Duke Ellington yielded an Oscar nomination for his score to Sidney Poitier drama *Paris Blues*, which was adapted from Harold Flender's 1957 novel of the same name. The narrative has African American music embedded in its very DNA: Poitier plays an expatriate jazz saxophonist living in the French capital, and the movie features appearances from the likes of Louis Armstrong.

Ellington was the first-ever African American composer to be nominated in the category of Best Original Score, exposing the shocking disparity that had existed in Hollywood up until this time. (He lost to Henry Mancini's buoyant *Breakfast at Tiffany's*.) Even after this landmark moment, the accolades were disappointingly spotty regarding artists of color. This clearly indicated the American movie industry's struggle to embrace a multitude of different, non-white voices. Although this paid off (to admittedly short-lived effect) with the eventual Blaxploitation era, one laments the sheer amount of time it took to reach a suitably equitable level.

Other landmark scores from black musicians prior to the Blaxploitation era include Quincy Jones's *In Cold Blood*. The score, written for the 1967 Truman Capote adaptation, yielded an Oscar nomination, but no win. (That year it was a split win between Original Score for Elmer Bernstein's *Thoroughly Modern Millie* and Alfred Newman's Original Score Adaptation for *Camelot*.) *In Cold Blood* absorbs not just a sense of jazz heritage (throaty alto sax solos; pizzicato double-bass) but also many of the harsh mannerisms shared by the likes of Jerry Goldsmith, including piercing, high-register strings and turbulent snare drum solos. All the better for capturing the era-defining horror of this shocking true crime story.

In the wake of *Shaft* and *Super Fly*, many of the era's pre-eminent music stars were empowered to take up arms on the recording stage. One of them was the revered Marvin Gaye who turned to film scoring for the first, and only, time with 1972's *Trouble Man*, written for the film of the same name. The movie, directed by Ivan Dixon, centers on an authority-defying private detective, named Mr. T. (Robert Hooks), and is very much in line with works such as *Shaft*.

In truth, the film is largely forgotten today, and would likely be a footnote in the annals of Blaxploitation were it not for Gaye's involvement. The score came in the wake of Gaye's eleventh studio album, *What's Going On*, a turbulent and angry reaction to the Vietnam War, among other things, and released via the Tamla label. This was the label that had allowed Gaye to assert his credentials as a hip, funky purveyor of easily digestible yet socially conscious and politically incisive soul records. *Trouble Man*, however, was something a bit different.

Quite apart from its inherent status as a film score, meaning it was subservient to the needs of the picture, *Trouble Man* dropped the allegorical notions of *What's Going On*. Yet *Rolling Stone*'s original 1973 review praises Gaye's ability to craft a musical narrative that both serves its primary purpose and stands alone as an autonomous listening experience. Gaye "created a score strong enough to be completely independent of the film. It's not a lot of fluff wrapped around some slick images and obvious themes; mostly, it's sweet and churning jazz that abstracts the action rather than decorating or interpreting it."[6]

It's interesting to note the dismissal of "obvious themes" in *Rolling Stone*'s write-up. This was indicative of many film scores of the time where texture, tone and attitude ruled the day, as opposed to melodic signifiers signaling important story beats. Gaye, like his contemporaries, sought to create a unity of mood that would speak to African American audiences, and there's no doubt he succeeded. The *Trouble Man* soundtrack reached number 12 on America's Billboard 200 chart, perhaps boosted above and beyond other such film scores by virtue of Gaye's own celebrity status.

Despite this success, *Trouble Man* would be Gaye's only film score. For that reason, it stands alone as an experiment in his illustrious career, while offering yet more evidence of a crossover between pop music and film scoring. As ever, it was apparent that many huge record stars of the day could be imported into the fabric of a movie and boost its appeal in the eyes of the audience.

Rolling Stone observes the clarity of Gaye's instrumental choices in the score: "Most of the music carries on in a similar vein from *What's Going On*, although here it's a little more hard-edged (heavy drum punctuation, sharp horns and a staccato of hand-clapping or tambourines predominate) and at times self-consciously dramatic. The 'Main Theme' is handsome if slightly overdrawn; I wouldn't miss the strings if they were cut from the arrangement, however. 'T' Plays It Cool' is more successful and gripping: *hard* drumming, a Moog line and energetic sax work intertwining like hot electric wires over a sweet, almost mournful piano and light horns."[7]

The towering and influential James Brown also made his mark on the Blaxploitation soundtrack movement. He scored 1973's *Black Caesar*, directed by Larry Cohen and starring Fred Williamson as gangster Tommy Gibbs. Amusingly, Brown never watched, or engaged with, the movie during the production, merely using the opportunity to boost his profile.[8] The soundtrack, a collaboration between Brown, trombonist Fred Wesley, Jan Hammer (later of *Miami Vice* fame) and others, received mixed reviews at the time. That said, the score yielded several enduring Brown numbers, including "Down and Out in New York City," released as a single, and "The Boss" (heard in Guy Ritchie's 1998 crime comedy *Lock, Stock and Two Smoking Barrels*).

More than ever, specific instruments and tonalities were being deployed within cinema to convey contemporary tastes. If a score like *Gone with the Wind* is relatively ageless thanks to its symphonic approach, works like *Shaft*, *Super Fly* and *Trouble Man* were expressly designed to push buttons precisely at the moment of their release. Film music of the early 1970s was sophisticated enough to latch onto, and reflect, audience trends very quickly, although the longevity of those trends couldn't be guaranteed. Film scores often find themselves anchored to cinematic styles that reach their sell-by dates very quickly, and in the case of Blaxploitation, the craze had expired by the middle of the 1970s.

Elsewhere, the Western was continuing to prove a hotbed of alternative film score choices. Once embraced for its sweeping sense of adventure, the Western score had, as mentioned in the previous chapter, turned in on itself with the quirky scores of Ennio Morricone and Jerry Fielding during the 1960s. Then, in 1973, the genre got a significant cultural boost when Bob Dylan agreed to score Sam Peckinpah's *Pat Garrett and Billy the Kid*, a collaboration that would yield the hit "Knockin' on Heaven's Door."

The movie is a typically prickly offering from Western veteran Peckinpah, who once again indulges his love of nihilistic violence (à la 1969's *The Wild Bunch*). It stars James Coburn as the eponymous Pat Garrett, a real-life figure who lived in infamy for executing notorious outlaw, and former friend, Billy the Kid (Kris Kristofferson). In line with the other revisionist Westerns of the period, there's no glory in killing, and no easy sense of valor and heroism as the ageing Garrett must reckon with the brutalities of the Old West.

The movie's production was troubled, plagued by Peckinpah's alcoholism, clashes with the studio and tendency towards chaos, and Dylan's relative inexperience as a film composer didn't help matters. (He also appeared in the movie as hired killer Alias.) When MGM wrestled control of the movie from Peckinpah, they asserted a new cut of the film that significantly altered the emphasis of Dylan's music, although Peckinpah's original edit was later restored in 1984. For all of Dylan's star status, it seems his appointment on the film didn't sit easily with everyone, although Kristofferson would later praise his input.

"'Knockin' On Heaven's Door' was in that scene where Slim Pickens was dying and it was the strongest use of music that I had ever seen in a film," Kristofferson recalled. "Unfortunately Sam didn't include it in his director's cut. Sam had a blind spot there. He thought that the producer had forced Bob on him to make the film commercial and I don't think he appreciated who Bob was. I thought Dylan was great in the film, he looked great and you couldn't take your eyes off him, and his music was fantastic."[9]

Whatever Peckinpah's misgivings, Dylan's music is a richly evocative and melodic depiction of Western mythology. The main theme, named "Billy," mixes a typically expressive acoustic guitar with tapping castanets and double-bass, signaling a gentle canter across a vast landscape while also approximating the folk music traditions of the American interior a la Aaron Copland. It's said that this stirring piece, when performed for Peckinpah, is what got Dylan the acting gig as Alias.

Even so, "Knockin' on Heaven's Door" is what lingers in the memory. Released as a single in July 1973, it would become one of Dylan's most famous tracks, a chart-topping hit later covered by the likes of Guns N' Roses. Its impact may have been diluted by decades of covers and remixes, but it remains startlingly effective in the context of the movie. The piece acts as an elegy for death and destruction as Slim Pickens' Sheriff Colin Baker meets his maker, another example of how anachronistic music choices could imbue a cinematic narrative with added meaning.

Less anachronistic, but no less effective, was Martin Scorsese's use of pop tunes in his 1973 crime drama *Mean Streets*. With this film, Scorsese established his hallmarks: roving camerawork, nimble editing and an ability to coax volatile, electrifying performances from his actors. And then, of course, there is the soundtrack, which does so much of the storytelling on its own terms. The film centrally focuses on Charlie (Harvey Keitel), essentially an autobiographical stand-in for the director, who is torn between his Catholic heritage and the violent impulses of the New York streets. ("You don't make up for your sins in church. You do it on the streets," he says in the opening narration, which is delivered by Scorsese himself.)

This spiritual disparity directly informs the soundtrack, one of tonal and harmonic extremes. The Ronettes' exuberant "Be My Baby" casts a Day-Glo sheen over the convivial atmosphere shared between Charlie and his friends. The song emphasizes a sense of bonhomie and honor among thieves and hustlers. Sitting alongside this is the raw energy of the Rolling Stones' "Tell Me," which accompanies a famous tracking shot through the blood-red lighting of Charlie's local joint. The track crackles with urgency and suggests the combustible spirit of Charlie's incendiary best friend, Johnny Boy (Robert De Niro), setting in motion the repeated use of the Stones' music in future Scorsese films (including the oft-repeated "Gimme Shelter," used in 1990's *Goodfellas*, 1995's *Casino* and 2006's *The Departed*).

Popular music is often deployed by Scorsese in ironic contrast to brutal on-screen violence, including the use of The Marvelettes' "Please Mr. Postman" during a scrappy pool hall fight. Elsewhere, bubblegum pop and jazz favorites cast a sense of childlike glee, which is especially apposite when it comes to the Johnny Boy character, gleefully bombing mailboxes and firing guns from the rooftops.

The Shells' "Baby Oh Baby" and The Nutmegs' "The Ship of Love" are just two examples of how Scorsese deployed overlooked retro hits and set them against broiling, angry narratives, deliberately provoking an audience as to the necessary emotional response. Should the cumulative register be happy or sad? In Scorsese's world, these two extremes often coexist at the same time. When for instance, an exuberant jukebox track plays out over a scene of savagery, the disparity can indicate a number of things—perhaps a ruthless gangster's emotional remove from the violence he's carrying out, or the fact that such individuals derive feel-good glee from these actions.

Whatever one's view, our emotional response to the characters is informed and emboldened on an implicit level by Scorsese's superlative music choices. This approach would prove hugely influential on future generations of filmmakers, including the likes of Quentin Tarantino whose 1994 black comedy *Pulp Fiction* similarly balanced flippant, optimistic pop music against scenes of rampant violence and drug use.

Back within the recognizably orchestral realm, many of the era's composers were assimilating the darkly turbulent mood of the times. Many films decided to dispense with non-diegetic music altogether to craft a stronger sense of verisimilitude, and it's startling to note the trust placed in audiences of the early 1970s. Around this time, many filmmakers were keen to avoid using obvious music cues and melodramatic statements to influence the emotions. The spotting of cues led to lengthy intervals where dialogue and ambient effects became the dominant features in the soundscape. This was in line with the times: in an era of mistrust, corruption, surveillance and failed foreign policy, a loud film score would seem like an imposition, a fantastical distraction from the realities faced by millions of Americans every day.

One of the period's preeminent directors was Alan J. Pakula who made headlines with his critically acclaimed "Paranoia Trilogy." This encompassed *Klute* (1971), *The Parallax View* (1974) and *All the President's Men* (1976). The films variously grapple with fictional and factual narratives, but all are connected by a brooding sense of unease, of what it means to be destabilized in a world seemingly spinning out of control.

Another aspect the movies share in common is a relatively sparing use of music. Pakula's decidedly non-flamboyant camerawork, not to mention his politically incisive narratives, didn't exactly lend itself to a Korngold-style symphony. But that's not to say that film scores can only operate at the rousing end of the spectrum. The central tenet of a film score is to tailor itself to a given narrative, and in this sense Pakula's soundtracks, most commonly from Michael Small and David Shire, worked like a charm.

When it came to making *All the President's Men*, Pakula was grappling with the biggest political explosion in recent American history. The film traces the efforts of Bob Woodward (Robert Redford) and Carl Bernstein (Dustin Hoffman), the Washington Post journalists who follow a trail of breadcrumbs to expose President Richard Nixon's culpability in the Watergate scandal. In an objective, evidence-driven movie such as this, the dialogue leads the way and takes on its own form of musicality, which comes courtesy of an Oscar-winning William Goldman. It's perhaps best for the score to stay out of the way in a film such as this, lest it impose a sense of schematic emotion on the steady drip-feed of facts and revelations.

Nevertheless, Pakula enlisted the help of David Shire to subtly augment the sense of shock as Woodward and Bernstein inch closer towards their goal. Nervy piano chords and dissonant strings vanquish any sense of melody—this is a minimalist score of tone and suggestion, almost invoking a hushed sense of dawning realization. It was encouraging to note that filmmakers hadn't completely lost faith in film scores around this time. Nevertheless, it was another reminder that composers had to be adaptable to the moral, social and political temperature of the era in line with the movies themselves.

Shire was one of the masters of such scores. One of his most celebrated works is 1974's *The Conversation*, the Francis Ford Coppola classic starring Gene Hackman as paranoid surveillance man Harry Caul. The film doesn't just deploy Shire's piano-heavy score to craft a sense of melancholy around Caul's life, it also presents a series of ironic binary oppositions within the narrative. Caul is a saxophonist, and his bluesy riffs are an organic, urgent contrast with his lonely, mechanized life of surveillance. This is particularly during the chilling final shot of the film as he sits playing the saxophone amidst the wreckage of his apartment, evidence of his aborted, obsessive search for a bug.

The film also contorts diegetic sound into its own form of overwrought fear. Tracking a couple through San Francisco's Union Square, Caul alights on a fragment of the song "When the Red Red Robin Comes Bob Bob Bobbin' Along." This piece of audio, innocuous on its own terms, is isolated by Caul and therefore played back repeatedly in his search for clues, meaning we, the audience, hear it along with him. Its very repetition almost attains a mocking quality, as we step vicariously into Caul's shoes and attempt to discover a more insidious meaning beneath the flippancy.

In many films of this period, organic sounds were as rich in meaning as the standard symphonic film score, the placement of voices and the hubbub of traffic, among other things, connecting audiences to a profoundly visceral sense of objective reality. Scores were designed to arise out of these recognizable sounds, melding with them to almost imperceptible effect. Shire's excellent work in this area was, several decades later, called upon by director David Fincher who sought the composer's voice on the true crime drama *Zodiac* (2007).

Clearly, Fincher sought to import the heritage of one of the defining 1970s thriller composers. After all, *Zodiac* begins in 1967, recounting the decades-long search for the notorious San Francisco serial killer of the title. The movie traverses the very same period when Shire rose to prominence as a composer, and he responds in kind with an eerie, sparing score very much in line with his past successes. Glissando strings capture the ominousness of Zodiac's elusive yet fame-hungry aura, while a noirish solo trumpet underscores the policemen who became consumed by the case, notably Dave Toschi (Mark Ruffalo).

That's not to say that all film scores of the early to mid-1970s abandoned lyrical and appealing principles. One need only cite John Barry's score for Nicolas Roeg's *Walkabout* (1971) to hear the lingering romantic influence of Max Steiner and other masters. The film is an impressionistic, elliptical story of innocence lost as a sister (Jenny Agutter) and her brother (Luc Roeg) are abandoned in the Australian Outback after their father commits suicide. They then come across an Aboriginal adolescent (David Gulpilil) who is undergoing his traditional rites of passage ceremony or "walkabout."

Barry's score is a hauntingly beautiful evocation of childhood transience, favoring his signature, resonant major key strings to pull the listener between catharsis and melancholy. These principles had already been put to use in the James Bond movies, plus the Oscar-winning likes of *Born Free* (1966) and *The Lion in Winter*. Barry's romantic idiom would later reach its apex in the Oscar-winning *Out of Africa*, but *Walkabout* remains an underrated gem. Although the film is fragmentary and dream-like in its editing style (typical of Roeg), Barry's music cuts to the quick and suggests those universal emotions shared by those who've left their childhood behind.

Around this time, orchestral principles were often put in the service of decidedly dark narratives. Stories of tragedy and violence were sometimes off set with warm tones, to either signify the inner spirit of a character, or suggest compassion within those appearing to lack it. Jerry Goldsmith's score for Franklin J. Schaffner's *Papillon* (1973) deploys a tender accordion and string waltz that deliberately contrasts with the storyline: that of brutal penal imprisonment on French Guiana. The ethnic tinge to the music also serves the source material: author Henri Charrière is French and wrote the book about his experiences, although its veracity has been disputed. In the movie, Charrière is played by Steve McQueen and Goldsmith's music becomes his inner voice of hope amidst a sea of despair, although careful spotting means that the first 20 minutes pass with no music at all.[10]

Just a year earlier in 1972, esteemed Italian composer Nino Rota, a regular collaborator with director Federico Fellini, had seemingly achieved the impossible: he crafted a score that made us feel the familial bonds within a dynasty of mobsters. The project was, of course, *The Godfather*, a landmark achievement by any standard. Francis Ford Coppola's sweeping crime epic, adapted from Mario Puzo's novel, is still considered by many to be the greatest gangster film of all time, and it's the film's level of intimacy that continues to fascinate.

Cold-blooded and avaricious murderers though they may be, the members of the Corleone crime family remain steadfastly loyal to one another. While watching the film, the audience is compelled to weigh up the ruthless actions of the characters versus the recognizable human principles of love, honor and respect. Coppola richly mines these contradictions, particularly via the performances including a career-reviving, and Oscar-winning, turn from Marlon Brando as Don Vito Corleone. Matching him scene for scene, although in much more wary, watchful fashion, is a star-making Al Pacino as Michael Corleone, the reluctant successor to his father's position who eventually calcifies into a feared crime lord.

Rota's score emphasizes this emotional dissonance brilliantly.

Centrally, his music is rooted in the traditions of Sicily, the island from which the Corleone family hails.[11] By off-setting gentle, folkish waltzes against the visuals of burgeoning 20th-century modernism, Rota demonstrates how long-standing crime traditions from one country have taken hold in another.

This is not music that's necessarily aligned with a wholly American perspective, and intentionally so: it shows us how the Corleone family members remain fiercely devoted to their roots in spite of their surroundings. All this, even as the family's adoptive country starts to feel the pernicious influence of their activities. Trumpets and accordions cast an ironically appealing glow, most famously in the central "Godfather Waltz," making the sudden plunge into wanton violence all the more shocking.

These thematic ideas are extended through the sequel, *The Godfather: Part II* (released in 1974), and trilogy capper *The Godfather: Part III* (1990). Rota maintains stylistic continuity throughout the series by returning to, and expanding on, the deceptively attractive main theme, further emphasizing the legacy of Corleone corruption as events become even more bleak. One scene from *Part II* particularly stands out: Michael's assassination of his feckless older brother Fredo (John Cazale). Rota deploys a string ensemble that approaches the level of a funeral dirge, perfectly underscoring Michael's slide into ruthlessness and evil.

Interestingly the most powerful scene of *Part III*, the climax, is scored not with Rota's music, but the deeply impassioned opera *Cavalleria Rusticana* (1890) by Pietro Mascagni. An enthusiast of Mascagni's opera since he was a child, Coppola used the *Cavalleria* to inform the tone of Rota's first *Godfather* score.[12] The piece (which also tops and tails Martin Scorsese's boxing classic *Raging Bull*, 1980) crafts a genuine aura of Shakespearean tragedy around the aged Michael, as he clings to his dead daughter Mary (Sofia Coppola). All that Michael knows and loves comes bursting out in a silent scream, Mascagni's strings nothing less than the sound of a heart breaking.

Naturally, when it comes to fine melodies, one must cite Ennio Morricone. The famously ubiquitous composer rarely caught his breath during the 1970s, delivering a string of exquisitely beautiful scores that have, in many instances, outlasted the films for which they were written. One such example is *La Califfa* (1970) aka *Lady Caliph*, a French-Italian drama starring Romy Schneider that would surely have sunk into obscurity were it not for Morricone's involvement. The composer's stunningly gorgeous main melody makes the oboe sing in a multitude of emotional tones, accompanied by a gentle string backing that is the essence of grace. Few composers could pierce to the heart as effectively as Morricone.

Also rising to prominence during this era was a certain John Williams. As previously mentioned, he had established himself in the 1960s as a jazz musician and session player for the likes of Henry Mancini. He received his first Oscar nomination for adapting André Previn's score for *Valley of the Dolls* (1967) and scored further nominations for *Goodbye Mr. Chips* (1969) and *The Reivers* (1969), cited in the previous chapter. Williams landed his first Oscar for the musical *Fiddler on the Roof* (1971), based on the 1964 Broadway production by Joseph Stein, Jerry Bock and Sheldon Harnick. Williams won the prize for Best Scoring Adaptation and Original Song Score, vindication for his sensitive handling of Bock's original compositions.[13]

It augured even greater things for Williams later in the decade, but prior to being pegged as the symphonic master, the composer delivered some of his most fascinating and experimental work in the first half of the 1970s. Williams' disturbing score for director Robert Altman's *Images* (1972) is possibly the closest he has ever come to a straight horror score, except, perhaps, for *War of the Worlds* (2005), composed for Steven Spielberg. A largely atonal work with clear echoes of Stravinsky, *Images* uses instrumental principles but in a way that approaches musique concrète, whereby organic sounds are used integrated into a score to blur the lines between musical and non-musical.

The sounds in question come from acclaimed Japanese percussionist Stomu Yamashta, who deploys a host of clattering and shaking effects that sit alongside Williams' equally unnerving compositions. More than that, they blend with them, crafting a complex soundscape that enlivens the film's narrative, in which Susannah York's children's author descends into paranoia at her remote country home. Williams' use of strings and woodwinds is extreme in nature, using high pitch to suggest the screeching and wailing of a human voice.

In line with Yamashta's input, Williams' score becomes very unsettling indeed, a singular, unusual work from a man widely considered as the best film composer of all time. Williams reunited with Altman for noir gumshoe movie *The Long Goodbye* (1973), the jazzy score for which inventively crosses the divide between the diegetic and the non-diegetic. Title song "The Long Goodbye," which features lyrics by Johnny Mercer, is heard in a variety of witty instrumental guises from a radio broadcast to a tango to a performance at a hippie party.

Yet Williams was expertly able to walk the divide between the frightening and the fulsome. His 1972 score for Mark Rydell's *The Cowboys* is the antithesis of the modernism heard in *Images*. Rousing and rollicking, it calls to mind Jerome Moross and Elmer Bernstein, a reminder that nostalgia was still a powerful tool in music at a time when rules were seemingly made to be broken.

Pitched somewhere between the darkness of *Images* and the orchestral weight of *The Cowboys* are Williams' disaster movie scores for Irwin Allen. The likes of *The Poseidon Adventure* (1972) use traditional orchestral set-ups and themes, but often in a sparing, somewhat somber manner. In this instance, Williams' approach befits the story of an ill-fated, upside-down ship that challenges its passengers to survive: it's a gloomy score but not one that aims to deploy music as a discordant series of sounds. After all, such an approach wasn't necessary in the context of a popcorn disaster film; a degree of emotional directness is needed in this realm. Similar principles were at work in Williams' score for the burning building epic *The Towering Inferno* (1974), starring Paul Newman and Steve McQueen.

Williams' versatility acts as a microcosm of this era of film music. That melodic scores were able to sit alongside more astringent soundtracks, plus pop and soul-infused album collections, is a testament to the proliferation of musical voices at this time. To coin a phrase, the atom had split open, allowing film music to branch off into a multitude of styles and approaches, each valid in terms of massaging an audience's reactions.

The old-fashioned sat alongside the new, the emotional directness of the orchestra vying with the striking use of chart favorites, but all soundtracks of the period aimed to elicit a more complex emotional response. It was proof that, in the years since the heyday of Max Steiner, film music had become one of the most dynamic and exciting art forms in the world.

Even so, Williams' early success stories were but an entrée for what was to come. The composer really hit the stratosphere towards the end of the decade when, for the first time, he ventured into a galaxy far, far away, in the process reigniting enthusiasm for the traditional symphonic score.

John Williams, *Star Wars* and the Commodification of Nostalgia

Born in Queens, New York, on February 8, 1932, John Towner Williams would go on to change the face of film music forever. Eventually, he would become the most celebrated soundtrack composer of his generation, if not all time.

As ever, there was a trickle-down of influence from the parents. Williams' father, Johnny, was a jazz drummer and percussionist with the Raymond Scott Quintette. The group was named after the composer and band leader of the same name whose music was adapted by Carl Stalling into countless cartoons. Interestingly enough, Scott was also a pioneer in the field of electronic instrumentation, and so acted as an influence (albeit indirectly) on several of the composers already mentioned in this book.

Raymond Scott's website observes that the Quintette (in fact sextet) came in 1936, when John Williams was just four years old. As with Bernard Herrmann and other musical pioneers of the time, the group established themselves with performances on CBS Radio, before eventually hitting the big time. To that end, it's noted on Scott's site that "RSQ's December '36 radio performance of 'Twilight in Turkey' on SNSC makes the band an overnight sensation."[14]

This enthusiasm for rhythm and melody must have made an impression on the younger John Williams. However, he wasn't to remain in New York. In 1948, he and his family moved to Los Angeles where he studied under another familiar name: Mario Castelnuovo-Tedesco, the same man who tutored Williams' contemporary (and eventual friend) Jerry Goldsmith. The family's inherent love of music, combined with expert tuition and an upbringing in the epicenter of Hollywood, must have fired up Williams' formative imagination.

Williams had his first taste of practical experience when he was drafted into the U.S. Air Force. Specifically, he was assigned to the Northeast Air Command Band with the U.S. Air Force, stationed at Fort Pepperell in St. John's, Newfoundland. Tasked with arranging the music for the U.S. Air Force Band, including concerts and radio performances, Williams, in fact, had his first brush with film composition at this time.

He was commissioned by Atlantic Films to make a local tourist movie about the area, titled *You Are Welcome*. Together with his fellow musicians in the U.S. Northeast Air Force Band, Williams fashioned the first soundtrack of his career.[15] However, he remained humble and insisted, "It was not an original score." Williams added: "I did not have a clue or an idea on how to do that. What I did was go to the library, it must have been in St. John's, and pick a Newfoundland folk song or two which formed the basis of what I arranged for that little film."[16]

Original or not, this unassuming corner of Canada had inspired the first film soundtrack from Williams, the man who would later come to embody the medium. In that sense, it was a truly historic moment. After finishing his military service, Williams returned to his home city of New York where he established himself as a jazz pianist, right at the moment where the idiom was starting to be incorporated into movies. At the same time, further education was attained at the esteemed The Juilliard School (where Bernard Herrmann had studied) and the Eastman School of Music in the city of Rochester.

Emboldened by his Air Force experience and the knowledge he gained from study, Williams ventured back to Los Angeles. He arrived in the late

1950s, right in the midst of an era hungry for jazz players and session musicians, and his career would benefit hugely from Hollywood's avaricious appetite. Even before one gets to Williams' solo compositional credits, it's remarkable to list his contributions on other people's soundtracks, which he racked up during the 1950s and early 1960s.

To name but a few: Williams was the piano performer on Elmer Bernstein's *Sweet Smell of Success* (1957), Henry Mancini's TV series *Peter Gunn* (1958–1961) and Jerry Goldsmith's *City of Fear* (1959). He was also the piano player on Bernard Herrmann's *The Twilight Zone* (1959), Jerome Robbins and Leonard Bernstein's Oscar-winning musical *West Side Story* (1961) and Elmer Bernstein's *The Magnificent Seven* (1960) and *To Kill a Mockingbird* (1962). He also served as an uncredited orchestrator on Dimitri Tiomkin's score for *The Guns of Navarone* (1961).[17] It's a truly enviable list of credits—and to think this was just Williams' tenure as a session musician. He had truly found his calling in the midst of the era's most celebrated film composers.

Of all those works just cited, one must single out *To Kill a Mockingbird*, by any measure one of the greatest dramatic scores of all time. The score accompanies the adaptation of Harper Lee's seminal novel, a Pulitzer Prize–winning work of childhood innocence beset by racial segregation. The movie is adapted by director Robert Mulligan and screenwriter Horton Foote, featuring an Oscar-winning Gregory Peck as noble lawyer and father Atticus Finch. It's almost certainly one of the finest book-to-screen adaptations of all time, and a large part of the film's success is down to the music.

Bernstein's proclivity for sensitive, intimate orchestral ensembles is very much on display, as piano, strings, harmonica and woodwind capture the naiveté of Atticus' daughter Scout (Mary Badham), who narrates the story as an older woman. It's a stunningly beautiful work, aided by Williams' exemplary piano playing that is evident right at the start of the lyrical main theme. One can sense the tonal sensitivity and phrasing that would later come in Williams' own scores. It takes a special composer to assert themselves in just a few bars of playing, but then Williams had already built up a head of steam by working on many scores for other celebrated musicians.

Fascinatingly given the scores that Williams is now known for, he began his solo career as a jazz artist. He was credited as Johnny Williams and delivered largely fluffy, comedic works for mostly forgotten caper and farce films. This period of his career was thrust back into the limelight in 2002 when the composer wrote the score for Steven Spielberg's *Catch Me If You Can*, a fact-based con-man caper starring Leonardo DiCaprio and Tom Hanks. Williams' finger-snapping, sax-led score was Oscar nominated and seen by many as something of a departure. Of course, it wasn't—instead, it circled back to a rather overlooked period in his career, igniting the enthusiasm of Williams completists and advocates at the same time that it caught casual listeners off-guard.

Like many of his contemporaries, Williams also exploited his talents in the field of television. An early sign of his melodic gifts came with *Lost in Space*, which ran from 1965 to 1968. The showrunner was Irwin Allen who, as already mentioned, would establish a rapport with Williams on the 1970s disaster films *The Poseidon Adventure* and *The Towering Inferno*. Williams composed the overarching theme music for *Lost in Space* and several scores for the individual episodes, imprinting his early signature on an eager new generation of science-fiction fans.

The series was revived in 2018 and executive producer Zack Estrin said it was vital that Christopher Lennertz's new score maintained tonal consistency with Williams original work. "We're maintaining the core spirit of the show—this great family survival adventure—and along with the rights to the show came this incredible trove of original John Williams compositions," Estrin explained. "We wanted you to feel like you were in a great Steven Spielberg experience of a movie, and what better way to feel that than to have a hint of John Williams?"[18]

In the midst of much experimental revolution, lasting from the 1960s into the 1970s, Williams delivered many idiosyncratic scores of his own, the aforementioned *Images* being one of them. However, in the mid–1970s, Hollywood began to swerve back towards conservative, comforting and exhilarating norms of storytelling. After many years of cynical cinematic disillusionment and rage against the establishment, popcorn entertainment was about to enter an exciting new phase.

At the epicenter was Williams, whose music was informed by these trends. As with all film composers, he had to go with the flow, and this meant an increasing emphasis on large-scale symphonic masterworks to suit increasingly grandiose tales of good versus evil. At the same time, so brilliant were these eventual Williams compositions that they took on a life of their own.

The composer effectively commodified a sense of nostalgia in his music, tapping into a sense of youthful derring-do that brought audiences full circle back to the early wonders of Steiner and Korngold. In the process, Williams added increased emotional (and commercial) value to studios and filmmakers looking to envelop viewers in memorable adventures. In short, he didn't reinvent the symphonic soundtrack score—rather, he reminded people of what it was they had been missing. In an era where lengthy intervals of silence, pop tracks and unusual effects tended to hold sway, Williams was about to reiterate Hollywood's early musical heritage.

Several filmmakers of the mid to late 1970s were re-connecting with the fantasy serials and stirring adventures they had enjoyed in their youth, including Steven Spielberg and George Lucas. Increasingly, this necessitated the need for symphonic melodies that weren't pegged to contemporary (and potentially short-lived or arbitrary) trends. Notions of heroism, valor and romance are illusory, having been etched on mankind's collective consciousness since time immemorial. And the symphony orchestra's tendency to avoid era-specific instrumentation and techniques allows it to accommodate this sense of ageless sweep.

Add to this Williams' inherent skill with harmony, melody, rhythm and counter-rhythm, and it's little wonder that he was well-positioned to deliver a near-constant stream of masterpieces from the mid–1970s onwards. The first of these to make a seismic impact was 1975's *Jaws*, the second of Williams' collaborations with Spielberg following 1974's *The Sugarland Express*.

The movie, naturally, needs little introduction. Spielberg's pioneering creature feature navigated a famously choppy production to emerge as the original summer blockbuster. Adapted from Peter Benchley's novel, *Jaws* makes a virtue of the limitations brought on by its three malfunctioning prop sharks (collectively named "Bruce," after Spielberg's lawyer). It deploys strong performances, a vivid sense of location and the propulsive menace of Williams' score to terrify audiences.

Not only did the movie scare subsequent generations of moviegoers away from the sea, but it also revolutionized cinema marketing. With its saturation release (over 400 screens, a first for any kind of movie) and aggressive merchandising tie-ins, *Jaws* rode the wave of hype to gross more than $470 million worldwide. The film was actively presented to audiences as less a movie and more an event, with t-shirts, beach apparel, games and, yes, soundtrack albums all adding to the mystique of the film's titular man-eater. Every other movie was left floundering in its wake.

As mentioned, the score was key to the film's impact. When all seemed lost amidst sinking sets and recalcitrant props, Williams' musical intuition gave Spielberg the coveted heartbeat of the dreaded shark, cleverly deploying the theme at key moments to suggest the creature's absence—or presence. It's hard to deny that this approach, although not the original intended one, elevated *Jaws* into the realm of Hitchcockian classic, as opposed to just another throwaway B-movie creature feature.

Jaws screenwriter Carl Gottlieb later authored *The Jaws Log*, widely considered one of the finest making-of accounts. In addition to detailing the movie's famously turbulent production, Gottlieb also remembers the moment that Williams got involved with the production and, arguably, saved it.

"Steven and John Williams had a close rapport," Gottlieb recalled.

John's name had come up even back on [Martha's Vineyard] when we had been shooting, and he was the first person to see the work print outside of the studio-executive level. He liked it and immediately got into deep discussions with Steven as they discussed how the music should be approached.

They agreed that it was a film of high adventure, and Johnny went to the classic movie scores of the past for a closer listen, with Steven playing Stravinsky and Vaughan Williams albums in his office every day, looking for analogies to what he felt should be the themes.[19]

Referring to Williams specifically, Gottlieb explained: "John ... worked out a dramatic four-note motif for the shark, and developed themes and motifs in a manner that is sorely missing from contemporary film scoring.... His capabilities were a known factor. In the liner notes to the soundtrack album, Steven commented that 'the music fulfilled a vision we all shared.'"[20]

Few movie themes are as famous as *Jaws*. The film opens with the Universal Studios logo and unsettling, sonar-like sounds. Steadily mounting double-bass guides the audience in as we cut to an underwater point-of-view shot, choppy strings melding with trenchant trombone to give a sense of pure single-minded purpose.

The full presentation of the theme, or "concert arrangement," actually melds the shark music with the nautical, swashbuckling theme for the Orca, the shark-hunting ship commandeered by fisherman Quint (Robert Shaw), police chief Brody (Roy Scheider) and marine biologist Hooper (Richard Dreyfus). The menace of Herrmann meets the bravado of Korngold in one of Williams' career-topping musical achievements (further emphasized in the thrilling cue "Man Versus Beast"), although there's a lot more to the score than just the central theme.

Black comedy is in order during the jaunty "Tourists on the Menu," accompanying scenes of eager yet unsuspecting holiday-makers arriving on the island of Amity like lambs to the slaughter. Swirling string arpeggios capture the menace and mystery of the deep in "Ben Gardner's Boat," leading to a hair-raising musical stinger as Gardner's head emerges from the hull in a notorious jump scare (actually shot as an afterthought in editor Verna Fields' swimming pool).

"The Indianapolis Story" is a masterclass in how to discreetly score a dialogue sequence, underlining Quint's blood-curdling monologue with eerie high-register strings that sound like screams echoing through memories of the past. And "The Shark Cage Fugue" anticipates the darker material to come later in *Jurassic Park* (1993), jabbing strings and swirling harp arrangements creating a chilling sense of frenzied urgency. It goes to show that *Jaws* is a far more diverse score than many give it credit for.

Williams won his second Oscar for the movie (it was his first for Best Original Score), and in the process re-established the relevancy of a symphonic approach. Of course, it helped that the music was foregrounded in the context of the narrative; no-one was going to miss the impact of the hair-raising main theme, because the score was designed to draw attention to itself, and therefore, by proxy, to the shark. In this sense, the *Jaws* score abandoned the self-consciousness that had marked so many film soundtracks of the 1970s. This was a score that unashamedly guided the audience's emotions in the old-fashioned manner of Korngold, enveloping and extending the narrative themes.[21]

Spielberg himself credited half of the film's impact to Williams.[22] The composer's work immediately made waves in Hollywood, indicating how judiciously applied melodies and countermelodies could further commercialize high-concept action-adventures. And Williams' next venture in this genre would prove intergalactically successful.

In 1976, writer-director George Lucas sought to create a distinctly old-fashioned homage to the *Flash Gordon* and *Buck Rogers* serials he'd treasured in his youth. At the time, Lucas was coming off the back of two critically acclaimed, low-budget films: the George Orwell–influenced dystopian sci-fi *THX 11–38* (1971), and the nostalgic, fifties-set coming-of-age drama *American Graffiti* (1973). Both movies had scored success in their own way—in fact, *American Graffiti*, which channeled Lucas' own youth, was hugely profitable, grossing 100 times its budget and showcasing classic rock and roll tracks, including "Rock Around the Clock."[23] It was, however, an amuse-bouche compared to Lucas' next project.

Lucas was one of a group of filmmakers known affectionately as the "movie brats." Along with Steven Spielberg, Francis Ford Coppola, Peter Bogdanovich, John Milius and Brian De Palma, Lucas was steeped in a nostalgic love of film, honed from years of TV watching as a youngster. This democratic system of home entertainment had instilled a deep love of cinema in a new generation of middle-class Americans, who went on to channel their passions as aspiring, and eventually successful, filmmakers.

Empire Magazine notes: "They were the first generation of filmmakers who hadn't come through the system or via theater, novels or television; instead they had learned film as film. Raised on watching movies on TV from an early age, they had learned their craft at film school—Coppola at UCLA, Lucas and Milius at USC, Scorsese at NYU and De Palma at Columbia, whereas Spielberg created his own movie curriculum by making films from 11—and as such were both technically proficient—listen out for the dense use of sound in the films of Coppola and Lucas—and steeped in film lore."[24]

All this knowledge and passion led Lucas into a project known as

Star Wars: A New Hope. The movie would reject years of darkly turbulent, politicized Hollywood filmmaking. Instead it would return to comforting fairy tale and fantasy archetypes, more in line with *The Wizard of Oz* and other clean-cut adventure stories from Hollywood's "Golden Era." Rather than dabbling in shades of grey, Lucas sought to fashion a black and white tale of good versus evil on an ambitious scale, mixing a myriad of characters, planets and scenarios and, in the process, connecting audiences to the material he had so cherished as a child.

The movie embraces many ageless fairy tale conceits, from the white knight hero (Mark Hamill's aspiring Jedi Luke Skywalker) to the wise wizard (Alec Guinness' veteran Jedi master Obi-Wan Kenobi) and the comic relief sidekick helpers (Anthony Daniels' C-3PO and Kenny Baker's R2-D2, both droids). Of course, there's a roguish wild card thrown in there as well in the form of Harrison Ford's Millennium Falcon pilot Han Solo, and his loyal Wookie friend Chewbacca (Peter Mayhew). The plot, meanwhile, is pure fairy tale, revolving around a quest to save a princess, Leia (Carrie Fisher) from evil Galactic Empire overlord Darth Vader (David Prowse, voiced by James Earl Jones).

It had been a long time since Hollywood filmmaking had embraced such archaic conceits on the grand scale that Lucas envisaged. As has been explained, movies of the period were generally more concerned with taking risks and plugging into grittier, messier realities and concerns. Lucas, however, sought to return adults to a childlike state of wonderment. And music was intrinsic to Lucas' vision.[25]

This wouldn't be an electronic or pop-infused soundscape, but instead a timeless tapestry that connected to those deep-seated themes of bravery and sacrifice. Initially, the filmmaker planned to use a patchwork of classical pieces a la Stanley Kubrick's *2001: A Space Odyssey* (1968). One of these works was intended to be Holst's *The Planets*,[26] but in the end, Lucas called on Williams at the suggestion of Spielberg who had greatly enjoyed his collaboration with Williams on *Jaws*. With the composer now flying high after his Oscar win, he seemed like the perfect choice for *Star Wars*.

Williams recalled the fateful meeting that would help launch him into the upper echelons of the greatest-ever film composers. "One day, Steven [Spielberg] called me and said, 'Do you know George Lucas?' I said, 'No, I have no idea who he is.' 'Well, he's got this thing called *Star Wars*, and he wants to have a classical'—his term, he didn't say romantic—'classical score, and I've convinced George he should meet you, because he admired the score for *Jaws*.' I came out here one night, to Universal Studios, and met George."[27]

Temp track suggestions, ranging from the aforementioned Holst to selections from Ligeti and more, remained as placeholders to help guide Williams' eventual compositions. There can be no denying that Williams fused these impulses with the melodic overtones as featured in the earlier likes of *The Reivers* and *Jane Eyre* (1970). However, the scale of the first *Star Wars* score was to play out on a Wagnerian canvas not experienced since the heyday of Max Steiner and Miklós Rózsa. The sheer plethora of character and location-specific themes and motifs put forward by Williams was simply staggering, a potent reminder of the power of orchestral storytelling.

Emilio Audissino is the author of the wide-ranging academic study *John Williams's Film Music*. He observes: "*Star Wars* is, in fact, more a 'super-genre' than a sci-fi film. Only a few elements of the sci-fi genre, such as robots, laser weapons and spaceships, are present *Star Wars* is rather a mixture of elements from Western, fantasy and swashbuckler films and instead of being similar to sci-fi films of its day, it was closer to the Warner Bros adventure films directed by Michael Curtiz, featuring Errol Flynn's prowess and Erich Wolfgang Korngold's opulent music."[28] This is the philosophy that would end up powering the score.

The most famous and imitated of all the *Star Wars* pieces is the opening brass fanfare, a heraldic statement of intent that leads us into, and through, the opening scroll. Williams recalled the creation of the theme with affection and self-deprecation: "That fanfare at the beginning, I think it's the last thing I wrote. It's probably a little overwritten—I don't know. The 30-second notes in the trombones are hard to get, in that register of the trombone. And the high trumpet part!"[29]

Williams cited the enthusiastic performance of the London Symphony Orchestra whose association with the *Star Wars* franchise stretched through the original and prequel trilogies.[30] "Maurice Murphy, the great trumpet player of the LSO—that first day of recording was actually his first day with the orchestra, and the first thing he played was that high C. There was a kind of team roar when he hit it perfectly. He's gone now, but I love that man."[31]

Lucas and Williams immediately established the *Star Wars* aesthetic through the portent and majesty of the score. It was essential for tuning audiences into the adventure to come, one of major key highs and dissonant lows, a popcorn rollercoaster ride designed to emphasize escapist thrills rather than earthly realities. And yet the opening fanfare is but one gem amidst a galaxy of musical treasures.

Williams applies soaring tonal majesty to the concept of the Force, famously in the "Binary Sunset" cue, which fuses the concept of the light and the dark to Luke Skywalker's destiny in the stars beyond. The composer dips into his jazz background for groovy source music in "The

Cantina Band," heard diegetically (within the scene) during the Mos Eisley spaceport sequence. Interestingly, Vader and the Death Star aren't treated to an extended theme, but rather a menacing little motif that would later be nostalgically reprised in Michael Giacchino's score for prequel film *Rogue One: A Star Wars Story* (2016). Williams' interplay of the various ideas is truly dazzling—rarely a moment goes by when key themes aren't interacting with one another, creating the distinct sense of an organic musical canvas.

The application of the opening fanfare throughout the score is particularly thrilling. The oft-imitated "TIE-Fighter Attack" off-sets the theme against insistent low horns and trombones to represent the Imperial forces. During "Rescue of the Princess," it melds with the tender, innocent woodwinds depicting Leia. The fanfare fuses with the noble sound of the Force theme during the climactic "The Battle of Yavin," accompanying Luke's destruction of the Death Star. Frantic strings and hair-raising timpani create a level of musical ruckus that elevates the rather basic effects, a mixture of back projection, actor close-ups and egg-crates (used to craft the Death Star trench). The realm of the technically competent is elevated into a truly seat-gripping battle of good versus evil thanks to Williams' input.

Likewise, during the climactic medal-giving scene ("Throne Room and End Title"), a simple, dialog-free sequence is elevated into the realms of cathartic, operatic majesty thanks to the performance of the LSO's brass section. This then leads into the end credits that wraps up all of the primary themes, a quick canter through a theme-studded masterwork (later to become a hallmark of the *Star Wars* scores) that causes one to exit the movie utterly giddy and exhilarated.

Audiences in 1977 were certainly left exhilarated. *Star Wars: A New Hope* soared to astonishing global grosses of more than $700 million worldwide, becoming the most successful movie of all time at the point of its release. Throughout the production, aspersions had been cast on Lucas' reclusive personality, causing friction with numerous cast and crew members. The project had also been written off as a folly, not least because science-fiction had somewhat fallen out of fashion at the time of the film's production. But, given Lucas had secured sequel and merchandising rights through his Lucasfilm label, the end result transformed him into one of the most successful, and financially savvy, businessmen in the history of Hollywood.[32]

It's impossible to overstate Williams' impact on the success of the finished film. The score envelops the audience in a swashbuckling sense of bravado, applying the tone of Korngold's seafaring adventures to the realm of outer space. This approach would prove hugely influential on the next generation of film composers, and secured Williams his second Oscar for Best Original Score (and his third overall).

During the AFI's (American Film Institute) 44th Life Achievement Award Gala Tribute, George Lucas paid tribute to the composer who imbued *Star Wars* with its soul. "*Star Wars* was meant to be a simple hero's journey," Lucas recalled, "a fantasy for young people. But then John's music raised the film to an art that would stand the test of time. I had so many ideas for other movies, but I never got to them because you ensured that *Star Wars* would live forever."[33]

There can surely be no finer tribute to the man who reignited interest in symphonic cinematic storytelling. Orchestral scores had been in good health prior to the release of the first *Star Wars*—one need only cite Williams' prior Oscar win for *Jaws*, Jerry Goldsmith's Oscar win for *The Omen* and many other fine orchestral works from the 1970s. However, it was the sheer scale, exuberance and good-natured optimism of the first *Star Wars* score that awoke the slumbering child inside many a movie executive and audience member.

Emilio Audissino notes: "Symphonic orchestral film music didn't entirely disappear in the modern-style years but it definitely became less common.... What became marginal was the classical Hollywood style. In particular, the old-style spatial perceptive function survived mostly in an exaggerated farcical form in some comedies ... or in the mannerist, thunderous stingers of some horror/thriller B-movies.... Not until *Star Wars* did there appear patent signs that the old style could still have something to say."[34]

Williams' music acted as a powerful reminder as to why audiences loved movies in the first place: escapism, fantasy and the boundless breadth of imagination, underscored with a sincere sense of empathy and compassion. There was a vivid connection to the early days of Hollywood symphonic scores yet underpinned with Williams' singular sense of orchestral sophistication. It was a meeting of the old and the new. By reviving the large-scale symphonic orchestra, Williams had successfully fused artistic credibility with commercial success, in turn establishing his enduring association with the *Star Wars* series.

In release order, the franchise encompassed *The Empire Strikes Back* (1980) and *Return of the Jedi* (1983) in the original trilogy, followed by *The Phantom Menace* (1999), *Attack of the Clones* (2002) and *Revenge of the Sith* (2005) in the prequel trilogy. Later, Williams renewed his association with the series in *The Force Awakens* (2015), *The Last Jedi* (2017) and *The Rise of Skywalker* (2019). Out of all these, it's commonly held that *Empire* represents the movies, and the accompanying Williams scores, at their apex.

Following the extraordinary success of the first *Star Wars*, Lucas retrospectively retitled the movie *Episode IV*. His reasoning: this would act as the middle chapter in a wider saga, one that would develop the before and after story of the dreaded villain Darth Vader, his creation and his later chokehold on power. Lucas elaborated on this framework when it came to making *The Empire Strikes Back* (known as *Episode V*), a movie that he didn't direct (instead, Irvin Kershner stepped in). However, Lucas remained the creative stalwart from the sidelines, variously approving and disapproving script treatments from the likes of sci-fi author Leigh Brackett and writer Lawrence Kasdan (who eventually took a screenwriting credit).

The crux of *The Empire Strikes Back* was Vader's relationship with burgeoning Jedi master Luke, the emphasis of which changed midway through principal photography in spectacular fashion. In a daring twist, it's revealed that Vader is, in fact, Luke's father, the product of a last-minute script rewrite shared only between Lucas, Kershner, Kasdan and actor Mark Hamill. Audiences wouldn't get the full ramifications of this until *Episode I: The Phantom Menace*, the first entry in Lucas' prequel trilogy of movies. Back in 1980, they simply had to imagine the reasons why the innocent Anakin Skywalker had turned into the galaxy's most feared individual.

All of this proved catnip to a composer of Williams' caliber who immediately seized upon the movie's darker, more mature tone. *The Empire Strikes Back* is a textbook example of how to score a sequel: use the existing symphonic parameters of old, embellish and tweak the original themes, and throw in a plethora of terrific new ideas that signal the change in emotional temperature.

Vader's musical identity takes shape for the first time in the form of the thunderous "Imperial March," a bombastic, militaristic statement of all-consuming might, and one of Williams' most famous pieces. Heavily influenced by the balletic structure of Prokofiev and Tchaikovsky,[35] this theme would be utilized in all of the subsequent *Star Wars* saga movies, including the aforementioned prequel trilogy.

For instance, "Young Anakin," heard in *The Phantom Menace*, brilliantly off-sets pastoral, childlike woodwinds against subtly foreboding inflections of the March, foreshadowing the slide from innocence into corruption. Given that the narrative spine of the prequels revolves around Vader's creation, the theme takes on more ballast with the adolescent Anakin (Hayden Christensen) in *Episode II: Attack of the Clones*, before reaching darkly operatic grandeur with the character's transition into Vader in *Episode III: Revenge of the Sith*.

The theme was also incorporated into the most recent *Star Wars* trilogy initiated by director J.J. Abrams. The theme is briefly, but chillingly, invoked in *Episode VII: The Force Awakens* when Adam Driver's warmongering Kylo Ren vows to adopt the mantle of his grandfather, Vader, staring at the obliterated fragments of the latter's helmet. It also makes subtle but impactful appearances in *Episode VIII: The Last Jedi* and *Episode IX: The Rise of Skywalker*.

Williams' ability to maintain thematic continuity across multiple trilogies throughout the decades, encompassing collaborations with an assortment of filmmakers, is truly remarkable, ensuring clarity of identification via music. Outside of Basil Poledouris' *Conan the Barbarian* (1982) and Howard Shore's *The Lord of the Rings* trilogy (2001–2003), it's arguably the most successful modern-day exponent of the Wagnerian symphony, the various leitmotifs creating, especially in the later films, a Pavlov's dog reaction of immediate gratification and nostalgia. One such example would be the spectacular eruption of "TIE-Fighter Attack" midway through "The Battle of Crait" cue in *The Last Jedi*, which translated familiarity into fan-pleasing eruptions of joy the world over.

Returning to *The Empire Strikes Back*, it unleashed a plethora of themes in addition to the one for Vader. Like "The Imperial March," these have been threaded throughout all of the subsequent saga movies. Ancient and endearing Jedi master Yoda (Frank Oz) is treated to a theme that walks a sublime line between delicacy and veneration, a piece said to be one of Williams' favorites.

This piece was reprised not just in the original trilogy closer *Episode VI: Return of the Jedi* (1983), but also much later in *The Last Jedi* when Yoda made a fan-pleasing appearance as a "Force ghost." Elsewhere, "Han Solo and the Princess" develops yearning affection between Han Solo and Leia, later heard with an increased dash of melancholy during their long-overdue reunion in *The Force Awakens*. Consistency of musical emotion is key to Williams' methodology throughout the franchise, and an important reason why the series is so beloved by millions of people around the world.

Even in Lucas' much-maligned prequel trilogy, criticized for its poor dialogue, over-reliance on CGI and wooden acting, Williams' music is widely considered to be the one consistently good element. In 1999, *The Phantom Menace* opened to dreadful reviews but unsurprisingly reignited the slumbering *Star Wars* behemoth to the tune of $900 m worldwide. One must consider the nostalgic factor of Williams' music in this. A mixed-voice choir erupts in Sanskrit majesty for "Duel of the Fates," a vocal battle between the light and dark sides of the Force. One can sense the composer working overtime to engage the audience's emotions in the face of overwhelming artifice and stilted staging.

In *Attack of the Clones*, Williams channels the romantic spirit of Nino Rota's *Romeo and Juliet* (1968) for the love theme "Across the Stars." Graceful harp and string scales join a delicate oboe accompaniment to inject some lifeblood into the relationship between teen Anakin and eventual wife Padmé (Natalie Portman). The latter's fate becomes central to the tone of the closing trilogy score *Revenge of the Sith*, arguably the darkest in Williams' *Star Wars* canon. Portentous choir takes on a host of guises to reflect Anakin's spiritual, and, eventually, physical, devastation, including subtly insidious statements of the evil Palpatine's (Ian McDiarmid) theme. The placement of the theme anticipates its use in the chronologically later *Return of the Jedi*, as Palpatine embraces his role as the Emperor.

Williams' music is so deeply embedded in the DNA of the series that it was considered imperative to bring him back for the most recent saga storyline. The newest *Star Wars* films focus centrally on Rey (Daisy Ridley), a character with whom Williams became fascinated. There is a bucolic sense of innocent charm to her flute-based theme, which then gains in stature through the brass and string sections as the theme anticipates her elevation to Jedi mastery. Williams said it was Rey's character that secured his involvement in the most recent trilogy: "I told [Lucasfilm president] Kathy Kennedy I'm happy to do it, but the real reason is, I didn't want anybody else writing music for Daisy Ridley."[36]

J.J. Abrams, who helmed *The Force Awakens* and *The Rise of Skywalker*, said that simply being in the room with Williams was an education in storytelling. "Watching [John Williams] talk to the orchestra is a lesson in expression," Abrams explained. "I was amazed by how gentle and kind and humble he is. He was like that every day we worked together."[37]

As ever, the true worth of a composer resides in their lasting influence on the later generations. In recent years, so-called "anthology" *Star Wars* movies have arisen alongside the new saga storyline. Although these anthology movies are narratively tangential, they cannot escape the tractor beam-style lure of Williams' music, so vast a shadow does it cast over the series. Even when Williams' original themes are not directly cited, newer pieces ape the rhythm, tonality and harmonies of his creations.

In 2016, audiences were treated to *Rogue One: A Star Wars Story*, the tale of how the Rebel Alliance stole the plans for the original Death Star. The climax of the movie acts as a narrative segue into the beginning of *A New Hope*. Composer Michael Giacchino (who replaced Alexandre Desplat) was tasked with mimicking the tone of Williams' music while only drawing subtly on the musical themes established in the original trilogy. After all, this story is about setting up what comes later on, and this naturally extends to the music.

Hence why Giacchino's "Imperial Suite," full of enjoyably menacing bluster, apes rather than outwardly borrows from Williams' "Imperial March." Giacchino's music indicates the early stages of the Galactic Empire before it became identified with Darth Vader's musical identity. However, Giacchino does use the march during the pivotal meeting scene between Vader and Death Star commander Krennic (Ben Mendelsohn), showing that the specter of Williams' music really is inescapable.

More than four decades after the release of the first *Star Wars* movie, it was impossible to separate Williams from the series. It indicated how closely bound up he was with the characters and wider mythology. In 2018, Ron Howard helmed the spin-off movie *Solo: A Star Wars Story*, which brought us the early years of the infamous space cowboy. Alden Ehrenreich stepped into the boots of Harrison Ford, while composer John Powell took the reins from John Williams.

In fact, the filmmakers simply couldn't resist employing Williams' services: he composed the rousing, brass-led "The Adventures of Han," which Powell then adapted to thrilling effect throughout the remainder of the score. Powell's work deploys a breathless sense of swashbuckling energy during pieces such as "Corellia Chase" and "Into the Maw." The soundtrack essentially hands the baton from the musical equivalent of the Jedi master to the enraptured protégé, Powell belonging to the current generation of composers who've been singularly influenced by Williams' output.

Like so many fans, J.J. Abrams said his nostalgic love of the franchise was inherently bound up with memories of Williams' music, particularly in *A New Hope*. When asked what his favorite *Star Wars* theme was Abrams replied, "There are so many." He then elaborated: "I mean, I guess the first one that made me cry was the Force theme, when Luke is looking over the Binary Sunset."[38]

"It was when *Star Wars* came out that I finally made the connection: 'Oh, there are people playing this music and a trumpet sounds like that, a French horn sounds like that' and so on," says *Rogue One* composer Michael Giacchino.[39]

> That solidified it but the inspiration came from the years prior to that. Monster movies, *Sinbad* movies and that stuff. I love all that.
> One of those themes would just put you back in the world of a particular film and I really enjoyed that. I liked the idea that I could sit there at night in my bedroom, put something on the record player and be instantly transported back to this place. Whether it be the world of *Superman* or *Sinbad* or *Star Wars*, whatever, it was always just a great way to put myself into a different place for a little while. It was almost like meditation, if you think about it.
> So I loved that, and I loved the fact that each film had their own identity. A lot of films these days lack a specific identity. They all feel very similar in

construction. There was a little bit of that going around when I grew up but for the most part.... If you think about the summers where we had the likes of *Poltergeist* (1982) and *Back to the Future* (1985) for example, there were all these different films with different stories and different musical identities.⁴⁰

It's a powerful sign of how much film music can imprint on generations of moviegoers and filmmakers, particularly during the ennobling, standalone statements of majestic themes. Intangible concepts, far-off planets and fantastical characters are transmogrified into something relatable and believable, something that we feel innately within our souls. For all of Williams' intergalactic sense of sweep, his *Star Wars* music works because (to contradict an earlier point), it pertains to distinctly earthbound feelings and emotions.

When discussing his own ability to harness nostalgia in film music, Giacchino says: "In short, I don't know how to do it any other way. I certainly wouldn't have any fun doing it the other way. I do my best to carry that tradition forward.... You know, we need to make sure we're still enjoying what we're doing. Most of us are here because we're doing what we did as kids. Many of us made movies when we were young, and we did it for fun. So to keep a bit of that feeling is important."⁴¹

For much of the 1970s, movies, and their accompanying scores, had emphasized a sense of verisimilitude. After the release of John Williams' score for *A New Hope*, it was again viable to engage with the "fantastical" conceit of a non-diegetic soundtrack that boldly expanded the parameters of a given narrative. Where was the music coming from? In a narrative like *Star Wars*, it didn't matter—the narrative was already one of archetypal whimsy, and one needn't question the existence of a soundtrack that tapped into, and deepened those invisible, irresistible notions of romantic adventure.

Of course, that's all well and good in theory. But the score for *A New Hope* also worked in practice, helping elevate its respective movie to lavish box office returns. Once again, a strange, cyclical pattern emerged: as a movie, *Star Wars* engaged with past forms of entertainment, and this, in turn, inspired a return to the musical norms of old, which further empowered the film's charm and impact. It was noted how Williams' music humanized a genre formerly known for its atonal strangeness and electronic experimentation, while also returning to the "Golden Age" conventions of saturation scoring, with rarely a minute going past without the music offering a form of emotional expression.⁴²

With movies and movie scores, it's often very difficult to know if the tail is wagging the dog, or vice versa. Regardless, the synergy of Lucas' and Williams' respective visions caused Hollywood to sit up and take notice. Nostalgia had been commodified and a brand-new era of blockbuster films, one emphasizing a strong relationship with thematic music, was about to begin.

The Influence of *Star Wars* on Blockbuster Scores of the 1980s

By the end of the 1970s, the wide-ranging impact of *Star Wars* had become apparent. It drew a line in the sand between politicized, angry filmmaking and feel-good escapist thrills, ushering in a new decade that reverted to more conservative modes of entertainment. Once more, the emphasis would be on widescreen escapism, fantastical scenarios and imaginative set-pieces, a return to the Hollywood of old. Inevitably, film music was headed down the same path. Whereas much of the 1970s had been marked by a diversity of experimental approaches, John Williams' success with *Star Wars* caused the symphonic orchestra to become standardized once more.

There was another key development at the end of the decade. In 1980, director Michael Cimino's *Heaven's Gate* was finally released in cinemas, having been marked with endless delays, budget overruns and production chaos. The alleged self-indulgence of Cimino's vision was greeted with savage reviews, and so disastrous was the movie that it effectively bankrupted its studio, United Artists. It was, in essence, a cautionary tale, a warning about what would happen when a bright young director (in this case an Oscar winner for 1978's *The Deer Hunter*) was granted too much autonomy.

Heaven's Gate effectively ended the "auteurist" period of director-driven movies. For much of the preceding decade, filmmakers had been empowered to put their uncompromising personal visions at the forefront, all the better for capturing the turbulence and darkness of the era. But like all great honeymoon periods, it ended with a whimper, not a bang, causing studios to rein in their talent and forcing directors to adhere to more traditional modes of narrative storytelling. Budgetary concerns were clearly key to this—it was now more imperative than ever that filmmakers rigidly remain within certain parameters while high-concept pitches sought out the biggest audience possible.

This may seem unrelated to the development of film music, but as ever, the ripples in the Hollywood pool radiated out towards the industry's finest composers. As American cinema reshaped itself around populist, conventional modes of storytelling, it was essential that soundtrack music picked up the slack, conveying an all-important sense of grandiosity and fantasy. Put simply, the success of *Star Wars*, and the failure of the experimental *Heaven's Gate*, placed a desire for nostalgic, tried-and-tested technique back at the center of the movie industry.

That's not to deny the musical quality of *Heaven's Gate*, nor is it to suggest that familiar orchestral techniques are inherently superior to offbeat, potentially anachronistic compositions. As always with film music, there's more than one way to skin a cat—the question is, how well does a particular film score suit a director's vision? In hindsight, the music of *Heaven's Gate*, composed by David Mansfield, is one of its finest facets, a lyrical, yearning ode to the passing of the American West. It just so happened to arrive at the worst possible moment, the score going down with the ship as Hollywood rejected everything the film stood for. One of the great tragedies of film music is that it's rarely immune when its respective movie goes down in flames.

The ensuing result was a brand-new decade, the 1980s, filled with some of the most memorable and exciting orchestral music ever put to film. Whereas many bemoaned the loss of idiosyncratic and quirky voices in film and film music, decrying the homogenized emphasis on mass-market spectacle, there's no denying that the eighties birthed some truly spectacular works in the field of musical narrative. In particular, the realms of sci-fi, fantasy and action-adventure would benefit enormously from this re-calibration. Recalling Erich Wolfgang Korngold's success back in the 1940s, popcorn action movies proved to be a real boon for film composers.

One must first address the lasting impact of *Star Wars* on John Williams' own career. For better or worse, it pigeonholed him as a practitioner of sweeping symphony scores, at the expense of more experimental, angular and difficult efforts like *Images*. That's not to say that Williams' most popular works are devoid of dark moments. It's just that these moments generally sit amidst musical narratives that are designed to comfort and placate in their sense of inherent nostalgic bravado.

In 1978, Williams effectively birthed the contemporary superhero score with *Superman*. Richard Donner's rousing DC Comics adaptation made good on its tagline: "You'll believe a man can fly." Bolstered by breakthroughs in green screen technology, which placed delightful star Christopher Reeve at the center of the spectacular aerial sequences, *Superman* treated its comic book source with an appreciably reverent and compassionate touch. And, as ever, Williams' score (on offer originally extended to Jerry Goldsmith) was key to the film's impact, in particular its brassy, celebratory main fanfare which wonderfully captures the bravado and nobility of the comic book icon.

"We had a completed version of *Superman*, and much like you do with any composer, we ran the picture and spotted it, deciding where the music should be," Donner recalled.

But John was so far ahead of us after seeing it just once that he kind of took charge emotionally. He read so much into the picture, almost more than we did.

The first recording session for *Superman* was the opening reel of the movie, and those brilliant titles that were done by Richard Greenberg came flying onto the screen. It demanded special music, but you didn't have to say that to John because when the title "Superman" came flying in, John made the music say, "Su-Per-Man!" If you listen to just that one little piece, you can literally hear the music say, "Superman." It brought tears to our eyes.

When he's conducting, you're usually looking at his back, because you are looking at the orchestra much like he is. But I would often go on the music stage, up behind drums and the top instruments, and watch John like the orchestra was watching him, and his face conveyed the whole movie. He must have studied acting because it was like he was living the entire piece. Very beautiful. It ended with this truly happy expression on his face as if to say, "Oh my God, that was good, and I did it."[43]

Williams' music was Oscar nominated, further cementing his credentials as Hollywood's prime purveyor of blockbuster thrills. He ultimately lost the award to Giorgio Moroder's electronically-oriented *Midnight Express*, which indicated that scores with a contemporary element hadn't entirely lost their stranglehold on the Hollywood market, despite the recent resurgence in symphonic grandeur.[44] The chart-busting success of 1977's *Saturday Night Fever*, set to the songs of the Bee Gees, and 1978's *Grease*, both starring John Travolta, also reinforced this thinking, particularly the latter movie which capitalized on a love of retro 1950s rock and roll. (It also demonstrated that nostalgia was just as strong in cinematic pop music as it was in the field of the orchestral score.)

One might imagine that Moroder's standing as a pre-eminent 1970s record producer, having worked with the likes of Led Zeppelin and Queen, curried favor with Oscar voters, an attempt to stay relevant, perhaps. (He would later become entrenched in the Jerry Bruckheimer stable with the Oscar-winning likes of "Take My Breath Away" for 1986's *Top Gun*.) Nevertheless, as has been stated, one rarely looks to the Oscars for artistic credibility. And if one truly wants to measure the *Superman* score's impact, one must look at the imitators it spawned.

In 1989, former Oingo Boingo musician turned film composer Danny Elfman took his lead from John Williams (plus a dash of Bernard Herrmann) with his score for *Batman*. It was Elfman's third collaboration with director Tim Burton, adhering to the symphonic orchestral tenets, established by Williams, of strong, memorable themes and vibrant action music. Of course, whereas *Superman* represented a kind of moral purity (qualities that pervaded Williams' score), *Batman* was a different prospect entirely. A far more brooding, Gothic tone (albeit knowingly self-aware) was in order.

The *Batman* score is similarly anchored by a propulsive and thunderous main theme, buoyed by powerful trumpets, horns and trombones. It speaks of the dichotomy at the heart of Michael Keaton's central portrayal: heroism tinged with an unmistakable air of dark menace. Just as Williams created immediate identification with *Superman* with his theme, so too did Elfman with *Batman*. It was another reminder of the importance of strong thematic writing, particularly in blockbuster action films. It's essential that the audience knows the character through the music, even before they've been officially introduced.

That said, Elfman's symphonic voice (in this instance, very much reliant on the nuances wrought by orchestrator Steve Bartek and conductor Shirley Walker) is different from Williams' approach. There's a carnivalesque, absurdist tone to the material for Jack Nicholson's deranged Joker, waltzing and parading with tongue in cheek abandon. The incidental cues favor jittery xylophone and timpani rhythms, skittering in a darkly comic fashion before giving way to expansive organ and choral arrangements that honor Burton's primary Gothic horror influences.

Interestingly, however, Elfman's work almost fell afoul of the Hollywood commercial machine. More than 20 years after *The Graduate*, the notion of importing a popular artist to sell both the movie and the accompanying soundtrack showed no signs of waning. Even in the midst of a rich and vibrant period for orchestral film scores, the *Batman* producers felt it necessary to draft in Prince to compose his own album of material (only two songs from which appear in the finished film). In fact, it was initially suggested that Elfman co-write his score with Prince, something the former vehemently rejected.

"I was willing to walk away from the film rather than compromise what I knew should be the sound of the film," Elfman explained. "I just wasn't willing to do it. I knew what the score was, and as much as I love Prince's music, I didn't feel that his score was going to be the right score sound for the *Batman* movie. And so I had to walk away and let that play out."[45]

Ultimately, a compromise was reached: Prince would have his own album of songs and Elfman would be solely responsible for the score. The composer said that he had no regrets: "I had to stick to my guns. My feeling at that point was that Prince was a great, great songwriter, but that he probably was not a film composer, and that he would come up with melodies, and I would essentially be turning those melodies into a score. And so my feeling is that I would end up being a glorified orchestrator or an arranger, not a composer on the project. And I just wasn't willing to do that."[46]

Batman proved to be an enormous success for Warner Bros, grossing more than $400 million worldwide (the biggest commercial hit of the year) as it rode the back of an extensive marketing campaign. One might imagine that Prince's involvement had something to do with this, even if his presence in the final movie was somewhat minimized. It's Elfman's music that opens the movie and takes precedence throughout, working harder than Prince's contribution to reinforce the sense of a non-stop rollercoaster ride. The movie effectively birthed the contemporary superhero epic, and Elfman's score re-established the parameters of the modern comic book score in the wake of *Superman*.

Film music critic Craig Lysy asserts that Elfman's *Batman* score was a watershed moment in pop culture—and, of course, the influence of John Williams was embedded in the genetic code of Elfman's work. "This score propelled Danny Elfman to tier one composer status and he has never looked back," writes Lysy. "Following in the tradition of John Williams, Elfman's anthem for *Batman* joins *Superman* as iconic superhero anthems, which have passed unto legend.

"In a masterstroke of conception, Elfman captured the emotional core of Burton's film, providing the power, mystery and darkness that was Batman."[47] Later efforts including Elfman's own *Dick Tracy* and *Darkman* (both 1990), Jerry Goldsmith's *The Shadow* (1994) and David Newman's *The Phantom* (1996) would owe themselves to the trendsetting Batman score.

As for John Williams, he found himself firmly in demand as the 1980s beckoned. One of his crowning achievements was, and still remains, the *Indiana Jones* series, initially a trilogy, and later expanded to a tetralogy, with a fifth movie now on the way (set to be scored by Williams). The movies were overseen by Williams' friends and collaborators Steven Spielberg, who directed, and George Lucas, who produced via his Lucasfilm label. Lucas devised the central character, the whip-wielding, fedora-wearing archaeologist-adventurer–Nazi basher Indiana Jones, as wonderfully brought to life by a ruggedly charming Harrison Ford.

The first movie in the series, 1981's *Raiders of the Lost Ark*, arose partly as a response to the *James Bond* franchise. Spielberg had harbored a desire to make a Bond film, only for Lucas to reveal that he'd been working on a hero of his own, at that point named Indiana Smith (later changed to Jones). Spielberg responded enthusiastically, not least because he was smarting from the stinging critical reaction to his madcap World War II satire *1941* (released in 1979 and scored by Williams). Like *Star Wars*, *Raiders* was intended as a jubilant, lighthearted (though frequently scary and gory) throwback to the B-movie adventure serials of old. And Williams' past form in this area meant he was the only choice to compose the soundtrack.

"My first task on *Raiders of the Lost Ark* was to create a recognizable theme for the Indiana Jones character," Williams explained.

> Every time Harrison jumps on the horse or does something heroic, I wanted to pay reference to this theme. I remember playing Steven a couple of options on the piano. He loved them and simply said, "Why don't you use both?" So those two tunes became the main theme and bridge of what we now call "The Raiders March."
>
> The interesting thing about "The Raiders March" is that it is a very simple little tune, but I spend more time on those bits of musical grammar than anything else. The sequence of notes has to sound just right so it seems inevitable, like it has always been with us. It was something that I chiselled away at for a few weeks, changing a note here and there, to find the correct musical shape. Those little simplicities are often the hardest things to capture.[48]

"Were it not for the many crucial bursts of dramatic symphonic accompaniment," said Spielberg, "Indiana Jones would surely have perished in a forbidding temple in South America, or in the oppressive silence of the great Sahara desert."

> Nevertheless, Jones did not perish, but listened carefully to the *Raiders* score. Its sharp rhythms told him when to run. Its slicing strings told him when to duck. Its several integrated themes told adventurer Jones when to kiss the heroine or smash the enemy. All things considered, Jones listened ... and lived. John Williams saves yet another life and gives our picture, *Raiders of the Lost Ark*, a new, refreshing life of its own.[49]

As with *Star Wars*, the *Indiana Jones* series benefited hugely from its sense of musical consistency. The "Raiders March" was threaded through all the subsequent films, *The Temple of Doom* (1984), *The Last Crusade* (1989) and *The Kingdom of the Crystal Skull* (2008), in the process cementing another of film music's most important character signifiers. And yet each of the *Indiana Jones* scores proved tonally diverse and distinct from the one that preceded it.

Whereas the *Raiders* score was underpinned with wrath of god portent centering around the Ark of the Covenant, follow-up *The Temple of Doom* (actually a prequel) deployed some of Williams' most intense action music. This was clearly an attempt to mirror the film's more cartoonish nature (the frenetic woodwind trills in "Mine Car Chase" are something to behold), and also to make up for the spiritual absence that had imbued Raiders with a genuine sense of awe. Chanting Sanskrit choir and frenetic writing for tabla drums lends a sense of eerie mystique to heart-ripping villain Mola Ram (Amrish Puri) and his Thuggee cult.

Said Spielberg: "*Indiana Jones and the Temple of Doom* is as much a replica of, as it is a departure from, *Raiders of the Lost Ark*.... We the audience take an unexpected detour to the far side of fear and fantasy. In this section of the adventure, all comforting themes vanish, and we become lost in the inner sanctums of The Temple of Doom with a secret voodoo cult thought extinct for over 100 years. This sinister setting offers [John Williams] leagues of musical opportunity, and he makes a feast of it in one of his best film scores ever."[50]

Spielberg added: "I am especially proud of John's 'Short Round's Theme' and the nightmare choral chant in The Temple of Doom. These particular sections of the score could be the only music in the world capable enough to knock the hat off Indiana Jones' head."[51]

By contrast, *The Last Crusade* is the warmest and most homely of all the scores, taking its central, noble "Holy Grail" theme and applying it to the real treasure: the relationship between Indy and his father Henry (Sean Connery). Spielberg praised the score for the way it emphasizes the emotional relationship between the two men "in a lyrical way without sentimentality."[52]

"John's music has always related in a kinetic fashion to the way I rhythmically pace my sequences," continued Spielberg.

> It gives the impression of one constant, adventurous trip. What is unique is that John's music rhythmically matches my action for almost 110 minutes and becomes a character in the story with as much importance as the heroes and the villains.
>
> What I think is different in many ways about this score is that only fragments of the familiar Indiana Jones theme are used. We felt the movies had grown up to the point that we didn't have to lean on your thrill button every time something heroic occurs as we had done in the previous two motion pictures.... John has outdone himself.... He gives new meaning to the phrase "audience involvement."[53]

Raiders of the Lost Ark, *The Temple of Doom* and *The Last Crusade* were Oscar nominated (losing, respectively, to Vangelis' *Chariots of Fire*, Maurice Jarre's *A Passage to India* and Alan Menken's *The Little Mermaid*). Williams' fourth Indiana Jones score, *The Kingdom of the Crystal Skull*, was more of a highlights reel, albeit a splendid one, of everything that had come before. The musical tapestry established by Williams is a treasure trove of interlocking themes and ideas, easily rivaling his work on the *Star Wars* saga. Even more significantly, the *Indiana Jones* scores inspired countless other 1980s family adventure soundtracks to drink from the same orchestral well.

Not that the reaction to Williams' compositions was always kind. In his review of *The Temple of Doom*, Variety critic Todd McCarthy disparaged the aural onslaught: "What with John Williams' incessant score and the library full of sound effects, there isn't a quiet moment in the entire picture, and the filmmakers have piled one giant set piece on top of another to the point where one never knows where it will all end."[54]

This is a criticism that has often been leveled at Spielberg and Williams. When does a score become too much? Certainly Spielberg has been accused of using music to galvanize, not just prop up, his narratives, leading many to wince at his alleged earnestness and sentimentality. It calls to mind Max Steiner's core philosophy, cited in Chapter Two, that a film score is easily over-written and over-emphasized, used as a crutch in lieu of poor storytelling and narrative contrivance.

Whatever one's feelings, the operatic majesty conjured by Spielberg and Williams for *E.T. the Extra-Terrestrial* (1982) remains a high watermark for the orchestral film soundtrack. Spielberg's deeply personal film is the story of lonely boy Elliott (Henry Thomas) and the endearing but stranded alien botanist with whom he bonds. It's a masterful example of Williams' ability to unlock profoundly human concerns within the realm of fantasy, the score largely ditching any overt musical allusions to the alien or the intergalactic.

Rather, the music crafts a bucolic, moving ode to friendship, tenets capable of spanning species boundaries across light years of time. The majestic final movement, titled "Adventures on Earth," is perhaps where Spielberg and Williams come closest to attaining a level of operatic purity—in fact, Spielberg edited the final 15 minutes of the film around Williams' score, an unusual move that speaks of implicit trust.

Craig Lysy writes: "Williams understood that the film is seen through a child's eyes, a fact reinforced by Spielberg's camera angles in shooting the film. He also understood that the film spoke to the bond formed between an alienated, grieving boy, and a young alien, stranded, and alone on a strange world. Through their friendship they are both healed and the music needed to speak to this for the film to succeed."[55]

Lysy continues: "[Williams] captures the mystery of the aliens, and the menace of sinister government agents. The use of the piccolo for the gentle and diminutive E.T. was also perfectly conceived. Lastly, the iconic 'Flying Theme' takes its place in the hallowed halls of the pantheon of legendary film score memories. In scene after scene Williams fleshes out the powerful emotions and drama unfolding on the screen. Iconic confluences of cinematography and music were achieved with the flying against the full moon, and flaming sun at sunset. The death scene and departure scenes offer testimony to Williams' mastery of his craft, and finally, the ending of the film may be the finest in cinematic history. This score is a masterpiece, one of the finest in Williams' canon, and an early Bronze Age gem."[56]

E.T. won Williams his third Oscar for Best Original Score, another flagpole in an illustrious career, and another totem of vibrant, orchestral beauty in an era largely seeking nostalgic cinematic comfort food. Away from the films of Spielberg and George Lucas, many other mass-market movies of the period resorted to clean-cut morality tales in which emotions were foregrounded, and good and evil clearly demarcated.

This encouraged a widespread resurgence of the orchestral tonality and phrasing that had been embedded in Hollywood since the early days, prized for its ability to guide (nay, manipulate) an audience's emotions. High-register strings would favor a sense of swooning romance while trumpets could mimic a call-to-arms, or an irresistible call to adventure. When narratives dipped their toe into darker material, the strings would dip down through their ranges, the brass giving way to trombones or horns, the woodwind section to bassoons and other instruments.

There's an emotional purity of expression to be found in a symphony orchestra—even if one cannot explain the impact, one can feel it deep in the synapses. Come the mid-1980s, the notion of the orchestral film score as a shortcut to an audience's feelings once again had strong currency.

One of the finest practitioners of such scores was James Horner. He arose out of Roger Corman B-movies such as *Battle Beyond the Stars* (1980), elevating trashy material with the kind of orchestral confidence that defied any sense of a limited musical budget. The galloping horns and trumpets on *Battle Beyond the Stars* owed a clear debt to the phrasing of *Star Wars*, but in Horner's own inimitable fashion. He would then translate this approach onto his first major career success, *Star Trek II: The Wrath of Khan* (1982).

Obviously, this was a score that drew on the legacy of a certain other sci-fi franchise, one that preceded *Star Wars* by a good few decades. For that reason, Horner was following in the footsteps of another illustrious composer, Jerry Goldsmith, whose wondrous, swirling score for 1979's *Star Trek: The Motion Picture* beautifully illustrated the concept of strange new worlds. (It also illustrated Alexander Courage's famous brass fanfare from the original TV series.) *The Wrath of Khan*, however, was different from its ponderous, cerebral predecessor, more akin to a swashbuckling adventure in space.

For that reason, while Horner's score honors Goldsmith's symphonic approach, tonally it sounds quite different. Horner substitutes Goldsmith's *Star Trek* theme for one of his own, decidedly more pumped up with a sense of brassy vigor as befitted Nicholas Meyer's acclaimed movie. *The Wrath of Khan* was fertile ground for Horner, its extended aerial effects sequences allowing the composer to unleash extended, balletic ebbs and flows of tension and catharsis ("The Battle in the Mutara Nebula" cue being a famous example).

"I decided this was the Navy in outer-space," recalled Meyer, "so everything got skewed towards that idea. So when I came to talk to [James Horner] about the music, I said, 'You have to think Debussy, *La Mer*—nautical but nice.' We were Gilbert and Sullivan—we understood each other very well."[57]

Horner sought to emphasize the deepening bond between William Shatner's Kirk and Leonard Nimoy's Spock. "I'm always looking for the core story, and that's what I narrate," he explained. "I wanted to tell the story of two men and their friendship and that's what I gleaned out of the series and out of the first movie. So the closer I could play that bond during the movie, the more I could make out of that bond separation, the more I could break the audience's heart at the end of the movie."[58]

Horner's penchant for sensitive introspection, as well as explosive set-pieces, meant he was well-placed to capitalize on this upsurge in family-friendly entertainment, veering between excitement and poignancy with ease. Empowered by the success of John Williams and *Star Wars*, he had many opportunities to paint on a multifaceted musical canvas.

Vanity Fair journalist Scott Beggs made the following observation in the wake of Horner's death in a plane crash in 2015: "The Oscar-winning film composer's work is so ingrained in our cultural memory that he will live on through each percussive trumpet blast and soaring woodwind swell. Before the word became so terribly overused, Horner's scores defined what it meant for a movie to be epic."[59]

"Yet he was also endlessly versatile," continues Beggs, "a dynamic composer who maintained a sure sense of what every scene needed to draw out and amplify its emotions. From Kate Winslet throwing her arms wide open on the bow of the Titanic to the crew of Apollo 13 engineering a space-age solution while gasping for air, Horner's music was a common element of making a cinematic moment into a memorable icon."[60]

Versatile was certainly the by-word for Horner. In 1986, he landed his first Oscar nomination for *Aliens*, his first collaboration with writer-director James Cameron (who, coincidentally, had worked as an effects designer on *Battle Beyond the Stars*). It was a brutal and humbling experience for the composer, the recording schedule compressed from six weeks into three at London's Abbey Road Studios, yielding multiple last-minute rewrites.[61]

One senses the collective frustrations being channeled into the tense tone of Horner's music, one of the most impressive militaristic action scores in Hollywood history that breaks out the assortment of snares, timpani, anvil and kettle drums. All the better to capture Ripley's (Sigourney Weaver) ongoing battle with the xenomorph.

That very same year, Horner also struck out into animation with *An*

American Tail. With Disney's fortunes waning at this point in time, many of the studio's ex-animators began to fill the vacuum with their own stories. Ex-Disney artist Don Bluth sought the services of Horner for this sweet story of a displaced Russian mouse looking for his family Stateside, and the composer responded with some fine, tender melodic writing, including the title song "Somewhere Out There."

In fact, animation often played to this particular composer's strengths. Rather than "Mickey Mouse" the on-screen action, Horner instead excelled at long-lined passages of musicality that played out over several minutes. This helped ensure a consistency of emotion, the music not breaking for regular intervals or haphazard key changes but instead gracefully supporting the overarching musical spine of a given sequence. Later scores such as *The Land Before Time* (1988), another Bluth production, demonstrated this beautifully, hitting a level of profundity that many other "surface level" animation scores lacked.

Towards the end of the decade, in 1989, Horner delivered two career-topping masterpieces that embodied the versatility of the film score as a medium. The first was his score for Edward Zwick's critically acclaimed American Civil War drama *Glory*, which dramatized the story of the all-black regiment, the 54th Massachusetts Infantry Regiment. Buoyed by Freddie Francis' cinematography and some fiercely committed performances, including an Oscar-winning Denzel Washington, the film gains added power and resonance from Horner's score.

Nominated for a Golden Globe, the *Glory* soundtrack deploys a haunting multitude of voices, both young and old, to suggest a lamentation for innocence lost. The film has the feel of an elegy, and Horner's score amplifies this feeling, deploying the Boys' Choir of Harlem, plus an additional adult ensemble, to further the connection with the black soldiers at the center of the story. Despite the film's title, there is no glory in its portrayal of conflict, just a lasting legacy of sadness tinged with nobility and resolve. The various choirs (heavily influenced by the works of Prokofiev) are put through a series of tonal and rhythmic changes, ranging from wistful to forcefully strident, to reflect the divisions and disruptions brought on by the appalling wartime scenario.

If *Glory* was an outward expression of emotion, Horner turned everything inwards to sublime effect with his other 1989 score. *Field of Dreams*, written and directed by Phil Alden Robinson, is the oft-quoted, dreamy story of an Iowa farmer (Kevin Costner) who is compelled by a disembodied voice to build a baseball pitch in his cornfield ("If you build it, he will come"). Part ghost story, part aw-shucks Americana fable, part story of father-son redemption, it's a deceptively complex movie that challenged Horner to compose one of his most distinctive works.

Never claiming to be a baseball fan, Horner mostly deployed eerie electronics, shakuhachi wood flute and a chamber-sized string ensemble, occasionally alternating with swing jazz and soft rock, to convey the steadily mounting realization of Costner's character as to his destiny. When it's all unveiled in the famously moving finale, Horner earns the right to unleash the full orchestra in a manner that's sentimental but never maudlin (a criticism that dogged him through his entire career). In the masterful track "The Place Where Dreams Come True," Horner transforms a story that is outwardly about baseball into something profoundly universal.

It was very likely this cue that garnered Horner an Oscar nomination, and trace elements of both *Glory* and *Field of Dreams* would arise in later Horner works. These included *Legends of the Fall* (1994), *Braveheart* (1995), *Apollo 13* (1995) and the Oscar-winning, chart-topping *Titanic* (1997), which remains the most successful orchestral soundtrack release of all time. (It has sold more than 26 million units worldwide.[62]) This was largely buoyed by the Oscar-winning closing title track "My Heart Will Go On," performed by Celine Dion, although the real musical heart of the film is Norwegian soprano Sissel who offers a haunting, melancholic lament for the victims of the Titanic disaster.

For a composer who had started the decade very much in thrall to John Williams, Horner emerged with his own distinct voice, one that would heavily influence the tone of dramatic blockbuster scores in the 1990s, particularly the new age-influenced *Titanic*. One can hear the lingering influence of Horner's score on many subsequent dramatic works, including sections of Howard Shore's *The Lord of the Rings* trilogy (particularly Enya's ethereal "May It Be" from 2001's *The Fellowship of the Ring*).

Many other composers of the period were heavily influenced by Williams while simultaneously emerging from his shadow. Backtracking to 1985, director Robert Zemeckis delivered a box office-busting hit in the form of *Back to the Future*. Developed by Zemeckis and co-writer Bob Gale, the movie posed an irresistible question: what if you could travel back in time, in a flying DeLorean no less, and rewrite the story of your mother and father's romance? The screwy set-up allowed Zemeckis to cross-reference both the 1980s and 1950s at once: the effects-laden philosophy of the former decade is melded with a nostalgic yearning for the latter, all seen through the eyes of plucky Marty McFly (Michael J. Fox in a career-defining performance).

For all its technological craziness, *Back to the Future* is, fundamentally, a very sweet story of friendship, anchored by the chemistry between Marty and DeLorean inventor Doc Brown (Christopher Lloyd). It's a movie that epitomizes the decade in which it was made, putting irreverent scenarios in the service of believable characters. It expands the imagination at the same time as it engages us with relatable concerns. On the soundtrack front, the movie scored extra publicity by being adorned with Huey Lewis and the News' "The Power of Love," the exuberant rock anthem now embraced the world over. However, it was a composer named Alan Silvestri who provided the true musical heart of the piece.

Zemeckis had first collaborated with Silvestri on action-comedy *Romancing the Stone* (1984) whose largely electronic score had not impressed *Back to the Future* executive Steven Spielberg. In fact, he wasn't sure if Silvestri was up to the job of scoring a movie such as this.[63] To quell Spielberg's doubts, Zemeckis told Silvestri to make the score as grand and expansive as possible, elevating the heroic dynamics of Marty and Doc. Interestingly, there were two variations of the score: when original Marty actor Eric Stoltz was on board, the initial musical approach leaned in a slightly darker direction.[64] However, Silvestri was later able to feed off the puppyish enthusiasm of Fox's portrayal, leading to a signature 1980s soundtrack that resonated with warmth.

Back to the Future is what's often described as a "themes and variations" score—as in, the backbone of the piece is dominated by one principal idea. This theme is then deconstructed, fragmented and scattered throughout the wider score, ensuring thematic continuity while reserving the fuller, more grandiose statements for key set-pieces. And what a theme it is: an opening horn fanfare leads into a robust orchestral performance that alternates rich brass with surging strings, approximating the feel of a frenzied, head-spinning trip through time.

However, it's the incredibly bustling and detailed orchestral make-up of the score that really dazzles. Celesta and tense strings anticipate the reveal of the immediately iconic DeLorean, low-register piano captures the menace of primary villain Biff (Thomas F. Wilson) and gentle, oboe-led variations on the main theme reinforce the sincerity of Marty and Doc's friendship. The interplay between honking tubas, prancing strings and prominently placed xylophones, conjures, appropriately enough, a fanciful and comic atmosphere, a harmonic language that is beautifully tailored to its respective movie, not least during the famously tense, closing clock tower sequence.

So good was Silvestri's score that Spielberg, upon hearing an early suite, assumed it was the temp track.[65] (This describes the music cues that are placed onto the initial edit of the movie, usually by the director and editor, to ostensibly aid the scoring process.) However, it was, in fact, Silvestri's own material, and it helped define the movie. The composer's profile was boosted enormously when the film rose to grosses of more than

$300 million worldwide (the biggest hit of the year), scoring an Oscar nomination for Best Original Screenplay in the process.

This is the sort of exposure that film composers crave when seeking to crack the Hollywood market. *Back to the Future*'s success established Silvestri's place in the ensuing trilogy, not to mention the distinct rhythmic meters and tones of acclaimed works including *Predator* (1987) and *The Abyss* (1989). *Back to the Future: Part II*, released in 1989, is a somewhat tense and bleak affair, dealing with the ramifications of an alternate 1985. However, *Part III* (1990) is set in the Wild West, allowing Silvestri to unleash his joyous Elmer Bernstein and Jerome Moross pastiche.

It's a clear sign of how the musicality of certain franchises can hit a multifaceted and varied range of tones. And yet, it would be remiss to suggest that only orchestral scores held sway during this period. For sure, there were overt John Williams pastiches, including Craig Safan's *The Last Starfighter* (1984), Bruce Broughton's *Young Sherlock Holmes* (1985) and Bill Conti's *Masters of the Universe* (1987). Earlier in the decade, Basil Poledouris conducted extensive research on European speciality instrumentation and folk music for *Conan the Barbarian* (1982), a thunderous interlocking of Wagnerian motifs that carves out a distinct tone amidst all the Williams imitators of the period. But the 1980s was also a time of great experimentation.

Jerry Goldsmith's burgeoning love of synths (including new-fangled Yamaha technology) saw electronics mixed with orchestra in intriguing ways. The zany tone of *Gremlins* (1984) and *The 'burbs* (1989), both composed for director Joe Dante, used synthesizers to approximate the sound of wailing cats, among other things, breaking the rule of Elmer Bernstein's *Airplane!* (1980) that comedy scores are best played straight. Goldsmith's crossover work in this decade anticipated his more sophisticated streamlining of the organic and the electronic in 1990s scores such as *Medicine Man* (1992).

Elsewhere, pop artists such as the aforementioned Giorgio Moroder and Tangerine Dream were being sought for their eerie approximation of tone and mood, rather than melody. The latter's work on William Friedkin's *Sorcerer* (1977) and Kathryn Bigelow's vampire-western *Near Dark* (1987) carved out distinct soundscapes of buzzing, humming and thrumming electronics that quietly sawed away at the nerves.

Another landmark synth score of the 1980s was Brad Fiedel's work on *The Terminator* (1984). James Cameron's nightmarish vision saw a humanoid cyborg (an unforgettable Arnold Schwarzenegger) being sent back through time to eliminate Sarah Connor (Linda Hamilton), the mother of the human race's savior. The movie birthed a subgenre of sci-fi known colloquially as "Tech Noir" (named after a nightclub featured in the film), locating fantastical concepts and time loops in recognizably grungy, neon-lit environments.

Made on a shoestring budget, *The Terminator* proved to be a hugely profitable hit for a multitude of reasons, including Stan Winston's unforgettably gruesome and believable make-up effects. And Fiedel's score does an important job in establishing a forbidding atmosphere of dread, most famously with its off-kilter time signature in the main theme.

"It was unusual in the way that I wrote it," Fiedel recalled, "but it became even more unusual, because it was all a little experiment that I literally did the day after I saw the film."

> Jim and [producer] Gale Ann Hurd had come to see me in my studio, and I started working on it the next day. I pretty much wrote the main theme on the piano, but then started to play... "Well, how do I get this metallic heartbeat?" The technology at that point was limited. It wasn't all MIDI, where you can just tie together ... you can do it all on your laptop now. Back then, it was individual keyboards.
>
> Some of them did have internal rhythm clocks, or the Prophet-10 that has that main "ba-bong-a-bong-a-bong-a-bon-BOM!," that part, was on a little tape loop inside the keyboard, and it didn't quantize—which means it was just a manual thing where you played something, you hit stop and the thing that made the time signature particularly weird is that I'd hit stop on that machine at less than perfect completion of the loop. So I thought, "I didn't hit that right." Then I'm listening to it and I think, "I love that." Because it's kind of falling forward—it's a machine, but it's not a perfect tick-tock clock. It kind of goes "tu-tuh-tu-ta-kah," you know? I thought that Jim's main objective was to just keep the film moving. So it was a combination of those wonderful mistakes that make things work.[66]

Fiedel's association with the series continued with 1991 blockbuster sequel *Terminator 2: Judgment Day*, which broke new ground with its liquid-metal CGI effects for the evil T-1000 (Robert Patrick). In this instance, the theme was heroically expanded into an orchestral realm with ghostly, ethereal voices, while organic, grinding sounds capture the menace of Patrick's villain.

In the 1980s, synths were very much in vogue to capture a sense of "otherness," a sense of alienation or disconnect from the world as we know it. John Carpenter's low-budget *Escape from New York* (1981) is just such an example, drawing on the tone of his earlier electronic slasher score *Halloween* (1978) and establishing a palette that would later be extended in the likes of *They Live* (1988).[67] For 1982's *The Thing*, arguably the director's masterpiece, Carpenter augmented Ennio Morricone's icy orchestral score with additional synth pulses and hums to bottle the dread of an alien creature that disguises itself within other people.

Four. Allegro

Electronic alienation was also at the forefront in Vangelis' score for *Blade Runner*, also composed in 1982. Ridley Scott's adaptation of Philip K. Dick's novel *Do Androids Dream of Electric Sheep?* broke new ground with its awe-inspiring vision of 2019 Los Angeles, cloaked in neon, acid rain, glittering buildings and chimneys belting jets of fire. The movie's detached sensibility, as seen through the eyes of Harrison Ford's android hunter Deckard, challenges us to the nature of what makes us human. Or, to quote the motto of the film's Tyrell Corporation, "more human than human."

Step forward one-time Yes member and electronic pioneer Vangelis, who'd already scored an Oscar in 1981 for his iconic, hopeful theme to *Chariots of Fire*. The optimism of that score is replaced in *Blade Runner* with a much more challenging and, frankly, interesting collision of sounds, conveying the notion of organic human emotion as pitted against a faceless, monolithic human society.

Piercing synth drones are juxtaposed with sultry saxophone solos and jazzy piano, the more humanistic organic elements warring with the processed and manipulated sounds. The score embodies the themes of the movie, with the climactic death of android Roy Batty (Rutger Hauer) set to a yearningly beautiful synth piece that speaks of his relative humanity when compared to the cold, closed-off Deckard. The latter's existence as either a replicant or human has been called into question throughout the various edits of *Blade Runner*, and Vangelis' score mines that sense of disquiet.

It is, perhaps, heartening, to come full circle and perceive the influence of pioneering composers like Wendy Carlos. In a period largely dominated by the influence of John Williams, there continued to be a multitude of alternative voices and approaches, all advancing the notion of the film score in line with technological breakthroughs. In the coming decades, the boundaries between organic sound and artificial enhancement would become increasingly blurred—for better or worse.

Five

Atonal

The Role of Film Music in the Era of Franchising

"I've seen a lot of films that I've loved that haven't used the orchestra. I can get the same feeling out of the first *Atlantic* album by Aretha Franklin. That's as much a work of art as Beethoven's *Fifth*. I can't see the difference. Different types of music can create the same feeling. That feeling of transcendence."—JOHN POWELL[1]

Blockbuster Scoring and Indie Artistry in the 1990s

The start of the 1990s saw a splintering of film music across a variety of areas. This would prove to be a complex decade for movies, veering between tried and tested populism and some genuinely bracing, not to mention controversial, new voices. And, of course, the diversification in terms of cinematic representation extended to the sheer range of musical approaches.

On the one level, there was a wholesale continuation of the trends that had proved so popular in the 1980s: grandiose symphonic storytelling that placed thrilling bombast and uplifting emotion at the center of some effective (and not so effective) narratives. Running in parallel with this was a bold new approach towards pop and rock music within the indie realm. Rising directors were able to put new, and often startling, spins on some evergreen classics.

The 1990s also saw the development of a new kind of hybrid score. Neither completely orchestral nor wholly synthesized, this organic-processed blend would very swiftly become standardized within the action and thriller genres. In the coming decades, many would claim that this is where the film score began something of a decline, overly reliant on artificial techniques and enhanced volume at the expense of nuance or memorable ideas.

To begin with, however, the 1990s started on a profoundly beautiful crescendo of emotion, courtesy of the revivified Walt Disney Animation Studios. The company had seen its fortunes waning throughout the 1970s and most of the 1980s, courtesy of misfiring attempts like *The Black Cauldron* (1985), scored, to portentous effect, by Elmer Bernstein. But in 1989, a joyous movie about a mermaid seeking human contact would crash onto the big screen, setting in motion important musical trends throughout the entirety of the ensuing decade, and beyond.

The Little Mermaid, inspired by the Hans Christian Andersen fairy tale of the same name, would prove to be Disney's biggest hit in decades. Perhaps comparable to *Star Wars*, the film unashamedly embraced feel-good, moralistic storytelling, putting its big-hearted characters in the service of eye-popping, pastel-colored animation from directors Ron Clements and Jon Musker. The film tells the story of Ariel (voiced by Jodi Benson), a flame-haired denizen of the deep who falls in love with Prince Eric (Christopher Daniel Barnes), her wish to become human facilitated by the scheming witch Ursula (Pat Carroll).

By fusing tender romance with cackling villainy and incipient heroism, it's little wonder that *The Little Mermaid* made a splash with grosses of $233 million against a $40 million budget. The soundtrack would prove to be another hugely significant factor in the film's success. In fact, many have retrospectively pointed to the work of composer Alan Menken and lyricist Howard Ashman as being primarily responsible for the so-called "Disney renaissance," defined as the wave of glossy, slickly produced and exuberantly scored Disney animated blockbusters that restored the studio's credibility.

Both men were Broadway veterans, having collaborated on the likes of *Little Shop of Horrors*, and they were able to bring that exuberant, oversized, theatrical approach when the badly flagging Disney needed it the most. At the time of the film's 30th anniversary, Menken recalled the moment when the soundtrack took shape for the first time: "[Ashman and I] were always in the same room. In the case of *The Little Mermaid*, it was looking at classic Disney in the vocabulary. Once Howard had the idea that we should make Sebastian not a stuffy English crab, but a Caribbean crab, that opened up a treasure trove of possible stylistic influences and calypso and reggae informed a lot of the storytelling. And then for Chef Louis, a little bit of French musical, but it was all very specific musical vocabulary that we drew from."[2]

The overall soundtrack threads together the songs with Menken's underscore melodies. The movie launched immediately recognizable tunes on an unsuspecting audience including the jaunty, calypso inspired "Under the Sea" and "Kiss the Girl" (both performed by Samuel E. Wright, voicing Sebastian), and booming villain's piece "Poor Unfortunate Souls" (delivered with relish by Carroll). For the first time in decades, perhaps since 1967's *The Jungle Book*, a Disney movie was empowered by songs that not only supported the narrative but acted as its primary selling point. Even so, the construction of the soundtrack was, occasionally, a fraught one, particularly when the film faced the dreaded test screenings.

"We were finding that when [the film] got to 'Part of Your World,' there was a lot of restlessness and squirming," recalled Menken. "Clearly, it was not holding [the audience] and [producer Jeffrey Katzenberg] said, 'Well, look, we should just lose that song.' And Howard knew that song was a huge tentpole for the kind of projects we wanted to be writing for Disney. You have to have dramatic tension, and so once we put in that Ariel was being witnessed by Sebastian, then that held the audience and saved us from losing the number. To not have her inner journey expressed in song really robbed it of being a legitimate musical. We fought Jeffrey on that and Jeffrey is a very smart man and said 'OK, try it,' and it worked."[3]

Regardless of the incidental travails, both Menken and Ashman would scoop Oscars for their work on *The Little Mermaid*, one for Best Original Score and the other for Best Original Song ("Under the Sea"). It was the first artistic success for Disney's music department (or any such department for that matter) in years, establishing the two men as trailblazers in the field of animated storytelling.

Sadly, the partnership wasn't to last. Midway through the production of 1991's *Beauty and the Beast,* Ashman passed away. Although he died before the completion of the soundtrack and the release of the film, Ashman was able to imprint his personality on the songs, most of which went on to enjoy the same levels of critical acclaim and commercial success as those featured in *The Little Mermaid*.

Given the fairy tale longing of *Beauty and the Beast*'s narrative, Menken and Ashman's work took on a decidedly more yearning quality, deviating every now and then into those showboating, show-stopping numbers that had swiftly become their stock in trade. These included the boisterous "Be Our Guest," led by candelabra Lumière (Jerry Orbach), a reprise of the Broadway aesthetic that had propelled *The Little Mermaid* to success. There is a tonal contrast of sorts when one reaches the soaring title track, which cements the love affair between bookish Belle (Paige O'Hara) and the outwardly monstrous yet inwardly compassionate Beast (Robby Benson).

Reminiscing on the soundtrack, Menken explained: "I am sure that emotion informed what we did. We worked with a palette of French and classical and Broadway music and it was a culmination of a certain kind of emotion for us. Also all these projects we do—whether it is *The Little*

Mermaid or *Beauty and the Beast* or *Aladdin*—are homages. This one is an homage to the most romantic parts of the Disney canon. Maybe I was channelling something special I don't know, but it was clearly romantic and timeless and I credit Howard with a lot of what we came up with."[4]

Menken's audience-pleasing winning streak was further cemented with three separate Oscar nominations for Best Original Song. "Be Our Guest," "Belle" and "Beauty and the Beast" were all recognized, with the last of those (performed in the film by Angela Lansbury as Mrs. Potts) translating into an Oscar win. Additionally, Menken won his second Oscar for Best Original score, recognition for the intricacy with which he stitched together both the song melodies and standalone orchestral compositions (including the tear-jerkingly powerful transformation finale).

Beauty and the Beast made history as the first animated film to be Oscar nominated for Best Picture. (The category for Best Animated Feature Film wouldn't be established until 2001, with *Shrek* claiming the Oscar.) One imagines that Menken and Ashman's contribution had a lot to do with that: the soundtrack not just underlines the emotional integrity of the story but consciously adds further layers of emotion, amplifying the story's inherent themes and plucking the heartstrings of the audience. The unashamedly fulsome nature of these new Disney soundtracks proved one thing absolute: the art of operatic musical storytelling was again being embraced by filmmakers, critics and audiences alike, a continuation of the principle that had been re-ignited by John Williams and *Star Wars*.

Menken's winning streak continued with 1992's *Aladdin*, a Disney blockbuster that allowed the late, lamented Robin Williams to let rip as the Genie. In lieu of Ashman, who was involved early in the production before his death, Menken turned to lyricist Tim Rice to absorb a different kind of musical atmosphere: that of the Middle East. Exotic woodwinds including the duduk, plus percussion and location-specific instruments such as the oud, conjure a bewitching atmosphere of magic and enchantment, perfectly suited to the story of the street urchin Aladdin (Scott Weinger) turned imitation prince via the power of the lamp.

Naturally songs would play a prominent role, variously authentic and anachronistic to capture the film's complex mixture of archaic Middle Eastern atmosphere and Williams' distinctly 20th-century comic riffing. Directors John Clements and Ron Musker had already established a strong working relationship with Menken on *The Little Mermaid*, although *Aladdin* went through a somewhat convoluted production process on the way towards the big screen.

"Howard and I were developing *Aladdin* while we were doing *The Little Mermaid*," explained Menken. "And then also, Howard's illness played into this period. Then, *Beauty and the Beast* kind of inserted itself, if I remember. Essentially, we developed [*Aladdin*], it was shelved, and then before *Beauty and the Beast* was done, it resumed. We had had such a great experience working with John and Ron, that we continued our collaboration."[5]

Clements and Musker expanded on Ashman's original musical treatment, after rejecting a song-free draft from screenwriter Linda Woolverton. "I guess you'd say there were three versions of *Aladdin*," Musker explained. "There was Howard's original version. Then, there was our first version, which included songs that are in the movie now, like 'Arabian Nights' and 'Friend Like Me.' And it included 'Proud of Your Boy,' which we really loved, [about] Aladdin's relationship with his mother."[6]

For all the energy and exuberance present in the music, the process of its creation was underscored with a profound sense of sobriety. Of the rousing "Prince Ali," Menken recalled: "It was actually written, sadly, on Howard's hospital bed. He was at St. Luke's. I brought him a keyboard and we were writing. And there was one other song that got cut. It was Howard's last song, pretty much, called 'Humiliate the Boy.'"[7]

The latter song, written for sneering villain Jafar (Jonathan Freeman), was ultimately cut from the movie. However, one can clearly sense Ashman's imprint resonating throughout every note of the finished soundtrack. Menken won his third Best Original Score Oscar and his third, shared with Tim Rice, for Best Original Song ("A Whole New World," the magic carpet ballad performed as a duet by Brad Kane and Lea Salonga, who provided the singing voices of Aladdin and Princess Jasmine). The film was boosted to enormous box office returns of more than $500 million worldwide against a $28 million budget.

Once again, the cyclical relationship between moving image and accompanying music reared its head: the success of *Aladdin* raised the profile of the soundtrack enormously, but one also senses that Menken's and Ashman's imprimatur was one of the key reasons for the film's world-conquering success in the first place. By this stage, the Disney soundtrack had become newly emboldened, almost a cottage industry on its own terms, capable of influencing and shaping a film's narrative, right from the earliest stages of production.

In many ways, the standard for 1990s orchestral film scores was set by the jubilant, unashamedly crowd-pleasing tone of these Disney works. As popcorn blockbuster concepts became more outlandish, necessitating extraordinary visual effects breakthroughs in the process, orchestral film scores were encouraged to paint with bold colors. The decade birthed a host of groundbreaking action and fantasy movies, meaning that the respective composers had a significant advantage in painting with the dynamic range of the symphony orchestra.

Once again, the enduring stylistics of John Williams (and, by extension, Erich Wolfgang Korngold), proved hard to shake off. It seemed that optimistic, major key phrasing and tonality in classical film scoring carried a sense of latent nostalgia. Indeed, it's oddly comforting witnessing a new movie release being contextualized in the form of the old and the familiar, especially as far as film scoring is concerned.

Few scores of the mid–1990s embody this philosophy more effectively than *Cutthroat Island*. Composed by John Debney for the film of the same name, its swashbuckling sense of rip-roaring action is intended as a blatant yet loving homage to the pirate genre that Korngold defined. As with all professional film scorers, Debney takes his lead directly from the movie itself, a somewhat creaky and hokey treasure chest of every nautical movie cliché one can think of. However the film, directed by Renny Harlin and starring his then-wife, Geena Davis, proved to be a disastrous flop and near-enough bankrupted its studio, Carolco.

One of the few to emerge from the flotsam and jetsam with his dignity intact was Debney. He is a chameleonic composer, adept at absorbing the styles of his predecessors and contemporaries (see, for example, his work on 2016's remake of *The Jungle Book*, assimilating the tone of original composer George Bruns). And his full-throttle approximation of Korngold's style reminded audiences of one thing: pirate film scores can be spectacularly entertaining, even when the film itself fails to meet the basic standards of entertainment.

At the same time, the intensity of the orchestration and performance (the score was performed by the London Symphony Orchestra) showcases a level of sophistication in line with modern scoring techniques. It's a much more aggressive and relentless score than anything Korngold would have put forward, necessitated, perhaps, by the film's frequent lapses in acting quality and narrative logic. There's nothing quite like an excellent film soundtrack to paper over the gaps of a bad movie.

Film score critic Christian Clemmensen notes the forthright performance of the ensemble, augmented by the stirring sound of the London Voices choir. "Part of the recording's success is owed to the phenomenally athletic performance by the London performers," he writes. "Only John Williams (and perhaps James Horner on a rare occasion) could work out this ensemble to such an ambitious level. Precise orchestrations led by Brad Dechter and even more precise performances by the group offer a resilient power that never yields in the score's major statements. The percussion section earns significant kudos; the performer on the cymbals alone must have been on his or her toes during the entire process."[8]

The application of heraldic brass, particularly in the trumpet section, to suggest a schooner or pirate ship scything through the high seas has been imprinted on the emotions of film fans since the earliest days of Hollywood. In fact, this principle has often leached through to other genres: Jerry Goldsmith was forced to rework his original theme for *Star Trek: The Motion Picture* after director Robert Wise complained that it evoked "sailing ships."[9] Bearing this heritage in mind, Debney's work is a successful fusion of age-old stylistic principles and distinctly modernistic underpinnings. It's Korngold taken to the nth degree: a score that openly acknowledges an audience's knowledge, no matter how passing, of pirate soundtrack conventions, amplifying them to give the badly flagging movie the shot in the arm it needs.

The large-scale orchestral soundtrack was also showcased in 1996 alien invasion epic *Independence Day*, scored by David Arnold (who, coincidentally, was involved with *Cutthroat Island* at an early stage). The film, directed by Roland Emmerich, repackaged creaky 1950s sci-fi tropes in a slick new vision for the 1990s crowd, replete with awe-inspiring practical and visual effects that pushed the boundaries of blockbuster technique.

For all of its scenes of apocalyptic devastation and city-sized spaceships (spare a thought for stars Will Smith, Bill Pullman and Jeff Goldblum, trying to valiantly project against the visual effects onslaught), the movie is, fundamentally, extremely old-fashioned. The morality of the film couldn't be clearer: plucky humans versus technologically advanced and marauding extra-terrestrials, a set-up that initiates age-old themes of underdog bravado against impossible odds. It was a concept that fired the imagination of eager young British composer Arnold, whose first collaboration with Emmerich was 1994's *Stargate*.

Independence Day is not a vehicle for subtlety, but that can often prove a boon to a film composer, allowing the individual to compose on a lavish scale. Upon hearing Arnold's unashamedly brassy and energetic score for the first time, producer and co-writer Dean Devlin wryly observed: "You can leave it up to a Brit to write some of the most rousing and patriotic music in the history of American cinema."[10] And yet, it was the familiarity of Arnold's melodic and harmonic choices that proved successful: as a film, *Independence Day* grapples with a fiendish threat from the other side of the galaxy, but the tone of the score is a classic swashbuckler, reminiscent of the aforementioned Errol Flynn/Erich Wolfgang Korngold movies from the 1940s. (One track on the album is even called "Jolly Roger," furthering the comparison.)

There is a grounding sense of relatable humanity in the music that transforms an outlandish concept into one that the audience can perceive emotionally. The opening of the film shows the American flag on the moon, rendered in homely patriotic trumpet tones (courtesy of noted player, and movie regular, Malcolm McNab). It creates an immediate association of human triumph. This is then undercut by the double-bass, trombone and, eventually, choir of the overpowering alien music—a classic example of how major and minor key configurations in scoring can sketch a battle of good versus evil. It's not original, but it's almost always effective.

The use of the triumphant brass, reinforcing the David versus Goliath pluck of the human characters, is deployed without irony, even during the oft-mocked speech by Pullman's President Whitmore. As with the movie, the score invites listeners to plant tongue firmly in cheek, perfectly evoking the outsized emotions of old-school Hollywood epics. *Independence Day* ultimately soared to global grosses of more than $800 million, the highest-grossing movie release of 1996, and it's not hard to imagine that its easy-to-digest sense of triumphalism was responsible, Arnold's music included. The score was nominated for a Grammy and set Arnold's Hollywood career in motion.

The following year, Arnold came on board one of the most enduring of all franchises: *James Bond*. The 007 series had been newly revived in the post–Cold War period with *GoldenEye* (1995), the first movie starring Pierce Brosnan as Bond, and in the process had absorbed the glossy, post–MTV visual aesthetic that typified many 1990s blockbusters (including the likes of Michael Bay's *Bad Boys*, also 1995, and *The Rock*, released in 1996). Yet, for all *GoldenEye*'s critical and commercial success, its score from French composer Eric Serra, largely reliant on echoing metallic percussion and synths, was considered out-of-kilter with the style of the series.

For 1997's *Tomorrow Never Dies*, a hybrid model was proposed, one that would fuse the romanticism of series veteran John Barry with the propulsive modernism of a hip young 1990s composer. Arnold got the gig after impressing producers Michael G. Wilson and Barbara Broccoli with his album of Bond cover themes, *Shaken and Stirred: The David Arnold James Bond Project*. This included a swaggering cover of *On Her Majesty's Secret Service* (1969) with electro group The Propellerheads (later to feature in 1999's *The Matrix*). The project also impressed Barry himself: "[David Arnold] was very faithful to the melodic and harmonic content, but he's added a whole other rhythmic freshness and some interesting casting in terms of the artists chosen to do the songs. I think it's a terrific album. I'm very flattered."[11]

Arnold's assured mixing of a throbbing techno beat with jazzy piano and the familiar Barry horn blasts (present in rollicking cues like "Backseat Driver") arrested the attention with its blend of the old and the familiar. These stylistics would be maintained throughout the remainder of Arnold's Bond scores for Pierce Brosnan: both *The World Is Not Enough* (1999) and *Die Another Day* (2002) became increasingly reliant on synth pads and textured sounds, occasionally alternating with languid, string-based love themes. Arnold's two scores for Daniel Craig's acclaimed iteration of 007, *Casino Royale* (2006) and *Quantum of Solace* (2008), deployed electronics relatively more sparingly, relying more on the organic weight of the orchestra to convey a more human, fallible and nuanced Bond compared to Brosnan's coiffured performance.

That said, it wasn't all plain sailing for Arnold on *Tomorrow Never Dies*. As ever, the corporate Hollywood machine butted heads with artistic creativity as the composer's proposed title track "Surrender," performed by k.d. lang, was relegated to the end credits. (Hence, why its sultry brass melody is interpolated into the majority of Arnold's underscore.)[12] In its place came Sheryl Crow's functionally effective "Tomorrow Never Dies," a track that lacked the sensual menace of lang's performance.

Such battles were hardly new in Hollywood (John Barry and original Bond producer Harry Saltzman locked horns in 1964 over 'Goldfinger,' performed by Shirley Bassey), but, increasingly, franchise owners and stakeholders had more of a vested interest in the role of music. As the 21st century beckoned, composers would have to undertake an increasingly complex high-wire act, all the while honoring their own impulses, those of the director and those of the corporate behemoths lurking in the background.

The 1990s proved to be a fertile period for action scores, both in terms of franchising and on an individual basis. At the very start of the decade, the ubiquitous Jerry Goldsmith delivered a genre-defining work in the form of *Total Recall* (1990), his first score for controversial Dutch director Paul Verhoeven who had previously collaborated with Basil Poledouris to successful effect (on 1985's *Flesh+Blood* and 1987's *RoboCop*).

The film is loosely adapted from Philip K. Dick's story "We Can Remember It for You, Wholesale." It stars Arnold Schwarzenegger as one of two things: either a construction worker who reawakens memories of his former life as a secret agent on Mars, or a man experiencing a particularly lucid dream. The movie's trippy premise yielded one of Goldsmith's crowning achievements, pushing the boundaries of orchestral and synthetic innovation like never before, putting the musicians through their paces with a barrage of relentless musical set-pieces that befitted the propulsively violent nature of the movie. At the same time, awe-inspiring synths warp the notion of what is real and what is imagined.

Total Recall's album producer Robert Townson notes the intensity of the score's recording process: "In a failed attempt to save money, the studio had insisted on recording the score in Munich. However, after four days of unproductive work with the Munich musicians, the plug was pulled. Goldsmith and his recording team moved onto London and, instead, recorded with Sidney Sax's National Philharmonic Orchestra, an orchestra much more familiar with the composer, and much more prepared for the demands that this score would place on its musicians."[13]

Goldsmith's collaboration with Verhoeven only ran to three movies (concluding with *Hollow Man* in 2000), but it was a productive and fruitful one. If *Total Recall* set the standard for 1990s action/fantasy/sci-fi scores, then *Basic Instinct* (1992) reset the bar for the erotic thriller soundtrack in the wake of John Barry's *Body Heat* (1981). The enormously controversial movie paired Michael Douglas with Sharon Stone for an overwrought, steamy story of a troubled cop's relationship with a crime writer who may or may not be a devious, ice pick-wielding serial killer.

Filled to the brim with Verhoeven's signature provocation, violence and sexuality, the movie shot to box office success. It also proved to be an especially challenging assignment for Goldsmith, Verhoeven pushing the composer to elicit a pitch-perfect tone for the story. The silky-smooth strings and icy woodwind arrangements, present in the main theme and the incidental cues, capture both the alluring beauty and latent menace of Stone's character Catherine Tramell, combining the classic sound of Bernard Herrmann with Goldsmith's signature mannerisms.

"It took us forever to find the main theme," Verhoeven recalled. "I think we spent a month going back and forward between all kinds of possibilities, and we could never settle for something that pleased me. It drove him crazy, I think. One day, [Goldsmith] came up with a little part for a certain scene where it didn't work but I suddenly thought, perhaps it works for another scene. We put it there and it worked and from there on he could write the score in one run. There were never any problems any more, it was just the tone of the music that was difficult to find, this kind of threat and this kind of charming, seductive tone that is, of course, the character of Sharon Stone."[14] The struggle was worth it: Goldsmith was Oscar-nominated for his efforts (losing to the aforementioned *Aladdin*).

Elsewhere, another director-composer partnership was producing similarly extraordinary results. In 1993, Steven Spielberg and John Williams delivered the remarkable double-whammy of *Jurassic Park* and *Schindler's List*, a microcosm of the sheer versatility required from film composers. The former became the highest-grossing movie of all time on its release, surpassing Spielberg's own *E.T. The Extra-Terrestrial* and breaking new ground with its CGI dinosaur effects mixed with lifelike animatronics (from creature effects veteran Stan Winston).

Jurassic Park yielded an especially rich score from Williams, showcasing not one but two themes: a pastoral theme for the creatures and a rip-roaring brass melody for the spirit of adventure. At the same time, the growling, near-atonal music for the dreaded velociraptors calls back to

Williams' work on *Close Encounters of the Third Kind* (1977), while also anticipating his darker, more aggressive writing to come in the later likes of Oliver Stone's *Nixon* (1995).

If *Jurassic Park* leaned into the popcorn fantasy side of the Spielberg-Williams brand (not exactly a surprise by this point), *Schindler's List* showcased a transition to assured artistic maturity. The film dramatized businessman Oskar Schindler's (Liam Neeson) rescue of 1,000 Jews from Nazi occupation during World War II and won Spielberg the artistic acclaim he had coveted for so long, including Oscars for Best Picture and Best Director (Spielberg's first awards in both categories). Shot in documentarian black and white, using largely hand-held camerawork from Janusz Kamiński, *Schindler's List* showed remarkable restraint from a director notorious for his earnestness (at least until the misjudged climax).

For his score, Williams similarly relied on sparing yet deeply affecting instrumental techniques, using the keening solo violin of the noted Itzhak Perlman to act the voice of Jewish anguish and remembrance. The score leans heavily on Jewish folk tradition and tonality and remains arguably Williams' most effective dramatic work (or, at the very least, his best since 1970's *Jane Eyre*). Interestingly, Williams expressed reservations about scoring the film, initially telling Spielberg that he needed a far better composer to do the narrative justice. "I know," Spielberg replied, "but they're all dead."[15]

Williams' concerns were unwarranted: he won his third Oscar for Best Original Score, delivering what many consider to be his crowning artistic masterpiece. It augured a change in tone as far as his works for Spielberg were concerned: World War II drama *Saving Private Ryan* (1998), for example, favored careful spotting (there's no music in the battle sequences), dirge-like bass sonorities and stunning choral requiems ("Hymn to the Fallen") to instill a sense of somber reflection. And yet, it wasn't just old hands like Williams and Jerry Goldsmith who were pushing the boundaries during this decade.

One of the most striking and influential scores of the period was *Alien³* (1992), composed by Elliot Goldenthal. Following Jerry Goldsmith's trend-setting *Alien* score in 1979 and James Horner's militaristic *Aliens* in 1986, the musical tone of the franchise was destined to change again. David Fincher's gloomy, controversial directorial debut, beset by production interference, plays it heavy with the religious imagery and violence, all the while coaxing a career-best from Sigourney Weaver as the haunted Ripley.

Goldenthal's breakout score proved to be a shock for unsuspecting listeners, pushing the brass and string sections to animalistic, atonal extremes, intentionally blurring the lines between music and sound. At the same time, Goldenthal cuts loose with some stunningly beautiful string and choral arias that capture Ripley's tragic connection to the xenomorph that has defined her life. The score's mixture of savage violence and melancholic despair was, Goldenthal explained, directly influenced by the Los Angeles Rodney King race riots that were occurring as the soundtrack was being recorded.[16] The composer described the score as a year-long experiment,[17] one that mutated and changed repeatedly in line with the chaotic and turbulent production.

Despite the critical and commercial failure of the movie, Goldenthal arrested the attention with his signature musical voice. His characteristic orchestral brutalism was carried into 1994's *Interview with the Vampire*, directed by Neil Jordan, where the harsher textures mixed with renaissance instruments including the viola da gamba.[18] In fact, Goldenthal replaced original composer George Fenton, suggesting that the producers were actively seeking a uniquely modernistic approach from a breakout new composer.

Goldenthal was Oscar nominated, although his musical apex was, arguably, for the 1999 Shakespeare adaptation *Titus*, directed by his partner, Julie Taymor. The mayhem of *Alien³* met a whole host of jazz and pop techniques befitting the anachronistic approach of the movie (it blends Shakespeare's words with modern props like cars and microphones). It embodies Goldenthal's signature philosophy: that of music as a violent collision of ideals, pulling in all manner of directions but centrally held together by a unique voice.

Another of the decade's most idiosyncratic musicians was Thomas Newman. As mentioned in Chapter Two, Newman is the son of the revered Alfred, but whereas his father defined a bedrock of Hollywood musical principles, the younger Newman struck out in decidedly original directions. Broadly speaking, he fuses a lushly pastoral approach, particularly favoring delicacy in the oboe and string sections, with bracing experimentalism that meshes a whole host of speciality instruments. Some of his most acclaimed 1990s scores include *The Shawshank Redemption* and *Little Women* (both 1994, and both Oscar-nominated), but his score for 1999's *American Beauty* proved to be his most enduringly influential work.

The directorial debut of Sam Mendes, *American Beauty* was scripted, to memorably dyspeptic and piercing effect, by Alan Ball. It's narrated from the afterlife by Kevin Spacey's disaffected suburbanite Lester Burnham, taking the satirical hatchet to crushing conformity and the curdled notion of the American dream. Mendes' confident direction, with its emphasis on blood-red hues and roses, clearly demanded a score that was somewhat unorthodox. Newman duly responded with a soundtrack that amalgamated the percussive touches of his prior scores, including *The*

Shawshank Redemption, cleverly giving a spiky, rebellious inner life to Lester even as his outer existence remains composed, even stultifying.

Detuned mandolin, marimba, tabla drum, xylophone, glockenspiel—these are just some of the instruments that give the *American Beauty* score its arrestingly resonant atmosphere.[19] Sitting alongside this is the dreamily expressive "Plastic Bag" theme for piano, which builds to the final moment of moving catharsis as Lester finally appreciates the sum total of his apparently pointless life. The very oddness of *American Beauty* saw Newman awarded with an Oscar nomination, but, as ever, its greatest influence was felt in the years that followed.

Only a certain number of film scores can claim to have been covered by popular artists. (Hugo Montenegro's covers of Ennio Morricone's Western scores are a notable example.) Newman's "Dead Already" main theme was later covered by English DJ Jakatta: dubbed "American Dream," it exposed Newman's work to an even wider audience. Unexpectedly this highly unusual, jaunty piece of film music, albeit in its tweaked form, became a staple of chill-out albums during the new millennium. *American Beauty* also established percussive and textural mannerisms that would be present throughout every one of Newman's subsequent scores, from drama (2002's *Road to Perdition*, also directed by Sam Mendes) to animation (2003's *Finding Nemo*) and action (James Bond movies *Skyfall* and *Spectre*, released in 2012 and 2015, and both directed by Mendes).

Evidently the 1990s was a fertile decade for all manner of film scores, with directors encouraging established veterans and relative newcomers to assert their stamp on the marketplace. From franchising to one-off dramas, the sheer range of tones, textures and approaches was striking and exciting. Yet, there continued to be an appetite for non-original film soundtracks, compilations essentially, which delivered both a nostalgic kick and a narrative boost to their respective film. This trend stretched back to the 1960s with the likes of *The Graduate*, but 1994's *Pulp Fiction* invigorated the philosophy to a startling degree.

The sophomore film from writer-director Quentin Tarantino, *Pulp Fiction* erupted onto the scene in a headline-grabbing blur of controversy, critical acclaim and artistic success. Following his 1992 thriller *Reservoir Dogs*, Tarantino sought to fashion a postmodern, blackly comic thriller, one that would act as a sly commentary on "pulp"—the trashy, lurid fictional material that had inspired so many of Tarantino's cinematic influences.

Pulp Fiction is, therefore, an interlocking, non-linear collection of vignettes (a Tarantino hallmark), and a self-referential statement on storytelling conventions, beginning with the opening epigraph on the meaning of pulp itself. The movie is unashamedly bold in style, mixing formal, stylized camerawork with coruscating language, explicit violence and hard drug use. And yet, Tarantino largely plays the material as provocatively funny, reveling in his ensemble of miscreants, drug users, gangsters and hitmen.

Rhetorical conversations on the nature of McDonald's versus Burger King mix with graphic scenes of overdosing. A violent criminal repents of his ways while wearing surf gear as he prevents the hold-up of a diner. And an extended dance sequence in a 1950s-movie-themed restaurant strikes a chord of bubblegum innocence amidst the chaos, a distillation of Tarantino's love of movie heritage. Buoyed by an outstanding cast, including John Travolta, Samuel L. Jackson and Uma Thurman, *Pulp Fiction* made a huge splash at the 1994 Cannes Film Festival before eventually enjoying a healthy box office run ($213 million against an $8 million budget).

The soundtrack was a critical factor in the film's success. It acted as the inner monologue of Tarantino's seedily entertaining creations, the rockabilly/surf guitar/retro pop wash lending an air of impish rebelliousness. Tarantino pitched his movie, although not exclusively, at cineliterate viewers, flattering, even, indulging, their awareness of cinematic artifice and convention, from the pop culture-laden dialogue (already established in *Reservoir Dogs*) to the music itself. The nature of Tarantino's soundtrack choices was designed to craft an explicit link between filmmaker and audience: he exhibited a curated brand of retro hits, many of them utterly obscure, and in the process shared the thrill of musical rediscovery with his audience. One senses this in his other movies, which gleefully utilize existing orchestral tracks from the likes of Ennio Morricone (1967's *Death Rides a Horse*, heard in 2003's *Kill Bill: Vol. 1*), Bernard Herrmann (1968's *Twisted Nerve*, also heard in *Kill Bill*) and Jerry Goldsmith (1983's *Under Fire*, heard in 2012's *Django Unchained*).

Tarantino regularly tinkers with the boundaries of this approach to amusing effect, such as the overt record scratching during *Pulp Fiction*'s opening credits as the music switches from Dick Dale's "Misirlou" to Kool & the Gang's "Jungle Boogie." The music in the film crosses the diegetic and non-diegetic boundaries to frequent and disorienting effect. The Statler Brothers' jaunty and innocent-sounding "Flowers on the Wall" is cued up by its appearance on a car radio, throwing us off the scent as to the violence and mayhem that occurs shortly afterwards. And there's an added layer of meta-commentary when we see Travolta's Vincent Vega dancing the shuffle to Chuck Berry's "You Never Can Tell" opposite Thurman's Mia Wallace, assimilating the heritage of *Saturday Night Fever* (1977) and *Grease* (1978).

As with Martin Scorsese, Tarantino delights in the juxtaposition of obscure pop hits against unpleasant, transgressive behavior—the exuberant tone of many of the songs on the soundtrack creates an ironic distancing effect, further provoking one's feelings of disgust or appalled laughter. This isn't just music that props up its respective movie—the soundtrack grants it a uniquely residual character, while also standing as a separate marketable commodity on its own terms. That Tarantino interweaves his own dialogue throughout his albums is yet more proof of an auteurist approach to soundtrack creation, his role extending beyond writer and director into, essentially, a greatest hits DJ spinning all manner of familiar and unfamiliar tracks for our delectation.

"The mixture of surf, soul and shit-talking that Quentin Tarantino assembled for *Pulp Fiction*'s soundtrack played out like one of the world's coolest mixtapes, which made it an instant classic when it came out," noted *Rolling Stone*'s review on the soundtrack's 20th anniversary. "As it happens, Tarantino had mixtape sequencing in mind when he executive produced the album in 1994, rearranging the way the songs play out on the track list the same way he played with chronology in the movie. 'This could easily be a Quentin tape,' he said at the time of its release."[20]

"The soundtrack made it to Number 21 on the Billboard 200 and has since sold more than three and a half million copies," added *Rolling Stone*. "It was so successful, in fact, that its five surf-rock offerings renewed interest in the genre, prompting surf label Del-Fi to put out a comp called Pulp Surfin' the next year, and its influence has continued to reverberate as the Black Eyed Peas sampled it on their 2006 single 'Pump it.'"[21]

From lushly melodic tapestries to offbeat acoustic gems, crowd-pleasing audience spectaculars to retro-tinged surf rock anthologies, there was no denying that the 1990s represented film music at its most mercurial. Sweeping symphonic anthems (Trevor Jones' *Last of the Mohicans*, 1992) were located alongside scores of arresting minimalist intent (Philip Glass' *Powaqqatsi*, 1988, and *Kundun*, 1997). Yet this period also served to underline the medium's limitations: whether drawing on original orchestral writing or pre-existing songs, soundtracks constantly fall prey to nostalgic trappings, whether it's the brassy heroics of *Independence Day* or the analog surf cool vibe of *Pulp Fiction*. This is, naturally, governed by the aesthetics of the film in question.

However, midway through this decade, changes were afoot that would come to dominate and redefine the entire philosophy of film music. In 1994, a runaway action-thriller called *Speed* became a huge box office sleeper hit, focusing on a bomb-rigged bus that mustn't drop below 50 mph or it will explode. It was the directorial debut of Jan de Bont, the cinematographer on 1988 action classic *Die Hard* (scored by Michael Kamen), who brought his skill with nimble cameras in claustrophobic environments to bear on this non-stop thrill ride. It proved a fine showcase for star Keanu Reeves, despite studio reservations regarding his casting, while co-star Sandra Bullock also found herself elevated into the big time.

Amidst the movie's twists, turns and set-pieces, one of its most influential elements turned out to be its score. Composed by former Yes producer Mark Mancina, *Speed* was the harbinger of a new kind of film soundtrack in which samples, loops and enhancement effects sat alongside a standard orchestra. More than that, the *Speed* score actively blurred the lines between artificial and organic: the pitch of the strings and brass is such that one perhaps cannot distinguish them from a synthetic undercurrent.

There is a noble main theme, which rises to its most prominently heroic, major key string crescendo as Reeves' Jack and Bullock's Annie finally escape the stricken bus, later dissolving into a tender piano-led love variation that leads into the end credits. However, this facet of the orchestra is often layered within an assortment of clanking, whirring and percussive effects, perhaps mirroring the mechanics of the bus or the constant roar of oncoming traffic. As opposed to the Jerry Goldsmith school of thought, in which the orchestra was almost always placed front and center with the electronics as a supporting element, Mancina's music sought to turn a traditional symphony into a more anthemic, synth-rock-flavored mix with a distinctly contemporary edge.

Mancina's score was concurrent with the work of composer Hans Zimmer, who similarly favored a wall-of-sound aesthetic where layers of volume and distortion could turn organic concepts into increasingly alien, artificial-sounding pieces of audio. This approach would become the signature sound of Zimmer's own recording studio Media Ventures Entertainment Group, later renamed Remote Control Productions, gracing films such as submarine thriller *Crimson Tide* (1995).

"[Mark Mancina's] score for *Speed* was effective in its capacity to generate excitement (and it was therefore a strong piece of music for the film), but it is even more of an interesting case study of how the general Media Ventures action sound got started," notes Christian Clemmensen.

> Zimmer had already established his dominance over the synthetic realm, and, by 1994, had produced the largely electronic *Beyond Rangoon* and *Point of No Return* with an elegant mastery of his machinery.
>
> For Mancina's *Speed*, however, you have the opportunity to hear structural ideas and electronic sampling of the Media Ventures era that was in its infancy. Many of the rhythmic loops, electronic substitutes for real instruments, and musical sound effects are all recognizable from later staples of the Media Ventures studio.[22]

If Mancina's score was somewhat overlooked amidst the aural hotchpotch of *Speed* (the movie won Oscars for Best Sound Mixing and Best

Sound Editing), it came to define a new kind of film score that actively distorted the principles of electronic and orchestral. Mancina would later develop these principles in the superior and sweepingly beautiful *Twister* (1996), also composed for De Bont. At the same time, the escalating popularity of Media Ventures clearly advocated a greater emphasis on ghost-writing in film music, a controversial, team-focused philosophy that threatened to undermine the very notion of authorship itself.

Hans Zimmer and the Changing Perception of Film Music in the 21st Century

Is there a right way or a wrong way to score a film? Throughout the course of this book a multitude of approaches has been explored, from orchestral to electronic to pop-focused, giving rise to the notion of the film soundtrack as a singularly varied medium. That said, the stylistic principles of a particular soundtrack are always beholden to the film in question, so surely the most potent question is this: how does a film score best serve its narrative?

Very often, a composer can apply unorthodox choices to the most unlikely of material. In 1989, German composer Hans Zimmer, then just four years into his Hollywood scoring career, conjured a distinctive and unusual sonic palette for Oscar-winning race relations drama *Driving Miss Daisy*. Adapted by Alfred Uhry from his own stage play, the movie, which begins in the mid–20th-century American Deep South, explores the decades-long friendship between an ailing Jewish widow (Jessica Tandy) and her black chauffeur (Morgan Freeman).

Zimmer's tender score approximates an organic tone, but all of the textures are, in fact, electronic, including the famous undulating clarinet that makes up the catchy title theme. There are undertones of blues and jazz in the score, but it's all conjured with samples, an approach that's intentionally anachronistic but certainly effective. Zimmer is not scoring the period of the film but instead its themes of friendship, prejudice and compassion, ageless concepts that transcend the story's historical context. The score is therefore liberated from the treacly clichés (surging strings et al.) that might drag the material into emotional glibness, instead possessing more of an intellectually abstract, but still charming, tone. It was an astute notion that helped guide the score to a Grammy nomination.

Driving Miss Daisy, along with the earlier, Oscar nominated *Rain Man* (1988), announced Zimmer as the most singular soundtrack voice in many years. Born in Frankfurt in 1957, Zimmer was, come the 1980s, well-poised to capitalize on the new-found electronic confidence and experimentation that was taking shape amidst the field of Hollywood soundtrack recording.

"I've come from a confused family," Zimmer later recalled. "My mother was very musical, basically a musician, and my father was an engineer and an inventor. So, I grew up modifying the piano, shall we say, which made my mother gasp in horror, and my father would think it was fantastic when I would attach chainsaws and stuff like that to the piano because he thought it was an evolution in technology. I think as a kid I started with one foot in the music camp and the other foot in the technology camp."[23]

In the early stages of his career, Zimmer was associated with many of the UK's pioneering new wave acts of the late 1970s and early 1980s. It was during this time that he first came to international prominence, collaborating with The Buggles on their synth pop cover of "Video Killed the Radio Star" in 1979. A chart-topping international success for Trevor Horn and Geoff Downes, its accompanying music video (directed by Russell Mulcahy, later to helm 1986's *Highlander*, scored by Michael Kamen) featured an appearance from Zimmer himself (he can be spotted playing the synthesizer).

Zimmer's anthemic, sweeping and genre-defying approach to film music owes itself, at least in part, to his work with leading rock groups. Zimmer served as a producer for English gothic rock group The Damned and worked with Ultravox's Warren Cann on new wave ensemble Helden. It was here that he first learned to harness the power of harmonic expanse and sheer volume, characteristics that would define many of his later action and superhero scores, not to mention his crowd-pleasing live concert performances of said scores.

Zimmer also imprinted himself on UK audiences with his exuberant theme for the BBC game show *Going for Gold*. It was an early outlier of Zimmer's capacity for emotionally direct and appealing rhythmic material, wrapped in an electronic package. He later told the BBC: "*Going for Gold* was a lot of fun. It's the sort of stuff you do when you don't have a career yet. God, I just felt so lucky because this thing paid my rent for the longest time."[24]

Even more significantly, Zimmer was poised to revolutionize the art of recording. After composing jingles for London's Air Edel recording studio, Zimmer decided to establish a space of his own. He formed Lillie Yard Studio with friend and fellow composer Stanley Myers (composer of the famous guitar piece "Cavatina," popularized in 1978's *The Deer Hunter*). Together, the two men essentially created a musical laboratory in which they could experiment with the limitations and capabilities of electronic sound. A 1986 description of the work space is amusingly quaint by today's standards: "Lillie Yard also has classic MIDI and pre–MIDI synthesisers ... the most expensive drum machine known to man, and a Fairlight. Most important of all, the studio has a truly post–MIDI design philosophy."[25]

This appraisal is, however, a fascinating time capsule, and an insight into the wider transition from relatively crude, early synthetic equipment to something more sophisticated. At the time many Hollywood scores were already at the epicenter of this change, from Harold Faltermeyer's *Top Gun* (1986) to Jerry Goldsmith's Oscar-nominated *Hoosiers* (also 1986). And before long, Zimmer would take his learnings from Lillie Yard and fashion his own Hollywood breakthrough.

The composer's idiosyncratic approach was immediately recognizable in his early Hollywood scores. *My Beautiful Laundrette* (1985) and *Paper House* (1988), both composed with Stanley Myers, plus solo projects *A World Apart* (1988) and *Rain Man* (1988), worked up an intriguing smorgasbord of electronics, sampled elements and exotic speciality instruments. For *Rain Man*, Zimmer composed the score specifically from the point of view of autistic character Raymond (Oscar winner Dustin Hoffman), who is kidnapped and taken on the road by his yuppie car salesman brother, Charlie (Tom Cruise).

Zimmer's mixture of haunting electronics, pan pipes and didgeridoo sought to capture Raymond's world: dislocated, distanced to an extent, yet perceptive and alive with the joy of discovery.[26] This hybrid organic/acoustic/electronic approach invested the movie with a distinctly wistful atmosphere that accentuated the growing bond between the two estranged brothers, generating Zimmer's first Oscar nomination.

More forceful variations on this formula came in the likes of *Black Rain* (1989), Zimmer's first collaboration with Ridley Scott, *Days of Thunder* (1990) and *Drop Zone* (1994), each of which leaned more explicitly into Zimmer's rock background with an emphasis on wailing electric guitar. A more elegiac, haunting twist on this style came in the Ridley Scott movie *Thelma & Louise* (1991), featuring a sublime electric guitar solo from blues artist Pete Haycock, and *Regarding Henry* (also 1991).

Tonality aside, Zimmer's most lasting, and controversial, contribution to film music has come with his Remote Control Productions recording studio. Founded in 1989 as Media Ventures, the studio space allows burgeoning Hollywood composers to both work on their own projects and collaborate with others, centrally overseen by Zimmer himself. Steven Kofsky, Zimmer's business partner, states: "These composers are independent, have their own businesses and secure their own movies."[27] At the same time, Kofsky says it's a "gently competitive environment" with "great creative synergy."[28]

Zimmer's team-focused approach has helped shatter the notion of the film composer as a lone wolf, although that's already something of a misnomer given the standard presence of conductors, orchestrators and mixers (assuming that the composer in question hasn't adopted at least one of those roles). One person who became associated with Zimmer in the 1990s was John Powell, now established as the noted composer of the *Bourne* series (2002–2016), the *How to Train Your Dragon* franchise (2010–2019) and *Solo: A Star Wars Story* (2018). Collaborating with Zimmer was, Powell said, a significant boost to his career.

"Hans used to work at the same music production company that I did in London, writing music for Air Edel," Powell recalled.

> He'd left by the time I started working there but he still had contacts. They took me on as one of 20 composers and within a couple of years at the agency I'd become this kid who spent all his money on gear. There were composers who were very good at composing advertising music but I was probably the kid who turned up with more tech than anybody else! I was using the tech in a way that others weren't necessarily bothering with. So when Hans came back and reached out for help on a project, my name came up because I was the kid that had lots of samplers. So the first time I met him was at Air Edel. He liked me and he gave me more sounds and samplers to help him try and do it.
>
> I ended up helping this other composer who was ghost-writing for [Zimmer]. We presented a demo, which nowadays is completely normal but back then no-one was doing it besides Hans. So once I took away information from that experience, I flourished. So I am very much a child of that technique, of demoing everything to the nth degree. It gives me control over the way I like to construct things. There are huge limitations and you have to fight against falling into lots of traps but I don't think I'd have a career if I hadn't been able to adapt those techniques that Hans pioneered.[29]

Zimmer's musical voice had already become standardized amidst the Hollywood action scene of the mid–1990s. This led to a ripple effect as producers requested that other composers mimic Zimmer's distinctive approach. This was the quandary that faced Powell on 1997's exuberantly operatic *Face/Off*, the John Woo–directed action behemoth starring John Travolta and Nicolas Cage. Brought onto the project as the composer, Powell was obligated to fill some big shoes.

"That was a gig that came into Media Ventures and they wanted Hans," said Powell. "They didn't want anyone else, they wanted Hans. He had worked with [John Woo] on *Broken Arrow* so he really wanted him to do it, but Hans couldn't. I'd been working with Hans at the time and he liked me and he gave them a guarantee, saying let this kid write some themes. So I did for about two weeks based on a whole load of footage and on a Friday afternoon I played the music to the editor, the producers and John himself.

I played them these demos and the editor was questioning whether or not Hans had written the tunes. He hadn't, although he had given me a lot of advice along the way. And they agreed to let me do it with Hans producing. That was a technique that he learned, I believe, from Stanley Myers, this idea to just let these kids try and compose something. He's a very good teacher. He'd have been a great teacher had he not gone into scoring.

So I learned so much from that. And in the process of scoring the rest of the film, obviously he was involved in making sure I didn't fuck it up! I learned a lot technically, I learned a lot emotionally. I also learned that I was there filling in for him, that I shouldn't try and step too far outside his genre. They wanted that Media Ventures sound, so within that organisation, when you're getting those gigs you're asking: do they want you or do they want Hans? In the early days it was like, we want Hans but can't get him, so let's get someone who sounds like him.[30]

For better or worse, Zimmer's Media Ventures aesthetic initiated a sea-change in the art of screen composition while also throwing some troublesome questions into the mix. What happens when a score openly mirrors, if not imitates, another? This was evident in many Zimmer works from the 1990s: the sonic qualities of the aforementioned *Crimson Tide* were self-evident in later scores like *The Peacemaker* (1997), right down to the processed choral effects and artificially bulked-out brass section. And who can claim to be the author of a film score if a project is initiated amidst a bustling team environment of orchestrators, ghost-writers and mixers? Is this, in fact, scoring by committee?

Addressing the latter point, it's important to note that many film composers, even going back to the earliest days of Hollywood, have sought help from a team of professionals. Take Max Steiner, cited in Chapter Two of this book, whose impossible deadlines on *Gone with the Wind* necessitated extra work from his orchestrators, including the likes of Hugo Friedhofer. Without them, the score would likely never have been finished (certainly not by Steiner, at any rate). Therefore, the team-focused principle of Media Ventures wasn't entirely new; rather, Zimmer absorbed established Hollywood practices and bolted them to pioneering breakthroughs in recording technology.

Using *The Peacemaker* as an example, Zimmer was credited as co-composer with Nick Glennie-Smith. However, on the Disney blockbuster *Pirates of the Caribbean: The Curse of the Black Pearl* (2003), the music was credited to Zimmer associate Klaus Badelt, allegedly because the former couldn't take official credit for contractual reasons.[31] Certainly, upon listening to the score one can hear wholesale rhythms, motifs and aesthetic selections from a raft of earlier Hans Zimmer works, from *Black Rain* to *Backdraft* (1991) and *Crimson Tide*, giving the impression that the work is essentially his in all but name. (Zimmer was officially listed as the composer for the next three *Pirates* films, compounding the sense that these were his themes all along.)

The question is this: what constitutes a Hans Zimmer score? One can attribute early efforts like *Rain Man* to him relatively easily, but the issue of authorship became significantly more complex in the Media Ventures (later Remote Control) era. It might help to draw parallels with Zimmer's early rock career: on an album, a record producer will always take some form of credit, even if they haven't been directly involved in the composition. Nevertheless, there's a degree of professional oversight and expertise from the individual in question, which helps thread together the logistical and technical challenges of the recording, not to mention the publicity upon its eventual release.

If, therefore, Zimmer is the de facto producer, at least on scores like *The Curse of the Black Pearl*, then who is the official composer? On the first *Pirates* score, Klaus Badelt took the primary credit but there's a small army of fellow composers and ghost-writers listed as contributors, including the aforementioned Nick Glennie-Smith and Geoff Zanelli.[32] (The latter would eventually take charge of the fifth *Pirates* score, *Dead Men Tell No Tales*, released in 2017.) One cannot imagine that there is a single, overriding personality at work in the score, at least until listening to the music whereupon Zimmer's unmistakable approach asserts itself. Is this an example of a composer channeling his own musical personality through others?

Perhaps the answer exists beyond the parameters of the recording studio. Reiterating John Powell's earlier point about *Face/Off*, one must look at the role of filmmakers and their demands for musical imitation. As Powell explained, the *Face/Off* score sought to import the overblown nature of Zimmer's *Broken Arrow* (1996). Zimmer's music was essentially being used as a creative shorthand by the producers: if one enjoyed the theatrics of *Broken Arrow*, one was also likely to enjoy *Face/Off*, and here was the prefabricated tonality of a Hans Zimmer score to reinforce the aesthetic association between the two films. In this instance, however, Zimmer wasn't available, compelling Powell to step up and fashion a musical imitation of his mentor.

In hindsight, it's another disheartening sign of how autonomy in film music has continued to be diluted in the face of blockbuster and franchise expectations. In the modern era composers are not only required to mimic other people but, bizarrely enough, their own work. Therefore, rather than point fingers at the musical artist, initiating a lazy blame game of facsimile versus original content, one must acknowledge the highly pressurized conditions in which the composer is operating.

This is especially challenging when a composer has to deal with an outsized personality like *Pirates* producer Jerry Bruckheimer, one of the most powerful individuals in Hollywood. Bruckheimer's template of slick, glossy entertainment had first been established in the 1980s MTV era when he partnered with fellow producer Don Simpson on the likes of *Top Gun*. Such was the nature of Bruckheimer's authority that, come the 1990s and 2000s, he essentially obtained musical approval over the heads of the directors.

During the production of the first *Pirates* movie it was Bruckheimer, not director Gore Verbinski, who elected Zimmer and Badelt to score the film, having deposed Verbinski's original choice, Alan Silvestri, in the process.[33] This was, perhaps, inevitable given that Bruckheimer's association with Zimmer stretched all the way back to *Days of Thunder*. It essentially supported the notion of the composer as a brand name: the familiar Zimmer sound, which had been utilized throughout so many of Bruckheimer's movies, was now actively sought by the producer to give *Pirates* a contemporary lick and also a dash of familiarity. Once again, nostalgia proved to be a powerful commodity.

However, was this modernistic approach to scoring a pirate movie showing contempt towards the classic seafaring Korngold tradition? Are movies in this particular genre beholden to a sense of musical heritage, or should they be free to transpose a distinctly 20th-century style onto a period pirate setting? Once again, one must look at the score's effectiveness in the movie, and there's no denying that Badelt and Zimmer's music adds a degree of propulsion, derivative and often distracting though it is.

Increasingly, it's the stakeholders, franchise owners and money makers that hold sway over cinematic musical choices, at least in the realm of big-budget entertainment. This tension isn't unique to Zimmer's scores—one can also sense it in the most recent *Star Wars* soundtracks from John Williams. Although the music is extraordinary on its own terms, one senses the familiar themes being used as a glib signifier in the films themselves, a quick and easy blast of nostalgia providing instant gratification.

Certainly, by the time *Episode IX: The Rise of Skywalker* (2019) arrived, the franchise seemed more intent on recalling the heritage of the past than focusing on story cohesion in the present. Williams himself had no charges to answer—all he could do was work with the material he was given. One must instead look to director J.J. Abrams and producer Kathleen Kennedy, the current President of Lucasfilm, who were seemingly using this feel-good music iconography as a distraction to mask deficiencies in the wider saga storyline. *The Rise of Skywalker* was intended as the culmination of a three-film road map that started with *The Force Awakens*. However, following the controversy over the creative decisions made in *The Last Jedi*, it all collapsed in a confused heap of fan-pleasing references and blatant nostalgia, an issue that also blighted the deployment of the score.

Zimmer's sound has also been imported into collaborations with other directors. And few are more significant than his partnership with Christopher Nolan. The British director has established a reputation for thoughtful, gripping thrillers and blockbusters that are challenging in their use of chronology and fascinating in terms of philosophy. In Nolan's hands, time is a malleable, mutable concept, and this idea has been parlayed into the acclaimed likes of *Memento* (2000), his *Dark Knight* trilogy (2005–2012) and World War II drama *Dunkirk* (2017).

This fusion of brawn and brain has yielded a near-unbroken stream of commercial success for Nolan, securing his position as one of Hollywood's most powerful and influential filmmakers. Having worked with composer David Julyan early in his career, Nolan then switched gears to Hans Zimmer, before alighting on Ludwig Göransson for *Tenet* (2020). Like Jerry Bruckheimer, Nolan appears to be an advocate of tonality in music, rather than nuance, blanketing entire sequences with Zimmer's characteristic, bass-heavy approach.

That said, the deployment of Zimmer's scores in Nolan's movies is more varied than many claim. In *Dunkirk*, the horrifying mechanization of warfare, on land, on sea and in the air, is replicated in the droning buzz of Zimmer's music. The composer utilizes the "Shepard Tone," which gives the unsettling illusion of a sustained rising pitch in the music. This is further assimilated into the sound elements, including the dive-bombing Stuka aircraft, to evoke a wall of sound that immerses the audience in the terror of the conflict.

For outer-space odyssey *Interstellar* (2014), Zimmer was given a dream assignment. Composers love writing for space precisely because there is no sound in a vacuum, meaning they're allowed to project all manner of provocative musical concepts. In the case of *Interstellar*, the intimate and the grandiose are connected as Matthew McConaughey's astronaut calls out for his daughter across oceans of time, allowing Zimmer to infuse a distinctly profound, even religioso, tone into the score. As a sign of confidence in his composer, during pre-production, Nolan gave Zimmer a note outlining nothing more than the film's central theme and asked him to spend a day sketching potential musical ideas.

"I really just wrote about what it meant to be a father," said Zimmer. "And [Nolan] came down and sat on my couch and I played it for him. He goes, 'Well, I better make the movie now.' And I'm going, what is the movie? And he starts describing this huge journey, this vast canvas of space and philosophy and science and all these things. And I'm going, 'Hang on. I've written you this tiny little thing here.' And he goes, 'Yes, but I now know what the heart of the story is.' So he was writing with this piece of music sort of keeping him company all the way through the writing process, all the way through the shoot."[34]

Interstellar is, therefore, a rare instance of a Nolan film that's actively shaped, not just supported, by its soundtrack. In the depths of space, the music becomes the sound. The score helped reinforce the Nolan-Zimmer collaboration as its own kind of marketable brand, an emblem of shared commercial success that, somewhat unusually, has allowed film music to cross niche boundaries to reach a truly global audience. Zimmer's overwhelming musical aesthetic, honed from his anthemic rock days, serves to underline the scale, portent and seriousness of Nolan's thematic intent, whether it's Gotham City being torn apart by the Joker (the Oscar-winning Heath Ledger) or the mind-melding power of dreams in *Inception* (2010).

Opinions on the individual Nolan and Zimmer scores may vary, but the collaboration between the two men is clearly something that the director values deeply. "We fight like cats and dogs but in the best, the most productive way," Nolan explains.

> We love each other, with everything that comes with that. We fight like brothers at times and we love like brothers.
> It's an extraordinary partnership and a wonderful creative collaboration, but we do things and dive into things fully. And when you do that, passions run high. Always with great respect for each other and great love for each other, but we do challenge each other, and we do fight about things. But I think in the best way possible.[35]

Nevertheless, is it necessarily the best approach to have a composer import their standardized sound from one movie to another? Naturally, one could argue that film composers have been doing this since time immemorial—the angular menace of Bernard Herrmann's *Psycho* was a clear influence on the composer's later *Cape Fear* (1962), later adapted by Elmer Bernstein for Martin Scorsese's 1991 remake. Likewise, the exuberance of John Williams' *Star Wars* paved the way for the similarly nostalgic *Indiana Jones* series. Is there anything inherently different in the way that Zimmer adapts his basic approach for the likes of Christopher Nolan and Jerry Bruckheimer? And ultimately, if the score in question serves the movie and pleases the director, who can speak out against the finished product?

The issue is surely more a philosophical than a technical one: does any film composer have a right to individuality? Or are they defined by their inherent sellability, translating familiar musical codes and conventions from one project to another to maximize audience involvement and box office potential? In the era of Hans Zimmer and his fellow composers, this isn't a new problem, but it's certainly intensified as the battle for budgets and box office has become increasingly fraught. Certainly, if one considers the record-shattering success of Nolan's *The Dark Knight* (2008), which took more than $1 billion at the global box office, one can imagine the pressure on Zimmer (who co-composed with James Newton Howard) to stick true to his musical approach for the remainder of the Batman movie series.

However, it's not the case that Zimmer is a one-size-fits-all composer. Looking outside of his franchise work, one discovers some of Zimmer's most extraordinary and thought-provoking scores. In 1994, he collaborated with Disney, Elton John and Tim Rice on the animated blockbuster *The Lion King*, a hugely successful artistic endeavor that won Zimmer his first Oscar for Best Original Score. The emotional canvas of the movie, a gorgeously designed, anthropomorphic twist on Shakespeare's *Hamlet*, clearly inspired the imaginations of all involved, Zimmer included. The composer was brought on board by directors Roger Allers and Rob Minkoff after they were impressed with his Africa-themed score *The Power of One* (1992).[36]

The spirit of the savannah is infused into the opening track "Circle of Life," vocalists Lebo M and Carmen Twillie celebrating the majesty of the African continent. Thereafter, Zimmer's impassioned score weaves its way between John and Rice's contributions (including the Oscar-winning romantic duet "Can You Feel the Love Tonight") as it emphasizes the destiny of outcast lion cub Simba. It's a testament to Zimmer's abilities that his familiar voice continues to resonate, even in the midst of an animated context. Once again, electronics, orchestra, choir (often used in the avant-garde manner of *Backdraft*) and synth percussion is carefully stitched together, although this score has a more organic, symphonic feel than many of Zimmer's works from the same period.

One scene in particular resonates with a near-liturgical weight: the tragic death of Simba's father, Mufasa (James Earl Jones) at the hands of his scheming brother, Scar (Jeremy Irons). Zimmer, who confessed to not being a Disney stalwart and unwilling to embrace the project at first, said that he channeled profoundly deep-seated emotions into the ensuing musical sequence.

"I never quite got the story until I was working on it," he recalled. "But then came the moment when the father [Mufasa] dies. And my dad died when I was a kid, so suddenly it became a lot more serious.... All I knew was you can never talk down to children. So, I thought OK, if this deals with the death of a father, I'm going to go and write a serious requiem."[37]

It's a superb example of how a distinguished composer can invest seemingly "frivolous" family entertainment with a remarkable amount of dramatic weight. Zimmer is not scoring the outward imagery but the inner themes of parenthood, sacrifice, nobility and courage, akin to what Jerry Goldsmith accomplished on the superb *The Secret of NIMH* (1982), a Don Bluth animation, and Disney's very own *Mulan* (1998). Upon its release, *The Lion King* became the most financially successful Disney animation of all time (oddly, top position now goes to the 2019 remake of *The Lion King*, also scored by Zimmer), and one can well imagine the soundtrack's role in all of that. It was a brilliantly effective continuation of the earlier Alan Menken/Howard Ashman principle of using the music to lead the narrative.

The Thin Red Line (1998) could be considered as Zimmer's crowning achievement. Stately, elongated string passages, subtle ethnic influences (including taiko drums) and carefully placed intervals beautifully capture the introspective nature of Terrence Malick's World War II drama, adapted from James Jones' book of the same name. Zimmer expertly conjures a somber and melancholic portrait of an island paradise, Guadalcanal, beset by man-made conflict, conjuring a score whose tone was to influence many of his later works (including *12 Years a Slave* in 2013). Zimmer wrote four hours of music for the film (augmented by traditional Melanesian choral chants) as the mercurial Malick repeatedly chopped and changed the edit; barely 50 minutes is presented on the final album, but it remains a high point in Zimmer's career.[38]

Another of Zimmer's key partners is director Ridley Scott, whose ability to construct awe-inspiring worlds has coaxed a wide range of styles and approaches from the composer. Their most famous collaboration is surely *Gladiator* (2000), the triumphant Roman epic that made an Oscar-winning star of Russell Crowe and revived the moribund swords and sandals epic. The movie traces the destiny of Maximus (Crowe), a Roman legionnaire turned slave and gladiator who vows revenge against the vicious Emperor Commodus (Joaquin Phoenix) who wronged him, interweaving a personal story against the turbulent political backdrop of the Roman Empire.

Little wonder it inspired Zimmer to conjure one of his most powerful scores, although controversy was never far away. Two of the film's battle sequences are sequenced with a barely disguised variation on Gustav Holst's "Mars" from *The Planets*, although given Mars was the Roman God of War, one can perhaps better appreciate Zimmer's intentions. The tone of the score's action sequences is far removed from genre masters like Miklós Rózsa: the nature of the harmonization, orchestration and recording is pure Zimmer, attaining a dense wall of sound and once again calling on a range of additional composers and ghost-writers including Klaus Badelt.

Far more interesting are the dramatic underscore cues for the dialogue sequences, various internecine betrayals and the ever-present beckoning of the afterlife, referred to in the movie as "Elysium." Sorcerous choir, celli and double bass capture the decadent air of Rome itself, not to mention the dissolution of the evil Commodus. Zimmer expertly off-sets these minor key, broiling tonalities with the piercing sounds of Lisa Gerrard, who here represents elysium. Gerrard's haunting, yearning vocals capture Maximus' yearning for his deceased wife and son, particularly in the climactic movement "Now We Are Free." It set in motion a trend for wailing ethnic vocals in turn-of-the-millennium Hollywood scores, including Zimmer's own *Mission: Impossible II* (2000), James Horner's *Troy* (2004) and John Williams' *Munich* (2005).

Zimmer's ability to champion and empower rising young film composers also deserves acclaim. He has, essentially, democratized the process of film music composition, acting as the overseer for many looking to break into a fiercely competitive industry. One of these artists is Lorne Balfe who, having collaborated with Zimmer for several years as a producer and co-composer, hit the big time with solo projects including Tom Cruise blockbuster *Mission: Impossible—Fallout* (2018). Mirroring the words of John Powell, Balfe says Zimmer's mentoring and advice has been pivotal throughout his career.

"The thing is, I still have to pinch myself when I'm writing with [Hans Zimmer]," Balfe says. "I have him on such a high pedestal, when I make a suggestion I still question why he's interested in my opinion. His background is from that commercial pop production, and the record industry is always about working with others and improvising and jamming. He taught me a lot about not being pressured about what we write. The film comes first, and if it doesn't work, you have to say goodbye to that music. We never talk about music, we talk about filmmaking. He's a filmmaker first and a composer second. He understands the concept of storytelling. He's been an amazing mentor, and still is."[39]

Balfe's appraisal underlines Zimmer's status as a singular figure within film music. Perhaps more than any other composer in the history of the medium, Zimmer possesses a sense of showmanship, honed from his early recording days, a sense of flamboyance and theatricality that comes across not just in the music, but also the way in which the music is presented. In recent years, Zimmer has taken his scores on tour throughout the world, transmogrifying them and presenting them in outsized rock venues complete with teeming crowds. This is the kind of sight that usually greets a chart-topping pop artist, not a film composer, but it speaks of Zimmer's popular ability to transcend those boundaries.

"I think they grew up with [my music]," Zimmer said of the crowds who attended his 2017 Coachella concert debut. "A large part of the audience wasn't even born when we did *The Lion King*. I keep running into people who've gone to college, and they all studied to my music. There are no words to distract [them]. I think that was part of the experiment—we go out there and not show any images from the movies. The subtext is what you felt at the time when you saw this or when you heard this for the first time. That was the big experiment for me. Can the music stand on its own two feet, or is it really just in the old fashioned way that film music used to be called background music? I just needed to find that out for myself."[40]

Nevertheless, Zimmer deflected the comparisons between himself and traditional festival acts. "I'm a composer, I'm not a performer," he explained. "I write music that is actually quite hard to play—because what I'm trying to do is write things which are interesting for the musicians to play. Now, I suddenly find myself in the position of regretting writing some of these things because they're slightly outside my technical ability."[41]

Returning to the subject of Christopher Nolan, his use of music and sound underlines a wider issue that has engulfed contemporary movies. At the best of times, both music and sound will be interwoven like a gordian knot, the organic subjectivity of the former mixing with the objective, non-melodious tone of the latter. But what happens when the aural mixture becomes soupy and overpowering? More specifically, where does this leave the score?

AIR Studios in London is a highly admired recording studio that has played host to many of Hans Zimmer's most celebrated scores, including *Gladiator*. The nature of the recording mix is critical to a score's impact, and a particular stage can add rich ambience to the symphonic performance. Mixer Olga Fitzroy explains: "AIR Studios has two great acoustic spaces. The best-known one is Lyndhurst Hall, a large hexagonal hall set underneath a big domed ceiling, that can accommodate around 100 musicians in normal times. It has a very warm four-second reverb time that just makes everything sound warm (lots of low frequencies) and lush."[42]

Fitzroy explains that there is an all-important distinction between recording dry sound ("no echo or reverberation") and wet sound ("a lot of reverberation and echo").[43] This subtle yet impactful decision can alter the entire character of a film soundtrack. Nevertheless, an audience's first exposure to a completed film score will likely be in digital surround sound at a multiplex cinema and, as fellow AIR engineer Geoff Foster explains, this presents its own range of complexities. The impact of a film's score and sound design in the context of a movie theater is, he says, highly subjective.

"When I sit in the cinema, I try and sit directly in the center to simulate what my experience would have been during the dubbing process," Foster explains. "Anyone else and you're going to get problems with the mix. You may have 20 to 30 surround speakers in the theater and they're not time-aligned for where you're sitting. So, you end with this weird coning, phasing effect. The information that you want to hear, which is usually the dialogue, is a little fuzzy. With music, it exists and persists for a longer period of time, moving around in the Atmos, and the brain is usually happy with it."[44]

The assaultive nature of modern sound design has been the subject of much ire regarding Nolan's film *Tenet*, where the underpowered dialogue mixture is competing with a barrage of effects and a sonorous musical approach from Ludwig Göransson. This isn't particularly helpful when the story is dealing with head-scratching concepts of entropy and time reversal, ideas that require absolute clarity of communication so the audience can keep up. However, this conflict may stem directly from Nolan's singular aesthetic choices, something that became apparent in 2015 when a 60-piece symphony orchestra, led by Hans Zimmer, played *Interstellar* live to picture at London's Royal Albert Hall. Geoff Foster supervised the sound dub and said it evoked a very different mood from the theatrical presentation.

"A lot of people came up to me afterward and said they'd picked up pieces of dialogue they didn't hear in the movie," recalled Foster. "But talking to [Chris Nolan], he commented that the dub was interesting, and it was fascinating to get another perspective on it. Chris' point of view on the movie mix was that you're not really meant to hear what's being said, least of all in the initial shuttle launch sequence, which is designed to be overwhelming and overpowering."[45]

In terms of the score as a conceptual entity, it's clearly the composer who will absorb the most criticism for the music being allegedly overbearing or overwritten. In the case of *Tenet*, Göransson's rhythmically adventurous music (albeit derivative of Zimmer, presumably at Nolan's behest) was dismissed by many as an indistinguishable extension of an already overbearing sound mixture. Regardless of one's opinion on the score itself, it's important not to overlook the complicated dynamics of film music production and the pressures on a given composer.

As this chapter has made clear, the delivery of a successful film score relies on a great deal of extenuating factors, many of which exist outside of the musician's control: collaborative demands, environmental variables, a successful mix and the climactic presentation of the movie in cinemas. What, therefore, does the future of film music hold when both artistic sensibilities and intangible passages of notes are increasingly at loggerheads with corporate behemoths?

The Rise of the Comic Book Movie Score and the Battle for Thematic Identity

The notion of clearly enunciated themes and motifs is a hotly contested subject in the modern-day film scoring environment. Are film scores, particularly those in the blockbuster realm, obligated to construct their narratives from obvious building blocks that consciously play on our emotions? And what does it mean when an attempt to establish thematic continuity is disrupted by an ensuing score from a different composer altogether?

The new millennium started on a superlative note for thematically driven film music. Both *The Matrix* (1999–2003) and *The Lord of the Rings* (2001–2003) trilogies were broadly concurrent with one other, and their respective scores, from Don Davis and Howard Shore, revived the notion of Wagnerian operatic bombast as a powerful narrative device. Of course, given that one of these franchises is set in an artificial, rule-breaking dream simulation, and the other in the fantastical realm of Middle-earth, the individual music approaches couldn't be more different.

Beginning with *The Matrix* as a trilogy, one becomes aware of symphonic film music as a bundle of contradictions, running the gamut from the orchestral to the electronically enhanced. Davis had a broad canvas on which to paint, working with directors the Wachowskis to give added resonance to their eye-widening science-fiction conceit. The first *Matrix* movie, released in 1999, proved to be enormously influential on the genre, fusing all manner of comic book influences and kung fu–flavored fight sequences with dense philosophical discourse on the nature of reality. Combine all this with groundbreaking developments in computer generated imagery (CGI), namely the oft-imitated "bullet time" effect, and it's little wonder that audiences were truly transported.

The story centers on apparently lowly hacker Neo (Keanu Reeves) who becomes aware that the world as he knows it is nothing more than a computer simulation. Unplugged from the mainframe, Neo joins forces with rebels Morpheus (Laurence Fishburne) and Trinity (Carrie-Anne Moss) to liberate the human race, which is essentially being used as a giant battery to power the terrifying futuristic world of the machines. It's a dazzling concept and one that many film composers would relish tackling. Davis, a veteran orchestrator who'd worked on James Horner's sweeping period epic *Legends of the Fall* (1994) and others, rose to the challenge, composing a distinctly avant-garde score that was far-removed from the in-vogue Hans Zimmer trends of the period.

Davis' style keenly evokes that of contemporary Elliot Goldenthal, particularly in the eerie brass "suspensions" and sustained chords, a recurring musical device that seems to imply a limitless realm of possibilities. Goldenthal's influence is writ large throughout the robust performance of the Hollywood Studio Symphony, which emphasizes clustered, low-register brass patterns, whirling strings and pounding anvil. Alternating with these moments are several sequences of wondrous choral grandeur, including the massed choir when Neo first awakens in the real world, and the delicate soprano vocal when his body is being repaired after first being decoupled from the Matrix. As an aside, Davis noted the Wachowskis' love of the percussive "pile driver" sound effect, which featured in their previous collaboration, *Bound* (1996).[46]

Davis also observed the Wachowskis' exacting demands for the music to sync up directly with the on-screen action, including the climactic reveal of Neo as "The One" in which he stops bullets in mid-air and reaches out to grab one. "As it and the rest of the bullets hit the carpet, the music hits each impact with a slam. That was at the Wachowskis' request," Davis recalled,[47] adding that such a beat-by-beat approach in the music is "something that film composers today tend to do a lot less of."[48]

Davis praised his collaboration with the Wachowskis, although he remembered the challenge of scaling back the tone of his opening Trinity chase sequence so that the sound of the police cars could be heard as she soars from roof to roof.[49] "As a composer, using an orchestra wasn't something I had to fight for. When they wanted something electronic, it was generally handled with needle drops, electronica tracks that they had licensed. But they did want a choir—that wasn't something I had anticipated using for the score."[50]

The Matrix was a critical, commercial and artistic success, winning several Oscars including Best Visual Effects. Davis' music was largely overlooked, perhaps because it does such an excellent job in establishing tone and texture without calling attention to itself. It's often said that the best kind of film score is one that the audience doesn't notice. But that was exactly the philosophy demanded in the full-throttle sequels *The Matrix Reloaded* (2003) and *The Matrix Revolutions* (also 2003). Seemingly caught unawares by the success of their sci-fi debut, the Wachowskis had to contend with all the mythology they'd initiated, arguably losing focus in a barrage of gaudy, effects-laden set-pieces and heavy-handed sermonizing.

"The Wachowskis' heads exploded with the enormous responsibility and expectations they were faced with when they shot the sequels, even though they somehow managed to actually gain more control," said Davis. "The first *Matrix* was in development at Warner Bros. for four or five years, yet when they followed that up with not one, but two films, they had to work out the scripts in a much shorter period of time, with little or no interference from the studio. As a result, they became much more micromanaging in the sequels ... that's not to underestimate their micromanaging on the first one, however."[51]

In contrast to the first *Matrix* score, which alternated Davis' orchestral soundtrack with needle-drop song selections (The Propellerheads, Rage Against the Machine and others), *The Matrix Reloaded* encouraged a hybrid blend in the composer's music. The familiar sense of atonality and discordant instrumentalism was still present, but this time the symphony orchestra was melded with the pulsating electronica of the group Juno Reactor. The end result was an intriguing mixture that, on the one hand, stood as a product of its time, and yet at the same time remained ageless. It implicitly supported the expansion of the *Matrix* universe, suggesting both the malleability of physics and the emergent heroism of Neo who, in this installment, becomes almost a Superman figure.

The final movie, *The Matrix Revolutions*, was by far the most expansive and impressive of Davis' three scores. One imagines that the Wachowskis were increasingly reliant on the music to convey a sense of allegorical profundity, qualities distinctly lacking in their incoherent screenplay. Unusually for a *Matrix* score, the electronics were largely dropped in favor of massive orchestral and choral forces suggesting the Messianic nature of Neo. This is where the Wagnerian impulses of Davis' music really come to the forefront, the composer tying up the various musical threads, including Neo's hero theme and the Neo-Trinity love theme, in explosively grand fashion.

Reinforcing the connection, the climactic battle between Neo and the villainous Smith (a scene-stealing Hugo Weaving) is set to a soaring cue named "Neodämmerung." This is a reference to Wagner's own opera *Götterdämmerung*, the fourth entry in the hugely influential *Rings Cycle* that inspired the use of the leitmotif within film music. The latter translates as "Twilight of the Gods" whereas Davis' variation reads as "Neo's Twilight," one of many allegorical allusions embedded deeply in the *Matrix* soundtracks.

The sheer volume and breadth of Davis' final *Matrix* score caps off a superb trilogy of music and positions it as a technically accomplished successor to the likes of *Star Wars* and *Conan the Barbarian*. Sadly, and not a little ironically, the better the scores got, the more overblown and forgettable the films became, and the soundtracks were perhaps not firmly instilled in the minds of audiences as much as they should have been. Disappointingly, director Lana Wachowski chose not to renew her collaboration with Davis for the fourth *Matrix* movie, although the composer has remained sanguine and said that post–*Revolutions*, both Lana and her sister Lilly were simply looking to move on with a new creative team.[52]

If Davis helped give weight to the notion of reality as a computer simulation, how does a composer breathe audible life into a landscape that bears no relation whatsoever to our own? That was the monumental challenge facing Howard Shore when, in 2000, he signed on to compose director Peter Jackson's *Lord of the Rings* trilogy. The New Zealand filmmaker, who had flip-flopped between DIY comedy-horror gore (1992's *Dead Alive*) and haunting true crime drama (1994's *Heavenly Creatures*) had, many claimed, bitten off more than he could chew.

The teeming world of author J.R.R. Tolkien's novel was said to be too multifaceted and complex for any filmmaker to do justice to it. Jackson, however, proved the naysayers wrong by exploiting the varied natural landscape of New Zealand, employing an excellent international cast and honing a seamless mixture of cutting-edge CGI, make-up effects, models and props. But the real success of the trilogy resided in its clear compassion and warmth for Tolkien's source: although Jackson and fellow writers Philippa Boyens and Fran Walsh made many changes to the text, they remained steadfastly loyal to the emotions and the characters.

Naturally, music was key to the emotional reach of *The Lord of the Rings* trilogy, which comprised *The Fellowship of the Ring* (2001), *The Two Towers* (2002) and *The Return of the King* (2003). Shore faced a gargantuan challenge, compelled to delineate between good and evil, landscape and character, set-piece and introspection. He also repeatedly returned to Tolkien's text and researched the languages originally devised by the author, including Elvish, and incorporated them in a multitude of choral guises. This level of intricate detail yielded an astonishing abundance of musical riches, arguably one of the greatest-ever accomplishments in the field of film scoring.

It has been noted that the sheer canvas of the *Lord of the Rings* trilogy required 170 hours of recording sessions, with Shore deploying symphony orchestras, instrumentalists and vocalists in both London and New Zealand.[53] The London Philharmonic Orchestra and New Zealand Symphony mix with a guttural Maori voice choir; pastoral pennywhistles and fiddles give way to the ethereal, haunting tones of soprano Isabel Bayrakdarian; and the mysterious, insidious strings of the central theme for the One Ring contrast superbly with the heraldic, triumphant brass of the theme for Rohan. It's a dazzling mixture of tones and textures across the major and minor key spectrums (with an emphasis on the latter), all seeking to capture a multitude of characters, incidents and emotional temperatures in the classic Wagnerian style.

Superstar names attached to the trilogy included Enya ("May It Be," for *The Fellowship of the Ring*), and Annie Lennox (the Oscar-winning "Into the West," from trilogy-closer *The Return of the King*). Yet what really impresses is the consistency of Shore's own musical voice. In the chilling bass onslaught for Mordor and Isengard, one can hear clear echoes of Shore's acclaimed works on disturbing thrillers such as David Cronenberg's *The Fly* (1986), *The Silence of the Lambs* (1991) and *Se7en* (1995). The persistent presence of pounding timpani and anvil in much of the villainous material apes the mechanization of industry and its intrusion on the natural landscape, forces of change that were feared by Tolkien himself.

At the same time, the delightful Celtic-inflected theme for Hobbiton and The Shire, embodied by the heroic Frodo Baggins (Elijah Wood), is quite unlike anything else in Shore's canon. It does, however, remind one of his lighter touch that has been put to use in terrific scores such as *Big* (1988), *Mrs. Doubtfire* (1993) and *Ed Wood* (1994). That said, it's the thunderous set-pieces that really arrest the attention, as Jackson and Shore's spotting works wonders. Very often, grace notes of optimism and beauty will arrive when one least expects it, a soprano vocal briefly yet delicately interrupting a minor key brass onslaught to suggest incipient moral purity amidst a world under grave threat. The score brilliantly absorbs the characteristics of the ever-changing landscape: the reveal of the multi-storied city of Minas Tirith, for example, is accompanied by ascending scales of brass that construct their own kind of musical edifice.

Musicologist Doug Adams collaborated with Shore on the comprehensive study *The Music of the Lord of the Rings Films*. He surmised that there were 93 motifs composed in total across the three movies,[54] quite possibly a record for any kind of theatrical franchise. The mutability of these themes is key to our understanding of Middle-earth's complexities. For instance, the presence of the One Ring's theme in the scenes with Gollum (Andy Serkis) suggests its malevolent influence on the former hobbit. In one of the trilogy's most powerful moments, the folksy overtones of the Shire theme reinforce the bond between the despairing Frodo and Sam (Sean Astin) as they make their arduous trek up the fiery precipice of Mount Doom.

The *Lord of the Rings* soundtracks extended a notable influence over subsequent movie epics. It's been noted that the minor key emphasis of much of Shore's work (a characteristic of the composer's wider career) is designed to convey an air of darkly broiling portent, something that carried across into James Horner's *Troy* and Vangelis' *Alexander* (2004).[55] This is in contrast with the relatively more optimistic pomp and pageantry of the swords and sandals scores from the 1950s and 1960s[56]; post–*Lord of the Rings*, the scoring of grandiose epics appears to have become self-consciously serious, lest relentlessly bright melodies drag the material into parody.

This is surely a sign of how contemporary audiences are hyper-aware of a score's ability to work on their emotions. Or, more accurately, it's a sign of how filmmakers make those assumptions on behalf of the audience, and then expect composers to fall into line. Either way, the scores for *Lord of the Rings* struck the kind of commercial chord not seen since the heyday of James Horner's *Titanic*. This was aided and abetted by the fact that the theatrical edits of each movie were soon followed by extended cuts on DVD that allowed greater luxuriation in Middle-earth and its multifaceted musical tapestry. Shore also released "Complete Recordings" of the scores for each of the three films, in total encompassing more than 10 hours of material. Hidden gems included the use of *Titanic* vocalist Sissel performing "Asëa Aranion" in "The Last Debate" cue from *The Return of the King*. Sissel would go on to tour with Shore during the 2004 "Lord of the Rings Symphony Tour" in the United States and Europe.

Shore won three Oscars for his work on the series: two for Best Original Score (*The Fellowship of the Ring* and *The Return of the King*) and one for Best Original Song (the aforementioned "Into the West"). Shore's wins, and those Oscars received elsewhere (most notably Best Picture for *Return of the King*), were most unusual for the fantasy genre, a field usually treated with snobbery and disdain by Academy voters; it was truly heartening to note how the integrity and emotional clarity of the franchise had crossed boundaries and struck hearts. And yet, the real triumph of *Lord of the Rings* is the collaboration established between director and composer: implicit trust went hand in hand with careful research and wise aesthetic choices to do justice to Tolkien's marvelous imagination.

Jackson lauded Shore's ability to embrace the "diversity" of Middle-earth, "giving life to the cultures of the elves, dwarves, hobbits and men in a shimmering symphony of immense beauty and power."[57] He added: "Howard's great strength as a composer is his ability to capture the emotional truth of the story—a story of friendship, love and sacrifice, which forms the very heart of the film; for his music reflects not only the truth and beauty of J.R.R. Tolkien's vision, but also its darkness ... and its soul."[58]

Shore responded in kind. "I could not have approached a work of this scope without great collaborators. Peter Jackson and Fran Walsh have led me on a journey through Middle-earth. They lit the dark corners of Tolkien's world and revealed to me its secrets and mythology.... At times, I must admit I felt like Frodo with the burden of the Ring in my vest pocket, but page by page, then note by note, I was able to uncover Tolkien's complex world. Special thanks to Philippa Boyens who created so many of the lyrics and authored poems for the film that were translated into Elvish, Dwarvish, Black Speech and Adunaic."[59]

Jackson later reunited with Shore for *The Hobbit* trilogy (2012–2014), which unconvincingly acted as both a standalone narrative and a prequel trilogy to *The Lord of the Rings*. As a result the *Hobbit* scores were forced, somewhat awkwardly, to integrate the themes from *The Lord of the Rings* into a canvas that, frankly, didn't require them. However, this is no slight on the composer; rather, it reflected the haphazard direction of travel on the part of Jackson, forever in thrall to the success of his earlier fantasy creation or, more specifically, its stupendous box office returns.

Both *The Matrix* and *The Lord of the Rings* soundtrack trilogies were a high watermark in the digital era of film music production. However, painful as it may be to admit, they were exceptions to the rule as far as interlocking thematic music was concerned. One only gets scores on this kind of a gargantuan, intelligent scale when they are aligned with movies whose conceptual ambition favors such an approach. If the films are destined to be a once-in-a-generation experience, then it stands to reason that the scores will be similarly anomalous.

In the years since both of the aforementioned trilogies, the emphasis on large-scale, demographic-driven franchise filmmaking has escalated. Somewhat ironically, at the same time the reliance on theme and motif-driven film scores has seemingly become bittier and more diffuse. Strong melodic ideas may surface in a given film on the assumption that they will be developed in a later chapter, only to be unceremoniously dropped. This has been thrown into sharp relief following the emergence of the Marvel Cinematic Universe (MCU), which started with 2008's *Iron Man*.

The Marvel franchise has achieved success in two important ways. Firstly, it has reinforced the lucrative sales value of so-called "B-tier" comic book characters, starting with the aforementioned Iron Man. Prior to the film's release, no-one could have predicted that billionaire-turned-flying-suit-developer Tony Stark would end up rivaling the DC likes of Superman and Batman in terms of big screen comic book supremacy. But thanks to pacy direction from Jon Favreau, a witty script and a career-reviving turn from Robert Downey Jr., the character of Iron Man went from zero to hero, becoming the de facto figurehead of an expanding blockbuster franchise.

Secondly, the MCU has popularized the notion of serialized cinematic storytelling, or, at the very least, has given it a new lease of life. Post-*Iron Man*, the franchise has acted as a drip-feed of both individual storylines and wider ensemble efforts that gather together a host of different characters. These various movies are grouped together in "phases" that, over time, have unveiled specific Marvel comic book characters and large-scale conflicts with deadly enemies, both of which serve to advance the overarching narrative. If something like HBO's *Game of Thrones* (2011–2019) unfolds in individual "seasons," then each phase of the MCU could be said to act as its own "season," albeit with episodes that unfold on a big-budget, theatrical scale two or three times a year.

Five. Atonal

One might imagine that musical consistency has been a bedrock of the MCU. Oddly enough, that's not been the case, at least not straight away. Coincidentally the first *Iron Man* movie was scored by Ramin Djawadi who has won over a global audience with his intricate scores for *Game of Thrones*. But whereas those works contemporize the notion of the symphony fantasy score (a la Djawadi's mentor, Hans Zimmer), *Iron Man* ditched the orchestra altogether. Instead, it takes a rock-centric approach, assimilating the gung-ho maverick bravado of its title character, albeit at the expense of memorable themes. Attitude, rather than nuance, is the emphasis.

From here, the MCU became a spotty patchwork of musical styles, employing a multitude of composers with a range of different voices. Sometimes, the results were impressive (Craig Armstrong's *Incredible Hulk*, from 2008), sometimes less so (John Debney's inconsistent melding of Djawadi and Jerry Goldsmith–aping brass anthems in 2010's *Iron Man 2*). Disconcertingly, individualistic composers have been drafted in to seemingly perform a facsimile of the Remote Control/Hans Zimmer aesthetic, a fate that befell Patrick Doyle on 2011's *Thor*, directed by his regular collaborator Kenneth Branagh. It's hard to reconcile the *Thor* score, occasionally sweeping though it is, with the richly orchestral tonalities of *Henry V* (1989), *Much Ado About Nothing* (1993), *Hamlet* (1996) and others.

What purpose does it serve if one imports a composer known for a specific style, and thereafter restricts the musician from deploying their voice? More alarmingly, how can one establish thematic consistency over a wide-ranging, and ever-expanding, franchise if composers are essentially on a revolving-door principle, giving way to predecessors with a very different style? This happened within the *Thor* franchise as Brian Tyler took over from Doyle for 2013's *Thor: The Dark World*, conjuring an enjoyably muscular, Norse-inspired score, but at the expense of Doyle's own material.

Arguably, it wasn't until 2012's *The Avengers*, directed by Joss Whedon, that the series attained any kind of musical spine at all. The film, a key episode in Marvel Phase One, was pivotal in bringing together the first generation of MCU heroes, characters who would ultimately form the Avengers initiative indicated in the title. This kind of Marvel team-up had never been attempted on the big screen before and the film's breezy sense of wit, largely driven by the antagonistic chemistry of its main players (Iron Man included), buoyed it to box office success and critical acclaim. Newly emboldened, Marvel used *The Avengers* as a test basis for all future ensemble epics in the MCU franchise.

In a musical sense, the production made the sage decision to import veteran Alan Silvestri. He was already a dab hand at thunderous, rhythmically adventurous symphonic scores, from *Back to the Future* (1985) *to Predator* (1987), *The Abyss* (1989) to *Judge Dredd* (1995). Not only did Silvestri have this singular orchestral heritage to his name, traits that would be infused in the soundscape of the *Avengers* movie, but he'd also scored a critical hit with his debut MCU score, just a year earlier. In 2011, Silvestri brought the first sense of memorable thematic unity to the MCU with *Captain America: The First Avenger*, whose retro World War II setting made it singularly perfect for a film composer with a distinctly old-fashioned sense of style. The movie was directed by Joe Johnston, who had already elicited a joyous superhero score from James Horner with *The Rocketeer* (1991).

The First Avenger charts the development of Steve Rogers (Chris Evans) from scrawny wannabe hero into buffed-up, near-invulnerable super-soldier, who takes on the evil Red Skull (Hugo Weaving). It's a stylized, nostalgic adventure, drawing on the tone of the *Indiana Jones* series and others, and Silvestri responds in kind with the propulsively exciting, militaristic "Captain American March," heard in bursts throughout and in full during the end credits. So strong is Silvestri's musical voice, from the rhythmic phrasing to the warm brass pitch and the compassionate nature of the strings, that one immediately feels strong identification with the title character a la Batman and Superman.

This theme and melody approach was exactly what was sought in *The Avengers*. Silvestri's characteristic mixture of powerful trumpets, horns and trombones, mixed with pulsating strings and inventive rhythms in the xylophone and timpani sections, is very much on full display. This musical style is emphasized first when the Avengers are at each other's throats, and then continued during the later action sequences when they realize the greater good of fighting their common enemy, Loki (Tom Hiddleston). The underscore cues are held together by a propulsive main theme, which consists of an A and B section. Part A has a militaristic bearing, as forceful strings mix with timpani and brass—this fragment is heard most often at the beginning of the film, essentially the formation material as Nick Fury (Samuel L. Jackson) seeks to bring the Avengers together.

Part B is what has commonly been adopted as the MCU's primary musical signifier for the Avengers team, a resoundingly virtuous passage for horns and trumpets that unifies our heroes and celebrates them as a world-saving collective. This is heard during the famous New York battle tracking shot sequence, the B section of the theme taking flight as Iron Man, Captain America, Thor (Chris Hemsworth), Hulk (Mark Ruffalo), Black Widow (Scarlett Johansson) and Hawkeye (Jeremy Renner) bring their disparate talents together.

That said, it took the MCU a long time to realize the potential of

Silvestri's theme as a binding emotional element. In 2015, the theme was adapted by Danny Elfman for *Avengers: Age of Ultron*, ostensibly as a musical bedrock for a new-look Avengers unit. (Elfman's theme sat alongside material from Brian Tyler.) However, it wasn't until 2018 that Silvestri was brought back into the Marvel fold, his theme gracing *Avengers: Infinity War*, directed by Joe and Anthony Russo. This was the first part of the "Infinity Saga," shot concurrently with *Avengers: Endgame* (2019), another installment that featured Silvestri's involvement.

Infinity War grapples with the threat of the ruthless Thanos (Josh Brolin) who threatens to obliterate half of all life in the universe with the power of the Infinity Stones. *Endgame* sees the disempowered Avengers leading the fight back. Both movies were gargantuan efforts, tasked with resolving not only a decade of MCU worldbuilding, but also individual character arcs. Director Anthony Russo championed the notion of heritage in the resulting soundtracks, saying that he and his brother tasked Silvestri with reprising several existing themes: "In terms of preserving themes from the MCU, we wanted to harness Alan's themes from *Captain America* as well as his previous *Avengers* work, specifically *Infinity War*, which has one particular cue tied to one of the stones."[60]

This cross-pollination of musical themes was only made possible by the emotional magnitude of the combined "Infinity Saga." The Russos' recognized the nostalgic register of Silvestri's music, no matter how spotty its deployment throughout the preceding MCU movies, and exploited it as an important emotional lightning rod, implicitly communicating heroism, valor and sacrifice in the face of overwhelming evil. Silvestri himself described the "Infinity Saga" soundtracks as a culmination of sorts, particularly given his established relationship with the Captain America character: "These are long-term relationships between the audience and these characters…. People have grown up with Iron Man, Captain America and Thor. I hope that tears come during the sad moments, as well as the victorious and heartwarming ones."[61]

It's a somewhat unusual example of musical loyalty in a franchise not known for it. Yet even within *Infinity War* and *Endgame*, one can sense a reluctance to fully merge the various character motifs together. Besides the "Captain America March," the odd brief motif from *Black Panther* (the 2018 score from Ludwig Göransson) and the *Ant-Man* films (scored in 2015 and 2018 by Christophe Beck), there's perhaps not as much thematic overlap as one would expect. Instead there's a sense of streamlining, the overarching Avengers theme becoming the dominant theme, either for reasons of distilling the musical soundscape (lest there be too many distracting musical identities), or simply because the MCU isn't traditionally in favor of the Wagnerian tapestry showcased in *Lord of the Rings*.

It must be said that the *Lord of the Rings* movies operate by a different set of principles than the MCU. *Lord of the Rings* is overseen by a single director and a single composer, and encompasses a single narrative, not a multitude. Perhaps this is the problem: there is an evolution to the Marvel films, but with a range of iconoclastic directors bringing their own specific demands for music, it's inevitable that there will be a lack of consistency from film to film. This pertains to the issue raised earlier with regard to Hans Zimmer: film composers are increasingly subject to extenuating corporate circumstances, meaning that, to use the MCU as an example, they can only assert limited creative control before they give way to someone else.

One must consider the presence of three composers on both the *Iron Man* series (Ramin Djawadi, John Debney and Brian Tyler for 2013's *Iron Man 3*) and the *Thor* series (Patrick Doyle, Brian Tyler and Mark Mothersbaugh on 2017's *Thor: Ragnarok*). Elsewhere, the *Captain America* series has been graced by one score from Alan Silvestri and two from Henry Jackman (2014's *The Winter Soldier* and 2016's *Civil War*). Even when there is composer consistency within certain MCU character strands (Michael Giacchino's work on *Spider-Man: Homecoming* in 2017, *Spider-Man: Far from Home* in 2019 and *Spider-Man: No Way Home* in 2021), there's frustratingly little thematic bleed-through in other movies showcasing said characters.

This isn't a problem that's unique to Marvel. The Warner Bros MonsterVerse franchise has developed parallel Godzilla and King Kong narratives, before finally bringing these classic movie monsters together to fight in *Godzilla vs. Kong* (2021). This franchise has showcased the input of Alexandre Desplat (2014's *Godzilla*), Henry Jackman (2017's *Kong: Skull Island*), Bear McCreary (2019's *Godzilla: King of the Monsters*) and Tom Holkenborg aka Junkie XL (*Godzilla vs. Kong*).

Although there are tonal allusions to the styles set down by the original composers of the Godzilla and Kong franchises (principally, Akira Ifukube and Max Steiner), each MonsterVerse movie is treated as its own self-contained entity on a musical basis. Once again, this means little music is shared from film to film, and even within the franchise, the harmonics and approaches of each score vary wildly, from the crisp, fortissimo orchestration of Desplat's take to the much more harshly industrial, post–Hans Zimmer approach of Holkenborg. One can see these principles at work in the *Harry Potter* series (2001–2011): initiated by John Williams, a series of other composers (Patrick Doyle, Nicholas Hooper and Alexandre Desplat) have brought their own styles to J.K. Rowling's world, albeit staying true to Williams' central "Hedwig's Theme."

The problem would, therefore, appear to be endemic within 21st-century franchise filmmaking. And yet, to play devil's advocate, there are plenty of recent blockbuster scores that have shown a degree of thematic unity. Composer Danny Elfman is ubiquitous within the comic book genre, and in 2002, he wrote the score for the first big-screen *Spider-Man* movie (one that wasn't affiliated with the MCU). Continuing his collaboration with *Darkman* director Sam Raimi, Elfman delivered a soaringly heroic theme that adapted the harmonic voice of the earlier *Batman* but in a more overtly optimistic vein. This theme was traced throughout Elfman's *Spider-Man 2* (2004) and Christopher Young's *Spider-Man 3* (2007), the latter a replacement for Elfman after he and Raimi fell out.

Likewise the increasingly successful *Mission: Impossible* series, fronted by Tom Cruise, has stayed loyal to the iconic TV series theme by Lalo Schifrin. That said, the treatment of the theme has undergone a host of different guises in line with each director's signature style. In 1996's *Mission: Impossible*, directed by paranoia master Brian De Palma, composer Danny Elfman's jittery, anxious score emphasized the bongos, piccolo flutes and unusual time signatures of Schifrin's creation. John Woo's flamboyant *Mission: Impossible II* (2000) was scored by Hans Zimmer and marked arguably the biggest deviation from the "traditional" sound, showcasing Zimmer's synth-rock-opera approach familiar from his 1990s action scores.

Michael Giacchino's two scores, *Mission: Impossible III* (2006), directed by J.J. Abrams, and *Mission: Impossible—Ghost Protocol* (2011), helmed by Brad Bird, restored the playful retro groove of Schifrin's music, as did Joe Kramer's dynamic and exciting *Mission: Impossible—Rogue Nation* (2015) for director Christopher McQuarrie. As cited earlier, Lorne Balfe's score for McQuarrie's *Mission: Impossible—Fallout* fell very much into the post–*Dark Knight*/*Inception* mode of heavily processed and sampled sound, albeit with traces of the organic quirks familiar to Schifrin.

In terms of Marvel's inconsistent musical methodology, it may be tempting to lay the blame at the feet of Kevin Feige, the President of production company Marvel Studios, and the overseer of the various cinematic threads of the MCU. Like Jerry Bruckheimer, he asserts a vast amount of creative control, but it may be incorrect to suggest that Feige similarly treats music as a cut and paste job. Michael Giacchino has said that the decision to open *Spider-Man: Homecoming* with an orchestral reprise of the original *Spider-Man* TV theme (composed in 1967 by Paul Francis Webster and Bob Harris) arose from a conversation with Feige. They decided to use it in the film and also as an introduction to the 2016 Marvel Comic-Con panel,[62] a clear demonstration of how music can bridge the divide between filmmakers and fans.

But who's to say that theme-driven comic book scores are the be-all and end-all? Circling back to Hans Zimmer, his scores for Christopher Nolan's *Dark Knight* trilogy have proved to be a divisive yet interesting case study in playing against the expectations of thematically driven superhero music. Beginning with *Batman Begins* in 2005, Zimmer's approach was very much in favor of darkly nebulous tone and texture, with a rising two-note phrase serving as the primary identity for Christian Bale's Bruce Wayne. The malleability of this theme meant it could drift in and out of the unremittingly oppressive soundscape, alleviated every now and then by co-composer James Newton Howard's relatively more appealing material for Wayne's wounded human psyche.

This aesthetic was carried into *The Dark Knight* with Zimmer fashioning a buzzing, angular sound for the Joker, less a theme and more a textural expression of imminent chaos. Newton Howard, meanwhile, got arguably the most interesting material for doomed lawyer Harvey Dent (Aaron Eckhart), steadily contorting a noble "white knight" theme into a churning, despairing piece for cello and double bass as the character is warped into the dreaded Two-Face.

Newton Howard's absence was keenly felt in the score for *The Dark Knight Rises* (2012), a solo Zimmer effort that emphasizes the most overbearing aspects of his work with Nolan. The primary new idea is a Sanskrit chant for the villain Bane (Tom Hardy), alluding to his prison upbringing and his plans to overthrow Gotham City. The vocals were crowd-sourced from fans online,[63] another indication of Zimmer's democratic approach to film scoring. Sadly this idea, and the remainder of the score's themes, are swamped by sheer bombast, a fault of the music, perhaps, but more likely down to Nolan's controversially aggressive sound mixing decisions.

Zimmer's Batman aesthetics have served to underline a sharp division between soundtrack critics and the merits of the artist in question. Zimmer has stressed his need for an "anti-heroic" theme that embodied Nolan's morally murky universe, as opposed to a more recognizably triumphant piece a la Danny Elfman,[64] and there's no doubt he succeeded in developing a singular voice for the overall *Dark Knight* trilogy. But does following a director's brief necessarily translate into a captivating score on its own terms? For casual film fans, the thought of listening to a soundtrack as a standalone listening experience is likely inconceivable; if the score serves its respective film, then all well and good.

However, is Zimmer's approach to Batman another example of flouting musical heritage, or even treating it with contempt? Danny Elfman has himself criticized Nolan and Zimmer's musical philosophy,[65] but even this stalwart of the comic book score isn't immune to messy franchise expectations or chaotic productions. For 2017's *Justice League*, Elfman was tasked with scoring director Joss Whedon's re-edit after original director

Zack Snyder left for reasons of personal tragedy. The ensuing hodgepodge of poserish seriousness and obviously tacked-on jokes resulted in a messy score that aimed to exploit earlier thematic material for emotional directness and nostalgic bravado, a vain attempt to salvage a doomed production.

Elfman's original *Batman* theme and John Williams' *Superman* theme both feature in the movie but to indistinct, confusing effect, a clear sign of a composer swamped by the franchise context in which he was operating. When Snyder returned in 2021 to deliver his *Snyder Cut* of *Justice League*, he chose to employ the anarchically aggressive tones of Tom Holkenborg aka Junkie XL, who evokes the tone of his barraging *Mad Max: Fury Road* score from 2015. Whatever one thinks of Holkenborg's music, it further compounded the slapdash history of the project and its detrimental effect on the art of film music.

Interestingly enough, Elfman has spoken out against the treatment of his original *Batman* film score, widely considered a classic of the genre. He said: "I was terribly unhappy with the dub in *Batman*. They did it in the old-school way where you do the score and turn it into the 'professionals' who turn the knobs and dub it in. And dubbing had gotten really wonky in those years."[66] The composer took aim at "so-called professionals" who "plunk [the music] off to the side and just get the dialogue."[67]

It's a somewhat sobering note on which to end this chapter. It's a reminder that film music is, at the best of times, a delicate and ephemeral construct, one that is all too often used and abused by an industry that fails to harness the art form to its fullest extent. But there is a historical precedent for this. Since the earliest days of Hollywood, composers have been subjected to the whims of tyrannical producers and directors, not to mention pressure-cooker studio expectations, their music often used as a last resort to bail out flagging productions. The difference now is that the individual films cost a lot more money in terms of their production and marketing spend, and more than ever it's harder for film composers to shout above the noise. So what does this mean for the art of film music as the 21st-century advances?

Six

Dissonance

Gender Disparity, Temp Scores and Rejected Scores

"There are just not enough women scoring the top box office movies."—LAURA KARPMAN[1]

Confronting the Gulf Between Male and Female Film Composers

In 1948, a British film named *Penny and the Pownall Case* was released in cinemas. A somewhat forgotten mystery thriller, it's directed by Slim Hand and tells of a glamor model who is hired by Scotland Yard to help apprehend a criminal gang. The film features Diana Dors and was produced by Highbury Productions, an affiliate of British institution The Rank Organization (associated with the films of Powell and Pressburger, and David Lean). Despite this pedigree, the film surely would have been lost to the annals of time were it not for two things. It was one of the first credited appearances from a certain Christopher Lee, soon to become a British acting icon with his striking appearances in Hammer Horror films such as *Dracula* (1958). More pertinently, it was the first-ever British feature film to be scored by a woman.[2]

Indeed it took nearly 60 years, from the inception of the cinematic medium to the release of *Penny and the Pownall Case*, for a woman to crack the UK's patriarchal scoring industry. It's a damning indictment of the gender divisions that existed at the time, and which still sadly continue to this day, in the UK, America and elsewhere. The composer in question was Elisabeth Lutyens, a maverick classical musician who made the successful leap into film and television. But, speaking truthfully, how many film score aficionados, let alone casual listeners, would be able to cite Lutyens' place in the history of the film soundtrack? Certainly, her contribution would appear to be eclipsed by the likes of John Williams and Hans Zimmer, but her story deserves to be reclaimed.

Born in 1906 to the aristocratic Lady Emily Bulwer-Lytton and noted English architect Edwin Lutyens (designer of the London Whitehall Cenotaph), she brought uncompromising, modernistic techniques to the musical landscape of post–World War II Britain.³ Dismissive of the pastoral, quintessentially "English" style of Ralph Vaughan-Williams ("The Lark Ascending") and others, describing it as "cowpat music,"⁴ Lutyens drew on her varied schooling at both the École Normale de Musique in Paris and the Royal College of Music in London.⁵ Lutyens' subsequent career saw her dividing time between standalone chamber pieces, operas and scores for film.

Lutyens was later married to BBC music producer and conductor Thomas Edward Clark, to whom she was introduced in 1938.⁶ Clark was a friend and former student of Austrian composer Arnold Schoenberg, and it's implied that the latter's pioneering technique of 12-tone (or dodecaphonic) serialism may have been extended through Clark, which in turn had an impact on Lutyens' own compositional style.⁷ Broadly speaking, serialism gives equitable importance to all 12 notes of the chromatic scale, in essence crafting a sense of atonality (music without an obvious major or minor tonal center). It was adopted by Lutyens to acclaimed, if dissonant, effect in her 1939 "Chamber Concerto" and many of her subsequent film works.⁸ However it would, perhaps, be misleading to suggest that she was defined, either directly or indirectly, by men.

By 1945, Lutyens' idiosyncratic approach had delivered a spectrum of classical works including string quartets, requiems, piano instrumentals and chamber concertos. She was then commissioned by esteemed composer William Walton, a noted member of the English music establishment, to compose a work of her choosing, sight unseen. The resulting piece, dedicated to Walton himself, was a chamber opera named *The Pit*, which made its debut in 1947 at London's Wigmore Hall. It was a strategic move for Lutyens, allowing her to pierce through the established hierarchy and assert her own singular voice. One year later, she found herself scoring *Penny and the Pownall Case*, although her most significant contribution to cinema came later, in 1963, with Hammer film *Paranoiac*, starring Oliver Reed.

Directed by Freddie Francis, the gifted cinematographer of classic ghost story *The Innocents* (1961), *Paranoiac* is an overcooked story of a man, long thought dead, who returns to reclaim his rightful inheritance. Once again, its significance is owed almost entirely to Lutyens' involvement, a rare example of a genre film from a major studio that is scored by a woman. The score is noted for its chamber orchestra dimensions, a striking contrast to the thunderously Gothic romanticism of Lutyens' male contemporaries such as James Bernard (*Dracula*).⁹ Nevertheless, it's noted how her relatively subtle musical approach complemented Francis' sound design.[10]

"Dialogue, commentary, music and sound effects should all work together," she later explained. "It is ideal—though not always done—to work in closest co-operation with the sound effects department. I do not think sufficient care is taken by the composer, scriptwriter and effects department to obtain a properly integrated soundtrack—more's the pity; music and dialogue often compete uncomfortably to the detriment of both."[11]

In her own way, Lutyens seemed to be anticipating the relatively more discreet, objective scoring of paranoid 1970s thrillers. The blurring of the lines between music and sound design was also being mirrored in the work of her contemporary Delia Derbyshire, the pioneering arranger of the BBC's *Doctor Who* theme. It was said that Lutyens didn't particularly rate her work on films, although she reportedly did enjoy her label of "the horror queen."[12] What she clearly relished was the exposure to her work: far more people became familiar with Lutyens' challenging musical aesthetic through cinema than any other medium. She later observed that "the audience for horror films accepted without a murmur shrill, atonal music, which they would have rejected with irritation in the concert hall."[13]

Interestingly, given that she was operating within such a patriarchal environment, Lutyens did occasionally find herself replacing some of Hollywood's most famous male composers. This occurred with 1967's *Theater of Death* (aka *Blood Fiend*), starring Christopher Lee. The film was originally meant to have been scored by Bernard Herrmann, and it's suggested, somewhat regrettably, that Lutyens' lower fee secured her the job.[14] The movie, directed by Samuel Gallu, is a Grand Guignol story of a theater owner whose establishment is connected to a series of grisly deaths, and although one imagines what Herrmann would have done with it, Lutyens' score came in for praise as one of her more accessible film score works.

It was one of several scores Lutyens composed for British production company Amicus, noted for their influential portmanteau horror movies (including 1965's *Dr. Terror's House of Horrors*, directed by Freddie Francis). It's noted that the score for *Theater of Death*, despite its typically singular percussion and ostinato patterns, strikes a more traditional tone than Lutyens' other Amicus scores with emphasis on grandiose brass and sonorous strings, perhaps more akin to her contemporary James Bernard.[15] The latter is a noted influence on the lavishly Gothic sound of Wojciech Kilar's acclaimed *Bram Stoker's Dracula* (1992), composed for Francis Ford Coppola.

Given her intriguing flouting of musical convention, her compositional skill and her association with the upper echelons of the British classical scene, why, therefore, is Elisabeth Lutyens not better known? She passed away in 1983, having made a considerable impact on the UK music hall and the cult horror film scene of the 1960s, but her valuable contribution is swamped by the onrush of male composers making their mark on the film industry around the same time (John Barry, Ennio Morricone, Jerry Goldsmith, Elmer Bernstein and so on).

Regrettably, it may simply be a case of numbers: there continues to be a disproportionate ratio of men to women in the film scoring sector, with the effect that the works of women composers tend to be negated or overlooked altogether. It may also be the quality of the projects to which women composers often find themselves attached; fascinating though Lutyens' horror soundtracks tended to be, the films she worked on tended to be cult offerings with the prime cuts seemingly reserved exclusively for men. Certainly, one might struggle to measure up the merits of *Theater of Death* with, say, *Cool Hand Luke*, the anti-establishment Paul Newman vehicle scored that very same year by Lalo Schifrin (to Oscar-nominated effect).

To be clear, that's no slight on the quality of Lutyens' compositions; it's just that exposure counts for many things, if not everything, in the Hollywood recording industry. The situation becomes even more stark with the following fact: it wasn't until 1981 that a female film composer scored a Hollywood film on their own. The musician in question was Suzanne Ciani, an electronic pioneer who wrote the music for Joel Schumacher's directorial debut *The Incredible Shrinking Woman*.[16] The was a critical and commercial flop and this has, unfortunately, tended to relegate Ciani's significance amidst the annals of Hollywood film music.

Just as shockingly, it wasn't until 1997 that a female composer won an Oscar. The musician in question was Rachel Portman, the movie being Jane Austen adaptation *Emma*, starring Gwyneth Paltrow.[17] Ironically enough, the category in 1997 was split between Musical or Comedy Score, for which Portman won her Oscar, and Original Dramatic Score, which went to Gabriel Yared for *The English Patient*.

To be clear, the Oscar category for Best Original Score was first established in 1935; it took a further 62 years for a man to give way to a woman in the field. How unfortunate it is that one has to single out skilled composers like Portman and position them as footnotes or marking points in Hollywood history, in the process illuminating the vast disparities that exist in the realm of film scoring. This has the detrimental effect of overshadowing the music itself, which in Portman's case is a sunny, quintessentially "English" distillation of Austen's comedy of manners. In that sense, Portman's ability to channel the pastoral likes of Vaughan Williams is the polar opposite to Elisabeth Lutyens' approach.

Whatever one's opinion on Portman's work (it has been derided as "fluffy" in certain quarters[18]), it opened the doors and essentially cemented her as the in-house composer for distributor Miramax, which released *Emma*. No other women composers at the time could claim to have defined a signature sound for a leading Hollywood studio, but Portman found herself very much in demand.

This, despite Shirley Walker's quietly pioneering work in the years beforehand: after several years of conducting other people's work, her breakout score was 1992's *Memoirs of an Invisible Man*, for director John Carpenter, followed by her acclaimed superhero score *Batman: Mask of the Phantasm* in 1993. Walker was the first woman to ever score a comic book movie, and she later experienced genre success with the *Final Destination* horror series, beginning in 2000; Walker's eerie main theme was continued throughout the remainder of the franchise after her death in 2006.

Rachel Portman's graceful harmonic choices, from skipping strings to dainty flutes and tender oboe variations, became the de-facto signature of so-called "Oscar-bait" Miramax movies such as *The Cider House Rules* (1999) and *Chocolat* (2000), both Oscar nominated for their score, *The Legend of Bagger Vance* (2000) and *The Human Stain* (2003). The prestigious nature of such pictures, upholstered with a crisp visual aesthetic, often sentimental narrative trajectories and star power to match, demanded a musical idiom that very much drew on classical tradition. Portman responded in kind with an approach that approximated tenderness and melancholy in equal measure.

Of the scores cited above, *The Legend of Bagger Vance* impresses with its more harmonically diverse palette. Portman interweaves a graceful solo trumpet (performed by Andrew Crowley) to accentuate the nostalgic story of a golfer (Matt Damon) and the eponymous mystery man (Will Smith), a caddy who helps guide him to victory. There's a resonant note of American patriotism and expanse in Portman's brass section, a sense of mystique and good old down home conservative values that ably supports director Robert Redford's aesthetic. That said, some of Portman's most interesting scores came before she won the Oscar for *Emma*. Her Asian-inflected score for Wayne Wang's *The Joy Luck Club* (1993) fosters an intoxicating atmosphere, while before that, she fashioned a spine-chilling atmosphere for the 1989 TV adaptation of Susan Hill's ghost story *The Woman in Black*.

Portman has said that film scoring can achieve "all sorts of things."[19] She then elaborated: "It can be an equal partner to the actors; it can be like another actor in the film. Also if it's used wisely, it can inform and affect the scene just as much as a lot of the dialogue. And that is what you should think to do if you're writing a score to a movie. It is a supporting role but an important one—and if you take it all away, there's no color in the film—it can feel like that. Of course, when it's used badly, it's the most annoying and irritating thing, if there's music that you find repellent. It's certainly over-used in films these days and I'm always fighting that. But there's a fear coming from filmmakers and studios these days—a fear of having scenes without music at all, a fear of silence. And if you think about this life we lead, how everyone walking down the street these days has music plugged into their ears: we live our lives to a soundtrack."[20]

A Portman score that highlights this dichotomy is *Never Let Me Go* (2010). Director Mark Romanek's haunting take on Kazuo Ishiguro's novel (adapted by Alex Garland) centers on three young people who have been raised from birth for a dreadful purpose, which only becomes clear to them during adolescence and early adulthood. The fine performances from Carey Mulligan, Andrew Garfield and Keira Knightley are tightly controlled, as is Romanek's tendency to withhold vital information about the surrounding context.

The score, meanwhile, is a gripping cello and double bass-driven depiction of imminent tragedy that flags up a dreadful sense of destiny foretold right from the opening scene. Is the music, therefore, telling us too much? It's certainly more operatic in its reach than either the visual aesthetic or the performances, and yet it crafts a sense of emotional directness that the otherwise chilly film would lack. It's a musical battle between restraint and earnestness, although the downbeat nature of Portman's music makes it a striking, and dramatically refreshing, change of pace from her usual work.

The same bucolic sense of "Englishness" can be heard in the soundtracks of Portman's contemporary Debbie Wiseman. In the 1990s, Wiseman achieved success with a string of period drama scores: *Tom & Viv* (1994), James Herbert adaptation *Haunted* (1995) and *Wilde* (1997). The last of these scores was met with critical acclaim, distilling the mixture of elegance and melancholy within Stephen Fry's performance as the titular Oscar Wilde. *Haunted* also impresses: nominally a ghost story score, it defies expectations with lyrical piano and string passages, only occasionally conceding to the supernatural with eerily spectral choir.

Wiseman's work has been compared with that of Patrick Doyle, often emphasizing chamber-sized ensembles, attractive themes and delicate restraint. Certainly, one can hear the parallels between *Haunted* and Doyle's score for Jane Austen adaptation *Sense and Sensibility*, composed the same year for director Ang Lee and screenwriter Emma Thompson. Whereas Doyle has continued his fruitful collaboration with Kenneth Branagh, Wiseman has experienced further critical success in the realm of television, including the BBC's *Wolf Hall* (2015), and live performance, including *Queen Elizabeth II's 90th Birthday Celebration*, performed by The National Symphony Orchestra.

A more troubling question is this: are women destined to score polite comedies and period dramas while men score action, fantasy and sci-fi? Are film scores codified to sound typically "masculine" or "feminine"? Anne Dudley is the noted composer and conductor of *The Crying Game* (1992) and *The Full Monty* (1997), for which she won an Oscar. Dudley has successfully traversed the divide between pop music and classical scoring; having been associated with the likes of The Buggles' Trevor Horn early in her career, she then became a founding member of avant-garde synth-pop group Art of Noise. Now an established collaborator with the provocative Paul Verhoeven (2006's *Black Book*, 2017's *Elle* and 2021's *Benedetta*), Dudley explained that gender dualities are writ large throughout the scoring industry.

"There still seems to be a barrier to women composing for these big action movies," said Dudley. "It's not as if women can't be composers because it requires a different level of strength to men. There are lots of women working as assistants on action films but there still seems to be a barrier."[21]

One composer who has bucked that particular trend is Pinar Toprak. The Turkish-American artist generated headlines when, in 2019, she scored the Marvel Studios movie *Captain Marvel*. In the process, she became the first woman to score a Marvel blockbuster. The film was positioned on several fronts as a comic book fantasy that would address the male-centric imbalance of the genre. This extended to the presence of a female composer on the recording stage. Brie Larson stars as intergalactic Kree warrior Vers who crash-lands on Earth in the 1990s and starts to remember fragments of her past life as human Air Force pilot Carol Danvers. Inexorably, her destiny starts to change, and she grows into the character eventually known as Captain Marvel.

Directed by Anna Boden and Ryan Fleck, the movie's feminist credentials are well-intentioned, if ultimately sunk by an overly familiar narrative. Nevertheless, the presence of Toprak as composer makes the film something of a historic milestone, and demonstrates that, contrary to glib Hollywood opinion, women are more than capable of taking the reins on a large-scale symphonic superhero score. Toprak channels the spirit of established Marvel composers like Alan Silvestri while also drawing on her own background in televisual comic book narratives, primarily *Superman* prequel series *Krypton* (2018–2019).

The score is very much anchored in traditional idioms, based around a heroic brass fanfare that is steadily teased out over the course of the narrative. This is in line with Vers' steadily awakening sense of realization, and the full Captain Marvel presentation is largely withheld until the climactic set-piece battle scene. Toprak also slyly incorporates analog synth samples to reinforce the film's retro sense of retro nostalgia. The composer recalled that thematic loyalty was central to her philosophy on the score.

"I made my intentions clear, and when the opportunity to demo came, I wanted to make sure that I made the best impression," Toprak explained. "I went and hired a 70-piece orchestra and did a big production of it so that they could see me in front of the orchestra conducting, and I did another video inside my studio where I talked about the character and the theme. I really wanted to put my best foot forward, and I'm very grateful it worked out."[22]

"There's so much weight on [the *Captain Marvel*] theme, and at first I was kind of psyching myself out," she added. "After two days of being in the studio and not being happy with anything I wrote, I went out for a walk, and I started humming a theme—and believe it or not, that's still in my voice memo, and that is the *Captain Marvel* theme."[23]

The *Captain Marvel* score invites us to confront the apparent gender dichotomy within film music. It's a score composed by a woman for a female character, and yet its brassy constructs are those commonly, if not glibly, associated with a sense of masculine bravado. This is perhaps due to long-standing Hollywood precedent, going all the way back to Erich Wolfgang Korngold's scores for Errol Flynn. Very often, brass has been used by male composers as a signifier for roguish, swashbuckling male characters (John Debney's *Cutthroat Island* being a rare exception), and these inherent biases have been instilled over the course of many decades.

If more women scored films in general, especially blockbusters, maybe these facile associations would not be so entrenched. As it stands, Toprak's ability to both secure the *Captain Marvel* gig and deliver a score worthy of her Marvel contemporaries is a significant achievement within the scoring industry. However it is a relatively isolated accomplishment— one waits to see if Toprak has set any kind of precedent, at least within the Marvel Cinematic Universe (MCU).

Later in 2019, Icelandic composer Hildur Guðnadóttir achieved significant artistic success with her score for DC's *Joker*. The movie, directed by Todd Phillips, reimagined the Clown Prince of Crime's origin story as a Martin Scorsese–inflected crime drama, plunging viewers into a seedy depiction of 1980s Gotham City. The movie rises high on the back of Joaquin Phoenix's intense central turn as Arthur Fleck, the emotionally troubled clown who begins a chilling transformation into Gotham's most feared anarchist.

Phoenix won an Oscar for his tightly wound performance, as did Guðnadóttir for her score. She was only the third woman to score any kind of comic book movie (after Toprak and Shirley Walker for *Batman: Mask of the Phantasm*), and the third woman to win an Oscar for film music.

The music plays against our expectations of comic book scores, in line with the narrative and the film's visual style. Guðnadóttir casts a wholeheartedly bleak sense of mood with an emphasis on celli and double-bass to lament Arthur's fall into despair. The string section is prevalent throughout—if brass and timpani are deployed, it's to accentuate a sense of human violence and frailty, the sense of one man raging against a world that has left him behind. Very often, Guðnadóttir's music overlaps with the bustling soundscape of Gotham City, the diegetic and non-diegetic mixing a la her Emmy-winning score for 2019 TV show *Chernobyl*.

Somewhat unusually, Guðnadóttir composed her initial impressions based on the script and sent them to Phillips. He then played them back on the set, which helped to inform Phoenix's portrayal (including the acclaimed, elegiac bathroom breakdown sequence).[24] The composer would later describe the experience as "magical," adding: "It was completely unreal to see the physical embodiment of that music. His hand gestures were the same types of movements that I felt when I wrote the music. It was one of the strongest collaborative moments I've ever experienced."[25]

Joker would go on to gross $1 billion worldwide, granting Guðnadóttir the thing that composers seek more than anything: exposure. Her artistic credentials were solidified by her Oscar win, but despite the success of the score, she said: "I'm not going to focus solely on films; I'd get really tired of that. I'm getting a lot of offers right now. But it's important for me to have space, because the work affects me so much. I just follow the curiosity carrot."[26]

Did Guðnadóttir's triumph, therefore, establish a new precedent? It's surely too soon to tell and it's worth pointing out that elsewhere in 2019, all other Marvel and DC comic book epics (and others not affiliated with those brands) were scored by men. That year, 10 comic book movies were released in total, and in terms of men to women, it was a ratio of eight to two. Emmy-winning composer Laura Karpman believes that success stories for women composers are, presently, something of a blip on the landscape. In-keeping with Pinar Toprak and Hildur Guðnadóttir, Karpman has experienced much success venturing into the kind of genre filmmaking usually withheld for men.

Her score for sci-fi series *Taken* (2002), backed by Steven Spielberg, and her multifaceted soundscape for HBO's sci-fi/horror/anthology/fantasy series *Lovecraft Country* (2020), adapted from Matt Ruff's book, showcase a willingness to experiment. The latter is a remarkable conflation of jazz, blues and celestial soundscapes, a disorienting experience that mirrors the journey of African American characters through a landscape populated with monsters both human and fantastical. Karpman believes there is a fundamental imbalance at the heart of the scoring industry. This is borne out in the paucity of Oscar wins for women composers, not to mention the arduous stretch of time between these incredibly isolated victories.

"Hildur's work was undeniably excellent and it was fantastic that she made it through everywhere," Karpman said of the situation. "However, there needs to be more than one. It was the same thing with Rachel Portman, and that was 25 years before *Joker* and Hildur. It's just not enough."[27]

There is, of course, a rich history of women composers pushing at the malleable boundaries of sound. Cited in Chapter Three, Wendy Carlos brought an icy sense of absurdist comedy to her classical music manipulations in Stanley Kubrick's *A Clockwork Orange*. This, in turn, established her as a singular electronic voice, leading to the later likes of *Tron* (1982), a film whose literalization of a digitized landscape required a radical, synthetic score to match. Carlos' legacy was subsequently honored in Daft Punk's thrilling sequel score *Tron: Legacy* (2010), a sophisticated merger of orchestral and electronic overseen by orchestrator Joseph Trapanese.

On the subject of Stanley Kubrick, he has elicited fine scores from female composers elsewhere. For 1999's *Eyes Wide Shut*, his final film, he collaborated with Jocelyn Pook, a former Massive Attack collaborator turned experimental classicist. Pook founded the chamber quartet Electra Strings and partnered with the likes of Dire Straits' Mark Knopfler (whose melancholic score for 1983's *Local Hero* mixes haunting synths with the sounds of a Ceilidh band). Electra Strings traversed the divide between the supposedly elitist classical realm and that of popular recording artists, singling out Pook as a mercurial artist keen to break down boundaries.

Eyes Wide Shut was Pook's debut film score and exposed listeners around the world to her maverick mixture of classical minimalism and electronic manipulation. The spirit of Philip Glass is present in the repetitive rhythmic cells of "Masked Ball," which reverses and distorts an Orthodox liturgical chant to chilling effect, conveying a sense of arcane ritual. This is entirely appropriate for the emotional latitude of the scene, which emasculates the incognito character of Bill, a doctor who, tormented by sexual inadequacy, finds himself seeking bacchanalian revelations. By extension, the visuals and music also emasculate that most macho of icons: star Tom Cruise.

In 2013, artist Mica Levi crossed from the realm of recording artist to film composer with critically acclaimed results. Her background in experimental group Micachu and the Shapes ensured she was well-established for the tone of sci-fi drama *Under the Skin*. Jonathan Glazer's abstract, impressionistic drama stars a revelatory Scarlett Johansson as an alien in human disguise who prowls Scotland preying on men. The film jumps between bold, otherworldly imagery and candid-camera style realism as a disguised Johansson picks up unsuspecting passers-by, their interactions seamlessly interwoven into the fractured narrative.

This was clearly not the kind of movie that demanded a conventional approach. In her debut film score, Levi deployed a host of microtonal strings, variously scraping, buzzing and throbbing to suggest any number of things, be it the birth of an alien consciousness or a sense of human compassion aiming to break through an alien façade. Levi's music, augmented occasionally by euphoric synth effects, brilliantly gives an inner voice to Johansson's subtle performance, aided by the relative dearth of dialogue. The music is a textural element that adds subtextual meaning about the divide between human and inhuman, emotionally remote and often unpleasant, but technically accomplished in how it elevates the film's narrative.

Despite these accomplishments by individual composers, Karpman believes that for change to occur, awareness must be raised within the industry first. Along with Michael Giacchino and other noted scoring figures, she uses her position to advocate for positive change. "I'm an [Academy of Motion Picture Arts and Sciences] governor," she explains. "In my other life, I work in advocacy. I started the Alliance for Women Film Composers with [composer of 2018 documentary *RBG*] Miriam Cutler and [composer of 2016's *Batman: The Killing Joke*] Lolita Ritmanis. We set out to make an effort to really change things in 2013, and I think we've made progress."[28]

The Alliance for Women Film Composers (AWFC), cited by Karpman, announces itself as "a community of composers and colleagues who strive to support and celebrate the work of women composers through advocacy and education."[29] Among the composers belonging to the organization is Lesley Barber, a Canadian artist whose work on the 2016 drama *Manchester by the Sea* met with praise. The film is directed by Barber's regular collaborator Kenneth Lonergan and deals with family tragedy and recrimination, but the composer avoids melodrama. Instead, she deploys minimalist repetition and a capella vocals to powerful effect, also drawing on the legacy of Calvinist hymns embedded in the history of the film's New England setting.[30]

Karpman says that the AWFC's mission extends beyond the parameters of the recording stage: "We've worked on harassment issues, which is a big part, particularly for young women who are being harassed in university and graduate school, and also on jobs working for other composers. So, they leave the field or otherwise make themselves small. It's an ecosystem that's not just about writing music. It's about an environment that needs to be broadened."[31] As an example of this, the 2016 "Women Who Score: Soundtracks Live" concert showcased dynamic work from leading female film composers including Karpman, Barber, Shirley Walker, Rachel Portman, Miriam Cutler and Lolita Ritmanis.[32]

Changing awareness within the industry is one thing, but will this lead to actual tangible scoring assignments for women? More importantly, will these be the kind of high-profile, creatively stimulating assignments so often withheld from female composers? "We've got to have more women working on big-budgeted shows like *Lovecraft Country*, and also movies like *Joker*," Karpman says. "We will continue to inhabit this space and I think that at the Academy, we've done a lot, myself and Michael Giacchino included. We've worked to diversify the branch and we need to continue that work. I started the Women's Initiative at the Academy; we have these incredible gatherings of women filmmakers. There's a lot that's going to be announced in the near-future."[33]

Changes are, perhaps, afoot within the industry. One can glimpse more think-pieces centering on women in film music,[34] even if the balance compared to male coverage remains frustratingly lopsided. Many recent interesting docudramas and documentaries have attempted to set the record straight on the involvement of women in some of our most fascinating and iconic soundscapes.

One need only look at *Delia Derbyshire: The Myths and Legendary Tapes*, released in 2020, for a flavor of such projects. Director Caroline Catz foregrounds the story of Derbyshire's involvement in *Doctor Who* and the wider BBC Radiophonic Workshop, giving a quietly revolutionary artist the voice she deserves. One can also look at Lisa Rover's film *Sisters with Transistors* (2020), a celebration of women within the electronic spectrum more generally. This again extends to Derbyshire, and also the aforementioned Suzanne Ciani. The fascinating documentary takes a close look at Ciani's electronic experimentation within commercials, including her use of a Buchla synth to create the Coca Cola "pop and pour" effect. It was one of the few creative spaces left open to her, given that the film industry was averse to both women composers and avant-garde experimentation.

On balance, there is, perhaps, reason for hope, and one can also derive optimism from the brilliant new voices emerging onto the scene. A diverse range of sounds have emerged in recent years from the likes of Brooklyn-born Tamar-kali, the person behind the spiky sound of Shirley Jackson biopic *Shirley* (2020),[35] and Nami Melumad, whose witty Jewish folk melodies adorned Seth Rogen comedy *An American Pickle* (2020). The relative eccentricity and individuality of these assignments, each defying the crass notions of "femininity" that have held sway for so long in

Hollywood film music, may demonstrate a shattering of the glass ceiling, or at the very least, cracks within.

The Specter of the Temp Score and the Rejected Score

There's an oft-cited truism in Hollywood circles that a film composer cannot truly understand the industry until they've had at least one of their scores rejected. While the motion picture industry is dotted with stories of rejected scores (see Alex North's *2001: A Space Odyssey*, cited in Chapter Three), the practice has become more commonplace and intensive in recent decades, as has the presence of the dreaded "temp score."

Ordinary working practices state that when a composer is brought onto a project, he or she will sit down and "spot" a movie, working with the director to locate the breakpoints in a sequence for the start and end of cues. However, very often a filmmaker will have edited the initial cut of their movie to a temporary music track, or temp score.

Film music historian Mervyn Cooke points out the difficulties that this creates for composers. "Unless composers stay ahead of the game by succeeding in getting into feature-film temp tracks demos of their own music that may serve as early discussion points with the director ... they will often be put under considerable pressure to provide music close in style to cues already assembled on a temp track, which might include classical works or existing film scores by others."[36]

There is an established precedent for using temp scores for Hollywood movies, and this can often yield unexpected results. Miklós Rózsa's characteristic use of the theremin in his score for Billy Wilder's *Lost Weekend* (1945) is said to have derived from temp track confusion. Jazz was initially used as a placeholder, which is said to have given the feel of a comedy, instead of a searing drama about the perils of alcohol addiction.[37] This prompted Rózsa to expand his instrumental palette and deploy wavering, woozy textures to convey the fractured mindset of Ray Milland's tormented central character.

Director Brian De Palma has made a career from assimilating the voyeuristic style of Alfred Hitchcock, albeit with significantly more sex, gore and flashy visual flamboyance. To that end, he went straight to the source and hired Hitchcock's old collaborator Bernard Herrmann to score his 1972 horror-thriller *Sisters*. De Palma recalled an amusing, if fraught, meeting where the typically bullish Herrmann reacted with horror at the use of his love theme from Hitchcock's *Marnie* (1964) in the temp track. De Palma was using it as a placeholder for the opening sequence but

Herrmann demanded it be switched off so he could come up with his own ideas.[38]

Herrmann was, however, singular in making such demands, such was the strength of his personality. Nowadays film composers have to be far more malleable, lest they be replaced entirely. Corporate interests in modern-day Hollywood often come at the expense of film music and the egos of the composers in question. Cooke observes: "With productions undertaken on an individual package basis and unable to be subsidized by the financial security of the old studio system, today's film composer is even more at the mercy of producers and market forces than in the Golden Age. Many scores are rejected seemingly on a whim, and often at the last moment."[39]

Very often, the fate of a film score won't be specifically decided by the filmmakers. Rather, the movie will be screened to a test audience, often around five or six times, a common practice from the mid–1990s onwards.[40] Reactions via questionnaire then lead to a further round of focus groups where the specific movie, and all aspects of its production, are put even further under the microscope.[41] Very often, this is where the score is singled out as the alleged weak element; in reality, it may be because the production is a misfire, the filmmakers know it and the music isn't perceived to have done a good enough job in covering up the cracks.

That said, it may simply be the case that certain composers find themselves out of step with popular trends or the director's needs. Let's begin with John Barry who started the 1990s with his career-defining masterpiece, *Dances with Wolves*. The film needs little introduction: Kevin Costner's directorial debut, based on Michael Blake's novel, it's an end-of-the-American-frontier epic about a Civil War Union soldier who integrates with a tribe of Lakota Sioux. Initially written off as a folly, the movie eventually became the toast of the 1991 Oscars season, winning seven Academy Awards and offering a fine showcase for Barry's signature romanticism.

The score encapsulated Barry's flair for rhythmic experimentation, lush themes and elegiac sweep, assigning a uniquely melancholic tone to the destiny of Costner's central character, John Dunbar. It was a maturation of his sound, from the *James Bond* scores to *Born Free* (1966) and *Out of Africa* (1985) and marked Barry's return to film scoring two years after life-saving esophageal surgery. "In a strange way, I don't call this a Western," Barry said of the project. "There's nothing at all in the picture that rings of the typical Western, which is what I liked about it. It's very much John Dunbar's story, a story that, to my knowledge, has never been told before."[42]

He added: "I approached the whole score from John Dunbar's point of view. It was his journey, from the end of the Civil War, to go out there and see the frontier. It was about his observations, how he found the Sioux tribe. The music reflects John Dunbar's assessment of the dignity and graciousness of these people. As he says in the movie: 'Nothing I have been told about these people is correct.' That is where the score lies."[43]

Barry won his fourth Oscar for Best Original Score (his fifth and final Oscar overall) and delivered what many consider to be his crowning achievement. However, it didn't set in motion a consistent string of achievements throughout the decade. Far from it: Barry's stately or, dare one say it, old-fashioned, style led him to be removed from several projects. This included Barbra Streisand's *The Prince of Tides* (1991), an assignment taken by James Newton Howard, *The Bodyguard* (1992), eventually scored by Alan Silvestri and *The Horse Whisperer* (1998), on which he gave way to Thomas Newman.[44]

A composer falling out of step with industry demands? An individual who refused to renege on a well-established musical style that had won him so much success in the past? Opinions will vary, but the ruthlessness of the Hollywood machine clearly doesn't allow individual prestige or heritage to cloud the filmmaking process. Backtracking several decades, two of Hollywood's most notorious examples of rejected (or, at the very least, heavily modified) scores befell Jerry Goldsmith. The first of these was *Alien*, the seminal 1979 sci-fi horror directed by Ridley Scott.

To reflect Scott's biomechanical nightmare of a film, which was augmented by the unforgettable xenomorph designs by Swiss surrealist H.R. Giger, Goldsmith dipped into the experimental bag of tricks for which he was so renowned. The composer put strings through an echoplex to create an eerie effect of depth, implicitly enhancing the span of the alien planet and the cavernous interior of the commercial towing vehicle Nostromo. For the titular alien, Goldsmith fused the sound of the didgeridoo with low, blatting horns and the serpent, an archaic wind instrument that creates an appropriately unsettling, snake-like effect. The final result is a score that embodies the twisted grandeur and horror of the imagery.

However, despite the success of Goldsmith's textural choices, he and Scott disagreed on the overarching structure of the score. Goldsmith aimed to introduce a warm-sounding trumpet melody and deconstruct it throughout the course of the score, suggesting humanity being riven by something parasitic and horrifying. Scott, on the other hand, thought this theme conveyed too much grandiosity and sweep, forcing Goldsmith to remove it from the opening credits and replace it with something more abstract. Hence why Goldsmith's main theme only appears in fits and starts throughout the movie, most notably in the LV-426 landing sequence.

Even more galling was the fact that Scott and editor Terry Rawlings were wedded to their temp track. The ventilation shaft sequence was temped to a sequence from Goldsmith's own *Freud* (1962), and this piece remained in *Alien* after Goldsmith's proposed track was turned down. With Goldsmith's original theme considerably dialed down in the final edit, it therefore didn't make sense for the theme to make a sudden, cathartic statement during the closing credits. Scott instead favored the Howard Hanson piece "Symphony No. 2 in D-flat Major: Romantic," denying the film's original composer the chance to put his stamp on the closing moments. (Somewhat ironically, elements of Goldsmith's *Alien* score ended up in the final edit for 1986 sequel *Aliens*, a combative experience for both James Horner and director James Cameron.)

Naturally, every director is free to do what they want with the score in their film. And there's no denying that the final presentation of the *Alien* score, including the butchered cues and alternate music, is devastatingly effective. But what does this say about the director's ability to communicate his wishes? After all, this is the bedrock of any great film soundtrack. Goldsmith himself expressed frustration at Scott's inability to convey what he wanted,[45] in the process turning an otherwise dream assignment into something arduous. The singularly brilliant atmosphere of *Alien* clearly demanded a score that was somewhat unorthodox, but here was an example of the show, don't tell battle than can exist between composers and directors.

Goldsmith's next collaboration with Scott was even more disastrous. *Legend* (1985) was designed as a stylized, otherworldly fantasy adventure, very much playing to Scott's strengths in terms of lush world-building. The movie blends an early performance from Tom Cruise with unicorns, goblins and the Lord of Darkness himself, played by a magisterial Tim Curry. Working from a script by William Hjortsberg (author of *Falling Angel*, inspiration for 1987's *Angel Heart*, scored by Trevor Jones), Scott clearly intended to add to a rich visual legacy that already included *The Duellists* (1977), *Alien* and *Blade Runner* (1982).

Sadly, the film was rocked by problems and crises of confidence. The stage on which the film was shooting, the 007 Stage at Pinewood Studios (initially built for 1977's James Bond movie *The Spy Who Loved Me*), burned down. And the scoring situation was no less fractious. Goldsmith was clearly enthralled by the scope and fantastical nature of the project, ultimately blurring string-led romanticism with ethereal synths in the pioneering manner of much of his 1980s work.

However, the American edit of the film saw Goldsmith's music replaced with a score from Tangerine Dream,[46] the synth-pop pioneers who were increasingly being used to foster connections with the lucrative youth audience. Following the test screening, the inevitable decision to remove Goldsmith's music was made by then Universal Studios president Sid Sheinberg,[47] a notorious meddler who, that very same year, had suggested that the *Back to the Future* title be changed to *Space Man from Pluto*.

Essentially, a passion project was junked overnight because the filmmakers got cold feet about the application of music on the project. It was, assuredly, a poor way to treat one of Hollywood's most distinguished composers, but should one point the blame solely at Scott? Certainly, one would expect the director to safeguard his choice of composer, particularly after the already difficult experience he and Goldsmith shared on *Alien*. However, it also exposes the relative impotency of directors when pitted against the clanking machinery of Hollywood expectations, test screenings and audience demographics, not to mention overbearing studio moguls.

Goldsmith's score was used in the European edit of the movie, but it was small potatoes. Little wonder he and Scott never worked together again. However, one of the great ironies of film music is that composers will often find themselves on both sides of the fence. Having suffered the ignominy of two misfiring Ridley Scott partnerships, Goldsmith later found himself doing the replacing on high-flying Harrison Ford action-adventure *Air Force One* (1997).

Directed by Wolfgang Petersen, a filmmaker not renowned for his subtlety, the film casts Ford as U.S. President James Marshall who is called into action when his plane is hijacked by diabolical Kazakh national Korshunov (a fiendish Gary Oldman). The movie plays its patriotism to the hilt and such material clearly demands music that will be played with a straight bat. Oddly enough, Petersen made the decision to hire Randy Newman, a songwriter and composer whose career had vacillated between light satire ("Short People"), Americana soundscapes (1990's *Avalon*) and frolicking, family-friendly fare (1995's Disney-Pixar masterpiece *Toy Story*, for which he composed the perennial favorite "You've Got a Friend in Me").

Outside of the climactic material in *Toy Story*, when Woody (Tom Hanks) and Buzz Lightyear (Tim Allen) are attempting to return to their owner Andy, Newman had rarely tackled action music before. He was an odd choice for *Air Force One*, to say the least, but clearly relished the opportunity to stretch his range. As far as Petersen was concerned, maybe he looked to invert expectations, aiming to elicit from the usually affable Newman an aggressive, full-throttle popcorn symphony.

Whatever the philosophy behind it, the decision didn't work. Newman's hectic score, including the overly peppy brass fanfare for Marshall's character, sat awkwardly over the initial edit of the film, appearing to parody its (admittedly ridiculous) sense of flag-waving bravado. This is what one would expect given Newman's sharp sense of humor, but it was wildly out of place with the dictates of the picture. It served to enhance the elusive divide between effective music and an effective film score; very often, the two are mutually exclusive, and what is often seen as compositionally, or technically, challenging on its own terms simply doesn't match with the flow or tone of a given visual sequence.

Hans Zimmer claimed at the time that he had never written action music as effective as Newman's material for *Air Force One*.[48] Regardless, Petersen wasn't impressed and, with mere weeks to go until the film's release, removed Newman from the project. Petersen later recalled: "[I thought,] 'Maybe we'll get something that's a little different, more daring.' Finally, it didn't really go together. At the end, it comes down to the filmmaker, what kind of taste he has. If I just have the feeling that it doesn't work for the picture I've done, then I have to make a hard decision."[49] He added: "It has nothing to do with the quality of the music. Randy's one of the greatest in the business, and a hugely talented man. We all know that. But it was not my taste, and finally I had to make that decision."[50]

Petersen then enlisted the services of the venerable Goldsmith. However, the deadline proved to be so tight (12 days in total) that Goldsmith was compelled to draw on the services of co-composer Joel McNeely. The latter would be tasked with scoring several set-piece action sequences and otherwise adapting Goldsmith's more traditionally flag-waving main theme. Said theme was a somewhat derivative, if rousing, effort from the composer, but it undeniably served the movie far better than Newman's attempt. And McNeely was well-versed in adapting the works of other composers: his score for *Star Wars: Shadow of the Empire* (1996) followed in the footsteps of John Williams but added some intriguing licks in the process. (McNeeley would later emulate Elmer Bernstein and Jerome Moross to sublime effect in his score for Seth McFarlane's 2014 Western comedy *A Million Ways to Die in the West*.)

Goldsmith vowed to never undertake such an arduous, last-minute assignment again,[51] but of course the saga of the rejected film score didn't stop there. Another Wolfgang Petersen epic, *Troy* (2004), ran into problems with its score when original composer Gabriel Yared was taken off the project after a year of work. Petersen's brawny take on Homer's *The Iliad* stars a bronzed, buffed and implausible Brad Pitt as Achilles, who leads the sacking of the city of Troy along with his Myrmidons.

Clearly, this was an attempt to cash in on the revived swords and sandals genre in the wake of *Gladiator*, employing good-looking A-list stars who had established currency with a contemporary audience. The movie was conjured on an epic budget of $175 million and obviously demanded a sense of sweep in its music. Yared enthusiastically responded, having only intermittently reached the heights of his Oscar-winning *The English Patient* back in 1996. This was the first historical action epic that the composer had tackled, and he devoted 12 months to researching authentic instrumentation, texture, rhythmic and harmonic choices to do justice to Homer's legacy. He then started recording the music in late 2003.

Mere weeks before the film's release in May 2004, however, and a rogue test screening threw the movie's musical philosophy into disarray. Reactions from said screening claimed that the music was too "old-fashioned" and the filmmakers and executives, despite Petersen's professed enthusiasm for the score, swiftly ended Yared's association with the movie.[52] It demonstrates the hypocrisy at the heart of the Hollywood studio system: the role of film music is said to be highly valued and regarded, particularly in terms of connecting the emotional jigsaw pieces, but it's the production element that most often becomes the scapegoat, sacrificed at the altar of a misfiring movie.

Realizing that time was running out, Petersen reached out to James Horner, his collaborator on *The Perfect Storm* (2000). The composer had just two weeks to fashion a sweeping score for this archetypal mythological adventure, and therefore one might be able to forgive its derivative flourishes (very characteristic of Horner's work). Yared, for his part, posted a letter on his website, along with a leak of the score itself, decrying how Warner Bros had jettisoned his passion project without allowing him to make any changes. However, this was met with widespread criticism and legal threats, and he was compelled to remove it.[53] It's perhaps telling that Yared hasn't received a Hollywood assignment as high-profile as *Troy* in the years since.

James Horner's replacement score for *Troy*, functionally effective given the circumstances, highlighted his notorious penchant for self-plagiarism (although, as mentioned, the severe time constraints perhaps made this inevitable). It's one thing for executives or directors to ask a film composer to mimic the sound or tone of a temp track, insulting as it may be. But what does it mean when a composer, entirely of their own volition, borrows notation, or even entire passages, from their own scores or the works of other people?

To be clear, this isn't referring to musical irony, such as Michael Kamen's witty use of Beethoven's "Ode to Joy" as the theme for the villainous Hans Gruber (Alan Rickman) in *Die Hard* (1988). To highlight the point, one can look at two James Horner scores, *Willow* (1988) and *Honey, I Shrunk the Kids* (1989). For *Willow*, a Ron Howard–directed, Lucasfilm-distributed fantasy-adventure, Horner loosely adapted a number of existing pieces including Robert Schumann's "1850 Rhenish Symphony No. 3" (used as the theme for the baby Elora Danan).⁵⁴ The performance of the London Symphony Orchestra and King's College Choir is robust and gorgeous, but one struggles to relax into the idea of Horner having authored the themes.

The frenetic score for Disney's shrinking adventure *Honey, I Shrunk the Kids* was even more contentious. Horner pilfered (or "adapted," based on one's point of view) Raymond Scott's 1937 jazz instrumental "Powerhouse," which had become associated with the Warner Bros *Looney Tunes* cartoons. Horner also deployed a thinly veiled reworking of Nino Rota's *Amarcord* (1973), composed originally for director Federico Fellini. This controversial approach got Disney sued on two fronts by the estates of the respective composers,⁵⁵ although it clearly didn't have a negative impact on Horner's career moving forward.

Horner didn't just plagiarize the works of other people. He wasn't averse to lifting key moments from his own soundtracks either. One can take the score for *Avatar* (2009) as a prime example. The score for James Cameron's blockbuster (currently the highest-grossing movie of all time) is practically a mixtape of Hornerisms, although perfectly enjoyable and nostalgic for all that. Tinkling piano melodies from *The Spitfire Grill* (1996) mix with the delicate chimes and vocal accents familiar from *Titanic* (1997). The infamous four-note horn theme of danger (lifted from Rachmaninoff's *Symphony No. 1*, composed in 1895), is also present and correct, having been a Horner mainstay since *Willow*. The tribal percussion and plosive vocal effects from *Apocalypto* (2006) are also evident.

Horner's music was nominated for an Oscar (the last nomination he received prior to his death in 2015). Mimicking the successful marketing strategy of *Titanic*, the score deploys a chart-topping pop artist during the end credits. Only this time, instead of Celine Dion and "My Heart Will Go On," it's X-Factor winner Leona Lewis, here performing "I See You" (the melody for which acts as the underscore's love theme between Sam Worthington's Jake Sully and Zoe Saldana's Neytiri).

The score's self-referential nature epitomizes the issue of individuality in film music; if one appreciates the music for *Avatar*, one surely has to question whether they are, in fact, enjoying the constituent elements of all the other scores being referenced. The difference with Horner was the overtness of the approach: he rarely cared to disguise his influences, whether they were derived from his own career or other people's. Other film composers are often more guarded and implicit in terms of such an approach, even when compelled to follow a temp track.

Opinions on Horner's methods vary sharply. Some continue to decry him for not visibly citing his inspirations while others say that Horner's self-plagiarism was a natural by-product of a composer in high demand from a ruthless industry.[56] New Yorker music critic Alex Ross takes a more tongue-in-cheek view, suggesting (in reference to *Troy*'s barely disguised use of Shostakovich and Benjamin Britten) that Horner's postmodern pilfering of other people's scores is an implicit commentary on the lack of individuality in modern culture. Either that or, Ross concludes, "the man is a hack."[57] The notion of authorship in film music has always been a sharply divisive one, but Horner transformed such discussions into their own kind of art-form.

A contrasting situation comes with Bill Conti's score for *The Right Stuff* (1983), directed by Philip Kaufman. Here was an example of a composer who was directly instructed to imitate the temp track by the film's producers. The temp in question was Holst's *The Planets*, somewhat appropriate given that the film's narrative centers around the early days of the American space race (the film was adapted from the novel by Tom Wolfe). This put Conti in a somewhat unenviable position: he had to oblige the filmmakers to keep the job (after John Barry had already walked away), while towing the line so as to avoid being sued.

To that end, Conti fashioned a spirited "tribute" to Holst, building on the brassy punch that he had established in Sylvester Stallone's rousing *Rocky* series (with the exception of 1985's *Rocky IV*, Conti would score all the films in the franchise up until 2006's *Rocky Balboa*). He was also careful to acknowledge the source of inspiration in the credits for the soundtrack album. In fact, Conti outright demanded the need for a citation credit, no doubt aware of the potential legal quagmire that lay ahead.[58] Conti would eventually win the Oscar for Best Original Score, maybe proving that imitation really is the sincerest form of flattery.

And yet, Hollywood is nothing if not deliciously ironic. The year after *Troy*, Horner himself was on the receiving end of rejection while working on Terrence Malick's *The New World* (2005). The director was nominally constructing a romantic story about the connection between early American settler John Smith (Colin Farrell) and Algonquin woman Pocahontas (Q'orianka Kilcher), but according to Horner this emotional purity was shredded during Malick's typically fastidious editing process. This also meant that the emotional core of Horner's score no longer had any relevance to the picture. Subsequently, Horner's lyrical music (eventually released in its entirety via album) gave way to tracked-in source cues from Wagner and others.

Years later, Horner gave a frank appraisal of the troubled situation. "Terrence Malick is an enigmatic filmmaker," he explained. "He's a brilliant photographer. He's a brilliant cinematographer. In a way, though, he doesn't know how to coalesce a story from beginning to end. When I first saw this movie it was an early edit. There was no reason this movie couldn't have been as successful as *Titanic*. It was cut that way. It was a story of this Native American girl meeting this guy and it was really romantic. In editing, Terry, as he does in his filmmaking, made much more of a dreamworld and he disassociated the scenes. There was no through-line any more. He lost the love story. He wasn't interested in that. He started telling a story about images and it didn't hold together. The movie didn't hold together for me, or for an audience."[59]

"I think that Terry's brilliant but he is an abstract painter," Horner continued. "You have to know going in that what you initially see—which is a real story—ends up looking more like a Picasso or an abstract painting and it's broken up and musically that doesn't work. You can't tell a linear story any more and he ends up cutting stuff and for an audience, emotionally, I just don't think that holds together. Visually, it's stunning but the storytelling—it's a book that can't be read."[60]

Very often, the rejection of a score, or even a multitude of scores, can be a harrowing experience for both the director and the composer. In 1973, director William Friedkin delivered what was arguably the first-ever horror blockbuster: *The Exorcist*. This disturbing adaptation of William Peter Blatty's novel elicited a stunning performance from Linda Blair as the possessed Regan whose soul hangs in the balance as Father Merrin (Max von Sydow) and Father Karras (Jason Miller) endeavor to save her from eternal damnation.

The Exorcist's blend of Catholic critique and shocking body horror, largely inflicted on an innocent pre-teen girl, generated immediate controversy. Inevitably, word of mouth and intense debate helped propel the film to remarkable grosses of $441.3 million (including re-releases) against a $12 million budget. It was also the first horror movie to be Oscar nominated for Best Picture. Despite this, the production was troubled with allegations of a curse hovering around the set, and several injuries (actress Ellen Burstyn suffered a permanent back injury after being pulled off a bed). And the creation of the music was no less tumultuous.

The documentary *Leap of Faith: William Friedkin on The Exorcist* (2019) offers a fascinating deep dive into the musically literate filmmaker's psyche. Keen to keep the score at a minimal level, so as not to disrupt the multifaceted sound design (which eventually won an Oscar), Friedkin first rejected an idea from Bernard Herrmann. After disparaging the rough cut of the film, Herrmann claimed he could save the picture with the use of the grandiose organ at St Giles Cripplegate church in London, the city where he was living at the time. Aghast, Friedkin ended the meeting.[61]

Friedkin then enlisted friend Lalo Schifrin to write an appropriately low-key score, which would mimic the minimalist temp track choices of

Krzysztof Penderecki and others. According to Friedkin, he was later horrified to hear what he perceived as an overbearing, rhythmic soundscape from Schifrin, and effectively ended their collaboration, and friendship, on the spot.[62] (Schifrin's music was used in a trailer for the film, later banned owing to its disturbing intensity.) The exacting Friedkin later found what he wanted by cycling through potential needle-drop solutions and alighting on Mike Oldfield's "Tubular Bells,"[63] which has since become a classic harbinger of impending doom and catastrophe.

Elmer Bernstein was another composer who had several scores rejected throughout his career. This included his work on Robert Redford's *A River Runs Through It* (1992), eventually scored, to Oscar-nominated effect, by Mark Isham. Bernstein had this to say about the nature of film music creation: "The position of a creator in motion pictures—writers are in a similar position—is that of a chattel, albeit well-paid. They buy music the way you buy a piece of furniture. So from a purely legal point of view, they've got every right to do whatever they want. But directors who are very successful either are people who admit their musical ignorance and defer to the composer or who themselves have a tremendous feeling for music."[64]

To craft beauty without a clear sense of ownership, to sacrifice individuality at the altar of collaboration, to see one's passion for music co-opted into the landscape of commerce and box office figures—such are the sacrifices made by film composers every single day. Rejected scores have become more commonplace but they serve to highlight the resilience of the individuals working in film scoring: the ability to bounce back and stay true to one's voice amidst a profit-hungry movie industry that, increasingly, has little patience for artistic scruples.

Coda

The Future of Hollywood Film Scoring

"If you play themes from contemporary films to people on the street, versus themes from the seventies, eighties or nineties, I wonder if they'd know what they were."—DAVID ARNOLD[1]

What has this book demonstrated in terms of the evolution of the film score? Hopefully it has demonstrated the majesty that can occur when picture and music fuse together in harmonious fashion. On a somewhat more disquieting note, it has, perhaps, also revealed the vulnerability of said music, particularly when it butts heads with the wider film industry. The delicacy of a graceful film melody is no match for the discordant aggression of the Hollywood marketing machine, which steamrollers all before it.

One might ask, what constitutes a perfect film score? In the opinion of this book's author, a perfect score must support, nay, enhance, its movie first and foremost. However, it also has the capacity to transcend the images as a standalone listening experience, communicating the ebb and flow of the film's narrative even when divorced from the visuals. In short, a perfect score conjures memories of the film's imagery through notation, melody, harmony, tone and texture, not to mention careful narrative sequencing. (To facilitate such a listening experience, many film score albums are sequenced differently to the presentation of the music in the movie.)

Plucking an example out of the air, I would cite Danny Elfman's *Edward Scissorhands* (1990), composed for director Tim Burton. Elfman's music is tremendous on its own terms, drawing on the heritage of Tchaikovsky's "Dance of the Sugar Plum Fairy" and demonstrating a sensitive awareness of fairy tale music convention in its use of waltzing strings, boys' choir (the Paulist Choristers of California), celesta and glockenspiel. One must also cite the crystal-clear mixing from the always-excellent

Shawn Murphy who has brought his magic touch to countless masterpieces including John Williams' *Jurassic Park* (1993).

Away from the context of the film, the soundtrack album is brilliantly sequenced to convey the emotional trajectory of Johnny Depp's tragic Edward, sliding from wide-eyed wonderment to fish-out-of-water comedy to eventual, heart-rending isolation and melancholy. It's an example of music that magnificently serves its primary context while also standing apart from it (something that a surprising amount of film scores struggle with).

Even so, what is the relative strength of film music in the modern age? Opinions vary widely. An especially damning indictment comes from the fine composer Mychael Danna who won an Oscar for his spiritually stirring score to *Life of Pi* (2012), directed by Ang Lee. Throughout his career, Danna has indulged in the slightly unorthodox and exotic, melding Eastern instrumentation such as the Indonesian gamelan (demonstrated in the music for *Life of Pi*) with offbeat rhythmic constructs (his work for director Atom Egoyan, including 1997's *The Sweet Hereafter*, demonstrates this).

"I don't think you would call this the Golden Age of film—or television—scoring," muses Danna. "There are a lot of forces at work that have made it more difficult to make scores that are serving the picture as well as they could, and second of all make the art movie forward."[2]

Danna then doubles down on his criticism: "Film music seems to be valued at its lowest point in at least a generation. You can tell that just in a simple market force way of budgets. It's common knowledge that Marvel low-balls. They pay very little for the music, much less than a film that is going to gross a $150 million at least in America. A music budget for a film like that 10 years ago—before the superhero craze—would have been a certain amount, and these are maybe half that, or less. Then you take the fact that they have a well-documented anti-thematic approach. Film music has really lost a great deal of its value. It's a dark time for film music."[3]

It's a stinging attack on modern industry standards from an esteemed and acclaimed composer. But do Danna's words tell the whole story? Mainstream awareness towards film music has been on the ascent in recent years with sold-out live performances at the likes of London's Royal Albert Hall. Concerts can take a host of guises, including feature-length orchestral performances of entire scores that are synced live to picture. Cited in Chapter Five: Hans Zimmer's gargantuan live staging of his *Interstellar* score in 2015. Other successful interpretations have included James Horner's *Aliens* (1986) and *Titanic* (1997), Alan Silvestri's *Back to the Future* (1985), and John Williams' *Raiders of the Lost Ark* (1981) and *Harry Potter and the Sorcerer's Stone* (2001).

Admittedly each of these scores holds something of a rarefied position, capable of enjoying greater levels of commercial success and awareness than other soundtracks (in large part down to the films to which they are attached). Nevertheless, for a film soundtrack to draw a large crowd must, on some level, speak to the instinctive, visceral power between music and image that has been instilled in people since the late 19th century. Many of the scores cited above are intensely bound up with a sense of nostalgia; a live performance of *Titanic*, for instance, can immediately transport an audience back to the film's heyday in 1997 when Horner's Celtic-inspired soundscapes first washed over cinema audiences in profound waves of romantic melancholy.

Composer David Arnold says that comforting familiarity is key to the appeal of certain film music. In June 2011, Arnold hosted a live tribute at the Royal Albert Hall to his James Bond idol John Barry, who had died in January of that year. Arnold recalls: "What I took away from the John Barry memorial, organized with Laurie Barry, EON and Barbara Broccoli, is that, come the end, we'd all sat through three minute pieces that everyone recognized. Every one was a drop dead, stone cold classic."[4]

Arnold reiterates the importance of thematic writing in establishing a strong emotional connection with the audience. These clearly defined building blocks, particularly the heroic and inspiring ones, are the kind of emotional signifiers that are capable of transcending the boundaries of the screen. Even away from the picture, such music plugs into our human nature on a profoundly primal and visceral level.

"Whenever you go to film music concerts, there's a reason why those big tunes keep coming back," Arnold says. "You're always going to hear *Raiders* and *Star Wars* and *Superman* and *E.T.* and the *Bond* theme and *The Good, the Bad and the Ugly*, *The Godfather*, *Rocky*.... People at film music concerts really don't want to hear three and six, revision seven or whatever. They want to hear the big themes. I know the specialists, those really into film music, would want to hear those things. But in a room the size of the Albert Hall, comprising 5,500 people, only 500 of them may be hardcore film music fans—the rest are the general public who want to hear something that they know. Or if they don't know it, that they would like."[5]

So how does the thematic integrity of past film scores match up against what we have today? Arnold muses: "I think what's interesting is when you think about contemporary film scoring, or things that are incredibly successful nowadays, I wonder how often that terrible cliché 'walking out of the screen whistling the theme' still happens? It's not always the fault of the composer. Very often we're asked to do things like that and we don't always have control over what's going on."[6]

Arnold says that opportunities in television are often more diverse and fulfilling, particularly in the era of streaming when a show can reach a mass audience more readily. This can help instill those all-important thematic identities, a process that Arnold has himself gone through with the BBC's *Sherlock* (2010–2017), co-composed with Michael Price, and Terry Pratchett/Neil Gaiman adaptation *Good Omens* (2019).

> "What's interesting about TV, and also video games as well, is it's episodic," he says. This means the music plays more frequently because over the course of six episodes, you get to hear the opening titles six times. There is more music in a six to 10 episode show than there is in a two and a half hour film. And there will be repetition of themes.
>
> Take *Game of Thrones*—I know that's been around for a long time, which helps it to be recognized, but it's got great exposure in terms of people being able to hear the music. It's very indicative of the success of a title sequence. *Sherlock* offered those same opportunities in terms of a title sequence. You hear it every week. Every time you watch the show, you hear that piece of music, and it's that sense of familiarity that can help you feel more attached to music.⁷

As something of a counter-swipe to Mychael Danna's Marvel criticism, composer Christophe Beck lauds the studio's musical vision. Having delivered two enjoyably retro scores for Marvel's *Ant-Man* on the big screen, Beck got to open his box of musical tricks with the acclaimed Disney+ series *WandaVision* (2021). The show focuses on Marvel characters Wanda Maximoff (Elizabeth Olsen) and Vision (Paul Bettany) in a sly approximation of various American TV hits, from *The Dick van Dyke Show* (1961–1966) to *Malcolm in the Middle* (2000–2006). This allows for an especially diverse soundscape and, Beck says, he has also been allowed to emphasize thematic continuity from the movies, something Marvel is said to lack.

"In *WandaVision*, there are definitely some musical Easter eggs sprinkled throughout that refer to other themes by other composers from other movies, including one that I will just say is you cannot miss," Beck explains.

> It's really one of the amazing things about working as a composer in the Marvel Family. A cinematic universe has never really been created like this before. I've worked with [Kevin Feige] enough now to see just how much attention he pays to those details. There's so much interconnectivity between them, and it really rewards the fans in a very meaningful way. It's just so much fun to be a part of that. So, of course, I'm really enthusiastic to reinforce this whole overarching franchise idea, musically, whenever I can.⁸

Former Disney executive Andy Hill takes a sanguine view towards contemporary film music. "Music for the screen has come of age," he writes, "and enjoys far greater respect than it once did, but there are also challenges that didn't exist in Elmer Bernstein's era. These are, in many ways, 'the best of times and the worst of times.' On the negative side of the ledger is the fact that music no longer enjoys the immunity it once had from the sausage factory aspects of motion picture entertainment. It's on the factory floor along with all the other entrails. Elmer once confessed to me that he was glad he hadn't come up in this period, when 'everyone's an expert and composers are more like order takers.' It is indeed harder to develop the kind of distinctive signature that such composers as Bernstein, Herrmann and Goldsmith had with a committee of people looking over your shoulder."[9]

Despite these reservations, Hill recognizes the many breakthroughs that have come with 21st-century film scoring. "On the plus side, however, is the undeniable fact that—to quote Lucasfilm's THX tagline—'the audience is listening.' [Hans Zimmer], [Danny Elfman], [John Williams] and [Howard Shore] are far better known to the general public than [Miklós Rózsa], [Dimitri Tiomkin] and [Franz Waxman] were in their day," Hill states. "Their music is being heard not only in cinemas, but in concert halls and arenas, as well as on smartphones and game consoles."[10]

Hill is also quick to cite the "growing number of festivals in Europe that have expanded the audience and enhanced the international cachet of film music—such festivals as Fimucité (in the Canary Islands), Film Fest Gent (in Ghent, Belgium), Transatlantyk (in Poznan, Poland), and the Film Musical Festival (FMF) in Kraków, Poland."[11] On the subject of the FMF, Hill observes "the 15,000-seat Tauron Arena is filled to capacity for live performances to picture of such scores as *Gladiator* and *Star Trek*."[12]

Such occasions also allow somewhat more out-of-the-box, challenging scores like Don Davis' *The Matrix* (1999) and *Perfume* (composed for the 2006 movie by director Tom Tykwer, plus Reinhold Heil and Johnny Klimek) to take center stage. Hill says that such scores, plus showcases of new works from maverick composers like Elliot Goldenthal, "have received receptions normally reserved for rock stars."[13] One can also see this in the reception accorded to Hans Zimmer at venues such as Coachella (cited in Chapter Five).

Ennio Morricone was another illustrious composer who was fiercely critical about the state of modern-day film music. In 2015, he cited a "deterioration of standards," adding: "The respect for a musical score must come from the director … If the director has no power and has to surrender to budgetary constraints, this is where we have the problem."[14]

Echoing the sentiments from Mychael Danna, Morricone then took aim at working practices within the industry: "Electronic instruments flatten everything. Maybe you can do everything with [them], but the result is quite similar—a kind of standardized music. The fact that people today tend to use too many electronic instruments or amateur composers is because they want to spend less money."[15]

Were one to take Morricone's statements at face value, it would write off a talented generation of young composers who have recently been pushing the boundaries in ways both familiar and unfamiliar. One such person is Daniel Pemberton, a British composer who has reveled in redefining his sound with every new film project. His score for Guy Ritchie's *The Man from U.N.C.L.E.* (2015) is one of the most delightful throwback scores in recent years, a cocktail of jazz and lounge influences that shakes up elements of John Barry, Lalo Schifrin and Morricone himself.

That same year, Pemberton rendered a shift from analog to digital sound in the score for *Steve Jobs*. Danny Boyle's acclaimed drama, starring Michael Fassbender as the titular Apple creative, tracks Jobs from the 1980s through to the 2000s, allowing Pemberton to transition from modular, retro synths to a more sophisticated blurring of organic and electronic sound.

Many of Pemberton's works feature some startlingly off-beat musical decisions, from the guttural breaths used as propulsive rhythms in *King Arthur: Legend of the Sword* (2017) to the sampled hip hop vibe of Oscar-winning animated comic book movie *Spider-Man: Into the Spider-Verse* (2018). At the other end of the scale, Pemberton's work on Netflix Sherlock Holmes spin-off *Enola Holmes* (2020) is among his most melodically appealing and beautiful, a distillation of Englishness with a scampering main theme that captures the energy of Millie Bobby Brown's central performance.

One can also point towards the likes of Ludwig Göransson, a composer who has translated his genre-defying approach with sampled sounds and electronics into the film score arena. Having collaborated extensively with Childish Gambino (most notably on 2018's urgent and topical "This is America"), Göransson went on to impress with his score for Marvel's *Black Panther* (2018). Dysrhythmic drums and the piercing vocals of Baaba Maal, both resulting from Göransson's research into Senegalese music culture, fused with the more traditionally bombastic symphonic approach heard in Western superhero scores. The compelling soundscape gave voice to the film's primary landscape, Wakanda, and went on to win Best Original Score, the first ever comic book movie soundtrack to do so.

Göransson's harsher side came out in the score for the Tom Hardy comic book movie *Venom* (2018), an anguished, churning onslaught of sound that approximated the feeling of being consumed by an alien symbiote. Göransson, like Christophe Beck, Ramin Djawadi and David Arnold, has also enjoyed much creative latitude in the realm of TV.

His score for the *Star Wars* Disney+ series *The Mandalorian* (2019–

present) does an effective job in emphasizing "dirty," gritty, sampled sounds, in line with the show's Spaghetti Western aesthetic and depiction of lawless vagabonds and bounty hunters. At the same time, Göransson is also loyal to the orchestral principles laid down by John Williams, albeit trickling it out carefully over the course of each season. In contrast to Göransson's experimentation, a more traditional symphonic set-up is evident in the score for Netflix hit *Bridgerton* (2021–present), whereby composer Kris Bowers steers his lushly romantic material around inventive covers of leading artists including Taylor Swift.

The presence of fresh musical voices like Göransson, Pemberton and Bowers gives one hope that the future of film and TV scoring is moving in a new direction, at once experimental and thematic. Challenging material has come from the pen of Mica Levi, not just with 2013's *Under the Skin* (cited in Chapter Six) but also the atmospheric *Jackie* (2016), which has an eerie, unresolved feeling arising from the titular Jackie Kennedy's (Natalie Portman) emotional turmoil. A striking array of choral accents have arisen from the scores of Michael Abels: both *Get Out* (2017) and *Us* (2019), composed for director Jordan Peele, brilliantly use voices to comment on a narrative's implicit themes, more often than not the sense of institutional racism and ideological bondage.

Another intriguing voice that has emerged in recent years: Radiohead guitarist turned classicist Jonny Greenwood, whose collaborations with director Paul Thomas Anderson have traversed the emotional spectrum. They first worked together, to memorably astringent, piercing effect on oil-seeking drama *There Will Be Blood* (2007), starring Daniel Day Lewis in a suitably volcanic performance. Anderson's elliptical, often bizarre narratives are well-served by Greenwood's discombobulated soundscapes, as the likes of *The Master* (2012) and *Inherent Vice* (2015) attest. For Anderson's *Phantom Thread* (2017), Greenwood delivered an altogether more palatable and attractive work, a stately evocation of Elgar and Vaughan Williams in line with Day-Lewis' measured, compelling portrayal of an isolated woman's tailor.

Another innovator is the composer Bear McCreary who has graduated from TV shows like *Battlestar Galactica* (2004–2009) and *The Walking Dead* (2010–present) to impressively mounted fantasy and thriller soundtracks. In 2016, he dusted off the blaster beam (familiar from Jerry Goldsmith's *Star Trek: The Motion Picture*, 1979) for *10 Cloverfield Lane*, mixing it alongside an onslaught of Herrmann-esque strings. For 2019's *Godzilla: King of the Monsters*, he deployed a raft of techniques including low-register Buddhist chanting and a choir incanting the names of Godzilla's key enemies, including Rodan. And for the 2019 remake of cult horror *Child's Play*, McCreary captured the essence of killer doll Chucky by sampling noises from a host of children's toys, in the process crafting a malicious lullaby.

The duo of Trent Reznor (of the rock group Nine Inch Nails) and Atticus Ross have also generated attention, largely for their collaborations with David Fincher. Their coldly pulsating musical depiction of Facebook founder Mark Zuckerberg in *The Social Network* (2010) won them an Oscar, and the same icy synthetic work was carried into *The Girl with the Dragon Tattoo* (2011) and *Gone Girl* (2014). Fincher's *Mank* (2020), a biopic of *Citizen Kane* (1941) writer Herman J. Mankiewicz, elicited an atypically orchestral, Oscar-nominated score from the pair that channeled the moody spirit of Bernard Herrmann, while also incorporating pastiches of era-appropriate jazz standards. The same year as *Mank*, Reznor and Ross brought a sense of abstraction to Disney-Pixar movie *Soul* (2020), interweaving their material with pieces from jazz artist Jon Batiste, and yielding their second Oscar in the process.

Whether one likes or appreciates these scores or not, it clearly demonstrates the level of creative diversity at play in Hollywood. Composer Nicholas Britell is another figure who can vacillate between minimalism (2016's *Moonlight*), lush romanticism (2018's *If Beale Street Could Talk*) and arrestingly unusual Disney scores (2021's *Cruella*). Sitting alongside these offbeat works are the more traditional symphonic accompaniments for blockbuster franchises. As articulated throughout this book, the Hollywood machine cannot resist the lure of nostalgia in film music, an approach that is now bifurcated along generational lines.

On the one hand, genre veterans like John Williams and Alan Silvestri are sought by modern-day franchise filmmakers because of their musical heritage. One doesn't just hire a composer: one hires an embodiment of symphonic film scoring history, an individual whose timeless sense of orchestral grandeur has the ability to connect contemporary franchises (whether it's *Star Wars*, Marvel or something else entirely) to a sense of archetypal myth.

On the other hand, there are the composers who grew up listening to such musical titans, and who now parlay that influence into their own film scores. One can hear this in the scores of Michael Giacchino who has been well-schooled in the John Williams theme-and-melody approach. Giacchino has proven adept at assimilating and tweaking the style of Hollywood musical masters, lacing a groundswell of thematic beauty with his own rhythmic quirks from the likes of TV show *Lost* (2004–2010).

Giacchino stepped into the shoes of Lalo Schifrin for *Mission: Impossible III* (2006) and *Mission: Impossible—Ghost Protocol* (2011), revising Schifrin's signature TV show theme and also his secondary theme "The Plot." For the *Jurassic World* series (2015–present), Giacchino supplemented John Williams' original *Jurassic Park* material with new creations of its own, a clear sign of how the past is inescapable, even in the realm of film music. (See also his score for 2016's *Rogue One: A Star Wars Story*, cited in Chapter Four.) And then there is Giacchino's contribution to the newly revived *Star Trek* franchise, which started with J.J. Abrams' *Star Trek* in 2009. Virtually all of the scores in the franchise, from Jerry Goldsmith to James Horner, Leonard Rosenman to Cliff Eidelman, have emphasized bold melodic statements, and this sat comfortably within Giacchino's wheelhouse, allowing him to indulge in passages of full-throttle action and awestruck grandeur.

Nostalgia is also a powerful marketing tool when considering the recent wave of live-action Disney remakes: *Maleficent* (2014), *The Jungle Book* (2016), *Pete's Dragon* (2016), *Beauty and the Beast* (2017), *Dumbo* (2019), *Aladdin* (2019), *The Lion King* (2019) and *Mulan* (2020). The movies will either employ the composer from the original Disney animation, or request that a new composer interpolates the ideas of the initial artist (for instance, John Debney and George Bruns on *The Jungle Book*).

Alan Menken's work on *Beauty and the Beast* was a direct adaptation of his 1991 score and worked around new songs ("Evermore," performed by Dan Stevens as the Beast). Likewise, Hans Zimmer revisited his own work on *The Lion King*, even as the familiar Elton John songs were updated ("Can You Feel the Love Tonight," now performed by Beyoncé).

The notion of the musical USP is particularly important to the Disney brand (as explored in Chapter Five); it conveys a sense of heritage to the audience, a safety blanket of musical familiarity. This allows older viewers to rekindle the sense of childhood awe they felt when first engaging with the animated properties, in turn passing such enthusiasm onto their own children.

A similar sense of nostalgia was channeled in Disney sequel *Mary Poppins Returns* (2018), as composer Marc Shaiman and lyricist Scott Wittman, working with *Hamilton* creator Lin-Manuel Miranda, both honored and updated the sound of the Sherman brothers from the 1964 original. Outside the sphere of Disney, a sense of nostalgic lyricism was also present in the soundtrack for the Oscar-winning musical *La La Land* (2016), composed by Justin Hurwitz with lyrics by Pasek and Paul. (The duo was also responsible for the hugely successful, pop-inflected musical *The Greatest Showman* in 2017.)

Two composers who crisscross the divide between the abstract and the emotionally direct are Thomas Newman and Alexandre Desplat. These two composers each bear a unique musical signature that is immediately recognizable to fans, a remarkable achievement in an era where composers are routinely encouraged to imitate one another. One might recognize a Newman score from little more than a wavering oboe solo (1995's *How to Make an American Quilt*, or 2008's Pixar movie *Wall-E*). Even more recognizable is his ability to mix up a host of speciality string and percussion elements, crafting a jaunty and quirky soundscape that can be translated into a host of genres, from war drama (2005's *Jarhead*) to action (Bond movies *Skyfall* in 2012 and *Spectre* in 2015).

Desplat, meanwhile, has a distinctly crystalline and metronomic approach to rhythm and melody, which has led to some accusations of intellectual skill above emotional impact. But that would underestimate the adaptability of his voice, which has graced everything from reincarnation drama (2004's *Birth*) to thunderous fantasy (*Harry Potter and the Deathly Hallows: Parts I* and *II*, released in 2010 and 2011). Desplat's intricacy and delicacy has yielded two Oscar wins: the delightful cimbalom/balalaika combination in *The Grand Budapest Hotel* (2014), composed for director Wes Anderson, and the yearning romanticism of *The Shape of Water* (2017), for director Guillermo del Toro.

Maverick, brilliant voices like Newman and Desplat make one hopeful for the future of film music. They have navigated choppy commercial waters, imposing deadlines and the micro-managing onslaught of the Hollywood machine without ever compromising their vision. Yet even the most experienced industry musicians have had to adapt to unprecedented change in the wake of the coronavirus pandemic. Compositional skill has had to match with technological advances such as Zoom in order so that orchestras can be recorded remotely. One can surely expect certain cost-effective elements of remote recording to become standardized in the film music industry, particularly if studios and producers are inclined to tighten their budgets.

Laura Karpman said this presented a unique challenge when constructing her score for HBO's *Lovecraft Country* (2020). She was compelled to close-mic the individual musicians, have them record their parts and later mix the various elements together into a symphonic whole ready for the final dub. However, rather than proving restrictive, Karpman said the process was liberating and gave her greater control over the sonic weight of certain instruments.

"For example, if you've got the same violinist playing first and second violin, you don't want to have both parts playing in unison, because then you're doing a useless dub," she explained. "I hate doubled strings, because they always sound fazy to me. So instead you might double first violins with the violas and have the second violins do something different. It's about having a contrabass clarinet doubling a tuba to give it more body on the bottom. You'd never usually hear it in the traditional orchestral setting, but we have the control here."[16]

Amidst all this discussion of Hollywood rhetoric, process and technique, one must surely ask: how do composers view themselves in the midst of a turbulent, ever-changing industry? The final word is left to James Horner who, prior to his death in 2015, eloquently expressed the paradoxical nature of film music, and his increased disillusion with the industry.

"Unlike anything else, when you write a score for a movie, somebody else owns the score; it's not mine," he reflected. "If I'm a writer and I write a story or if I'm a painter and I paint a painting, the idea of a proprietary, copyrighted thing doesn't occur as strictly as it does in music. You write a film score and you develop interesting ideas and you think you'd love to explore that more in your next score or in a serious piece—if you're a painter you can do a whole series of paintings on a theme…. In [film] music, once you've written it, it belongs to somebody else, and it's a very hard thing to come up with a completely different personality in every film. It's part of your nature, as it is in every art…[This is] the sort of thing that [film] music suffers from—that you can't continue a style or explore ideas you've explored before, because they don't belong to you. I would say, more recently, it's harder and harder to be completely fresh each time. No other discipline requires that quite as dramatically as the music does."[17]

Horner's words epitomize what is a uniquely contradictory art form. Film music is meant to foster stronger emotional connections between sound and vision but has the capacity to both tear apart creative collaborations and undermine the fabric of a given film. Such music is personal to the composer in question, but said composers are ultimately in the service of someone else's art.

Relatively innocent notes on a cue sheet can suddenly become a political football in the tussle between executives, audiences and the box office. Film music is both infused with, and devoid of, an autonomous personality. Hence why any score capable of navigating these particular minefields is something to be championed, from the highest rooftops. A successful film score has embedded within it the archetypal story of human endeavor: the need to balance one's vision in the face of overwhelming odds, with the hope that at least some residual personality will emerge intact to excite, enthrall and inspire future generations.

Chapter Notes

Chapter One

1. Sean Wilson, "Howard Shore on Capturing the Sound of *Funny Boy*," *Composer Magazine*, accessed April 28, 2021, https://composer.spitfireaudio.com/en/articles/howard-shore-on-capturing-the-sound-of-funny-boy.
2. "History: Clevedon's Historic Cinema," *Curzon*, accessed February 6, 2021, https://www.curzon.org.uk/heritage/history/.
3. Simon Trezise, "Historical Introduction," in *Music and Sound in Silent Film: From the Nickelodeon to The Artist*, edited by Ruth Barton and Simon Trezise (New York: Routledge, 2019), 5.
4. *Ibid.*
5. Mervyn Cooke, *A History of Film Music* (Cambridge: Cambridge University Press, 2008), 5.
6. *Ibid.*, 7.
7. *Ibid.*
8. *Ibid.*
9. *Ibid.*
10. *Ibid.*
11. *Ibid.*
12. "*Dickson Experimental Sound Film 1895*," *Filmsound*, accessed February 6, 2021, http://www.filmsound.org/murch/dickson.htm.
13. Martin Koerber, "Oskar Messter, Film Pioneer: Early Cinema Between Science, Spectacle and Commerce," in *A Second Life: German Cinema's First Decades*, edited by Thomas Elsaesser with Michael Wedel (Amsterdam: Amsterdam University Press, 1996), 54, https://www.jstor.org/stable/j.ctt45kfh9.6?seq=4#metadata_info_tab_contents.
14. Mervyn Cooke, *A History of Film Music* (Cambridge: Cambridge University Press, 2008), 8.
15. Simon Trezise, "Historical Introduction," in *Music and Sound in Silent Film: From the Nickelodeon to The Artist*, edited by Ruth Barton and Simon Trezise (New York: Routledge, 2019), 7.
16. *Ibid.*
17. *Ibid.*
18. Sean Wilson, "Howard Shore on Capturing the Sound of *Funny Boy*," *Composer Magazine*, accessed April 28, 2021, https://composer.spitfireaudio.com/en/articles/howard-shore-on-capturing-the-sound-of-funny-boy.
19. Simon Trezise, "Historical Introduction," in *Music and Sound in Silent Film: From the Nickelodeon to The Artist*, edited by Ruth Barton and Simon Trezise (New York: Routledge, 2019), 9.
20. *Ibid.*
21. Mervyn Cooke, *A History of Film Music* (Cambridge: Cambridge University Press, 2008), 10.
22. *Ibid.*
23. Simon Trezise, "Historical Introduction," in *Music and Sound in Silent Film: From the Nickelodeon to The Artist*, edited by Ruth Barton and Simon Trezise (New York: Routledge, 2019), 10.
24. Mervyn Cooke, *A History of Film Music* (Cambridge: Cambridge University Press, 2008), 15.
25. Simon Trezise, "Historical Introduction," in *Music and Sound in Silent Film: From the Nickelodeon to The Artist*, edited by Ruth Barton and Simon Trezise (New York: Routledge, 2019), 15.
26. *Ibid.*
27. Katharine M. Rogers, *L. Frank Baum: Creator of Oz: A Biography* (New

York: St Martin's Press, 2007), 184, https://play.google.com/books/reader?id=kxePw8MEs-oC&hl=en&pg=GBS.PA162.w.1.0.400.

28. Craig Lysy, "100 Greatest Scores of All Time: *L'Assassinat Du Duc De Guise*—Camille Saint-Saëns," *MovieMusicUK*, accessed February 6, 2021, https://moviemusicuk.us/2020/11/23/lassassinat-du-duc-de-guise-camille-saint-saens-2/.

29. Sean Wilson, "Howard Shore on Capturing the Sound of *Funny Boy*," *Composer Magazine*, accessed April 28, 2021, https://composer.spitfireaudio.com/en/articles/howard-shore-on-capturing-the-sound-of-funny-boy.

30. Craig Lysy, "100 Greatest Scores of All Time: *L'Assassinat Du Duc De Guise*—Camille Saint-Saëns," *MovieMusicUK*, accessed February 6, 2021, https://moviemusicuk.us/2020/11/23/lassassinat-du-duc-de-guise-camille-saint-saens-2/.

31. Katharine M. Rogers, *L. Frank Baum: Creator of Oz: A Biography* (New York: St Martin's Press, 2007), 224, https://play.google.com/books/reader?id=kxePw8MEs-oC&hl=en&pg=GBS.PA201.w.1.0.131.

32. *Ibid.*, 225.

33. Laraine Porter, "The Feminization of British Silent Cinema," in *Music and Sound in Silent Film: From the Nickelodeon to The Artist*, edited by Ruth Barton and Simon Trezise (New York: Routledge, 2019), 100.

34. Simon Trezise, "Historical Introduction," in *Music and Sound in Silent Film: From the Nickelodeon to The Artist*, edited by Ruth Barton and Simon Trezise (New York: Routledge, 2019), 15.

35. *Ibid.*

36. Mervyn Cooke, *A History of Film Music* (Cambridge: Cambridge University Press, 2008), 25.

37. *Ibid.*, 24.

38. Martin Marks, "The Well-Furnished Film: Satie's Score for *Entr'acte*," *Canadian University Music Review* 4 (1983): 248, https://www.erudit.org/fr/revues/cumr/1983-n4-cumr0428/1013906ar.pdf.

39. Laraine Porter, "The Feminization of British Silent Cinema," in *Music and Sound in Silent Film: From the Nickelodeon to The Artist*, edited by Ruth Barton and Simon Trezise (New York: Routledge, 2019), 100.

40. *Ibid.*

41. Sean Wilson, "Howard Shore on Capturing the Sound of *Funny Boy*," *Composer Magazine*, accessed April 28, 2021, https://composer.spitfireaudio.com/en/articles/howard-shore-on-capturing-the-sound-of-funny-boy.

42. Mervyn Cooke, *A History of Film Music* (Cambridge: Cambridge University Press, 2008), 34.

43. *Ibid.*, 36.

44. *Ibid.*

45. Charles Chaplin, *My Autobiography* (London: Penguin Modern Classics, 2003), 98.

46. *Ibid.*, 99.

47. *Ibid.*, 100.

48. *Ibid.*, 101.

49. *Ibid.*, 118.

50. David Robinson, *Chaplin: His Life and Art* (London: Penguin, 2001), 107.

51. *Ibid.*, 105.

52. *Ibid.*, 118.

53. Charles Chaplin, *My Autobiography* (London: Penguin Modern Classics, 2003), 145.

54. David Robinson, *Chaplin: His Life and Art* (London: Penguin, 2001), 147.

55. *Ibid.*, 282.

56. Charles Chaplin, *My Autobiography* (London: Penguin Modern Classics, 2003), 125.

57. David Robinson, *Chaplin: His Life and Art* (London: Penguin, 2001), 297.

58. Theodore Huff, "Chaplin as a Composer," *Charlie Chaplin*, accessed February 7, 2021, https://www.charliechaplin.com/en/articles/205-Chaplin-as-a-Composer.

59. *Ibid.*

60. Jeffrey Vance, "Chaplin the Composer," an excerpt from *Chaplin: Genius of the Cinema* (New York: Harry N. Abrams, 2003) in Variety Special Advertising Supplement, 20–21.

61. Charles Chaplin, *My Autobiography* (London: Penguin Modern Classics, 2003), 324.

62. *Ibid.*, 325.

63. David Raksin with Charles Berg, "'Music Composed by Charlie Chaplin': Auteur or Collaborateur?'" *Journal of the University Film Association* 31, no. 1 (1979): 48, http://www.jstor.org/stable/20687463.

64. David Robinson, *Chaplin: His Life and Art* (London: Penguin, 2001), 439.

65. *Quarterly Journal of the Library of*

Congress, Summer 1983, as cited in David Robinson, *Chaplin: His Life and Art* (London: Penguin, 2001), 499.
    66. David Robinson, *Chaplin: His Life and Art* (London: Penguin, 2001), 500.
    67. *Quarterly Journal of the Library of Congress*, Summer 1983.
    68. Sean Wilson, "The Sound of Cinema," *Composer Magazine*, accessed April 13, 2021, https://composer.spitfireaudio.com/en/articles/the-sound-of-cinema.
    69. Ibid.
    70. "Part 5—George Groves at Bell Labs and the Vitagraph Studios (1923–26)," *George Groves The Movie Sound Pioneer*, accessed February 6, 2021, https://www.georgegroves.org.uk/talking_films/belllabs/.
    71. Ibid.
    72. Mervyn Cooke, *A History of Film Music* (Cambridge: Cambridge University Press, 2008), 49.
    73. "Part 6—George Groves' Work on *Don Juan* (1926–27)," *George Groves The Movie Sound Pioneer*, accessed February 6, 2021, https://www.georgegroves.org.uk/talking_films/donjuan/.
    74. Ibid.
    75. Mervyn Cooke, *A History of Film Music* (Cambridge: Cambridge University Press, 2008), 49.
    76. "Part 7—*The Jazz Singer*: George Groves and Al Jolson (1927)," *George Groves The Movie Sound Pioneer*, accessed February 6, 2021, https://www.georgegroves.org.uk/talking_films/jazzsinger/.
    77. "The 1st Academy Awards Memorable Moments," *Academy of Motion Picture Arts and Sciences*, accessed February 6, 2021, https://www.oscars.org/oscars/ceremonies/1929/memorable-moments.
    78. Mervyn Cooke, *A History of Film Music* (Cambridge: Cambridge University Press, 2008), 290.
    79. "Part 7—*The Jazz Singer*: George Groves and Al Jolson (1927)," *George Groves The Movie Sound Pioneer*, accessed February 6, 2021, https://www.georgegroves.org.uk/talking_films/jazzsinger/.
    80. Ibid.
    81. Alex Greenberg and Malvin Wald, "Report to the Stockholders," *Hollywood Quarterly Magazine* 1, no. 4 (1946): 410–415, https://online.ucpress.edu/fq/article-abstract/1/4/410/37313/Report-to-the-Stockholders?redirectedFrom=fulltext.

Chapter Two

1. Sean Wilson, "In the Deep End with Desplat: Alexandre Desplat Talks *The Shape of Water* and Guillermo del Toro," *Film Score Monthly Online* 22, no. 11, November 2017. Accessed April 28, 2021, https://www.fsmonlinemag.com.
2. Paul F. Boller, Jr., "Music by Max Steiner," *Southwest Review* 51, no. 3 (1966): 260, https://www.jstor.org/stable/43467799?read-now=1&seq=5#page_scan_tab_contents.
3. Ibid.
4. Ibid.
5. Steven C. Smith, *Music by Max Steiner: The Epic Life of Hollywood's Most Influential Composer* (Oxford: Oxford University Press, 2020), xv.
6. Paul F. Boller, Jr., "Music by Max Steiner," in *Southwest Review* 51, no. 3 (1966): 260, https://www.jstor.org/stable/43467799?read-now=1&seq=5#page_scan_tab_contents.
7. Ibid.
8. Steven C. Smith, *Music by Max Steiner: The Epic Life of Hollywood's Most Influential Composer* (Oxford: Oxford University Press, 2020), 21.
9. Paul F. Boller, Jr., "Music by Max Steiner," *Southwest Review* 51, no. 3 (1966): 260, https://www.jstor.org/stable/43467799?read-now=1&seq=5#pagescan_tab_contents.
10. Steven C. Smith, *Music by Max Steiner: The Epic Life of Hollywood's Most Influential Composer* (Oxford: Oxford University Press, 2020), 39.
11. Paul F. Boller Jr., "Music by Max Steiner," *Southwest Review* 51, no. 3 (1966): 261, https://www.jstor.org/stable43467799?read-now=1&seq=5#page_scan_tab_contents.
12. Ibid.
13. Steven C. Smith, *Music by Max Steiner: The Epic Life of Hollywood's Most Influential Composer* (Oxford: Oxford University Press, 2020), 47.
14. "Music by the Reel," *Cue*, August 14, 1943. As cited in Steven C. Smith, *Music by Max Steiner: The Epic Life of Hollywood's Most Influential Composer* (Oxford: Oxford University Press, 2020), 48.
15. Steven C. Smith, *Music by Max Steiner: The Epic Life of Hollywood's Most*

Influential Composer (Oxford: Oxford University Press, 2020), 61.
16. Paul F. Boller, Jr., "Music by Max Steiner," *Southwest Review* 51, no. 3 (1966): 261, https://www.jstor.org/stable/43467799?read-now=1&seq=5#page_scan_tab_contents.
17. Mervyn Cooke, *A History of Film Music* (Cambridge: Cambridge University Press, 2008), 87.
18. *Ibid.*
19. Steven C. Smith, *Music by Max Steiner: The Epic Life of Hollywood's Most Influential Composer* (Oxford: Oxford University Press, 2020), 67.
20. Peter Wegele, *Max Steiner: Composing, Casablanca, and the Golden Age of Film Music* (Lanham, MD: Rowman & Littlefield, 2014), 10–11.
21. Steven C. Smith, *Music by Max Steiner: The Epic Life of Hollywood's Most Influential Composer* (Oxford: Oxford University Press, 2020), 74.
22. Max Steiner, *Notes to You*, Chapter XIII. As cited in Steven C. Smith, *Music by Max Steiner: The Epic Life of Hollywood's Most Influential Composer* (Oxford: Oxford University Press, 2020), 74.
23. Ray Morton to Seth Ambramovitch, "Origin of 'Kong': The Unbelievable True Backstory of Hollywood's Favorite Giant Ape," *The Hollywood Reporter*, accessed May 23, 2021, https://www.hollywoodreporter.com/movies/movie-news/king-kong-unbelievable-true-story-hollywoods-favorite-giant-ape-984785/.
24. *Ibid.*
25. *Ibid.*
26. Steven C. Smith, *Music by Max Steiner: The Epic Life of Hollywood's Most Influential Composer* (Oxford: Oxford University Press, 2020), 100.
27. Max Steiner to Tony Thomas, "Max Steiner: Vienna, London, New York and Finally Hollywood," in *The Max Steiner Collection* (Provo: Brigham Young University, 1996).
28. Mervyn Cooke, *A History of Film Music* (Cambridge: Cambridge University Press, 2008), 88.
29. *Ibid.*, 89.
30. Sean Wilson, "Exclusive Interview—*A Perfect Planet* Composer Ilan Eshkeri on Capturing Nature Through Music," *Flickering Myth*, accessed February 7, 2021, https://www.flickeringmyth.com/2021/01/a-perfect-planet-interview-composer-ilan-eshkeri/.
31. *Ibid.*
32. Steven C. Smith, *Music by Max Steiner: The Epic Life of Hollywood's Most Influential Composer* (Oxford: Oxford University Press, 2020), 101.
33. Mervyn Cooke, *A History of Film Music* (Cambridge: Cambridge University Press, 2008), 88.
34. MS to Warner, April 5, 1939. From the collection of JWM.
35. Steven C. Smith, *Music by Max Steiner: The Epic Life of Hollywood's Most Influential Composer* (Oxford: Oxford University Press, 2020), 229.
36. David O. Selznick to Max Steiner and Lou Forbes, "*Gone with the Wind* (1936–1941)," in *Memo from David O. Selznick*, edited by Rudy Behlmer (New York: Modern Library, 2000), 240–241.
37. Max Steiner to Tony Thomas, "Max Steiner: Vienna, London, New York, and Finally Hollywood," in *The Max Steiner Collection* (Provo: Brigham Young University, 1996).
38. Max Steiner, "Setting Emotions to Music," *Variety*, July 31, 1940.
39. "Jerry Goldsmith," *The Times*, accessed February 7, 2021, https://www.thetimes.co.uk/article/jerry-goldsmith-6tkpzm023pn.
40. Steven C. Smith, *Music by Max Steiner: The Epic Life of Hollywood's Most Influential Composer* (Oxford: Oxford University Press, 2020), 240.
41. David O. Selznick to John Hay Whitney, "*Gone with the Wind* (1936–1941)," in *Memo from David O. Selznick*, edited by Rudy Behlmer (New York: Modern Library, 2000), 253–254.
42. "Top Lifetime Adjusted Grosses," *Box Office Mojo*, accessed June 2, 2021, https://www.boxofficemojo.com/chart/top_lifetime_gross_adjusted/?adjust_gross_to=2020.
43. Sean Wilson, "In the Deep End with Desplat: Alexandre Desplat Talks *The Shape of Water* and Guillermo del Toro," *Film Score Monthly Online* 22, no. 11, November 2017. Accessed April 28, 2021, https://www.fsmonlinemag.com.
44. *Ibid.*
45. Mervyn Cooke, *A History of Film Music* (Cambridge: Cambridge University Press, 2008), 95.

Notes—Chapter Two

46. *Ibid.*
47. Alex Ross, "Erich Wolfgang Korngold, the Opera Composer Who Went Hollywood," *The New Yorker*, accessed May 26, 2021, https://www.newyorker.com/magazine/2019/08/19/erich-wolfgang-korngold-the-opera-composer-who-went-hollywood.
48. *Ibid.*
49. Mervyn Cooke, *A History of Film Music* (Cambridge: Cambridge University Press, 2008), 168.
50. Craig Lysy, "*Captain Blood*," *Movie MusicUK*, accessed May 26, 2021, https://moviemusicuk.us/2020/03/30/captain-blood-erich-wolfgang-korngold/.
51. *Ibid.*
52. Mervyn Cooke, *A History of Film Music* (Cambridge: Cambridge University Press, 2008), 94–95.
53. *Ibid.*
54. *Ibid.*, 96.
55. *Ibid.*
56. Craig Lysy, "*The Adventures of Robin Hood*," *MovieMusicUK*, accessed May 27, 2021, https://moviemusicuk.us/2015/11/16/the-adventures-of-robin-hood-erich-wolfgang-korngold-2/.
57. Rudy Behlmer, "Robin Hood on the Screen: From Legend to Film," in *Robin Hood: An Anthology of Scholarship and Criticism*, edited by Stephen Knight (Suffolk: Boydell & Brewer, 1999), 458–459.
58. Kevin Courrier, *Randy Newman's American Dreams* (Toronto: ECW Press, 2005), 200.
59. Mervyn Cooke, *A History of Film Music* (Cambridge: Cambridge University Press, 2008), 104.
60. *Ibid.*
61. Jon Burlingame, "L.A. Music's First Family," *Variety*, accessed May 30, 2021, https://variety.com/1997/music/markets-festivals/l-a-music-s-first-family-1116677018/.
62. Craig Lysy, "*How the West Was Won*," *MovieMusicUK*, accessed May 30, 2021, https://moviemusicuk.us/2017/10/16/how-the-west-was-won-alfred-newman/.
63. Jon Burlingame, "L.A. Music's First Family," *Variety*, accessed May 30, 2021, https://variety.com/1997/music/markets-festivals/l-a-music-s-first-family-1116677018/.
64. Liner notes for *The Robe*, by Alfred Newman. Nick Redman. La-La Land Records, LLLCD 1203, 2012, compact disc.
65. Steven C. Smith, *A Heart at Fire's Center: The Life and Music of Bernard Herrmann* (Oakland: University of California Press, 1991), 43.
66. *Ibid.*
67. Robert Metz, *CBS: Reflections in a Bloodshot Eye* (New York: Signet, 1975), 45.
68. Steven C. Smith, *A Heart at Fire's Center: The Life and Music of Bernard Herrmann* (Oakland: University of California Press, 1991), 59.
69. Mervyn Cooke, *A History of Film Music* (Cambridge: Cambridge University Press, 2008), 123.
70. *Ibid.*
71. Andy Hill, *Scoring the Screen: The Secret Language of Film Music* (Lanham, MD: Rowman & Littlefield, 2017), 300.
72. *Ibid.*
73. Steven C. Smith, *A Heart at Fire's Center: The Life and Music of Bernard Herrmann* (Oakland: University of California Press, 1991), 66.
74. *Ibid.*
75. Steven C. Smith, *A Heart at Fire's Center: The Life and Music of Bernard Herrmann* (Oakland: University of California Press, 1991), 67.
76. "The 100 Greatest Films of All Time," *British Film Institute*, accessed June 1, 2021, https://www2.bfi.org.uk/greatest-films-all-time.
77. Jon Burlingame to David Mermelstein, "Daring and Original, Bernard Herrmann Changed Movie Music," *The Washington Post*, accessed June 1, 2021, https://www.washingtonpost.com/entertainment/music/daring-and-original-bernard-herrmann-changed-movie-music/2011/06/21/AGG0YXjH_story.html.
78. Steven C. Smith, *A Heart at Fire's Center: The Life and Music of Bernard Herrmann* (Oakland: University of California Press, 1991), 76.
79. *Ibid.*, 80.
80. *Ibid.*, 79.
81. *Ibid.*, 131.
82. *Ibid.*, 220–221.
83. *Ibid.*, 222.
84. Mervyn Cooke, *A History of Film Music* (Cambridge: Cambridge University Press, 2008), 208.

85. *Ibid.*
86. E.W. Cameron, *Sound and the Cinema* (London: Routledge, 1980), 133.
87. *Ibid.*
88. Ratcliffe, "Composing 'Emotional Scenery.'" As cited in Steven C. Smith, *A Heart at Fire's Center: The Life and Music of Bernard Herrmann* (Oakland: University of California Press, 1991), 241.
89. Bernard Herrmann to Misha Donat, 1973. As cited in Steven C. Smith, *A Heart at Fire's Center: The Life and Music of Bernard Herrmann* (Oakland: University of California Press, 1991), 239.
90. Danny Elfman to David Mermelstein, "Daring and Original, Bernard Herrmann Changed Movie Music," *The Washington Post*, accessed June 1, 2021, https://www.washingtonpost.com/entertainment/music/daring-and-original-bernard-herrmann-changed-movie-music/2011/06/21/AGG0YXjH_story.html.
91. Mervyn Cooke, *A History of Film Music* (Cambridge: Cambridge University Press, 2008), 209.
92. *Ibid.*
93. Scorsese, 1-24-89. As cited in Steven C. Smith, *A Heart at Fire's Center: The Life and Music of Bernard Herrmann* (Oakland: University of California Press, 1991), 352.
94. Jon Burlingame to David Mermelstein, "Daring and Original, Bernard Herrmann Changed Movie Music," *The Washington Post*, accessed June 1, 2021, https://www.washingtonpost.com/entertainment/music/daring-and-original-bernard-herrmann-changed-movie-music/2011/06/21/AGG0YXjH_story.html.
95. Sean Wilson, "In the Deep End with Desplat: Alexandre Desplat Talks *The Shape of Water* and Guillermo del Toro," *Film Score Monthly Online* 22, no. 11, November 2017. Accessed April 28, 2021, https://www.fsmonlinemag.com.

Chapter Three

1. Sean Wilson, "Blanchard: Scoring the Struggle: Terence Blanchard on Spike Lee's historical crime joint, BlacKkKlansman," *Film Score Monthly Online* 23, no. 9, September 2018. Accessed April 28, 2021, https://www.fsmonlinemag.com.
2. "Jazz on Film: *A Streetcar Named Desire*," *Jazzwise*, accessed February 7, 2021, https://www.jazzwise.com/features/article/jazz-on-film-a-streetcar-named-desire.
3. Annette Davison, *Alex North's A Streetcar Named Desire: A Film Score Guide* (Lanham, MD: Scarecrow Press, 2009), 6.
4. *Ibid.*
5. "Alex North: Hollywood Film Composer," *Jazz Professional*, accessed February 8, 2021, http://www.jazzprofessional.com/interviews/Alex%20North.htm.
6. Annette Davison, *Alex North's A Streetcar Named Desire: A Film Score Guide* (Lanham, MD: Scarecrow Press, 2009), 6.
7. *Ibid.*, 23.
8. David Meeker, "Jazz on the Screen," Library of Congress Music Division, accessed February 8, 2021, https://memory.loc.gov/diglib/ihas/html/jots/jazzscreen-overview.html.
9. *Ibid.*
10. *Ibid.*
11. *Ibid.*
12. Craig Lysy, "A Streetcar Named Desire," *MovieMusicUK*, accessed February 9, 2021, https://moviemusicuk.us/2017/03/13/a-streetcar-named-desire-alex-north/.
13. "The 58th Academy Awards Memorable Moments," *Academy of Motion Picture Arts and Sciences*, accessed February 9, 2021, https://www.oscars.org/oscars/ceremonies/1986/memorable-moments.
14. Craig Lysy, "Spartacus," *MovieMusic UK*, accessed February 10, 2021, https://moviemusicuk.us/2017/07/31/spartacus-alex-north/.
15. *Ibid.*
16. Henry Mancini and Gene Lees, *Did They Mention the Music? The Autobiography of Henry Mancini* (Lanham, MD: Cooper Square Press, 2001), 141.
17. *Ibid.*
18. Sean Wilson, "Blanchard: Scoring the Struggle: Terence Blanchard on Spike Lee's historical crime joint, BlacKkKlansman," *Film Score Monthly Online* 23, no. 9, September 2018. Accessed April 28, 2021, https://www.fsmonlinemag.com.
19. *Ibid.*
20. *Ibid.*
21. Sanya Shoilevska Henderson, *Alex North, Film Composer: A Biography, with*

Analyses of A Streetcar Named Desire, Spartacus, The Misfits, Under the Volcano and Prizzi's Honor (Jefferson, NC: McFarland, 2009), 72.

22. Ibid., 72–73.

23. Mervyn Cooke, *A History of Film Music* (Cambridge: Cambridge University Press, 2008), 184.

24. Ibid.

25. Ibid., 185.

26. Stephan Eicke, *The Struggle Behind the Soundtrack: Inside the Discordant New World of Film Scoring* (Jefferson, NC: McFarland, 2019), 18.

27. Ibid.

28. Florent Groult, "Goldsmith by Beltrami: Master and Student," *Underscores*, accessed February 13, 2021, http://www.underscores.fr/rencontres/interviews-vo/2008/08/interview-with-marco-beltrami/.

29. Jon Burlingame, "Jerry Goldsmith: An Appreciation," *Film Music Society*, accessed February 13, 2021, http://www.filmmusicsociety.org/news_events/features/2004/080204.html.

30. Ibid.

31. Randall D. Larson, "Interview with Jerry Goldsmith," *CinemaScore: The Film Music Journal* 11/12 (July 15, 1982): 4.

32. Andy Hill, *Scoring the Screen: The Secret Language of Film Music* (Lanham, MD: Rowman & Littlefield, 2017), 71.

33. Ibid.

34. Liner notes for *The Magnificent Seven*, by Elmer Bernstein. Jerry McCulley. VSD-6559, 2004, compact disc.

35. Ibid.

36. Ibid.

37. Andy Hill, *Scoring the Screen: The Secret Language of Film Music* (Lanham, MD: Rowman & Littlefield, 2017), 52.

38. Craig Lysy, "Planet of the Apes," *MovieMusicUK*, accessed February 16, 2021, https://moviemusicuk.us/2018/02/26/planet-of-the-apes-jerry-goldsmith/.

39. Ibid.

40. Tim Grieving, "Jerry Goldsmith, 'The Composer's Composer,' Honored with Hollywood Star," *NPR*, accessed February 17, 2021, https://www.npr.org/2017/05/09/527575323/jerry-goldsmith-the-composers-composer-honored-with-hollywood-star?t=1621585217617.

41. Liner notes for *Star Trek: The Motion Picture: 20th Anniversary Collector's Edition*, by Jerry Goldsmith. David Hirsch, Ford A. Thaxton. Columbia, COL 489929 2, 1999, compact disc.

42. James Southall, "Tora! Tora! Tora!," *Movie-wave*, accessed February 18, 2021, http://www.movie-wave.net/tora-tora-tora/.

43. Mervyn Cooke, *A History of Film Music* (Cambridge: Cambridge University Press, 2008), 459.

44. Deena Weinstein, *Rock'n America: A Social and Cultural History* (Toronto: University of Toronto Press, 2015), 57.

45. Todd Leopold, "The 50-Year-Old Song that Started it All," CNN, accessed February 20, 2021, https://edition.cnn.com/2005/SHOWBIZ/Music/07/07/haley.rock/.

46. "TCM's 15 Most Influential Film Soundtracks," *TCM*, accessed February 20, 2021, https://web.archive.org/web/20100315120648/http://www.tcm.com/dailies/.

47. Patrick Humphries, *Elvis the #1 Hits: The Secret History of the Classics* (Kansas City: Andrews McMeel, 2003), 52.

48. Liner notes for *Lawrence of Arabia*, by Maurice Jarre. Geoff Leonard. CIN CD 008, 1999, compact disc.

49. Ibid.

50. Ibid.

51. Craig Lysy, "Ben-Hur," *MovieMusic UK*, accessed February 22, 2021, https://moviemusicuk.us/2017/09/18/ben-hur-miklos-rozsa-2/.

52. Mervyn Cooke, *A History of Film Music* (Cambridge: Cambridge University Press, 2008), 400.

53. Mark Harris, *Pictures at a Revolution* (London: Penguin, 2008), 360–361.

54. Dave Simpson, "How We Made Steppenwolf's 'Born to Be Wild,'" *The Guardian*, accessed February 25, 2021, https://www.theguardian.com/music/2018/jul/31/how-we-made-steppenwolf-born-to-be-wild.

55. Ibid.

56. Mervyn Cooke, *A History of Film Music* (Cambridge: Cambridge University Press, 2008), 374.

57. Ibid., 199.

Chapter Four

1. Sean Wilson, "Michael Giacchino Interview: The Art of Scoring Movies," *Den*

of Geek, accessed April 28, 2021, https://www.denofgeek.com/movies/michael-giacchino-interview-the-art-of-scoring-movies/.

2. "Compose Your Own *Doctor Who* Theme," *BBC Bitesize*, accessed March 5, 2021, https://www.bbc.co.uk/bitesize/topics/zhdfscw/articles/zkkrbdm#:~:text=Back%20in%20the%201960s%2C%20there,create%20the%20eerie%20futuristic%20music.

3. Jude Rogers, "She Made Music Jump Into 3D: Wendy Carlos, The Reclusive Synth Genius," *The Guardian*, accessed March 4, 2021, https://www.theguardian.com/music/2020/nov/11/she-made-music-jump-into-3d-wendy-carlos-the-reclusive-synth-genius.

4. Rob Bowman, *Soulsville U.S.A.: The Story of Stax Records* (New York: Schirmer Trade, 2003), 229–233.

5. Richard Brody, "Louis Malle's *Elevator to the Gallows*, and Its Historic Miles Davis Soundtrack," *New Yorker*, accessed June 8, 2021, https://www.newyorker.com/culture/richard-brody/louis-malles-elevator-to-the-gallows-and-its-historic-miles-davis-soundtrack.

6. Vince Aletti, "*Trouble Man/M.P.G.*" *Rolling Stone*, accessed March 6, 2021, https://www.rollingstone.com/music/music-album-reviews/trouble-man-m-p-g-192399/.

7. *Ibid.*

8. Mervyn Cooke, *A History of Film Music* (Cambridge: Cambridge University Press, 2008), 401.

9. Spencer Leigh, "Kris Kristofferson," accessed March 7, 2021, https://web.archive.org/web/20120415001040/http://www.spencerleigh.demon.co.uk/Interview_Kristofferson.htm.

10. Mervyn Cooke, *A History of Film Music* (Cambridge: Cambridge University Press, 2008), 459.

11. *Ibid.*, 378.

12. *Ibid.*, 379.

13. *Ibid.*, 414.

14. "Raymond Scott Timeline," *RaymondScott.net*, accessed March 12, 2021, https://www.raymondscott.net/timeline/.

15. Heather Barrett, "*Star Wars* Composer John Williams' First Score a 1952 Newfoundland Film," *CBA*, accessed March 12, 2021, https://www.cbc.ca/news/canada/newfoundland-labrador/star-wars-composer-john-williams-first-score-a-1952-newfoundland-film-1.3241603.

16. *Ibid.*

17. "Other Works," *Jwfan*, accessed March 12, 2021, http://www.jwfan.com/?page_id=3928.

18. Jon Burlingame, "Netflix's *Lost in Space* Reboot Borrows Grandeur of Original Score," *Variety*, accessed March 13, 2021, https://variety.com/2018/artisans/production/lost-in-space-score-1202749940.

19. Carl Gottlieb, *The Jaws Log: 25th Anniversary Edition* (New York: Faber & Faber, 2001), 181–182.

20. *Ibid.*

21. Mervyn Cooke, *A History of Film Music* (Cambridge: Cambridge University Press, 2008), 461.

22. Laurent Bouzereau, "A Look Inside *Jaws* ['Music by John Williams']," *Jaws: 30th Anniversary Edition* DVD (2005): Universal Home Video.

23. Mervyn Cooke, *A History of Film Music* (Cambridge: Cambridge University Press, 2008), 410.

24. Willow Green, "Movie Movements That Defined Cinema: The Movie Brats," *Empire*, accessed March 15, 2021, https://www.empireonline.com/movies/features/movie-brats-movie-era/.

25. Mervyn Cooke, *A History of Film Music* (Cambridge: Cambridge University Press, 2008), 455.

26. Alex Ross, "Listening to *Star Wars*," *New Yorker*, accessed March 15, 2021, https://www.newyorker.com/culture/cultural-comment/listening-to-star-wars.

27. Alex Ross, "The Force Is Still Strong with John Williams," *New Yorker*, accessed March 15, 2021, https://www.newyorker.com/culture/persons-of-interest/the-force-is-still-strong-with-john-williams.

28. Emilio Audissino, *John Williams's Film Music: Jaws, Star Wars, Raiders of the Lost Ark, and the Return of the Classical Hollywood Music Style* (Madison: University of Wisconsin Press, 2014), 72.

29. Alex Ross, "The Force Is Still Strong with John Williams," *New Yorker*, accessed March 15, 2021, https://www.newyorker.com/culture/persons-of-interest/the-force-is-still-strong-with-john-williams.

30. Mervyn Cooke, *A History of Film Music* (Cambridge: Cambridge University Press, 2008), 462.

31. Alex Ross, "The Force Is Still Strong with John Williams," *New Yorker*, accessed March 15, 2021, https://www.newyorker.com/culture/persons-of-interest/the-force-is-still-strong-with-john-williams.

32. Mike Fleming, Jr, "'*Star Wars*' legacy II: An Architect of Hollywood's Greatest Deal Recalls How George Lucas Won Sequel Rights," *Deadline*, accessed March 16, 2021, https://deadline.com/2015/12/star-wars-franchise-george-lucas-historic-rights-deal-tom-pollock-1201669419/.

33. "Steven Spielberg, George Lucas, Kobe Bryant & More Salute John Williams," *American Film Institute*, accessed March 18, 2021, https://www.afi.com/news/watch-steven-spielberg-george-lucas-kobe-bryant-more-salute-john-williams/.

34. Emilio Audissino, *John Williams's Film Music: Jaws, Star Wars, Raiders of the Lost Ark, and the Return of the Classical Hollywood Music Style* (Madison: University of Wisconsin Press, 2014), 68.

35. Mervyn Cooke, *A History of Film Music* (Cambridge: Cambridge University Press, 2008), 463.

36. Jon Burlingame, "AFI Honoree John Williams Looks Back on Six Decades of Iconic Themes," *Variety*, accessed March 18, 2021, https://variety.com/2016/film/spotlight/john-williams-afi-1201792072-1201792072/.

37. "Steven Spielberg, George Lucas, Kobe Bryant and More Salute John Williams," *AFI*, accessed March 18, 2021, https://www.afi.com/news/watch-steven-spielberg-george-lucas-kobe-bryant-more-salute-john-williams/.

38. Ibid.

39. Sean Wilson, "Michael Giacchino Interview: the Art of Scoring Movies," *Den of Geek*, accessed April 28, 2021, https://www.denofgeek.com/movies/michael-giacchino-interview-the-art-of-scoring-movies/.

40. Ibid.

41. Ibid.

42. Mervyn Cooke, *A History of Film Music* (Cambridge: Cambridge University Press, 2008), 462.

43. Gregg Kilday, "Steven Spielberg and Fellow Directors Reveal the Stories Behind John Williams' Iconic Scores," *The Hollywood Reporter*, accessed March 21, 2021, https://www.hollywoodreporter.com/news/steven-spielberg-fellow-directors-reveal-900829.

44. Mervyn Cooke, *A History of Film Music* (Cambridge: Cambridge University Press, 2008), 467.

45. Lyndsey Parker, "Batman Composer Danny Elfman Says Turning Down Prince Was 'Biggest, Most Stressful Gamble' of His Career," *Yahoo!*, accessed March 22, 2021, https://www.yahoo.com/entertainment/batman-composer-danny-elfman-says-turning-down-prince-was-biggest-most-stressful-gamble-of-his-career-192951834.html.

46. Ibid.

47. Craig Lysy, "Batman," *MovieMusic UK*, accessed March 22, 2021, https://moviemusicuk.us/2018/12/31/batman-danny-elfman-2/.

48. "*Indiana Jones* and Me: John Williams," *Empire*, accessed March 21, 2021, https://www.empireonline.com/movies/features/indiana-jones-john-williams/.

49. Liner notes for *Indiana Jones: The Soundtracks Collection—Raiders of the Lost Ark*, by John Williams. Steven Spielberg. Concord Records, CRE-31002–02, compact disc, 2008.

50. Liner notes for *Indiana Jones: The Soundtracks Collection—Indiana Jones and the Temple of Doom*, by John Williams. Steven Spielberg. Concord Records, CRE-31003–02, compact disc, 2008.

51. Ibid.

52. Liner notes for *Indiana Jones: The Soundtracks Collection—Indiana Jones and the Last Crusade*, by John Williams. Steven Spielberg. Concord Records, CRE-31004–02, compact disc, 2008.

53. Ibid.

54. Todd McCarthy, "*Indiana Jones and the Temple of Doom*," *Variety*, accessed March 21, 2021, https://variety.com/1984/film/reviews/indiana-jones-and-the-temple-of-doom-1200426218/.

55. Craig Lysy, "*E.T. the Extra-Terrestrial*," *MovieMusicUK*, accessed March 23, 2021, https://moviemusicuk.us/2018/07/30/e-t-the-extra-terrestrial-john-williams/.

56. Ibid.

57. Liner notes for *Star Trek II: The Wrath of Khan*, by James Horner. Jeff Bond, Alexander Kaplan and Lukas Kendall. Retrograde Records-Film Score Monthly, FSM 80128–2, compact disc, 2009.

58. *Ibid.*
59. Scott Beggs, "Seven Scenes Made Epic by James Horner, the King of the Movie Music World," *Vanity Fair*, accessed March 24, 2021, https://www.vanityfair.com/hollywood/2015/06/james-horner-epic-moments.
60. *Ibid.*
61. Tim Grieving, "Why the *Alien* Franchise Has Such a Dramatic Musical Past," *Vulture*, accessed March 24, 2021, https://www.vulture.com/2017/05/why-the-alien-franchise-has-such-a-dramatic-musical-past.html.
62. "James Horner: 10 Best Movie Soundtracks—*Titanic*," *Classic FM*, accessed March 25, 2021, https://www.classicfm.com/composers/horner/music/james-horner-ten-best-movie-soundtracks/titanic-8/.
63. Christian Clemmensen, "*Back to the Future*," *Filmtracks*, accessed March 26, 2021, https://www.filmtracks.com/titles/back_future.html.
64. *Ibid.*
65. *Ibid.*
66. Ryan Lambie, "Brad Fiedel Interview: Composing *Terminator 2*'s Iconic Score," *Den of Geek*, accessed March 27, 2021, https://www.denofgeek.com/movies/brad-fiedel-interview-composing-terminator-2s-iconic-score/.
67. Mervyn Cooke, *A History of Film Music* (Cambridge: Cambridge University Press, 2008), 470.

Chapter Five

1. Sean Wilson, "John Powell Interview: Scoring *Bourne*, Hans Zimmer, *Face/Off* and More," *Den of Geek*, accessed March 28, 2021, https://www.denofgeek.com/movies/john-powell-interview-scoring-bourne-hans-zimmer-faceoff-and-more/.
2. Mackenzie Nichols, "*The Little Mermaid* Turns 30: Inside the Disney Classic's Rocky Journey," *Variety*, accessed March 28, 2021, https://variety.com/2019/film/news/oral-history-the-little-mermaid-1203379538/.
3. *Ibid.*
4. Robert Greenberger, "Alan Menken Revisits *Beauty and the Beast*," *Comic Mix*, accessed March 29, 2021, https://www.comicmix.com/2010/10/02/alan-menken-revisits-beauty-and-the-beast/.
5. Jeff Labrecque, "*Aladdin* Directors and Alan Menken Remember Robin Williams," *Entertainment Weekly*, accessed March 30, 2021, https://ew.com/article/2015/10/13/aladdin-roundtable/.
6. *Ibid.*
7. *Ibid.*
8. Christian Clemmensen, "*Cutthroat Island*," *Filmtracks*, accessed March 30, 2021, https://www.filmtracks.com/titles/cutthroat_island.html.
9. Charlie Brigden, "Looking Back at the Music of *The Motion Picture*," *Star Trek (Official Site)*, accessed March 30, 2021, https://intl.startrek.com/news/looking-back-at-the-music-of-the-motion-picture.
10. Christian Clemmensen, "*Independence Day*," *Filmtracks*, accessed March 30, 2021, https://www.filmtracks.com/titles/id4.html.
11. Jon Burlingame, "Bonding with the Score: David Arnold Blends the Traditional with the Modern in Music for *Tomorrow Never Dies*," *L.A. Times*, accessed April 2, 2021, https://www.latimes.com/archives/la-xpm-1997-dec-18-ca-65184-story.html.
12. Christian Clemmensen, "*Tomorrow Never Dies*," *Filmtracks*, accessed April 2, 2021, https://www.filmtracks.com/titles/tomorrow_never.html.
13. Liner notes for *Total Recall: The Deluxe Edition*, by Jerry Goldsmith. Robert Townson. Varèse Sarabande, VSD 6197, 2000, compact disc.
14. Liner notes for *Basic Instinct*, by Jerry Goldsmith. Gary Kester. Prometheus, XPCD 154, 2004, compact disc.
15. Craig Lysy, "*Schindler's List*," *MovieMusicUK*, accessed April 3, 2021. https://moviemusicuk.us/2019/02/18/schindlers-list-john-williams/.
16. *Alien 3*, "Music, Editing and Sound," DVD, directed by David Fincher (Century City, CA: 20th Century Studios, 1992).
17. James Southall, "*Alien 3* Soundtrack Review," *Movie-wave.net*, accessed April 4, 2021. http://www.movie-wave.net/titles/alien3.html.
18. Jon Broxton, "Interview with the Vampire," *MovieMusicUK*, accessed April 4, 2021. https://moviemusicuk.us/2009/09/12/interview-with-the-vampire-elliot-goldenthal/.
19. Jon Burlingame, "Spotlight on

Thomas Newman," *Variety*, accessed April 4, 2021. https://variety.com/2000/music/news/spotlight-thomas-newman-111776 1178/.

20. Kory Grow, "Surf Music and Seventies Soul: The Songs of *Pulp Fiction*," *Rolling Stone*, accessed April 6, 2021. https://www.rollingstone.com/movies/movie-lists/pulp-fiction-soundtrack-songs-tarantino-14045/.

21. *Ibid.*

22. Christian Clemmensen, "*Speed*," *Filmtracks*, accessed April 6, 2021. https://www.filmtracks.com/titles/speed.html.

23. Frank Berkman, "Hans Zimmer: The Computer Is My Instrument," *Mashable*, accessed April 7, 2021. https://mashable.com/2013/02/05/hans-zimmer-vjam/?europe=true#eioz.pe62ZqD.

24. Mark Savage, "Talking Shop: Hans Zimmer," *BBC News*, accessed April 7, 2021. http://news.bbc.co.uk/1/hi/entertainment/7526033.stm.

25. Matthew Vosburgh, "Yards Ahead," *muzines.co.uk*, accessed April 7, 2021. http://www.muzines.co.uk/articles/yards-ahead/978.

26. *Rain Man*, "The Journey of *Rain Man*," DVD, directed by Barry Levinson (Los Angeles: MGM, 1988).

27. Jon Burlingame, "Remote Control Prods.: Hans Zimmer's Music Factory as a Breeding Ground," *Variety*, accessed April 9, 2021. https://variety.com/2014/music/news/remote-control-prods-music-factory-as-breeding-ground-1201173763/.

28. *Ibid.*

29. Sean Wilson, "John Powell Interview: Scoring *Bourne*, Hans Zimmer, *Face/Off* and More," *Den of Geek*, accessed April 9, 2021. https://www.denofgeek.com/movies/john-powell-interview-scoring-bourne-hans-zimmer-faceoff-and-more/.

30. *Ibid.*

31. Christian Clemmensen, "*Pirates of the Caribbean: The Curse of the Black Pearl*," *Filmtracks*, accessed April 10, 2021. https://www.filmtracks.com/titles/pirates_caribbean.html.

32. *Ibid.*

33. Dan Goldwasser, "Battling Monsters with Alan Silvestri," *Soundtrack.net*, accessed April 11, 2021. https://www.soundtrack.net/content/article/?id=137.

34. Tim Appelo, "Composer Hans Zimmer Talks *Interstellar* Origin, Punk Influence on *Dark Knight*," *The Hollywood Reporter*, accessed April 11, 2021. https://www.hollywoodreporter.com/news/composer-hans-zimmer-talks-interstellar-745891.

35. Andrew Collins, "'We Fight Like Cats and Dogs, But in the Best, the Most Productive Way': Christopher Nolan Speaks Exclusively About His Extraordinary Partnership With Composer Hans Zimmer," *Classic FM*, accessed April 11, 2021. https://www.classicfm.com/composers/zimmer/music/christopher-nolan-interview/.

36. James Southall, "*The Lion King* Soundtrack Review," *Movie-wave.net*, accessed April 13, 2021. http://www.movie-wave.net/the-lion-king/.

37. Maddy Shaw Roberts, "Hans Zimmer on *The Lion King* Score: 'The Death of a Father Needs a Serious Requiem,'" *Classic FM*, accessed April 13, 2021. https://www.classicfm.com/composers/zimmer/hans-lion-king-remake-new-soundtrack-interview/.

38. Christian Clemmensen, "*The Thin Red Line*," *Filmtracks*, accessed April 13, 2021. https://www.filmtracks.com/titles/thin_red.html.

39. Adam Chitwood, "*Mission: Impossible—Fallout* Composer Lorne Balfe on Crafting an Epic Score," *Collider*, accessed April 13, 2021. https://collider.com/mission-impossible-fallout-lorne-balfe-interview/.

40. Matt Miller, "Why Hans Zimmer Emerged from Behind the Screen," *Esquire*, accessed April 13, 2021. https://www.esquire.com/entertainment/music/news/a54981/hans-zimmer-live-tour-coachella-2017-interview/.

41. *Ibid.*

42. Sean Wilson, "The Sound of Cinema," *Composer Magazine*, accessed April 13, 2021. https://composer.spitfireaudio.com/en/articles/the-sound-of-cinema.

43. *Ibid.*

44. *Ibid.*

45. *Ibid.*

46. Marc V. Ciafardini, "*The Matrix* Composer Reveals Secrets from His Score, 20 Years Later," *The Hollywood Reporter*, accessed April 14, 2021. https://www.hollywoodreporter.com/heat-vision/matrix-composer-reveals-one-scene-was-cut-1198353.

47. *Ibid.*
48. *Ibid.*
49. *Ibid.*
50. *Ibid.*
51. *Ibid.*
52. *Ibid.*
53. Mervyn Cooke, *A History of Film Music* (Cambridge: Cambridge University Press, 2008), 497.
54. Doug Adams, *The Music of The Lord of the Rings Films* (Los Angeles: Carpentier/Alfred Music, 2010), 11.
55. Mervyn Cooke, *A History of Film Music* (Cambridge: Cambridge University Press, 2008), 498.
56. *Ibid.*
57. Liner notes for *The Lord of the Rings: The Fellowship of the Ring*, by Howard Shore. Peter Jackson. Reprise Records, 9362-48110-2, 2001, compact disc.
58. *Ibid.*
59. Liner notes for *The Lord of the Rings: The Fellowship of the Ring*, by Howard Shore. Howard Shore. Reprise Records, 9362-48110-2, 2001, compact disc.
60. Byron Burton, "*Avengers: Endgame* Composer on Finding a Poignant Ending for the Journey," *The Hollywood Reporter*, accessed April 20, 2021. https://www.hollywoodreporter.com/heat-vision/avengers-endgame-composer-his-poignant-journey-score-1204799.
61. *Ibid.*
62. Sean Wilson, "Michael Giacchino Interview: The Art Of Scoring Movies," *Den of Geek*, accessed April 21, 2021. https://www.denofgeek.com/movies/michael-giacchino-interview-the-art-of-scoring-movies/.
63. Darren Franich, "*Dark Knight Rises*: Hans Zimmer Wants You to Chant," *Entertainment Weekly*, accessed April 22, 2021. https://ew.com/article/2011/11/10/dark-knight-rises-soundtrack-chant-zimmer/.
64. Dan Goldwasser, "Breaking the Rules with Hans Zimmer," *Soundtrack.net*, accessed April 22, 2021. https://www.soundtrack.net/content/article/?id=210.
65. Byron Burton, "Danny Elfman Hates When Reboots Scrap Classic Themes," *The Hollywood Reporter*, accessed April 22, 2021. https://www.hollywoodreporter.com/heat-vision/justice-league-danny-elfman-hates-reboots-scrap-classic-themes-1059262.
66. Cory Wong, Jason Shadrick, "Danny Elfman Goes Psycho!" *Wong Notes Podcast*, accessed May 19, 2021. https://www.premierguitar.com/podcast/wong-notes/danny-elfman.
67. *Ibid.*

Chapter Six

1. Sean Wilson, "H.P. Karpman Country: Laura Karpman Discusses Her Work on the New HBO Project From J.J. Abrams and Jordan Peele," *Film Score Monthly* 25, no. 9, September 2020. Accessed April 28, 2021, https://www.fsmonlinemag.com.
2. David Huckvale, *Hammer Film Scores and the Musical Avant-Garde* (Jefferson, NC: McFarland, 2009), 54.
3. *Ibid.*
4. *Ibid.*, 56.
5. *Ibid.*, 57.
6. Laurel Parsons, "Early Music and Ambivalent Origins of Elisabeth Lutyens' Modernism," in *British Music and Modernism, 1895–1960*, edited by Matthew Riley (London: Routledge, 2016), 289.
7. *Ibid.*, 290.
8. *Ibid.*
9. David Huckvale, *Hammer Film Scores and the Musical Avant-Garde* (Jefferson, NC: McFarland, 2009), 58.
10. *Ibid.*
11. Elisabeth Lutyens, quoted in Roger Manvell and John Huntley, *The Technique of Film Music* (London: Focal Press, 1957), 229.
12. David Huckvale, *Hammer Film Scores and the Musical Avant-Garde* (Jefferson, NC: McFarland, 2009), 5.
13. Humphrey Searle, "*Quadrille with a Raven*: Chapter 11—Leslie and Rosie's Pub." Accessed April 27, 2021, http://www.musicweb-international.com/searle/lesley.htm.
14. David Huckvale, *Hammer Film Scores and the Musical Avant-Garde* (Jefferson, NC: McFarland, 2009), 68.
15. *Ibid.*
16. Kate Hutchinson, "Making Sounds with Suzanne Ciani, America's First Female Synth Hero," *The Guardian*, accessed May 9, 2021. https://www.theguardian.com/music/2017/may/20/suzanne-ciani-america-female-synth-hero.
17. "The 69th Academy Awards," Academy of Motion Picture Arts and Sciences,

accessed April 26, 2021. https://www.oscars.org/oscars/ceremonies/1997.

18. Christian Clemmensen, *"Emma,"* *Filmtracks*, accessed April 26, 2021. https://www.filmtracks.com/titles/emma.html.

19. John Caps, "Rachel Portman: Composing for Stage and Screen," *MFiles*, accessed April 26, 2021. https://www.mfiles.co.uk/composers/Rachel-Portman-interview.htm.

20. *Ibid.*

21. Adam Sherwin, "Women Composers Frozen Out of Hollywood Blockbuster Soundtracks Says British Oscar-Winner," *iNews*, accessed April 26, 2021. https://inews.co.uk/culture/film/women-composers-frozen-out-hollywood-blockbuster-soundtracks-anne-dudley-394788.

22. Scott Huver, *"Captain Marvel* Composer Hired a 70-Piece Orchestra to Become First Woman to Score an MCU Film," *Vulture*, accessed April 27, 2021. https://www.vulture.com/2019/03/captain-marvel-pinar-toprak-first-female-composer.html.

23. Maddy Shaw Roberts, "Pinar Toprak: Everything You Need to Know About Marvel's First Female Film Composer," *Classic FM*, accessed April 27, 2021. https://www.classicfm.com/discover-music/periods-genres/film-tv/pinar-toprak-captain-marvel-composer/.

24. Alex Godfrey, *"Joker* and *Chernobyl* Composer Hildur Guðnadóttir: 'I'm Treasure Hunting,'" *The Guardian*, accessed April 28, 2021. https://www.theguardian.com/music/2019/dec/13/joker-and-chernobyl-composer-hildur-gunadottir-im-treasure-hunting.

25. *Ibid.*

26. *Ibid.*

27. Sean Wilson, "H.P. Karpman Country: Laura Karpman discusses her work on the new HBO project from J.J. Abrams and Jordan Peele," *Film Score Monthly* 25, no. 9, September 2020. Accessed April 28, 2021, https://www.fsmonlinemag.com.

28. Sean Wilson, "H.P. Karpman Country: Laura Karpman Discusses Her Work on the New HBO Project from J.J. Abrams and Jordan Peele," *Film Score Monthly* 25, no. 9, September 2020. Accessed April 28, 2021, https://www.fsmonlinemag.com.

29. "About the AWFC," *The AWFC*, accessed April 28, 2021. https://theawfc.com/about.

30. Jon Burlingame, "Mother and Daughter Collaborate on Music for *Manchester by the Sea*," *Variety*, accessed April 30, 2021. https://variety.com/2016/artisans/production/manchester-by-the-sea-music-1201925153/.

31. Sean Wilson, "H.P. Karpman Country: Laura Karpman Discusses Her Work on the New HBO Project from J.J. Abrams and Jordan Peele," *Film Score Monthly* 25, no. 9, September 2020. Accessed April 28, 2021, https://www.fsmonlinemag.com.

32. Melinda Newman, "The Women Who Score Concert, Featuring Award-Winning Female Composers Set for Aug. 19," *Billboard*, accessed April 30, 2021. https://www.billboard.com/articles/news/7401442/the-women-who-score-concert.

33. Sean Wilson, "H.P. Karpman Country: Laura Karpman Discusses Her Work on the New HBO Project from J.J. Abrams and Jordan Peele," *Film Score Monthly* 25, no. 9, September 2020. Accessed April 28, 2021, https://www.fsmonlinemag.com.

34. Tim Grieving, "Female Composers Are Trying to Break the Sound Barrier," *N.Y. Times*, accessed April 30, 2021. https://www.nytimes.com/2019/01/10/movies/female-film-composers.html.

35. Emma Warren, "Tamar-kali on Scoring for Film, Chamber Orchestra & DIY Punk Bands," *Composer Magazine*, accessed April 30, 2021. https://composer.spitfireaudio.com/en/articles/tamar-kali-on-scoring-for-film-chamber-orchestra-diy-punk-bands.

36. Mervyn Cooke, *A History of Film Music* (Cambridge: Cambridge University Press, 2008), 494.

37. *Ibid.*, 113.

38. Steven C. Smith, *A Heart at Fire's Center* (Oakland: University of California Press, 1991), 321.

39. Mervyn Cooke, *A History of Film Music* (Cambridge: Cambridge University Press, 2008), 492.

40. *Ibid.*

41. *Ibid.*

42. Liner notes for *Dances with Wolves*, by John Barry. Jon Burlingame. Epic/Legacy, EPC 515132 2, 2004, compact disc.

43. *Ibid.*

44. Mervyn Cooke, *A History of Film Music* (Cambridge: Cambridge University Press, 2008), 493.

45. *Alien*, "Future Tense: Scoring and Editing," DVD, directed by Ridley Scott (Century City, CA: 20th Century Studios, 1979).
46. Mervyn Cooke, *A History of Film Music* (Cambridge: Cambridge University Press, 2008), 469.
47. Jon Broxton, "*Legend*," *MovieMusic UK*, accessed May 4, 2021. https://moviemusicuk.us/2016/04/21/legend-jerry-goldsmithtangerine-dream/.
48. Christian Clemmensen, "*Air Force One*," *Filmtracks*, accessed May 4, 2021, https://www.filmtracks.com/titles/air_force_one.html.
49. Jon Burlingame, "Music You Won't Hear at the Movies," *L.A. Times*, accessed May 5, 2021. https://www.latimes.com/archives/la-xpm-1997-jul-15-ca-12822-story.html.
50. *Ibid*.
51. Christian Clemmensen, "*Air Force One*," *Filmtracks*, accessed May 4, 2021. https://www.filmtracks.com/titles/air_force_one.html.
52. Mervyn Cooke, *A History of Film Music* (Cambridge: Cambridge University Press, 2008), 492.
53. *Ibid*.
54. Jon Broxton, "*Willow*," *MovieMusic UK*, accessed May 6, 2021. https://moviemusicuk.us/2018/05/24/willow-james-horner/.
55. James Southall, "*Honey, I Shrunk the Kids*," *Movie-wave.net*, accessed May 6, 2021. http://www.movie-wave.net/honey-i-shrunk-the-kids/.
56. Mervyn Cooke, *A History of Film Music* (Cambridge: Cambridge University Press, 2008), 495.
57. Alex Ross, "Das Lied von der Brad," *The Rest Is Noise*, accessed May 6, 2021. https://www.therestisnoise.com/2004/05/symphony_of_brad.html.
58. Christian Clemmensen, "*The Right Stuff*," *Filmtracks*, accessed May 7, 2021. https://www.filmtracks.com/titles/right_stuff.html.
59. Sophie Monks Kaufman, "James Horner Reveals the Story Behind Five of His Classic Film Scores," *Little White Lies*, accessed May 7, 2021. https://lwlies.com/articles/james-horner-reveals-the-story-behind-five-of-his-classic-film-scores/.
60. *Ibid*.
61. *Leap of Faith: William Friedkin on The Exorcist*, directed by Alexandre O. Philippe. (Denver: Exhibit A Pictures, 2019).
62. *Ibid*.
63. *Ibid*.
64. Jon Burlingame, "Music You Won't Hear at the Movies," *L.A. Times*, accessed May 8, 2021. https://www.latimes.com/archives/la-xpm-1997-jul-15-ca-12822-story.html.

Coda

1. Sean Wilson, "Exclusive Interview— Composer David Arnold discusses *Good Omens*," *Flickering Myth*, accessed May 11, 2021. https://www.flickeringmyth.com/2019/06/david-arnold-good-omens-soundtrack-interview/.
2. Stephan Eicke, *The Struggle Behind the Soundtrack: Inside the Discordant New World of Film Scoring* (Jefferson, NC: McFarland, 2019), 1.
3. *Ibid*.
4. Sean Wilson, "Exclusive Interview— Composer David Arnold discusses *Good Omens*," *Flickering Myth*, accessed May 11, 2021. https://www.flickeringmyth.com/2019/06/david-arnold-good-omens-soundtrack-interview/.
5. *Ibid*.
6. *Ibid*.
7. *Ibid*.
8. Amon Warmann, "Christophe Beck on Scoring Different Eras for *Wanda Vision*," *Composer Magazine*, accessed May 13, 2021. https://composer.spitfireaudio.com/en/articles/christophe-beck-on-scoring-different-eras-for-wandavision.
9. Andy Hill, *Scoring the Screen: The Secret Language of Film Music* (Lanham, MD: Rowman & Littlefield, 2017), 384.
10. *Ibid*.
11. *Ibid*.
12. Andy Hill, *Scoring the Screen: The Secret Language of Film Music* (Lanham, MD: Rowman & Littlefield, 2017), 385.
13. *Ibid*.
14. Dalya Alberge, "Ennio Morricone: Good Film Scores Have Been Replaced by the Bad and the Ugly," *The Guardian*, accessed May 13, 2021. https://www.theguardian.com/music/2015/jun/03/ennio-morricone-good-film-scores-replaced-by-bad-and-ugly.
15. *Ibid*.

16. Sean Wilson, "H.P. Karpman Country: Laura Karpman Discusses Her Work on the New HBO Project from J.J. Abrams and Jordan Peele," *Film Score Monthly* 25, no. 9, September 2020. Accessed April 28, 2021, https://www.fsmonlinemag.com.

17. Jeff Bond, "Horner Revealed," in *Film Score Monthly* 9, no. 2, edited by Lukas Kendall (Los Angeles: Vineyard Haven, 2004): 17–18. Accessed May 25, 2021, https://fsmonlinemag.com.

Bibliography

"About the AWFC." Accessed April 28, 2021. https://theawfc.com/about.

Academy of Motion Picture Arts and Sciences. Accessed February 6, 2021. https://oscars.org/.

Adams, Doug. *The Music of The Lord of the Rings Films*. Los Angeles: Carpentier/Alfred Music, 2010.

Alberge, Dalya. "Ennio Morricone: Good Film Scores Have Been Replaced By the Bad and the Ugly." Accessed May 13, 2021. https://www.theguardian.com/music/2015/jun/03/ennio-morricone-good-film-scores-replaced-by-bad-and-ugly.

Aletti, Vince. "*Trouble Man/M.P.G.*" Accessed March 6, 2021. https://www.rollingstone.com/music/music-album-reviews/trouble-man-m-p-g-192399/.

"Alex North: Hollywood Film Composer." Accessed February 8, 2021. http://www.jazzprofessional.com/interviews/Alex%20North.htm.

Alien. DVD, directed by Ridley Scott. Los Angeles: 20th Century Studios, 1979.

Alien 3. DVD, directed by David Fincher. Los Angeles: 20th Century Studios, 1992.

Appelo, Tim. "Composer Hans Zimmer Talks *Interstellar* Origin, Punk Influence on *Dark Knight*." Accessed April 11, 2021. https://www.hollywoodreporter.com/news/composer-hans-zimmer-talks-interstellar-745891.

Audissino, Emilio. *John Williams's Film Music: Jaws, Star Wars, Raiders of the Lost Ark, and the Return of the Classical Hollywood Music Style*. Madison: University of Wisconsin Press, 2014.

Barrett, Heather. "*Star Wars* Composer John Williams' First Score a 1952 Newfoundland Film." Accessed March 12, 2021. https://www.cbc.ca/news/canada/newfoundland-labrador/star-wars-composer-john-williams-first-score-a-1952-newfoundland-film-1.3241603.

BBC Bitesize. "Compose Your Own *Doctor Who* Theme." Accessed March 5, 2021. https://www.bbc.co.uk/bitesize/topics/zhdfscw/articles/zkkrbdm#:~:text=Back%20in%20the%201960s%2C%20there,create%20the%20eerie%20futuristic%20music.

Beggs, Scott. "Seven Scenes Made Epic By James Horner, the King of the Movie-Music World." Accessed March 24, 2021. https://www.vanityfair.com/hollywood/2015/06/james-horner-epic-moments.

Behlmer, Rudy. "Robin Hood on the Screen: From Legend to Film." In *Robin Hood: An Anthology of Scholarship and Criticism*, edited by Stephen Knight, 458–459. Suffolk: Boydell & Brewer, 1999.

Berkman, Frank. "Hans Zimmer: The Computer Is My Instrument." Accessed April 7, 2021. https://mashable.com/2013/02/05/hans-zimmer-vjam/?europe=true#eioz.pe62ZqD.

Boller, Paul F., Jr. "Music by Max Steiner." *Southwest Review* 51, no. 3 (1966): 256–271. https://www.jstor.org/stable/43467799?read-now=1&seq=5#page_scan_tab_contents.

Bond, Jeff. "Horner Revealed." In *Film Score Monthly*, edited by Lukas Kendall, Vol. 9. No. 2 (Los Angeles: Vineyard Haven, 2004): 17–18. https://filmscoremonthly.com/backissues/viewissue.cfm?issueID=95.

Bond, Jeff, Alexander Kaplan, and Lukas Kendall. Liner notes for *Star Trek II: The Wrath of Khan*, by James Horner.

Retrograde Records-Film Score Monthly, FSM 80128-2, compact disc, 2009.

Bowman, Rob. *Soulsville U.S.A.: The Story of Stax Records.* New York: Schirmer Trade, 1997.

Box Office Mojo. Accessed June 2, 2021. https://www.boxofficemojo.com/chart/top_lifetime_gross_adjusted/?adjust_gross_to=202.

Brigden, Charlie. "Looking Back at the Music of *The Motion Picture.*" Accessed March 30, 2021. https://intl.startrek.com/news/looking-back-at-the-music-of-the-motion-picture.

British Film Institute. "The 100 Greatest Films of All Time." Accessed June 1, 2021. https://www2.bfi.org.uk/greatest-films-all-time.

Brody, Richard. "Louis Malle's *Elevator to the Gallows,* and Its Historic Miles Davis Soundtrack." Accessed June 8, 2021. https://www.newyorker.com/culture/richard-brody/louis-malles-elevator-to-the-gallows-and-its-historic-miles-davis-soundtrack.

Broxton, Jon. "*Interview with the Vampire.*" Accessed April 4, 2021. https://moviemusicuk.us/2009/09/12/interview-with-the-vampire-elliot-goldenthal/.

Broxton, Jon. "*Legend.*" Accessed May 4, 2021. https://moviemusicuk.us/2016/04/21/legend-jerry-goldsmithtangerinedream/.

Broxton, Jon. "*Willow.*" Accessed May 6, 2021. https://moviemusicuk.us/2018/05/24/willow-james-horner/.

Burlingame, Jon. "AFI Honoree John Williams Looks Back on Six Decades of Iconic Themes." Accessed March 18, 2021. https://variety.com/2016/film/spotlight/john-williams-afi-1201792072-1201792072/.

Burlingame, Jon. "Bonding with the Score: David Arnold Blends the Traditional with the Modern In Music for *Tomorrow Never Dies.*" Accessed April 2, 2021. https://www.latimes.com/archives/la-xpm-1997-dec-18-ca-65184-story.html.

Burlingame, Jon. "Daring and Original, Bernard Herrmann Changed Movie Music." Accessed June 1, 2021. https://www.washingtonpost.com/entertainment/music/daring-and-original-bernard-herrmann-changed-movie-music/2011/06/21/AGG0YXjH_story.html.

Burlingame, Jon. "Jerry Goldsmith: An Appreciation." Accessed February 13, 2021. http://www.filmmusicsociety.org/news_events/features/2004/080204.html.

Burlingame, Jon. "L.A. Music's First Family." Accessed May 30, 2021. https://variety.com/1997/music/markets-festivals/l-a-music-s-first-family-1116677018/.

Burlingame, Jon. Liner notes for *Dances with Wolves,* by John Barry. Epic/Legacy, EPC 515132 2, 2004, compact disc.

Burlingame, Jon. "Mother and Daughter Collaborate on Music for *Manchester by the Sea.*" Accessed April 30, 2021. https://variety.com/2016/artisans/production/manchester-by-the-sea-music-1201925153/.

Burlingame, Jon. "Music You Won't Hear at the Movies." Accessed May 5, 2021. https://www.latimes.com/archives/la-xpm-1997-jul-15-ca-12822-story.html.

Burlingame, Jon. "Netflix's *Lost in Space* Reboot Borrows Grandeur of Original Score." Accessed March 13, 2021. https://variety.com/2018/artisans/production/lost-in-space-score-1202749940.

Burlingame, Jon. "Remote Control Prods.: Hans Zimmer's Music Factory as a Breeding Ground." Accessed April 9, 2021. https://variety.com/2014/music/news/remote-control-prods-music-factory-as-breeding-ground-1201173763/.

Burlingame, Jon. "Spotlight on Thomas Newman." Accessed April 4, 2021. https://variety.com/2000/music/news/spotlight-thomas-newman-1117761178/.

Burton, Byron. "*Avengers: Endgame* Composer on Finding a Poignant Ending for the Journey." Accessed April 20, 2021. https://www.hollywoodreporter.com/heat-vision/avengers-endgame-composer-his-poignant-journey-score-1204799.

Burton, Byron. "Danny Elfman Hates When Reboots Scrap Classic Themes." Accessed April 22, 2021. https://www.hollywoodreporter.com/heat-vision/justice-league-danny-elfman-hates-reboots-scrap-classic-themes-1059632.

Cameron, E.W. *Sound and the Cinema.* London: Routledge, 1980.

Caps, John. "Rachel Portman: Composing for Stage and Screen." Accessed April 26, 2021. https://www.mfiles.co.uk/composers/Rachel-Portman-interview.htm.

Bibliography

Chaplin, Charles. *My Autobiography*. London: Penguin Modern Classics, 2003.

Chitwood, Adam. "*Mission: Impossible—Fallout* Composer Lorne Balfe on Crafting an Epic Score." Accessed April 13, 2021. https://collider.com/mission-impossible-fallout-lorne-balfe-interview/.

Ciafardini, Marc V. "*The Matrix* Composer Reveals Secrets From His Score, 20 Years Later." Accessed April 14, 2021. https://www.hollywoodreporter.com/heat-vision/matrix-composer-reveals-one-scene-was-cut-1198353.

Clemmensen, Christian. "*Air Force One.*" Accessed May 4, 2021. https://www.filmtracks.com/titles/air_force_one.html.

Clemmensen, Christian. "*Back to the Future.*" Accessed March 26, 2021. https://www.filmtracks.com/titles/back_future.html.

Clemmensen, Christian. "*Cutthroat Island.*" Accessed March 30, 2021. https://www.filmtracks.com/titles/cutthroat_island.html.

Clemmensen, Christian. "*Emma.*" Accessed April 26, 2021. https://www.filmtracks.com/titles/emma.html.

Clemmensen, Christian. "*Independence Day.*" Accessed March 30, 2021. https://www.filmtracks.com/titles/id4.html.

Clemmensen, Christian. "*Pirates of the Caribbean: The Curse of the Black Pearl.*" Accessed April 10, 2021. https://www.filmtracks.com/titles/pirates_caribbean.html.

Clemmensen, Christian. "*The Right Stuff.*" Accessed May 7, 2021. https://www.filmtracks.com/titles/right_stuff.html.

Clemmensen, Christian. "*Speed.*" Accessed April 6, 2021. https://www.filmtracks.com/titles/speed.html.

Clemmensen, Christian. "*The Thin Red Line.*" Accessed April 13, 2021. https://www.filmtracks.com/titles/thin_red.html.

Clemmensen, Christian. "*Tomorrow Never Dies.*" Accessed April 2, 2021. https://www.filmtracks.com/titles/tomorrow_never.html.

Collins, Andrew. "'We Fight Like Cats and Dogs, But in the Best, the Most Productive Way': Christopher Nolan Speaks Exclusively About His Extraordinary Partnership With Composer Hans Zimmer." Accessed April 11, 2021. https://www.classicfm.com/composers/zimmer/music/christopher-nolan-interview/.

Cooke, Mervyn. *A History of Film Music*. Cambridge: Cambridge University Press, 2008.

Courrier, Kevin. *Randy Newman's American Dreams*. Toronto: ECW Press, 2005.

Curzon Cinema and Arts. "History: Clevedon's Historic Cinema." Accessed February 6, 2021. https://www.curzon.org.uk/heritage/history/.

Davison, Annette. *Alex North's A Streetcar Named Desire: A Film Score Guide*. Lanham, MD: Scarecrow Press, 2009.

"Dickson Experimental Sound Film 1895." FilmSound.org. Accessed February 6, 2021. http://www.filmsound.org/murch/dickson.htm.

Eicke, Stephan. *The Struggle Behind the Soundtrack: Inside the Discordant New World of Film Scoring*. Jefferson, NC: McFarland, 2019.

Elfman, Danny, to David Mermelstein. "Daring and Original, Bernard Herrmann Changed Movie Music." Accessed June 1, 2021. https://www.washingtonpost.com/entertainment/music/daring-and-original-bernard-herrmann-changed-movie-music/2011/06/21/AGG0YXjH_story.html.

Fleming, Mike, Jr. "'*Star Wars*' Legacy II: An Architect of Hollywood's Greatest Deal Recalls How George Lucas Won Sequel Rights." Accessed March 16, 2021. https://deadline.com/2015/12/star-wars-franchise-george-lucas-historic-rights-deal-tom-pollock-1201669419/.

Franich, Darren. "*Dark Knight Rises*: Hans Zimmer Wants You to Chant." Accessed April 22, 2021. https://ew.com/article/2011/11/10/dark-knight-rises-soundtrack-chant-zimmer/.

"George Groves: The Movie Sound Pioneer." Accessed February 6, 2021. https://www.georgegroves.org.uk/.

Godfrey, Alex. "*Joker* and *Chernobyl* Composer Hildur Guðnadóttir: 'I'm Treasure Hunting.'" Accessed April 28, 2021. https://www.theguardian.com/music/2019/dec/13/joker-and-chernobyl-composer-hildur-gunadottir-im-treasure-hunting.

Goldwasser, Dan. "Battling Monsters with Alan Silvestri." Accessed April 11, 2021. https://www.soundtrack.net/content/article/?id=137.

Goldwasser, Dan. "Breaking the Rules with Hans Zimmer." Accessed April 22, 2021. https://www.soundtrack.net/content/article/?id=210.

Gottlieb, Carl. *The Jaws Log: 25th Anniversary Edition*. New York: Faber & Faber, 2001.

Green, Willow. "Movie Movements that Defined Cinema: The Movie Brats." Accessed March 15, 2021. https://www.empireonline.com/movies/features/movie-brats-movie-era/.

Greenberg, Alex, and Malvin Wald. "Report to the Stockholders." *Hollywood Quarterly* 1, no. 4 (1946): 410–415. https://online.ucpress.edu/fq/article-abstract/1/4/410/37313/Report-to-the-Stockholders?redirectedFrom=fulltext.

Greenberger, Robert. "Alan Menken Revisits *Beauty and the Beast*." Accessed March 29, 2021. https://www.comicmix.com/2010/10/02/alan-menken-revisits-beauty-and-the-beast/.

Grieving, Tim. "Female Composers Are Trying to Break the Sound Barrier." Accessed April 30, 2021. https://www.nytimes.com/2019/01/10/movies/female-film-composers.html.

Grieving, Tim. "Jerry Goldsmith, 'The Composer's Composer,' Honored with Hollywood Star." Accessed February 17, 2021. https://www.npr.org/2017/05/09/527575323/jerry-goldsmith-the-composers-composer-honored-with-hollywood-star?t=1621585217617.

Grieving, Tim. "Why the *Alien* Franchise Has Such a Dramatic Musical Past." Accessed March 24, 2021. https://www.vulture.com/2017/05/why-the-alien-franchise-has-such-a-dramatic-musical-past.html.

Groult, Florence. "Goldsmith by Beltram: Master and Student." Accessed February 13, 2021. http://www.underscores.fr/rencontres/interviews-vo/2008/08/interview-with-marco-beltrami/.

Grow, Kory. "Surf Music and Seventies Soul: The Songs of *Pulp Fiction*." Accessed April 6, 2021. https://www.rollingstone.com/movies/movie-lists/pulp-fiction-soundtrack-songs-tarantino-14045/.

Harris, Mark. *Pictures at a Revolution*. London: Penguin, 2008.

Henderson, Sanya Shoilevska. *Alex North, Film Composer: A Biography, with Analyses of A Streetcar Named Desire, Spartacus, The Misfits, Under the Volcano and Prizzi's Honor*. Jefferson, NC: McFarland, 2009.

Herrmann, Bernard, to Misha Donat. 1973.

Hill, Andy. *Scoring the Screen: The Secret Language of Film Music*. Lanham, MD: Rowman & Littlefield, 2017.

Huckvale, David. *Hammer Film Scores and the Musical Avant-Garde*. Jefferson, NC: McFarland, 2009.

Huff, Theodore. "Chaplin as a Composer." Accessed February 7, 2021. https://www.charliechaplin.com/en/articles/205-Chaplin-as-a-Composer.

Humphries, Patrick. *Elvis the #1 Hits: The Secret History of the Classics*. Kansas City: Andrews McMeel, 2003.

Huntley, John, and Roger Manvell. *The Technique of Film Music*. London: Focal Press, 1957.

Hutchinson, Kate. "Making Sounds with Suzanne Ciani, America's First Female Synth Hero." Accessed May 9, 2021. https://www.theguardian.com/music/2017/may/20/suzanne-ciani-america-female-synth-hero.

Huver, Scott. "*Captain Marvel* Composer Hired a 70-Piece Orchestra to Become First Woman to Score an MCU Film." Accessed April 27, 2021. https://www.vulture.com/2019/03/captain-marvel-pinar-toprak-first-female-composer.html.

"*Indiana Jones* and Me: John Williams." Accessed March 21, 2021. https://www.empireonline.com/movies/features/indiana-jones-john-williams/.

Jackson, Peter. Liner notes for *The Lord of the Rings: The Fellowship of the Ring*, by Howard Shore. Reprise Records, 9362–48110–2, 2001, compact disc.

"James Horner: 10 Best Movie Soundtracks—*Titanic*." Accessed March 25, 2021. https://www.classicfm.com/composers/horner/music/james-horner-ten-best-movie-soundtracks/titanic-8/.

Jaws, DVD, directed by Steven Spielberg. Los Angeles: Universal Studios, 1975.

"Jazz on Film: *A Streetcar Named Desire*." Accessed February 7, 2021. https://www.jazzwise.com/features/article/jazz-on-film-a-streetcar-named-desire.

"Jerry Goldsmith." Accessed February 7, 2021. https://www.thetimes.co.uk/article/jerry-goldsmith-6tkpzm023pn.

Kaufman, Sophie Monks. "James Horner Reveals the Story Behind Five of His Classic Film Scores." Accessed May 7, 2021. https://lwlies.com/articles/james-horner-reveals-the-story-behind-five-of-his-classic-film-scores/.

Kester, Gary. Liner notes for *Basic Instinct*, by Jerry Goldsmith. Prometheus, XPCD 154, 2004, compact disc.

Kilday, Gregg. "Steven Spielberg and Fellow Directors Reveal the Stories Behind John Williams' Iconic Scores." Accessed March 21, 2021. https://www.hollywoodreporter.com/news/steven-spielberg-fellow-directors-reveal-900829.

Koerber, Martin. "Oskar Messter, Film Pioneer: Early Cinema Between Science, Spectacle and Commerce." In *A Second Life: German Cinema's First Decades*, edited by Thomas Elsaesser with Michael Wedel, 51–61. Amsterdam: Amsterdam University Press, 1996. https://www.jstor.org/stable/j.ctt45kfh9.6?seq=4#metadata_info_tab_contents.

Labrecque, Jeff. "*Aladdin* Directors and Alan Menken Remember Robin Williams." Accessed March 30, 2021. https://ew.com/article/2015/10/13/aladdin-roundtable/.

Lambie, Ryan. "Brad Fiedel Interview: Composing *Terminator 2*'s Iconic Score." Accessed March 27, 2021. https://www.denofgeek.com/movies/brad-fiedel-interview-composing-terminator-2s-iconic-score/.

Larson, Randall D. "Interview with Jerry Goldsmith." *CinemaScore: The Film Music Journal* 11/12 (July 15, 1982): 4.

Leap of Faith: William Friedkin on The Exorcist, directed by Alexandre O. Philippe (Denver: Exhibit A Pictures, 2019).

Leigh, Spencer. "Kris Kristofferson." Accessed March 7, 2021. https://web.archive.org/web/20120415001040/http://www.spencerleigh.demon.co.uk/Interview_Kristofferson.htm.

Leonard, Geoff. Liner notes for *Lawrence of Arabia*, by Maurice Jarre. Cinephile, CIN CD 008, 1999, compact disc.

Leopold, Todd. "The 50-Year-Old Song That Started It All." Accessed February 20, 2021. https://edition.cnn.com/2005/SHOWBIZ/Music/07/07/haley.rock/.

Lysy, Craig. "*The Adventures of Robin Hood*." Accessed May 27, 2021. https://moviemusicuk.us/2015/11/16/the-adventures-of-robin-hood-erich-wolfgang-korngold-2/.

Lysy, Craig. "*Batman*." Accessed March 22, 2021. https://moviemusicuk.us/2018/12/31/batman-danny-elfman-2/.

Lysy, Craig. "*Ben-Hur*." Accessed February 22, 2021. https://moviemusicuk.us/2017/09/18/ben-hur-miklos-rozsa-2/.

Lysy, Craig. "*Captain Blood*." Accessed May 26, 2021. https://moviemusicuk.us/2020/03/30/captain-blood-erich-wolfgang-korngold/.

Lysy, Craig. "*E.T. the Extra-Terrestrial*." Accessed March 23, 2021. https://moviemusicuk.us/2018/07/30/e-t-the-extra-terrestrial-john-williams/.

Lysy, Craig. "*How the West Was Won*." Accessed May 30, 2021. https://moviemusicuk.us/2017/10/16/how-the-west-was-won-alfred-newman/.

Lysy, Craig. "100 Greatest Scores of All Time: *L'Assassinat Du Duc De Guise*—Camille Saint-Saëns." Accessed February 6, 2021. https://moviemusicuk.us/2020/11/23/lassassinat-du-duc-de-guise-camille-saint-saens-2/.

Lysy, Craig. "*Planet of the Apes*." Accessed February 16, 2021. https://moviemusicuk.us/2018/02/26/planet-of-the-apes-jerry-goldsmith/.

Lysy, Craig. "*Schindler's List*." Accessed April 3, 2021. https://moviemusicuk.us/2019/02/18/schindlers-list-john-williams/.

Lysy, Craig. "*Spartacus*." Accessed February 10, 2021. https://moviemusicuk.us/2017/07/31/spartacus-alex-north/.

Lysy, Craig. "*A Streetcar Named Desire*." Accessed February 9, 2021. https://moviemusicuk.us/2017/03/13/a-streetcar-named-desire-alex-north/.

Mancini, Henry, with Gene Lees. *Did They Mention the Music? The Autobiography of Henry Mancini*. Lanham, MD: Cooper Square Press, 2001.

Marks, Martin. "The Well-Furnished Film: Satie's Score for *Entr'acte*." *Canadian University Music Review* 4 (1983): 245–277, https://www.erudit.org/fr/revues/cumr/1983-n4-cumr0428/1013906ar.pdf.

McCarthy, Todd. "*Indiana Jones and the Temple of Doom*." Accessed March 21, 2021. https://variety.com/1984/film/reviews/indiana-jones-and-the-temple-of-doom-1200426218/.

McCulley, Jerry. Liner notes for *The Magnificent Seven*, by Elmer Bernstein. Varèse Sarabande, VSD-6559, 2004, compact disc.

Meeker David. "Jazz on the Screen." Accessed February 8, 2021. https://memory.loc.gov/diglib/ihas/html/jots/jazzscreen-overview.html.

Metz, Robert. *CBS: Reflections in a Bloodshot Eye*. New York: Signet, 1975.

Miller, Matt. "Why Hans Zimmer Emerged from Behind the Screen." Accessed April 13, 2021. https://www.esquire.com/entertainment/music/news/a54981/hans-zimmer-live-tour-coachella-2017-interview/.

Morton, Ray. "Origin of 'Kong': The Unbelievable True Backstory of Hollywood's Favorite Giant Ape." Accessed May 23, 2021. https://www.hollywoodreporter.com/movies/movie-news/king-kong-unbelievable-true-story-hollywoods-favorite-giant-ape-984785/.

MS to Warner, April 5, 1939. From the collection of JWM.

"Music by the Reel." *Cue*, August 14, 1943.

Newman, Melinda. "The Women Who Score Concert, Featuring Award-Winning Female Composers Set For Aug. 19." Accessed April 30, 2021. https://www.billboard.com/articles/news/7401442/the-women-who-score-concert.

Nichols, Mackenzie. "*The Little Mermaid* Turns 30: Inside the Disney Classic's Rocky Journey." Accessed March 28, 2021. https://variety.com/2019/film/news/oral-history-the-little-mermaid-1203379538/.

"Other Works." Accessed March 12, 2021. http://www.jwfan.com/?page_id=3928.

Parker, Lyndsey. "*Batman* composer Danny Elfman Says Turning Down Prince Was 'Biggest, Most Stressful Gamble' of His Career." Accessed March 22, 2021. https://www.yahoo.com/entertainment/batman-composer-danny-elfman-says-turning-down-prince-was-biggest-most-stressful-gamble-of-his-career-192951834.html.

Parsons, Laurel. "Early Music and Ambivalent Origins of Elisabeth Lutyens' Modernism." In *British Music and Modernism, 1895–1960*, edited by Matthew Riley, 269–293. London: Routledge, 2016.

Porter, Laraine. "The Feminization of British Silent Cinema." In *Music and Sound in Silent Film: From the Nickelodeon to The Artist*, edited by Ruth Barton and Simon Tresize, 93–109. New York: Routledge, 2019.

Quarterly Journal of the Library of Congress, Summer 1983.

Rain Man. DVD, directed by Barry Levinson. Los Angeles: MGM, 1988.

Raksin, David, with Charles Berg. "'Music Composed by Charlie Chaplin': Auteur or Collaborateur?" *Journal of University Film Association* 31, no. 1 (Winter 1979): 47–50, http://www.jstor.org/stable/20687463.

"Raymond Scott Timeline." Accessed March 12, 2021. https://www.raymondscott.net/timeline/.

Redman, Nick. Liner notes for *The Robe*, by Alfred Newman. La-La Land Records, LLLCD 1203, 2012, compact disc.

Roberts, Maddy Shaw. "Hans Zimmer on *The Lion King* score: 'The Death of a Father Needs a Serious Requiem.'" Accessed April 13, 2021. https://www.classicfm.com/composers/zimmer/hans-lion-king-remake-new-soundtrack-interview/.

Roberts, Maddy Shaw. "Pinar Toprak: Everything You Need to Know About Marvel's First Female Film Composer." Accessed April 27, 2021. https://www.classicfm.com/discover-music/periods-genres/film-tv/pinar-toprak-captain-marvel-composer/.

Robinson, David. *Chaplin: His Life and Art*. London: Penguin, 2001.

Rogers, Jude. "She Made Music Jump Into 3D: Wendy Carlos, the Reclusive Synth Genius." Accessed March 4, 2021. https://www.theguardian.com/music/2020/nov/11/she-made-music-jump-into-3d-wendy-carlos-the-reclusive-synth-genius.

Rogers, Katharine M. *L. Frank Baum: Creator of Oz: A Biography*. New York: St. Martin's Press, 2007. https://play.google.com/books/reader?id=kxePw8MEsoC&pg=GBS.PP1.

Ross, Alex. "Das Lied von der Brad." Accessed May 6, 2021. https://www.therestisnoise.com/2004/05/symphony_of_brad.html.

Ross, Alex. "Erich Wolfgang Korngold, the Opera Composer Who Went Hollywood." Accessed May 26, 2021. https://www.newyorker.com/magazine/2019/

08/19/erich-wolfgang-korngold-the-opera-composer-who-went-hollywood.
Ross, Alex. "The Force Is Still Strong with John Williams." Accessed March 15, 2021. https://www.newyorker.com/culture/persons-of-interest/the-force-is-still-strong-with-john-williams.
Ross, Alex. "Listening to *Star Wars*." Accessed March 15, 2021. https://www.newyorker.com/culture/cultural-comment/listening-to-star-wars.
Savage, Mark. "Talking Shop: Hans Zimmer." Accessed April 7, 2021. http://news.bbc.co.uk/1/hi/entertainment/7526033.stm.
Searle, Humphrey. "*Quadrille With a Raven*: Chapter 11—Leslie and Rosie's Pub." Accessed April 27, 2021. http://www.musicweb-international.com/searle/lesley.htm.
Selznick, David O. "*Gone With the Wind* (1936–1941)." In *Memo from David O. Selznick*, edited by Rudy Behlmer, 149–275. New York: Modern Library, 2000.
Sherwin, Adam. "Women Composers Frozen Out of Hollywood Blockbuster Soundtracks Says British Oscar-Winner." Accessed April 26, 2021. https://inews.co.uk/culture/film/women-composers-frozen-out-hollywood-blockbuster-soundtracks-anne-dudley-394788.
Shore, Howard. Liner notes for *The Lord of the Rings: The Fellowship of the Ring*, by Howard Shore. Reprise Records, 9362-48110-2, 2001, compact disc.
Simpson, Dave. "How We Made Steppenwolf's 'Born To Be Wild.'" Accessed February 25, 2021. https://www.theguardian.com/music/2018/jul/31/how-we-made-steppenwolf-born-to-be-wild.
Smith, Steven C. *A Heart at Fire's Center: The Life and Music of Bernard Herrmann*. Oakland: University of California Press, 1991.
Smith, Steven C. *Music by Max Steiner: The Epic Life of Hollywood's Most Influential Composer*. Oxford: Oxford University Press, 2020.
Southall, James. "*Alien 3* Soundtrack Review." Accessed April 4, 2021. http://www.movie-wave.net/titles/alien3.html.
Southall, James. "*Honey, I Shrunk the Kids*." Accessed May 6, 2021. http://www.movie-wave.net/honey-i-shrunk-the-kids/.

Southall, James. "*The Lion King* Soundtrack Review." Accessed April 13, 2021. http://www.movie-wave.net/the-lion-king/.
Southall, James. "*Tora! Tora! Tora!* Soundtrack Review." Accessed February 18, 2021. http://www.movie-wave.net/tora-tora-tora/.
Spielberg, Steven. Liner notes for *Indiana Jones: The Soundtracks Collection—Indiana Jones and the Last Crusade*, by John Williams. Concord Records, CRE-31004-02, compact disc, 2008.
Spielberg, Steven. Liner notes for *Indiana Jones: The Soundtracks Collection—Indiana Jones and the Temple of Doom*, by John Williams. Concord Records, CRE-31003-02, compact disc, 2008.
Spielberg, Steven. Liner notes for *Indiana Jones: The Soundtracks Collection—Raiders of the Lost Ark*, by John Williams. Concord Records, CRE-31002-02, compact disc, 2008.
Steiner, Max. "Max Steiner: Vienna, London, New York and Finally Hollywood." *The Max Steiner Collection*. Provo: Brigham Young University, 1996.
Steiner, Max. *Notes to You*, Chapter XIII.
Steiner, Max. "Setting Emotions to Music." *Variety*, July 31, 1940.
"Steven Spielberg, George Lucas, Kobe Bryant & More Salute John Williams." Accessed March 18, 2021. https://www.afi.com/news/watch-steven-spielberg-george-lucas-kobe-bryant-more-salute-john-williams/.
"TCM's 15 Most Influential Film Soundtracks." Accessed February 20, 2021. https://web.archive.org/web/20100315120648/http://www.tcm.com/dailies/.
Thaxton, Ford A., and David Hirsch. Liner notes for *Star Trek: The Motion Picture: 20th Anniversary Collector's Edition*, by Jerry Goldsmith. Columbia, COL 489929 2, 1999, compact disc.
Townson, Robert. Liner notes for *Total Recall: The Deluxe Edition*, by Jerry Goldsmith. Varèse Sarabande, VSD 6197, 2000, compact disc.
Tresize, Simon. "Historical Introduction." In *Music and Sound in Silent Film: From the Nickelodeon to The Artist*, edited by Ruth Barton and Simon Tresize, 1–23. New York: Routledge, 2019.
Vance, Jeffrey. *Chaplin: Genius of the Cinema*. New York: Harry N. Abrams, 2003.

Variety Special Advertising Supplement, 20–21.

Vosburgh, Matthew. "Yards Ahead." Accessed April 7, 2021. http://www.muzines.co.uk/articles/yards-ahead/978.

Warmann, Amon. "Christophe Beck on Scoring Different Eras for *Wanda Vision*." Accessed May 13, 2021. https://composer.spitfireaudio.com/en/articles/christophe-beck-on-scoring-different-eras-for-wandavision.

Warren, Emma. "Tamar-kali on Scoring for Film, Chamber Orchestra & DIY Punk Bands." Accessed April 30, 2021. https://composer.spitfireaudio.com/en/articles/tamar-kali-on-scoring-for-film-chamber-orchestra-diy-punk-bands.

Wegele, Peter. *Max Steiner: Composing, Casablanca, and the Golden Age of Film Music*. Lanham, MD: Rowman & Littlefield, 2014.

Weinstein, Deena. *Rock'n America: A Social and Cultural History*. Toronto: University of Toronto Press, 2015.

Wilson, Sean. "Blanchard: Scoring the Struggle: Terence Blanchard On Spike Lee's Historical Crime Joint, *BlacKkKlansman*." *Film Score Monthly Online* 23, no. 9, September 2018. Accessed April 28, 2021. https://www.fsmonlinemag.com.

Wilson, Sean. "Exclusive Interview—A *Perfect Planet* Composer Ilan Eshkeri on Capturing Nature Through Music." Accessed February 7, 2021. https://www.flickeringmyth.com/2021/01/a-perfect-planet-interview-composer-ilan-eshkeri/.

Wilson, Sean. "Exclusive Interview—Composer David Arnold discusses *Good Omens*." Accessed May 11, 2021. https://www.flickeringmyth.com/2019/06/david-arnold-good-omens-soundtrack-interview/.

Wilson, Sean. "Howard Shore on Capturing the Sound of *Funny Boy*." Accessed April 28, 2021. https://composer.spitfireaudio.com/en/articles/howard-shore-on-capturing-the-sound-of-funny-boy.

Wilson, Sean. "H.P. Karpman Country: Laura Karpman Discusses Her Work on the New HBO Project From J.J. Abrams and Jordan Peele." *Film Score Monthly Online* 25, no. 9, September 2020. Accessed April 28, 2021. https://www.fsmonlinemag.com.

Wilson, Sean. "In the Deep End with Desplat: Alexandre Desplat Talks *The Shape of Water* and Guillermo del Toro." *Film Score Monthly Online* 22, no. 11, November 2017. Accessed April 28, 2021. https://www.fsmonlinemag.com.

Wilson, Sean. "John Powell Interview: Scoring *Bourne*, Hans Zimmer, *Face/Off* and More." Accessed March 28, 2021. https://www.denofgeek.com/movies/john-powell-interview-scoring-bourne-hans-zimmer-faceoff-and-more/.

Wilson, Sean. "Michael Giacchino Interview: the Art of Scoring Movies." Accessed April 28, 2021. https://denofgeek.com/movies/michael-giacchino-interview-the-art-of-scoring-movies/.

Wilson, Sean. "The Sound of Cinema." Accessed April 13, 2021. https://composer.spitfireaudio.com/en/articles/the-sound-of-cinema.

Wong, Cory, and Jason Shadrick. "Danny Elfman Goes Psycho!" *Wong Notes Podcast*. Accessed May 19, 2021. https://www.premierguitar.com/podcast/wong-notes/danny-elfman.

Index

Abbey Road Studios 149
Abels, Michael 229
Abrams, J.J. 136, 137, 138, 178, 197, 231
Academy Awards 20, 25, 27, 41, 49, 51, 57, 67, 75, 90, 100, 106, 108, 113, 114, 123, 130, 134, 147, 158, 159, 160, 166, 167, 181, 191, 203, 214, 219, 220; *see also* Oscar nominations; Oscars
Adams, Doug 190
Addison, John 65
The Adventures of Robin Hood 45, 47, 50, 51, 52
Agnes of God 43
The Agony and the Ecstasy 80
Air Edel Studio 173, 175
Air Force One 216, 217
AIR Studios 22, 184
Airplane! 153
Aladdin 159, 160, 165, 231
Alexander Nevsky 14, 75
Alexander's Ragtime Band 51
Alfred Hitchcock Presents 64
Alien 214–215
*Alien*³ 166, 167
Aliens 149, 166, 215, 224
All About Eve 55
All the President's Men 119
Alliance for Women Film Composers 210–211
Altman, Robert 123
American Beauty 57, 167, 168
"American Dream" 168
American Graffiti 130
American Society of Composers, Authors and Publishers 81
An American Tail 150
Amicus 202
Anatomy of a Murder 76, 82
animation 6, 18, 25, 26, 36, 57, 73, 77, 149, 150, 157–159, 181–182, 231; *see also* Disney
Ant-Man 195, 226

Anthony Adverse 49–50
Appalachian Spring 60
Argento, Dario 105
Armstrong, Louis 70, 74, 104, 114
Arnold, David 4, 36, 162, 163, 223, 225, 228
The Arrival of a Train at La Ciotat 6
ASCAP *see* American Society of Composers, Authors and Publishers
Ashman, Howard 157, 158, 159, 160, 182
The Assassination of the Duke of Guise 9, 10
atonal music 89, 108, 123, 139, 165, 166, 188, 201, 202; *see also* Lutyens, Elisabeth; Schoenberg, Arnold; serialism
The Audion 22
Audissino, Emilio 132, 134
Avatar 219
"Ave Satani" 89
The Avengers 2, 193–195
Avengers: Age of Ultron see The Avengers
Avengers: Endgame see The Avengers
Avengers: Infinity War see The Avengers
AWFC *see* Alliance for Women Film Composers

Bach, Johann Sebastian 29, 105, 110, 111
Bacharach, Burt 106, 112
Back to the Future see Back to the Future trilogy
Back to the Future: Part II see Back to the Future trilogy
Back to the Future: Part III see Back to the Future trilogy
Back to the Future trilogy 139, 151, 152, 153, 194, 216
Badalamenti, Angelo 79
Badelt, Klaus 176, 177, 178, 282
Balfe, Lorne 183, 197
ballyhoo 5
The Bar-Kays 113
Barber, Lesley 210
Barry, John 20, 37, 40, 84, 85, 86, 87, 104,

259

105, 120, 163, 164, 165, 203, 213, 214, 220, 225, 228
barker *see* ballyhoo
Bartek, Steve 143
Basic Instinct 165
Bassey, Shirley 85, 164
Bates, Tyler 96
Batman (movie) 65, 66, 142–144, 197, 199
Batman Begins see The Dark Knight trilogy
Batman: Mask of the Phantasm 204, 208
Battle Beyond the Stars 148
The Battle of Algiers 105
Battleship Potemkin 11
Baum, L. Frank 9, 10
Bayrakdarian, Isabel 189
BBC Radiophonic Workshop *see Doctor Who*
"Be My Baby" 118
The Beatles 100
Beau Ideal 32
The Beautiful Greek Girl 29
Beauty and the Beast 158–159
Beck, Christophe 195, 226, 228
Bee Gees 100, 142
Beethoven, Ludwig van 29, 111, 156, 218
Bell Labs *see* synchronized sound
Beltrami, Marco 82, 89
Ben-Hur 76, 99
Berklee College of Music 78
Berlin, Irving 24, 51, 54
Bernard, James 201, 202
Bernstein, Elmer 56, 73, 76, 78, 81, 85, 87, 92, 107, 114, 123, 126, 153, 157, 180, 203, 217, 222, 226
Berry, Chuck 169
best music—scoring *see* Academy Awards
best original dramatic score *see* Academy Awards
best original score *see* Academy Awards
best original song *see* Academy Awards
best original song score *see* Academy Awards
The Big Country 87, 106, 123
Bill Haley & His Comets 95
billboard chart 96
The Bird with the Crystal Plumage 105
The Birds 64
The Birth of a Nation 11–12, 13
Black Caesar 116
Black Eyed Peas 170
Black Panther 195, 228
Blackboard Jungle 93–97
Blade Runner 13, 155, 215
Blanchard, Terence 4, 69, 78, 79
blaster beam 91, 229
Blaxploitation 112–116

block booking 81
"The Blue Danube" 29, 79
The Blue Max 85–86
Bluth, Don 150, 182
Body Heat 165
The Bondman 30
Born Free 121, 213
"Born to Be Wild" 103–104
Boston Pops Orchestra 92
Bowers, Kris 229
Boys' Choir of Harlem 150
Brando, Marlon 26, 69, 70, 74, 94, 121
Breil, Joseph Carl 11–12
Bridgerton 229
Brittell, Nicholas 2, 230
Britten, Benjamin 220
Broadway 30, 31, 46, 54, 55, 69, 123, 157, 158
Broken Arrow 175, 177
Bronze Age 147
Broughton, Bruce 153
Brown, James 116
Bruckheimer, Jerry 142, 177, 178, 179, 180, 187
buchla *see* synthesizer
The Buggles *see* Horn, Trevor
Bullitt 77–78
Burlingame, Jon 56, 57, 61, 66
Burton, Tim 67, 142, 143, 223
Butch Cassidy and the Sundance Kid 105–107

La Califfa 122
Calloway, Cab 42, 73
Cameron, James 149, 153, 215, 219
Capote, Truman 94, 114
Captain America 194–196
Captain America: Civil War see Captain America
Captain America: The First Avenger see Captain America
Captain America: The Winter Soldier see Captain America
Captain Blood 47–49, 50, 52, 72
Captain Marvel 206–207
Carlos, Wendy 13, 110–112, 155, 209
"Carnival of the Animals" 9
Carpenter, John 154, 204
Casablanca 40, 47
Casino Royale see James Bond
Castelnuovo-Tedesco, Mario 83, 125
Cavalleria Rusticana 122
"Cavatina" 173
CBS *see* Columbia Broadcasting System
CBS Orchestra 60–62
"Celluloid Commandos" 26
Chaplin, Charles 14–20, 53
The Charge of the Light Brigade 38, 49
Chariots of Fire 146, 155

Index

Childish Gambino 228
"The Chimes of Normandy" 6
Chinatown 78, 90, 91
Chopin, Frédéric 103
christie organ *see* organ
Ciani, Suzanne 203, 211
Cimarron 32
Cimino, Michael 140
Cinerama 57
Citizen Kane 60–62, 70
City Lights 16–19, 53
Civil Rights Movement 102, 112, 113
Clemmensen, Christian 161, 171
click track 31–32, 35, 45, 93
A Clockwork Orange 109–111, 209
Close Encounters of the Third Kind 166
Coachella 183
Cole, Nat King 18, 19
Columbia Broadcasting System 59, 125
"Come and Get Your Love" 96
Conan Doyle, Arthur 33
Conan the Barbarian 136, 153, 188
concert hall 49, 52, 60, 82, 83, 173, 224, 225, 227
conductor 8, 25, 30, 31, 49, 54–56, 58, 83, 143, 175, 201, 206
Conti, Bill 153, 220
The Conversation 119–120
Cooke, Mervyn 48, 212
Cool Hand Luke 203
Cooper, Merian C. *see* King Kong
Copland, Aaron 60, 85, 117
Coppola, Francis Ford 119, 121, 122, 130, 202
Costner, Kevin 51, 150, 151, 213
Courage, Alexander 148
The Cowboys 123, 124
Crimson Tide 171, 176
Cronenberg, David 190
Cruise, Tom 174, 183, 197, 209, 215
cue sheet 8, 233
Curtiz, Michael 47, 50, 132
Curzon Clevedon 5
Cutler, Miriam 211
Cutthroat Island 161–162, 207

Daft Punk 209
Dali, Salvador 63
Dances with Wolves 213–214
Danna, Mychael 224, 226, 227
The Dark Knight *see* *The Dark Knight trilogy*
The Dark Knight Rises *see* *The Dark Knight trilogy*
The Dark Knight trilogy 179, 181, 197, 198
Davis, Carl 17, 19
Davis, Don 186–188

Davis, Miles 28, 114
The Day the Earth Stood Still 56, 62, 110
Days of Heaven 9
The Dead City see *Die Tote Stadt*
Dean, James 76, 94
Death Rides a Horse 169
Debney, John 161–162, 193, 196, 207, 231
Debussy, Claude 29, 149
Decca Records 95
Delerue, Georges 28, 43, 67
Delia Derbyshire: The Myths and Legendary Tapes 211
Dell'Orso, Edda 86
Del Toro, Guillermo 67, 232
De Niro, Robert 66, 118
De Palma, Brian 130, 197, 212
Derbyshire, Delia 110, 202, 211
Desplat, Alexandre 4, 28, 36, 43, 53, 67, 137, 196, 231, 232
The Diary of Anne Frank 55, 57
The Dickson Experimental Sound Film 6
Die Another Day see *James Bond*
diegesis 8, 15, 31, 32, 34, 35, 58, 78, 99, 103, 118, 120, 123, 133, 139, 169, 208
diegetic music see diegesis
"Dies Irae" 13
Dion, Celine 151, 219
Dirty Harry 78
Disney 25, 26, 42, 150, 157, 158, 159, 160, 176, 181, 182, 216, 219, 226, 228, 230, 231; *see also* animation
Dixiana 31
Django Unchained 169
Djawadi, Ramin 193, 196, 228
Doctor Dolittle 87
Doctor Who 110–111, 202, 211
Dollars Trilogy 86
Don Juan 22–24
Donner, Richard 89, 141
"Down and Out in New York City" 116
Doyle, Patrick 193, 196, 205
Dracula 200, 201, 202
Dream Street 24, 25
Driving Miss Daisy 172
dry sound *see* mixing
dubbing 22, 32, 185, 199
Dudley, Anne 206
Dunkirk 179
Dylan, Bob 104, 116–117

Eastwood, Clint 78, 86
Easy Rider 102–104, 105
École Normale de Musique 201
Edison, Thomas 6, 8–9
Edison Kinetogram *see* Edison, Thomas
Eduorade, Carl 26

Index

Edward Scissorhands 65, 223
The Egyptian 58
"Eighteen Fifty Rhenish Symphony No. 3" 219
Eisenstein, Sergei 11
El Cid 56, 63
electronic music 13, 56, 62, 63, 64, 82, 83, 92, 96, 109, 110, 125, 131, 142, 151–155, 164, 171–174, 181, 186, 187, 188, 203, 209, 211, 212, 227, 228; see also synthesizer
Elevator to the Gallows 114
Elfman, Danny 65, 66, 67, 142–144, 195, 197, 198, 199, 223, 227
Elinor, Carli 11
Ellington, Duke 73, 76, 114
Emma 203–204
Emmerich, Roland 36, 162
Enola Holmes 228
Entr'acte 12, 13
Enya 151, 189
Escape from New York 154
Eshkeri, Ilan 34, 35
E.T. The Extra-Terrestrial 147–148, 165
The Exorcist 221–222
expressive scoring 8, 17, 46, 60, 64, 117, 168
Eyes Wide Shut 209

Face/Off 175–177
Fairbanks, Douglas 16, 54
The Fairylogue and Radio-Plays 9
Faltermeyer, Harold 174
Feige, Kevin 197, 226
Fellini, Federico 121, 219
The Fellowship of the Ring see The Lord of the Rings trilogy
Fiddler on the Roof 123
Fiedel, Brad 153–154
Field of Dreams 150–151
Fielding, Jerry 107, 108, 116
Film Fest Gent 227
Film Musical Festival 227
film noir 18, 94, 120, 123
Fimucité 227
Fincher, David 120, 166, 220
Finding Nemo 168
Fireworks: A Celebration of Los Angeles 92
A Fistful of Dollars see Dollars Trilogy
Five Easy Pieces 102–103
Die Fledermaus 29, 46
Flynn, Errol 44, 47–51, 132, 162, 207
For a Few Dollars More see Dollars Trilogy
Forbstein, Leo F. 49
Ford, Glenn 94, 95
Ford, Harrison 131, 138, 144, 145, 155, 216
Ford, John 32, 38, 41, 56
Francis, Freddie 150, 201, 202

Friedhofer, Hugo 41, 50, 63, 176
Friedkin, William 153, 221, 222
From Russia with Love see James Bond
"furniture music" 12

The Gadfly 14
Gambino, Childish 228
Game of Thrones 192, 193, 226
Garfunkel, Art see Simon and Garfunkel
Garland, Judy 41
Gaye, Marvin 115–116
The General 17
Gerrard, Lisa 183
Gershwin, George 30, 54
The Ghost and Mrs Muir 56, 62
The Ghost and the Darkness 90
Giacchino, Michael 4, 109, 133, 137, 138, 139, 196, 197, 210, 211, 230, 231
Gimpel, Jakob 83
Gladiator 2, 182–183, 184, 217, 227
Glass, Philip 90, 170, 209
Glory 150, 151
The Godfather see The Godfather trilogy
The Godfather: Part II see The Godfather trilogy
The Godfather: Part III see The Godfather trilogy
The Godfather trilogy 121–122, 225
Godzilla 36, 196, 229
Going for Gold 173
"Golden Age" 48, 53, 54, 55, 62, 65, 67, 131, 139, 213, 224
"Golden Era" see "Golden Age"
GoldenEye see James Bond
Goldenthal, Elliot 166, 167, 186, 187, 227
Goldfinger see James Bond
Goldman, William 105, 119
Goldsmith, Jerry 3, 13, 41, 53, 66, 78, 79, 80, 81–93, 115, 121, 126, 134, 141, 144, 148, 153, 162, 164, 165, 166, 169, 171, 174, 182, 193, 203, 214, 215, 216, 217, 227, 229, 231
Gone with the Wind 38–42, 47, 50, 62, 87, 113, 116, 176
Good Omens 226
The Good, the Bad and the Ugly see Dollars Trilogy
Goodwin, Ron 66, 86
Göransson, Ludwig 179, 185, 195, 228, 229
Götterdämmerung see Der Ring des Nibelungen
Gottlieb, Carl 128, 129
Gottschalk, Louis Ferdinand 10
The Graduate 65, 101–105, 143, 168
Grauman's Chinese Theater 36
Grauman's Egyptian Theater 23
Grease 142, 169

Index 263

The Great Escape 85
The Greatest Showman 231
Greenwood, Jonny 229
Gremlins 90, 92, 153
Griffith, D.W. 11, 12, 16, 19, 24
Groves, George *see* synchronized sound
Grusin, Dave 102
Guardians of the Galaxy 96, 97
Guðnadóttir, Hildur 207, 208
Gunn, James 96
"Gymnopedie No. 1" 12

Haley, Bill *see* Bill Haley and his Comets
Halloween 154
Hammer 200, 201
Hanson, Howard 215
A Hard Day's Night 100
Hardy, Tom 198, 228
harmonium 6
Harry Potter 196, 224, 232
The Hateful Eight 75
Havilland, Olivia de 41, 46, 48, 49, 50, 52
Hayes, Isaac 112–113
HBO 192, 208, 232
Heaven's Gate 140, 141
Herrmann, Bernard 28, 53, 56, 58–67, 70, 82, 83, 90, 91, 93, 98, 110, 125, 126, 129, 142, 165, 169, 180, 202, 212, 213, 221, 227, 229, 230
Highlander 173
Hill, Andy 60, 86, 226
Hitchcock, Alfred 59, 61–67, 83, 128, 212
Hepburn, Audrey 26
Heston, Charlton 80, 87, 88, 89, 99
Hisaishi, Joe 17
The Hobbit trilogy 192
Hoffman, Dustin 101, 108, 119
Holiday, Billie 73
Holkenborg, Tom 196, 199
Hollywood Studio Symphony 187
Holst, Gustav *see The Planets*
Honey, I Shrunk the Kids 218, 219
"The Honeysuckle and the Bee" 18
Hoosiers 174
Hopper, Dennis 103–104
Horn, Trevor 173, 206
Horner, James 3, 53, 148, 149, 161, 166, 183, 186, 190, 191, 184, 215, 218, 219, 231, 233
"Hound Dog" 97
House Un-American Activities Committee 81
How the West was Won 56–57
H.U.A.C. *see* House Un-American Activities Committee
Huey Lewis and the News 152
Hugo 6, 7–8

The Hunchback of Notre Dame 55
Hurwitz, Justin 231
Huppertz, Gottfried 13

Ifukube, Akira 36, 196
illustrated songs 6
illustrative scoring 8, 12, 17, 60
Images 20, 123, 124, 127, 141
In Cold Blood 94, 114
The Incredible Shrinking Woman 203
Independence Day 162–163, 170
Indiana Jones 3, 144–147, 180, 194
Indiana Jones and the Kingdom of the Crystal Skull see Indiana Jones
Indiana Jones and the Last Crusade see Indiana Jones
Indiana Jones and the Temple of Doom see Indiana Jones
Indigo and the Forty Thieves 29
The Informer 38
Interstellar 179–180, 185, 224
Interview with the Vampire 167
Iron Man 192–196
Iron Man (movie) *see Iron Man*
Iron Man 2 see Iron Man
Iron Man 3 see Iron Man
Isham, Mark 79, 222

Jackman, Henry 37–38, 196
The Jackson 5 96
Jackson, Peter 37, 189, 191
Jackson, Wilfred 26
Jailhouse Rock 97–100
Jakatta 168
James Bond 37, 84, 104, 121, 144, 163, 168, 213, 225
Jane Eyre 132, 166
Jarre, Maurice 28, 67, 92, 98, 146
Jason and the Argonauts 62
Jaws 35, 36, 108, 128–130, 131, 134
The Jaws Log see Jaws
jazz 69–79, 86, 104, 105, 106, 108, 112, 114, 115, 118, 123, 124, 125, 126, 132, 167, 172, 208, 212, 219, 228, 230
The Jazz Singer 22, 24–26
Jenkins, Barry 2
John, Elton 181, 231
Joker 207–209, 211
Jolson, Al 24–26
Jones, Quincy 114
Jones, Trevor 170, 215
Juilliard School 59, 71, 125
The Jungle Book 158, 161, 231
Junkie XL *see* Holkenborg, Tom
Juno Reactor 188
Jurassic Park 36, 129, 165, 166, 224, 230, 231

Jurassic World see *Jurassic Park*
Justice League 198–199

Kamen, Michael 51, 170, 173, 218
Karno, Fred 15
Karpman, Laura 4, 200, 208–211, 232
Kasdan, Lawrence 135
Kazan, Elia 69, 72, 74
Keaton, Buster 17
Kennedy, Kathleen 137, 178
Keystone Studios 15
Kid Auto Races at Venice 16
Kilar, Wojciech 202
Kill Bill: Volume 1 169
Kinetograph 6
Kinetoscope 6
The King and I 56
King Kong 27, 28, 32–38, 45, 47, 48, 55, 70, 85, 196
"Knockin' on Heaven's Door" 116–117
Knopfler, Mark 209
Kong: Skull Island see *King Kong*
Kool & the Gang 169
Korngold, Erich Wolfgang 12, 43–53, 54, 55, 59, 61, 70, 71, 72, 81, 85, 93, 127, 130, 132, 133, 141, 161, 162, 178, 207
Korzeniowski, Abel 13
Kosmograph 7
Kristofferson, Kris 116–117
Kubrick, Stanley 13, 75, 79, 109–112, 131, 209

La La Land 231
La-La Land Records 57
The Land Before Time 150
Lang, Fritz 13
"The Lark Ascending" 201
Last of the Mohicans 170
The Last Starfighter 153
Laura 18, 56
Lawrence of Arabia 92, 98–99
Lean, David 4, 98, 200
Leap of Faith: William Friedkin on The Exorcist 221
Lee, Spike 78
Legend 215–216
The Legend of Bagger Vance 204
Legends of the Fall 151, 186
Legrand, Michel 113, 114
Leigh, Vivien 39, 42, 69, 74
leitmotif 12, 13, 18, 29, 34, 49, 51, 136, 188; see also *Der Ring des Nibelungen*; Wagner, Richard
Lennox, Annie 189
Leone, Sergio 2, 86
Levi, Mica 209, 229
Lewis, Leona 219

libretto 45
Ligeti, György 79, 132
Lillie Yard Studios 173–174
Limelight 20
The Lion in Winter 121
The Lion King 181–182, 184, 231
Liszt, Franz 48
The Little Mermaid 146, 157–159
The Little Tramp 15–16
Little Women 167
live accompaniment 5–9, 11, 12, 13, 23, 31, 34, 54, 92, 173, 185, 211, 224, 225, 227
The Living Daylights see *James Bond*
Lloyd, Harold 17
Local Hero 209
London Philharmonic Orchestra 99, 189
London Symphony Orchestra 132, 161
The Long Goodbye 123
The Lord of the Rings trilogy 2, 136, 151, 186, 189–192, 195, 196
Lost in Space 127
Lost Weekend 212
The Lost World 33
The Love of Queen Elizabeth 12
Lovecraft Country 208, 211, 232
Lucas, George 128, 130, 131, 134, 144, 148
Lucasfilm 133, 147, 144, 178, 227
Lumière, Auguste Marie Louis Nicolas see Lumière brothers
Lumière, Louis Jean see Lumière brothers
Lumière brothers 6, 7
Lutyens, Elisabeth 200–203; see also atonal music; serialism
Lynch, David 79
Lysy, Craig 9, 10, 48, 51, 144, 147

Maal, Baaba 228
Mabel's Strange Predicament 16
Mad Max: Fury Road 199
Magic Fire 52
magic-lantern projection 5, 9
The Magnificent Seven 60, 85, 87, 126
Mahler, Gustav 29, 44, 45, 51
Malick, Terrence 9, 182, 220
The Man from U.N.C.L.E. 84, 228
The Man with the Golden Arm 73, 76
Manchester by the Sea 210
Mancina, Mark 171–172
Mancini, Henry 76, 83, 90, 114, 123, 126
The Mandalorian see *Star Wars*
Manhattan Opera House 23
Mann, Nathaniel D. 9
Mansfield, David 141
Maraval, Emile 6
"The Marseillaise" 13, 14
Marvel see Marvel Cinematic Universe

Marvel Cinematic Universe 32, 96, 192–197, 206–208, 224, 226, 228, 230; see also superhero
Mascagni, Pietro 122
Masters of the Universe 153
The Matrix see *The Matrix* trilogy
The Matrix Reloaded see *The Matrix* trilogy
The Matrix Revolutions see *The Matrix* trilogy
The Matrix trilogy 163, 186–188, 192, 227
Mayfield, Curtis 113
McCarthy, Sen. Joseph 81
McCreary, Bear 196, 229
McNab, Malcolm 162
McNeely, Joel 217
McQueen, Steve 77–78, 107, 121, 124
Mean Streets 117–118
Media Ventures see Remote Control Productions
Medicine Man 153
Meet Me In St. Louis 41
Meisel, Edmund 11
Méliès, Georges 6, 7
Melumad, Nami 211
Mendelssohn, Felix 46, 52
Menken, Alan 146, 157–160, 182, 231
Le Mépris 43
Messter, Oskar 6, 7
Metro-Goldwyn-Mayer 38, 41, 73, 97, 113, 117
Metropolis 13–14
Meyer, Nicholas 148, 149
MGM see Metro-Goldwyn-Mayer
"mickey-mousing" 17, 18, 47
Middle-earth see *The Lord of the Rings* trilogy
MIDI see synthesizer
Midnight Express 142
A Midsummer Night's Dream 46, 48, 52
Minnelli, Vincente 41
Minnie the Moocher 73
Miranda, Lin-Manuel 231
The Mission 43
Mission: Impossible 84, 183, 197, 230
Mission: Impossible (movie) see *Mission: Impossible*
Mission: Impossible (TV series) see *Mission: Impossible*
Mission: Impossible II see *Mission: Impossible*
Mission: Impossible III see *Mission: Impossible*
Mission: Impossible—Fallout see *Mission: Impossible*
Mission: Impossible—Ghost Protocol see *Mission: Impossible*

Mission: Impossible—Rogue Nation see *Mission: Impossible*
Mitchell, Margaret 38
mixing 20–27, 32, 54, 106, 163, 175, 176, 184, 185, 223, 229
Modern Times 16, 18, 19
MonsterVerse 196
Montenegro, Hugo 168
Moroder, Giorgio 13, 142, 153
Moross, Jerome 87, 106, 123, 153, 217
Morricone, Ennio 2, 43, 49, 75, 86, 87, 105, 107, 116, 122, 154, 168, 169, 203, 227, 228
Mothersbaugh, Mark 196
MTV 163, 178
Mulan 182, 231
Murphy, Shawn 224
"Music for the Funeral March of Queen Mary" 111
musicals 20, 24, 26, 27, 30, 31, 41, 54, 56, 87, 123, 126, 158, 160, 231
My Fair Lady 26
"My Heart Will Go On" 151, 219
Myers, Stanley 173, 174, 176

National Philharmonic Orchestra 80, 165
Near Dark 153
The New Babylon 14
New Orleans 69, 70, 73, 78
The New World 220–221
New York Philharmonic Orchestra 23
New Zealand Symphony 189
Newman, Alfred 18, 31, 51, 53–58, 59, 63, 93, 114, 167
Newman, David 57, 144
Newman, Lionel 55, 57
Newman, Paul 65, 105, 124, 203
Newman, Randy 57, 216–217
Newman, Thomas 57, 78, 167, 214, 231
Newton Howard, James 37, 198, 214
Nichols, Mike 101–102
Nicholson, Jack 90, 102, 103, 143
nickelodeon cinema 7, 30
"A Night in an English Music Hall" 15
Nolan, Christopher 179–181, 184, 198
non-diegetic music see diegesis
Norman, Monty 84
North, Alex 69–80, 86, 105, 212
North by Northwest 64
Nyman, Michael 11

O'Brien, Willis 28, 33
"Ode to Joy" 218
Oldfield, Mike 222
"Olympic Fanfare" 92
The Omen 89–90

Index

On Her Majesty's Secret Service see *James Bond*
Once Upon a Time in the West 86–87
One Night of Love 27
opera *see* operatic music
operatic music 8, 12, 24, 27, 29, 30, 43, 45, 46, 47, 50, 51, 52, 60, 64, 82, 86, 90, 105, 107, 122, 133, 135, 147, 159, 186, 188, 201, 205
orchestrator 14, 17, 21, 30, 31, 41, 50, 69, 126, 143, 161, 175, 176, 182, 186, 196, 209
organ *see* live accompaniment
Oscar nominations 8, 42, 56, 75, 102, 123, 159; *see also* Academy Awards; Oscars
Oscars 27, 42, 49, 69, 74, 142, 158, 166, 171, 187, 191, 213; *see also* Academy Awards; Oscar nominations
Out of Africa 37, 40, 121, 213
"Over the Rainbow" 41
The Oz Film Manufacturing Company 10

Pakula, Alan J. 119–120
Pantomimes lumineuses 6
Papillon 121
Paramount Studios 33
Paris Blues 114
Pat Garrett and Billy the Kid 116–117
Paulin, Gaston 6
Peckinpah, Sam 107–108, 116, 117
Pemberton, Daniel 228, 229
Penderecki, Krzysztof 222
Penny and the Pownall Case 200–201
"The Perfect Song" 12
Perlman, Itzhak 166
Petersen, Wolfgang 216–218
phonograph 5, 6, 7
pianist *see* live accompaniment
The Pink Panther 77
Pirates of the Caribbean 176–178
Pixar 57, 216, 230, 232
Planet of the Apes 13, 66, 79, 87–89, 92, 107
The Planets 131, 182, 220
Planquette, Robert 6
Poitier, Sidney 94, 113, 114
Poledouris, Basil 136, 153, 164
Poltergeist 90
Pook, Jocelyn 209
Portman, Rachel 203–204, 211
The Poseidon Adventure 20, 124, 127
Powaqqatsi 170
Powell, John 4, 138, 156, 175, 177, 183
"The Power of Love" 152
Pratt, Chris 96
"Prelude in E Minor" 103
Preminger, Otto 18, 76, 82
Presley, Elvis 97, 99, 101
Previn, André 83, 123

Prima, Louis 73
Prince 100–101, 143–144
Prokofiev, Sergei 14, 72, 75, 135, 150
The Propellerheads 163, 188
Psycho 64–65, 82, 180
Puccini, Giacomo 44, 46, 51
Pulp Fiction 118, 168–170
Purcell, Henry 111
Purple Rain 100

Quantum of Solace see *James Bond*

Rachmaninoff, Sergei 219
radio *see* Columbia Broadcasting System
Radio-Keith-Orpheum *see* RKO Pictures
Raging Bull 122
Raiders of the Lost Ark see *Indiana Jones*
Raimi, Sam 197
Rain Man 172, 174
"Raindrops Keep Falling On My Head" 106
Raksin, David 18, 19, 56
Rasch, Raymond 20
Reaching for the Moon 54
Rebecca 62
Rebel Without a Cause 76, 95
Redford, Robert 105, 119, 204
Redman, Nick 57
Reeves, Keanu 171, 186
Regent Theater 8
The Reivers 106–107, 123, 132
rejected scores 65, 79, 80, 91, 98, 212–222
Remote Control Productions 171–177, 193
Reservoir Dogs 169
The Return of the King see *The Lord of the Rings* trilogy
Reynaud, Émile 6
Reznor, Trent 230
"Rhapsody in Blue" 30
Rice, Tim 159–160, 181
Richard, Cliff 84, 100
The Right Stuff 220
The Ring Cycle see *Der Ring des Nibelungen*
Der Ring des Nibelungen 12, 188; *see also* leitmotif; Wagner, Richard
The Ring of Polycrates 45
Rio Rita 31
The Rite of Spring 36, 88
Ritmanis, Lolita 210, 211
A River Runs Through It 222
RKO Pictures 31–33, 38, 39, 61
Road to Perdition 168
roadshow 11
The Robe 56, 57
Robin Hood: Prince of Thieves 51
rock and roll 93–104, 108, 130, 142, 170
The Rocketeer 194

Rocky 220, 225
Rogue One: A Star Wars Story see *Star Wars*
Rolling Stone 115, 116, 170
The Rolling Stones 118
romantic music see romanticism
romanticism 3, 12, 16, 18, 28, 29, 30, 33, 34, 37, 39, 40, 42, 43, 49, 51, 56, 59, 60, 70, 71, 74, 83, 120, 121, 131, 137, 159, 163, 181, 201, 213; see also Vienna
The Ronettes 118
Ross, Alex 220
Ross, Atticus 230
Rossini, Gioachino 111
Rota, Nino 28, 121, 137, 219
Roundtree, Richard 112
Royal Albert Hall 185, 224, 225
Royal College of Music in London 201
Royal Scottish National Orchestra 80
Rózsa, Miklós 56, 63, 76, 83, 99, 132, 182, 212, 227
Russo brothers 195

Saint-Saëns, Camille 9–10, 13
St. Matthew Passion 105
Satie, Erik 12–13, 17
Saturday Night Fever 100, 142, 169
Saving Private Ryan 166
Schaffner, Franklin J. 87, 89, 121
Schauspiel-Ouvertüre 45
Schifrin, Lalo 77–78, 84, 197, 203, 221–222, 228, 230
Der Schneemann 45
Schoedsack, Ernest B. see *King Kong*
Schoenberg, Arnold 59, 201
Schumann, Robert 219
Scorsese, Martin 6, 7, 66, 117, 118, 130, 169, 180, 207
Scott, Raymond 125, 219
Scott, Ridley 13, 137, 155, 174, 182, 214, 216
Scream 82, 89
Screen Composers' Association 81
The Sea Hawk 44
The Searchers 32
The Secret of N.I.M.H. 182
Selznick, David O. 33, 38, 39, 41, 42, 62
Sennett, Mack 15–16
serialism 201; see also atonal music; Lutyens, Elisabeth
Serra, Eric 163
Shaft 112–113, 114, 115, 116
Shaken and Stirred: The David Arnold James Bond Project 163
Shakespeare, William 46, 167, 181
The Shape of Water 67, 232
The Shawshank Redemption 167–168
Sherlock 226

The Shining 13, 111
Shire, David 119, 120
Shore, Howard 1, 2, 4, 8, 10, 13, 31, 37, 136, 151, 186, 189–192
Shostakovich, Dimitri 9, 14, 220
Silvers, Louis 24, 27, 49
Silvestri, Alan 2, 3, 67, 152, 178, 194, 195, 196, 206, 214, 224
Simon, Paul see Simon and Garfunkel
Simon and Garfunkel 65, 101–102, 108
Singin' in the Rain 20–21
Sissel 151, 191
Sisters 212, 213
Sisters with Transistors 211
Skyfall see *James Bond*
Smith, Steven C. 29, 31, 32
Snow White and the Seven Dwarfs 26
The Snowman see *Der Schneemann*
Snowpiercer 89
Snyder, Zack 199
Sorcerer 153
The Sound of Music 87
"The Sound of Silence" 65, 101
sound on disc technology see synchronized sound
Spartacus 75–76, 79
Spectre see *James Bond*
Speed 170–172
Spellbound 62, 83, 99
Spider-Man 196, 197, 228
Spider-Man movie see *Spider-Man*
Spider-Man 2 see *Spider-Man*
Spider-Man 3 see *Spider-Man*
Spider-Man: Far from Home see *Spider-Man*
Spider-Man: Homecoming see *Spider-Man*
Spider-Man: Into the Spider-Verse see *Spider-Man*
Spider-Man: No Way Home see *Spider-Man*
Spielberg, Steven 2, 36, 67, 126, 127, 128, 130, 131, 144, 145, 146, 147, 148, 152, 165, 166, 208
"spotting" 10, 34, 35, 56, 61, 78, 89, 91, 98, 114, 119, 121, 141, 166, 190
Stagecoach 41
Stalling, Carl 32, 124
Star Trek 13, 90, 91, 148, 162, 227, 229, 231
Star Trek II: The Wrath of Khan see *Star Trek*
Star Trek V: The Final Frontier see *Star Trek*
Star Trek: First Contact see *Star Trek*
Star Trek: Insurrection see *Star Trek*
Star Trek: Nemesis see *Star Trek*
Star Trek: The Motion Picture see *Star Trek*
Star Trek: The Next Generation see *Star Trek*
Star Trek: Voyager see *Star Trek*

268　Index

Star Wars 10, 42, 50, 53, 77, 106, 108, 109, 124, 131–140, 141, 144, 145, 146, 148, 149, 157, 159, 175, 178, 180, 188, 217, 225, 228, 230, 231
Star Wars: Episode I—The Phantom Menace see Star Wars
Star Wars: Episode II—Attack of the Clones see Star Wars
Star Wars: Episode III—Revenge of the Sith see Star Wars
Star Wars: Episode IV—A New Hope see Star Wars
Star Wars: Episode V—The Empire Strikes Back see Star Wars
Star Wars: Episode VI—Return of the Jedi see Star Wars
Star Wars: Episode VII—The Force Awakens see Star Wars
Star Wars: Episode VIII—The Last Jedi see Star Wars
Star Wars: Episode IX—The Rise of Skywalker see Star Wars
Stax Records 112–113
Steamboat Willie 25–26
Steiner, Gabor 29
Steiner, Max 12, 27, 28–43, 45, 47, 48, 49, 50, 54, 55, 59, 70, 76, 85, 91, 93, 106, 120, 124, 132, 147, 176, 196
Steiner, Maximilian Raoul 28, 29
Steppenwolf 103–104, 108
Stothart, Herbert 31, 41
Strauss, Johann II 29, 79
Strauss, Richard 29, 44, 51, 79
Stravinsky, Igor 36, 88, 123, 129
A Streetcar Named Desire 69–77, 80, 105
studio orchestra 73, 81
StudioCanal 53
Die Stumme Serenade 52
subjective scoring 23, 44, 72, 108, 184
Summer Holiday 99–100
Super Fly 113–114, 115, 116
superhero 141, 144, 173, 194, 198, 204, 206, 224, 228; see also Marvel Cinematic Universe
Superman 138, 141–144, 194, 199, 225
Sursum Corda 51
Sweet Smell of Success 73, 76, 126
Switched-On Bach 110–111
Symphonic Serenade in B-flat major, Op. 39 52
Symphony No. 1 219
Symphony No. 2 in D-flat Major: Romantic 215
Symphony No. 9 111
syncronization see synchronized sound
synchronized sound 6, 7, 22–25, 26, 30, 31, 32, 35, 38, 45, 47, 65, 93

synthesizer 92, 104, 111, 153, 154, 173, 174; see also electronic music
"Take My Breath Away" 142
talkies" 20, 21, 58, 59
Tamar-kali 211
Tamla 115
Tangerine Dream 153, 215
Tarantino, Quentin 75, 118, 168–170
Tauron Arena 227
Taxi Driver 66, 90
Tchaikovsky, Pyotr Ilyich 135, 223
television 3, 17, 81, 82, 83, 90, 99, 100, 110, 127, 200, 205, 225
temp track 131, 212–222
The Ten Commandments 56, 76, 81, 87
Tenet 179, 185
Tennant, Neil 11
The Terminator 153–154
Terminator 2: Judgment Day 154
test screenings 158, 213, 216, 218, 219, 220, 221
theremin see electronic music
They Live 154
The Thing 154
Thor 193–196
Thor: Ragnarok see Thor
Thor: The Dark World see Thor
"Thus Spake Zarathustra" 79
Tierney, Harry 31
The Tik-Tok Man of Oz 10
Tiomkin, Dimitri 9, 31, 56, 126
Titanic 149, 151, 191, 219, 221, 224, 225
Titus 167
To Kill a Mockingbird 76, 126
Tolkien, J.R.R. 189–191
Tomorrow Never Dies see James Bond
Top Gun 142, 174, 178
Top Hat 54
Toprak, Pinar 206–208
Tora! Tora! Tora! 91
Torn Curtain 65, 98
Total Recall 90, 164–165
Die Tote Stadt 45–46
The Towering Inferno 124, 127
Townson, Robert 164
Transatlantyk 227
Travolta, John 142, 169, 175
Tristan und Isolde 64
"Trolley Song" 41
Tron 111, 209
Tron: Legacy 209
Trouble Man 115–116
The Trouble with Harry 63
Troy 183, 190, 217–218, 220
"Tubular Bells" 222

Turner Classic Movies 96
twelve-tone music *see* serialism
Twentieth Century Fox *see* Twentieth Century Studios
Twentieth Century Pictures *see* Twentieth Century Studios
Twentieth Century Studios 53, 55, 57, 73
The Twilight Zone 82, 126
Twisted Nerve 169
Twister 172
Two Thousand and One: A Space Odyssey 79–80, 131, 212
The Two Towers see *The Lord of the Rings* trilogy
Tyler, Brian 53, 193, 195, 196

Ultravox 173
Under Fire 169
Under the Skin 209, 229
United Artists 16, 140
U.S. Supreme Court 81
Universal Studios 53, 129, 131, 216

Vangelis 146, 155, 190
vaudeville 5, 7, 15, 17, 24, 54
Vaughan-Williams, Ralph 129, 201, 203, 229
Venom 228
Verhoeven, Paul 164–165, 206
Vertigo 61, 63–64
Vienna 29, 30, 44–47, 64, 92; *see also* romanticism
Vietnam War 102, 107, 109, 115
Violanta 45
VistaVision 87
Vitaphone *see* synchronized sound
A Voyage to the Moon 7

Wachowskis 186–188
Wagner, Richard 12, 13, 14, 18, 29, 34, 52, 64, 70, 82, 89, 132, 136, 153, 186, 188, 189, 195; *see also* leitmotif; *Der Ring des Nibelungen*
Wagnerian *see* Wagner, Richard
Walkabout 120–121
Walker, Shirley 143, 204, 208, 211
Waller, Fats 9, 74
Walton, William 201
WandaVision 226
The War of the Worlds 60; *see also* War of the Worlds

War of the Worlds 36, 123; *see also The War of the Worlds*
Warner, Jack L. 38
Warner Brothers 23, 25, 38, 48, 49, 73, 74, 132, 143, 187, 196, 218, 219
Watergate 107, 109, 119
Waxman, Franz 62, 63
Way Down East 24
"We Have All the Time in the World" 104–105
Webb, Roy 31
Wegele, Peter 31
Welles, Orson 60–62
West Side Story 126
wet sound *see* mixing
What's Going On 115
Where Eagles Dare 86
White Christmas 54
The Wild Bunch 107–108, 116
The Wild One 94
"William Tell Overture" 111
Williams, John 2, 3, 10, 20, 24, 35, 36, 50, 53, 56, 66, 67, 77, 78, 83, 92, 106, 123–155, 159, 161, 165, 178, 180, 183, 196, 199, 200, 203, 217, 224, 227, 229, 230, 231
Williams, Tennessee 69, 70, 74
Wiseman, Debbie 205–206
The Wizard of Oz 9, 10, 41, 131
The World Is Not Enough see James Bond
World War II 26, 30, 52, 72, 85, 89, 94, 166, 179, 182, 194, 201
Wray, Fay 34
Wurlitzer *see* live accompaniment

Yamaha *see* synthesizer
Yamashta, Stomu 123
Yared, Gabriel 203, 217–218
You Only Live Twice see James Bond
Young, Christopher 197
Young Sherlock Holmes 153

Zanuck, Daryl F. 25, 55
Zemeckis, Robert 67, 151, 152
Ziegfeld, Florenz 30
Zimmer, Hans 2, 24, 171–185, 186, 193, 196, 197, 198, 200, 217, 224, 227, 231
Zodiac 120

www.ingramcontent.com/pod-product-compliance
Lightning Source LLC
Chambersburg PA
CBHW032034300426
44117CB00009B/1057